DORLING KINDERSLEY
—HANDBOOKS—

MUSHROOMS

DORLING KINDERSLEY
—HANDBOOKS—

MUSHROOMS

THOMAS LÆSSØE

Photography by
NEIL FLETCHER

Editorial Consultant
GORDON RUTTER

A Dorling Kindersley Book

Dorling DK Kindersley

LONDON, NEW YORK, DELHI, JOHANNESBURG,
MUNICH, PARIS and SYDNEY

Important Notice
The author and publishers strongly advise
anyone gathering fungi for eating to seek the
help of an experienced mycologist. Never eat
any fungus unless you are 100% certain of its
identity. We accept no responsiblity for
readers who do not follow this advice.

Project Editor Jo Weeks
Project Art Editor Colin Walton
Picture Research Mollie Gillard
and Sean Hunter
Production Controller Michelle Thomas
Managing Editor Jonathan Metcalf
Managing Art Editor Peter Cross

First published in Great Britain in 1998
by Dorling Kindersley Limited,
9 Henrietta Street, London WC2E 8PS
Reprinted with corrections in 2000

2 4 6 8 10 9 7 5 3 1

A CIP catalogue record for this book is
available from the British Library

ISBN 0-7513-2717-4

Reproduction by Colourscan, Singapore
Text film output by The Right Type, England

Printed and bound in Singapore
by Kyodo Printing Co.

www.dk.com

CONTENTS

INTRODUCTION

The fungal kingdom is enormous, with fungi occurring in all habitat types all over the world. Ranging in size from microscopic yeasts to large, fleshy mushrooms, fungi also have highly diverse lifestyles, some forming beneficial relationships with living plants, others degrading or even killing their hosts. All play a vital role in the processes that govern life on our planet.

THE STUDY of the fungal kingdom is referred to as mycology. Until comparatively recently, fungi were simply considered to be a lower form of plant life and were studied as part of botany. They were also often regarded with suspicion due to their habit of appearing seemingly out of nowhere after rain. These factors perhaps help to explain why there are so many fungi as yet undescribed, although the sheer volume of species is also an important reason. Current estimates put the number of species in the fungal kingdom at approximately 1.5 million, in comparison with, for example, flowering plants at 250,000 species.

Mycologists believe that only about 80,000 of these species have been properly documented – less than five percent of the estimated total number in existence. Of the hitherto undescribed species, many are thought to inhabit tropical rainforest areas, but even in much more accessible regions, such as northern Europe, which have been quite closely studied, new species are still being discovered, including some that are large and fleshy.

△ FLY AGARIC
The colourful but poisonous Amanita muscaria *is perhaps the best known of all fungus species.*

SECRET LIFE

Most of us are familiar with mushrooms and toadstools, found mainly in wooded areas in the autumn, but fewer people are aware that each of these is simply the "fruitbody" of a much larger organism,

◁ FUNGUS COUNT
This pie chart represents the world's 1.5 million species of fungi. The "slices" show species identified so far: 28,700 macro- (fruitbody-forming) fungi; 24,000 rusts, smuts, and moulds, and 13,500 lichens.

KEY
- Macro-fungi
- Rusts, smuts, moulds
- Lichens
- Not described

LICHENS ▷

*A lichen is a compound organism, the result of an association between a fungus and algae. Lichens survive on nutrients filtered from the air, aided by the photosynthesis of the algal partner. They also take up air pollutants, so are a useful indicator of air quality. The picture shows the very common lichen Yellow Scales (*Xanthoria parietina*).*

Useful Fungi ▷

Fungi are an essential part of life, playing vital roles in many areas. They are used as a food, as flavouring, and to produce alcohol. Antibiotics are made from them, and they contain enzymes that are used in washing powder.

DETERGENT
The cleaning agents in clothes washing powders contain enzymes that have been extracted from fungi.

PENICILLIN
Penicillium *moulds produce a chemical that kills bacteria and is used in antibiotics.*

BLUE CHEESE
The flavouring in blue cheese is produced by the mould Penicillium roqueforti.

SALAMI SAUSAGES
Salami is flavoured and protected by the mould Penicillium nalgiovense.

which is concealed in the soil, wood, or other material (substrate) on which the fruitbody is growing. Fruitbodies are produced to enable the dispersal of spores, by which fungi reproduce. However, there are many other species that never produce fruitbodies. Most of these are moulds, such as those that occur on old foods like stale bread.

BEER
Beer is brewed using yeast, for example Saccharomyces carlsbergensis.

BREAD
Bread dough rises through the action of the yeast fungus Saccharomyces.

Macro-fungi

Only those fungi that produce more or less conspicuous fruitbodies are featured in this book. Mycologists refer to them as "macro-fungi", but most are popularly known as mushrooms or toadstools. They are diverse in form, varying from the well-known cap and stem type to those species with shelf-like fruitbodies and those that grow flat (see pp.12–13). Despite this diversity, the fruitbodies of some closely related fungi can look very similar and require careful examination for accurate identification. This book will assist the process of identification, and increase your understanding and enjoyment of the fungal kingdom.

Edible Fungi

Although not common in all cultures, the gathering of fungi for eating is an ancient practice. The Shii-take (*Lentinula edodes*) has been cultivated in China and Japan for hundreds of years, and, in Europe, the "Mushroom" (*Agaricus bisporus* p.161) has long been grown commercially. Today, oyster mushrooms (*Pleurotus* species pp.178–79) and several other species are widely cultivated, while huge quantities of morels, chanterelles, and boletes are collected from the wild and sold worldwide.

Before eating any mushroom from the wild be sure that it is correctly identified as edible (see also p.23). If poisoning is suspected, seek medical advice, taking along a sample of the fungus.

SHII-TAKE MUSHROOMS

AGARICUS BISPORUS

OYSTER MUSHROOMS

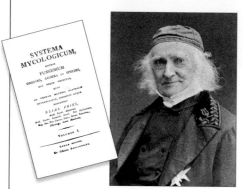

△ ELIAS FRIES *(1794–1878)*
Elias Fries was an outstanding early mycologist.
His Systema Mycologicum *(1832) laid the*
foundations for the modern classification system.

EATING WILD FUNGI

As well as making identification easier,
the species section of this book also
details edibility. However, it is strongly
recommended that beginners take
along an experienced forager if they are
gathering mushrooms for eating, as
many fungi are or can be poisonous.
There are also some edible species that
look very similar to poisonous ones (see
p.23). The species entries warn of any
specific dangers relating to each fungus.
The effects of eating a poisonous
mushroom vary from a
stomach upset to severe or
even fatal liver damage,
so it is not advisable
to experiment.

◁ DEADLY SPECIES
Amanita virosa *(far*
left) and Amanita
phalloides *(left) cause*
severe liver damage or
death if they are eaten.

CLASSIFICATION OF FUNGI

Our understanding and study of the
natural world is made easier by dividing
it into at least five kingdoms, one of
which is the fungal kingdom. Within
each kingdom further subdivisions
have been made, breaking the units
into smaller, more numerous groups.

Within the fungal kingdom there
are three phyla (see p.11). These are
divided into classes, then orders.
Within orders, fungi with similar traits
are grouped into families and then
genera, which link closely related
species. Each of these subdivisions has
its own scientific (Latin) name; the
name for individual species consists of
the genus name followed by a specific
(species) epithet. Many familiar species
also have another name, the so-called
common name.

As an example, the full scientific
classification for the widespread
Common Chanterelle (*Cantharellus
cibarius* p.28) is shown below.

KINGDOM
Fungi

PHYLUM
Basidiomycota

CLASS
Hymenomycetes

ORDER
Cantharellales

FAMILY
Cantharellaceae

GENUS (PLURAL GENERA)
Cantharellus

SPECIES
Cantharellus cibarius

*Cantharellus
cibarius* ▷

HOW THIS BOOK WORKS

THE FUNGI FEATURED in this book are placed in one of 16 main sections, based on their most obvious visual characteristics (see pp.24–27). To make identification even simpler, the larger sections are divided into subsections according to more detailed traits. Most of the fungi are shown at slightly smaller than life size; a few are enlarged to show more detail. ∎

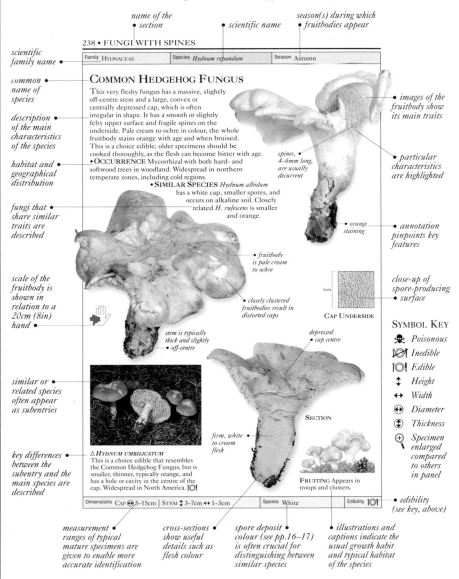

name of the section

scientific name

season(s) during which fruitbodies appear

238 • FUNGI WITH SPINES

scientific family name

Family HYDNACEAE | Species Hydnum repandum | Season Autumn

common name of species

COMMON HEDGEHOG FUNGUS

description of the main characteristics of the species

This very fleshy fungus has a massive, slightly off-centre stem and a large, convex or centrally depressed cap, which is often irregular in shape. It has a smooth or slightly felty upper surface and fragile spines on the underside. Pale cream to ochre in colour, the whole fruitbody stains orange with age and when bruised. This is a choice edible; older specimens should be cooked thoroughly, as the flesh can become bitter with age.

habitat and geographical distribution

• **OCCURRENCE** Mycorrhizal with both hard- and softwood trees in woodland. Widespread in northern temperate zones, including cold regions.

fungi that share similar traits are described

• **SIMILAR SPECIES** *Hydnum albidum* has a white cap, smaller spores, and occurs on alkaline soil. Closely related *H. rufescens* is smaller and orange.

images of the fruitbody show its main traits

particular characteristics are highlighted

spines, 4–6mm long, are usually decurrent

orange staining

annotation pinpoints key features

fruitbody is pale cream to ochre

scale of the fruitbody is shown in relation to a 20cm (8in) hand

closely clustered fruitbodies result in distorted caps

CAP UNDERSIDE

close-up of spore-producing surface

stem is typically thick and slightly off-centre

depressed cap centre

SYMBOL KEY

☠ Poisonous

⛔ Inedible

🍴 Edible

↕ Height

↔ Width

⊕ Diameter

⊕ Thickness

🔍 Specimen enlarged compared to others in panel

similar or related species often appear as subentries

firm, white to cream flesh

SECTION

△ HYDNUM UMBILICATUM
This is a choice edible that resembles the Common Hedgehog Fungus, but is smaller, thinner, typically orange, and has a hole or cavity in the centre of the cap. Widespread in North America. 🍴

key differences between the subentry and the main species are described

FRUITING Appears in troops and clusters.

Dimensions CAP ⊕ 5–15cm | STEM ↕ 3–7cm ↔ 1–3cm | Spores White | Edibility 🍴

edibility (see key, above)

measurement ranges of typical mature specimens are given to enable more accurate identification

cross-sections show useful details such as flesh colour

spore deposit colour (see pp.16–17) is often crucial for distinguishing between similar species

illustrations and captions indicate the usual growth habit and typical habitat of the species

WHAT IS A MUSHROOM?

IN POPULAR USAGE, mushrooms are fungi that produce conspicuous fruitbodies. Often the only visible part of a fungus, fruitbodies vary from the well-known cap and stem type shown below, to the variety illustrated on pp.12–13. Their function is to produce sexual spores, and mycologists divide all fungi species into three groups, or phyla, according to the way in which they do this (see p.11). The majority of species in this book belong to Basidiomycota; most of the others to Ascomycota. Zygomycota is represented by two mushroom parasites.

ANATOMY OF A FRUITBODY

Every fungus, including its fruitbodies, consists of masses of minute threads called hyphae. Hidden in the substrate, the hyphae form into mycelia, which produce fruitbodies on the surface when conditions are favourable. All fruitbodies have an area of fertile, spore-producing tissue, known as the hymenium, which is often supported by a fleshy structure, such as a cap on a stem.

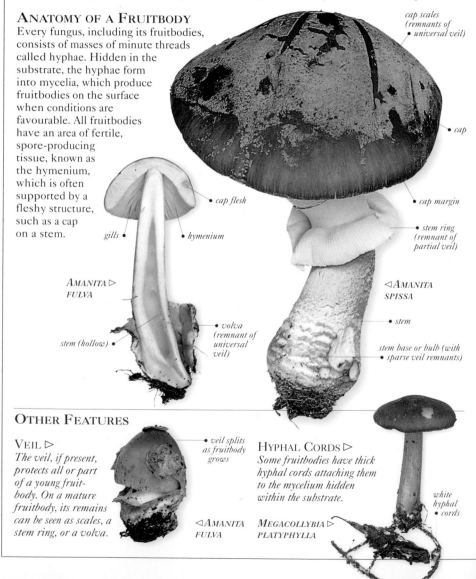

cap scales (remnants of universal veil)

cap

cap flesh

cap margin

stem ring (remnant of partial veil)

gills

hymenium

AMANITA ▷
FULVA

◁ AMANITA
SPISSA

stem

stem (hollow)

volva (remnant of universal veil)

stem base or bulb (with sparse veil remnants)

OTHER FEATURES

VEIL ▷
The veil, if present, protects all or part of a young fruit-body. On a mature fruitbody, its remains can be seen as scales, a stem ring, or a volva.

veil splits as fruitbody grows

◁ AMANITA
FULVA

HYPHAL CORDS ▷
Some fruitbodies have thick hyphal cords attaching them to the mycelium hidden within the substrate.

MEGACOLLYBIA ▷
PLATYPHYLLA

white hyphal cords

ASCOMYCOTA

Ascomycetes form spores inside tiny sac-like structures called asci, each typically producing eight spores. Asci are sited within the hymenium. The hymenium may be on the outside of the fruitbody, such as in morels, or the asci may be loosely distributed inside the fruitbody, as they are in truffles. Many ascomycetes do not produce fruitbodies, but reproduce by asexual spores (conidia).

COMMON MOREL ▷
Morchella esculenta *forms spores within asci lining the honeycomb-like structure of the cap.*

CUP-FUNGUS ASCI ▷
Here, some of the asci have discharged their spores, while others still contain spores that are not yet mature.

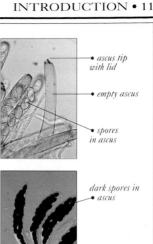

- ascus tip with lid
- empty ascus
- spores in ascus

FALSE FLASK-FUNGUS ASCI ▷
Once the spores in these asci have reached maturity, they are released through an opening in the top.

- dark spores in ascus
- asci are within the hymenium

BASIDIOMYCOTA

Nearly all basidiomycetes produce fruitbodies. The hymenium consists of club-shaped cells (basidia) with outgrowths (sterigmata) at one end, on which the spores are formed. On each basidium there are typically four sterigmata, each producing one spore. Many basidiomycetes are further distinguished from other fungi by clamp connections between their hyphae.

COMMON PUFFBALL ▷
Lycoperdon perlatum *forms spores on basidia in the hymenium, which is in the top of the fruitbody.*

GILL SURFACE ▷
Basidia with spores at different stages of maturity can be seen on this gill surface.

- basidium with four mature spores

hymenium •

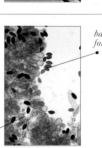

HYPHAL CLAMP ▷
Clamp connections between hyphae are a typical feature of many basidiomycetes.

- hypha
- clamp connection

hypha •

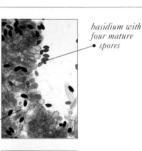

ZYGOMYCOTA

Zygomycetes do not have fruitbodies. Their sexual spores (zygospores) are long lived and able to wait for perfect conditions before germination. Zygomycetes also form asexual spores in structures called sporangia at the end of thread-like sporangiophores. The grey moulds found on foods or dung are mainly zygomycetes.

SPINELLUS FUSIGER ▷
This species consists of masses of thread-like sporangiophores.

Spinellus *growing on* Mycena

- sporangiophores
- sporangia containing asexual spores

FRUITBODY SHAPES

FUNGAL FRUITBODIES occur in a wide range of forms, with several different ways of arranging the spore-producing hymenium. This may be found on gills, in tubes, or on smooth surfaces on the fruitbody; in some fungi it is concealed inside. When the fruitbody is mature the spores are dispersed either actively or passively (see also pp.16–17). The shape of the fruitbody can reveal the method of spore dispersal. For example, tuber-like, rounded fruitbodies, found below ground (pp.258–59), have internal spores that are passively dispersed.

CAP AND STEM ▷
The hymenium lines the sides of the gills under the cap. The spores are actively discharged.

STEM OFF-CENTRE OR ABSENT ▷
The hymenium lines the gills under the cap. The spores are actively discharged.

SADDLE-LIKE CAP ▷
The hymenium lines the folds of the cap. The spores are actively discharged.

HONEYCOMB-LIKE CAP ▷
The hymenium lines the cavities in the cap. The spores are actively discharged.

BRACKET-LIKE ▷
The underside is smooth or has tubes lined with the hymenium. The spores are actively discharged.

SKIN-LIKE, GROWING FLAT OR CRUST-LIKE ▽
The hymenium covers most of the fruitbody surface. The spores are actively discharged.

◁ CLUB-SHAPED
The hymenium either covers the surface or is situated in flasks embedded in the flesh. The spores are actively discharged.

PHALLUS-LIKE ▷
The hymenium is formed within an egg-like structure and is then elevated on a stem. The slimy spore mass is dispersed by flies.

◁ **ANTLER-LIKE**
The hymenium covers most of the surface. The spores are actively discharged.

CORAL-LIKE ▷
The hymenium covers most of the surface. The spores are actively discharged.

ROUNDED ▷
The hymenium is formed internally or in flasks. The spores are passively or actively discharged.

◁ **PEAR- TO PESTLE-SHAPED**
The hymenium is formed internally. The spores are passively dispersed, often via raindrops.

△ **CUP- OR DISC-SHAPED**
The hymenium lines the inner or upper side. The spores are actively discharged.

CUP-SHAPED CONTAINING "EGGS" △
The "eggs" have an internal hymenium. The whole "egg" is propelled by rain splashes.

◁ **TRUMPET-SHAPED**
The hymenium is on the smooth to wrinkled outer surface. The spores are actively discharged.

STAR-SHAPED ▷
The hymenium is formed in a closed structure that splits. The spores are dispersed by rain splashes or flies.

CAGE-LIKE ▷
The hymenium is within a structure that splits into a mesh. The spores are dispersed by insects.

EAR-LIKE ▷
The hymenium is on the surface of the lobes. The spores are actively discharged.

LOBED AND GELATINOUS ▷
The hymenium is on the surface of the lobes. The spores are actively discharged.

CAP FEATURES

T HE CAP can provide lots of clues to the identity of a species. Its overall shape and features on the surface, such as scales or marginal threads (indicating remains of the veil) are important. Key characteristics include any structures on the underside of the cap, such as gills or pores, and their attachment to the stem.

CAP SHAPES AND SURFACES

Cap shape and surface texture can change as the fruitbody matures, so try to examine several specimens. A usually sticky surface may become non-sticky in dry weather. Test it by touching it with a moistened lower lip (the "kiss" test). If it sticks to the lip, it will have been sticky in more humid conditions.

CONVEX
Cap is more or less the shape of a bun

CONICAL
Cap is cone- or near cone-shaped

FUNNEL-SHAPED
Cap has a depressed centre

UMBONATE
Raised boss in centre of cap

LOOSE SCALES
Removable veil scales

PLEATED
Surface of cap is folded radially into pleats

SCALY
Cap skin is covered with fixed scales

STRIATE
Striations are gills seen through cap skin

GROOVED MARGIN
Distinct radial ridges at edges of cap

CONCENTRIC ZONES
Different colour zones

SHAGGY
Dense layer of long, fibrous scales on cap

STICKY
Cap skin is sticky-slimy (may dry up)

INROLLED MARGIN
Cap edge rolls inwards, especially when young

FOLDED
Whole cap consists of many folds of flesh

SADDLE-SHAPED
More or less folded cap, shaped like a saddle

HONEYCOMBED
Cap with indented cells similar to a honeycomb

GILLS IN SECTION

If the cap has gills it is vital to note how, and if, they are attached to the stem (if present). This is seen by making a section with a sharp knife. Free gills are not connected to the stem, which can often be loosened from the cap by twisting. If only a very narrow part of the gill runs down the stem, this is often called decurrent with a tooth.

DECURRENT
Gills run down stem, slightly or markedly

ADNATE
Broadly attached gills

ADNEXED
Narrowly attached gills appear almost free

FREE
Gills not joined to stem, which can be removed

NOTCHED
Gills indented just before joining stem

SINUATE NOTCHED
Curved and indented before joining stem

GILLS FROM BENEATH

Taking note of the cap underside can be useful in identification. For example, the proportion of full-length gills to shorter gills is an important feature, as is the number of gills and the distance between them.

EQUAL
All gills reach stem and are the same length

UNEQUAL
Full-length gills mixed with shorter ones

FORKED
Gills divide one or several times

CROWDED
Gills are arranged very close together

WIDELY SPACED
Gills are far apart from each other

JOINED TO COLLAR
Gills joined at a collar instead of reaching stem

RADIATING
Gills radiate from the margin of the cap

OTHER SPORE-PRODUCING SURFACES

Instead of having gills, some cap and stem fungi and bracket-like species have the hymenium on surfaces that are smooth to wrinkled, toothed, or in tubes. Rounded to angular pores on the fruitbody underside indicate that the hymenium is in tubes.

GILL-LIKE VEINS
Hymenium covers folds and wrinkles on the undersurface

TUBES WITH PORES
Hymenium lines tubes, which are vertical with pore-like openings

SPINES
Hymenium positioned vertically on spine-shaped structures

SPORES AND SPORE DISPERSAL

FUNGI PRODUCE SPORES to colonize suitable substrates, and just one fruitbody can produce billions of them. Spores can be asexual or sexual. Asexual spores (conidia) may produce individual mycelia that can then grow on their own. Sexual spores can sometimes establish independent mycelia but often a fusion with another mycelium has to take place before they can continue to grow.

HOW SPORES ARE DISPERSED

Spores can be dispersed either passively or actively. Passive dispersal relies on animals, wind, or water; active discharge occurs when the fruitbody itself has a special mechanism that ejects or propels the spores when they reach maturity.

EJECTION
In flask-fungi, including this Xylaria, *the mature asci eject the spores some distance through the mouths of the tiny fruitbodies.*

BY ANIMAL
Sticky spore masses, such as on this Phallus *species, are eaten by insects. Some spores stick to the insects and are borne away.*

BY WATER AND WIND
As rain falls on the fruitbodies of puffballs like this Lycoperdon, *they compress and the spores are released, to be dispersed by wind.*

SPORE DEPOSITS

A useful way of confirming the genus to which a fungus belongs is to find out the colour of its spore deposit. Taking a spore deposit from a gilled mushroom (agaric) is an easy process and can produce fascinating results, as it reveals both the pattern of the gill spaces and the colour of the spores. Cut the cap from a fresh specimen and place it gill-side down on paper. Use black paper to take pale spore deposits; for unknown colours, place the cap half over white paper and half over black paper.

1 COVERING THE CAP
Remove the stem and place the cap, gills down, on the paper. A drop of water on the top keeps it moist. Cover with glass – a bowl or tumbler – and leave for several hours or overnight.

2 REMOVING THE CAP
Gently lift the glass then the cap to reveal the spore deposit. The thicker the deposit, the easier it is to get an accurate idea of the spore colour. The deposit should be observed in natural light.

SPORE COLOUR

Species within a genus typically have spore deposits of more or less the same colour, so the genus of a specimen can be revealed by its spore colour. For example, all *Agaricus* species have spores in dark brown shades. In some genera, such as *Russula* (pp.120–31), the spore colour can also be used to differentiate between similar species. Spore deposits are usually black, white to cream, or red, purple, or brown shades. Exceptions include *Chlorophyllum molybdites* (p.166), which has a green deposit.

PINKISH TO RED

OCHRE TO CLAY

BLACK

WHITE TO CREAM

PURPLE-BROWN

RUST-BROWN

SPORE SHAPE AND SIZE

Spore shape and size can be very important in the final correct identification of a species. Most spores are less than 20 microns (µm) long or wide (0.02mm) and many are smaller than 5µm, although some can be up to about 2mm in diameter. Their shape varies according to the method of their dispersal: actively discharged spores are typically asymmetrical whereas those dispersed by passive means tend to be symmetrical. The spore chart on pp.284–88 gives spore shapes and average sizes, as well as other details, for species in this book.

eyepiece with inbuilt micrometer

stage for slides

focusing knob

inbuilt light source

◁ MICROSCOPE
To identify spore shapes and sizes, you will need a good-quality, though not necessarily very expensive, microscope. Ideally, enlargement should be × 1000, but good results can be obtained at only × 400. An inbuilt light source is very useful.

all of these close-ups are × 2000 life size

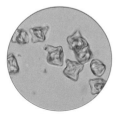

ENTOLOMA CONFERENDUM
Entoloma *species have angular spores. Those of* E. conferendum *are star-like in shape and many faceted.*

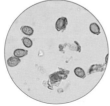

GANODERMA APPLANATUM
G. applanatum *has rough-textured spores that are truncated at one end and have a double skin.*

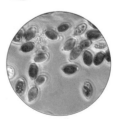

COPRINUS ATRAMENTARIUS
Like many Coprinus *species, the black spores of this species each have a tiny pore from which the hyphae germinate.*

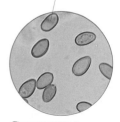

CONIOPHORA PUTEANA
The ellipsoid spores of C. puteana *have a smooth surface and appear yellow-brown in colour.*

MUSHROOM LIFESTYLES

Once a mushroom has established itself by forming a mycelium, it has to find a way to continue to grow and live. Different types of fungi have different methods of survival. Many have to form a mutually beneficial, or mycorrhizal, relationship with a living partner, such as a tree, which enables both to survive; others, known as saprotrophs, degrade (break down) dead material. There are also some fungi that kill plants or animals. These are called necrotrophs. Through their ability to break down dead matter or provide suitable growing conditions for other living things, fungi play a vital role in the ecological balance of the environment.

◁ THE HOST TREE
A single tree species can provide different fungi with what they need to survive. The spruce, shown here, can support mycorrhizal fungi, saprotrophs can live off its litter, and necrotrophs may kill it then live off its remains.

MYCORRHIZAL

Mycorrhizae are the basis for a close beneficial relationship between the tree and the fungus, in which the tree gives the fungus sugars, while the fungus provides water and nutrients. A mycorrhizal relationship is formed when the hyphae of fungi species, including some agarics and most boletes, penetrate roots of a suitable, living, host tree.

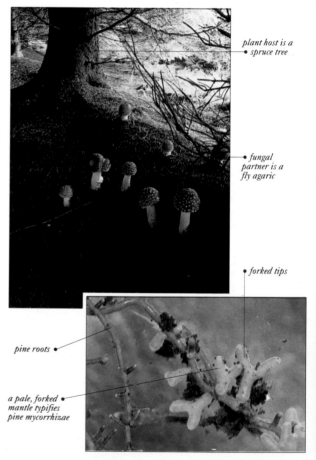

plant host is a
• spruce tree

• fungal
partner is a
fly agaric

• forked tips

SPECIAL RELATIONSHIP ▷
These fruitbodies of Amanita muscaria *(p.146) are near a spruce tree with which they may have formed mycorrhizae. Other trees, such as birch and oak, also form mycorrhizae with fungi.*

BELOW GROUND ▷
Where there is a mycorrhizal partnership, the fungus grows a mantle around the tiniest tree roots and a net of hyphae in between the outer root cells. Nutrients are exchanged between the partners via complex chemical pathways.

pine roots •

a pale, forked •
mantle typifies
pine mycorrhizae

SAPROTROPHIC

With the aid of enzymes, which they release externally, saprotrophic fungi degrade many types of dead organic matter, including fungi and animals. Some saprotrophs, such as *Strobilurus esculentus* (right), only occur on one substrate, in this case a spruce cone. Others are wider in their range. Some fungal species are even present in a passive form in living plants, waiting to start their activity once the plant dies.

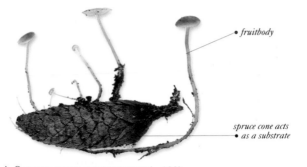

• *fruitbody*

spruce cone acts
• *as a substrate*

△ *STROBILURUS ESCULENTUS* (p.133)
This specialized saprotroph degrades only fallen spruce cones. It produces fruitbodies after obtaining the materials it needs from the substrate.

NECROTROPHIC

Necrotrophs live off and eventually kill living plants. Some kill their host by blocking or destroying the plant's water and nutrient transport system with hyphae or specially-produced, yeast-like cells; others use toxins. After killing the plant, the necrotroph acts like a saprotroph (see above), degrading the plant as a substrate. Necrotrophs include *Fomes fomentarius* (p.219), and *Armillaria* species (pp.42 and 80).

stump of
• *spruce tree*

• *fruitbody*

△ *HETEROBASIDION ANNOSUM* (p.222)
This species causes extensive damage in spruce plantations, spreading from tree to tree via the roots. Following the death of the tree, the wood is degraded by the fungus and brackets are produced.

BIOTROPHIC

Like mycorrhizal fungi, biotrophic fungi, such as rusts and mildews, depend on a living host. However, in this case, the plant does not benefit. Special hyphae are often produced by the fungus, which penetrate the host cells and transport the nutrients back to the fungus. Although the plant is not killed, its life processes may be affected. For example, spores may contaminate seed and germinate in seedlings.

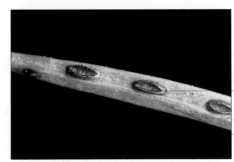

fruitbody with
• *slit-like opening*

• *diseased*
spruce needle

△ *LOPHODERMIUM PICEAE*
This tar-spot fungus produces black marks on spruce needles. Other Lophodermium *species may cause severe leaf fall on pines and other trees.*

MUSHROOM HABITATS

FUNGI OCCUR throughout the world, but most of the species in this book can be found in the northern temperate zones. Some are widespread, occurring in North America, Europe, and Asia; others are restricted to a single continent or a very localized region within it. Most fungi are confined to a very specific environment, so it is important to be able to recognize the main habitats, including their indigenous plants, and which mushrooms occur in them.

WOODLAND

The many varieties of woodland support different types of fungal life. Alkaline loam dominated by ash trees tends to contain non-mycorrhizal species, such as *Lepiota*. Acid, peaty soil, with beech or birch trees, has a high proportion of mycorrhizal fungi, such as boletes, knight-caps, and russules. Mineral-laden soil, along paths or beside ditches, can support species of *Lepiota*, *Psathyrella*, and *Peziza*, which thrive on comparatively small amounts of organic matter.

△ PINE WOODLAND
Sandy pine woods are home to many boletes, such as Suillus bovinus *(p.200), as well as russules (pp.120–29). Wetter, mossy pine forests are also rich in fungi.*

△ SUILLUS BOVINUS

◁ OAK WOODLAND
Mycorrhizal fungi and sapro-trophs, such as Fistulina *species, occur with oak trees. Some of the same species are also found growing with sweet chestnuts.*

◁ FISTULINA HEPATICA

SOFTWOOD TREES

Most softwood trees, or conifers, form important mycorrhizal relationships with fungi. Many fungus species are only found under one particular type of conifer, so knowing the tree's name makes an accurate identification of the fungus more likely. The trees shown are among the most important.

LARCH (*LARIX*)   SPRUCE (*PICEA*)   PINE (*PINUS*)

GRASSLAND

There are many types of grassland, from the basic monocultures of wheat and barley to heavily fertilized pastures or near-natural, unfertilized but grazed or mown grassland. The mushrooms in such habitats may be directly associated with the grass or other plants in the turf, or they may be dung-fungi, living on the droppings of the animals that graze there. Soil composition is also important, with different fungi species occuring in very acid grassland compared to more neutral or very alkaline soils.

△ FERTILIZED PASTURE
Typically grazed by farm animals, and with limited flora other than grass, fertilized pasture is a suitable habitat for many species of Agaricus, Coprinus, *and* Panaeolus, *which like dung-rich environments.*

△ AGARICUS
CAMPESTRIS

◁ UNFERTILIZED MEADOW
This type of grassland is rich in plant and mushroom species. Dominant fungi include species of Clavaria, Entoloma, *and* Hygrocybe, *which do not thrive in fertilized pasture, possibly because they cannot compete with other fungi that*
◁ HYGROCYBE *flourish where nutrient*
PUNICEA *levels are high.*

HARDWOOD TREES

Mycorrhizal relationships often exist between fungi and the hardwood, or deciduous, trees shown here. There are several other important hardwoods, including ash, elm, and sycamore, which have less direct relationships with fungi.

BIRCH (*BETULA*)

BEECH (*FAGUS*)

OAK (*QUERCUS*)

FORAYING FOR MUSHROOMS

WHEN LOOKING FOR FUNGI, remember to leave some fruitbodies in place so that they can mature, and, after your studies, throw leftovers on a compost heap or put them back in woodland. Check for maggots before gathering edibles.

EQUIPMENT
A sharp knife and a basket or a compartmentalized collection box are essential equipment for forayers. Tweezers are helpful for handling tiny specimens, and a hand lens reveals small details. A camera and note pad are useful for documenting finds.

FLAT BASKET

KNIFE **TWEEZERS**

COLLECTION BOX WITH COMPARTMENTS

HAND LENS

CAMERA WITH MACRO LENS

NOTE PAD AND PENCILS

HOW TO PICK
Although most species can be gathered using a knife, secateurs or a small pruning saw can be useful for collecting specimens on twigs or pieces of wood. Once picked, keep the fungi in closed containers so that important features are not lost and they do not dry out. Take a sniff when opening the container to detect diagnostic smells. Avoid picking poisonous or endangered species by making a preliminary attempt at identification before lifting specimens.

CUTTING WITH A KNIFE
When picking a mushroom, use a knife to lift out the stem base. Do not handle specimens more than absolutely necessary as this could damage or destroy useful identification characteristics.

THINGS TO NOTE

• **STAINING** Scratch with a finger nail to test for colour changes.
• **TEXTURE** Rub the flesh between your fingers to check its texture.
• **SMELL** Check for any distinctive fragrance.
• **TASTE** Only test with a tiny piece and always spit the sample out.
• **CHEMICAL TESTS** Join a local mycology group to get help with chemical tests, which can be very useful in identification.

TAKING MEASUREMENTS

Standard measurements for different types of fungi are shown here. Although mushrooms vary in size, and can grow quite a lot before they are fully mature, it is useful to take measurements as an aid to identification. The dimensions given in the species descriptions are of average mature specimens.

distance from front to back

depth from top to bottom

width from side to side

BRACKET THICKNESS ⊕

BRACKET WIDTH BY DEPTH ⊕

measure largest diameter

height from top to bottom of cap

measure to just under cap

STEM WIDTH ↔

STEM HEIGHT ↕

width of base

CAP DIAMETER ⊕

CAP HEIGHT ↕

POISONOUS OR EDIBLE?

Some poisonous mushrooms look similar to edible ones, so forayers are strongly advised to familiarize themselves with the dangerous species. Never eat anything you cannot identify accurately. If you suspect poisoning seek medical advice, taking along a sample of the fungus. Of the fungi here, *Amanita pantherina* can be lethal; *Agaricus xanthoderma* and *Russula mairei* produce minor poisonings. Note also: *Amanita phalloides* p.151, *A. virosa* p.150, *Cortinarius rubellus* p.72, and *C. orellanus* p.73.

AMANITA PANTHERINA p.149

AMANITA RUBESCENS p.147

RUSSULA MAIREI p.129

RUSSULA XERAMPELINA p.127

AGARICUS XANTHODERMA p.159

AGARICUS ARVENSIS p.158

IDENTIFICATION

To IDENTIFY A MUSHROOM, use the keys on the following pages to find out what type it is and where it is most likely to be described in the species section. Answer the simple question (right), then follow the instructions and illustrations to the end. If at any point you become "stuck", return to the start and double-check each characteristic. Note: remember, never eat a mushroom unless you are absolutely certain of its identity.

DOES IT HAVE A CAP AND STEM?

YES

SEE BELOW ▽

NO

SEE PAGE 26 ▷▷

CAP AND STEM FUNGI: MAIN TYPES

Examine the cap, especially the underside, and choose the most similar illustration below to progress to the next step. If the underside has gills, decide whether they are decurrent, adnexed to adnate, or free. A section will reveal this more clearly. If there are pores or spines instead (see p.15), choose a different illustration. Also check the stem is central. Note: the illustrations are for example only, your specimen could differ in colour or shape.

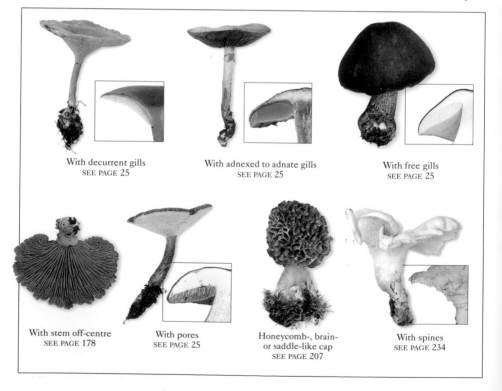

With decurrent gills
SEE PAGE 25

With adnexed to adnate gills
SEE PAGE 25

With free gills
SEE PAGE 25

With stem off-centre
SEE PAGE 178

With pores
SEE PAGE 25

Honeycomb-, brain- or saddle-like cap
SEE PAGE 207

With spines
SEE PAGE 234

CAP AND STEM FUNGI: OTHER CHARACTERISTICS

In this book, cap and stem fungi with gills or pores are divided into the subsections shown below. Choose the illustration and description that is closest to the fruitbodies you wish to identify, then turn to the page given. Be prepared to try again with any fruitbodies that fit more than one subsection. Spore colour and size is often required to confirm identity.

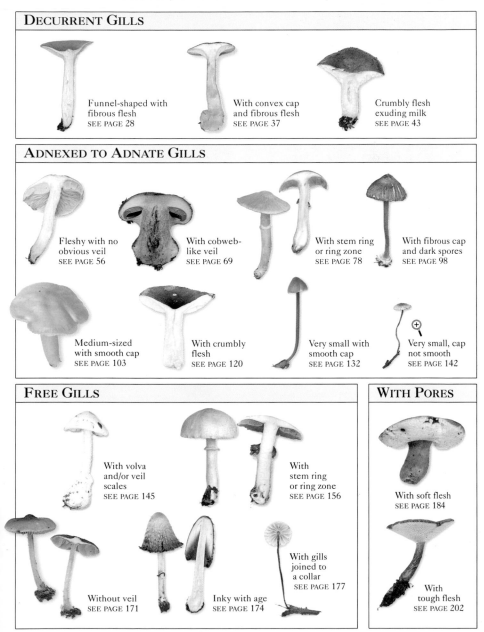

DECURRENT GILLS

Funnel-shaped with fibrous flesh
SEE PAGE 28

With convex cap and fibrous flesh
SEE PAGE 37

Crumbly flesh exuding milk
SEE PAGE 43

ADNEXED TO ADNATE GILLS

Fleshy with no obvious veil
SEE PAGE 56

With cobweb-like veil
SEE PAGE 69

With stem ring or ring zone
SEE PAGE 78

With fibrous cap and dark spores
SEE PAGE 98

Medium-sized with smooth cap
SEE PAGE 103

With crumbly flesh
SEE PAGE 120

Very small with smooth cap
SEE PAGE 132

Very small, cap not smooth
SEE PAGE 142

FREE GILLS

With volva and/or veil scales
SEE PAGE 145

With stem ring or ring zone
SEE PAGE 156

Without veil
SEE PAGE 171

Inky with age
SEE PAGE 174

With gills joined to a collar
SEE PAGE 177

WITH PORES

With soft flesh
SEE PAGE 184

With tough flesh
SEE PAGE 202

OTHER FUNGI: MAIN TYPES

This part of the key features fungi that do not combine a cap and stem and are not, for the most part, the traditional "mushroom" shape. The best first clue to their identity is to decide on their shape and appearance, followed by other features such as texture or where they grow (see p.27). Compare your specimen with the shapes illustrated and choose the closest example, bearing in mind that there are many variations, some of which can be seen in the final part of the key on p.27. Do not expect to see the exact replica of what you have found illustrated here, and do not be put off by differences in colour or details. Turn to the pages indicated to learn about variations in shapes and sizes within each section.

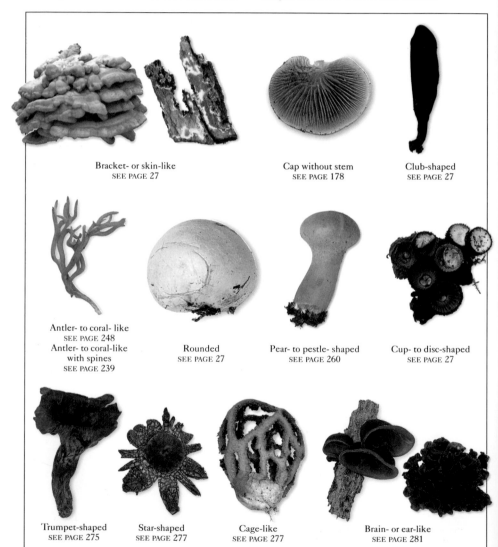

Bracket- or skin-like
SEE PAGE 27

Cap without stem
SEE PAGE 178

Club-shaped
SEE PAGE 27

Antler- to coral- like
SEE PAGE 248
Antler- to coral-like
with spines
SEE PAGE 239

Rounded
SEE PAGE 27

Pear- to pestle- shaped
SEE PAGE 260

Cup- to disc-shaped
SEE PAGE 27

Trumpet-shaped
SEE PAGE 275

Star-shaped
SEE PAGE 277

Cage-like
SEE PAGE 277

Brain- or ear-like
SEE PAGE 281

OTHER FUNGI: OTHER CHARACTERISTICS

In this book, the sections that contain a wide variety of forms are further subdivided. The subsections for fungi that are not the familiar cap and stem shape are illustrated below. Pick the illustration and description most similar to the fruitbodies you have found then turn to the page given. It is helpful to use a hand-lens to check whether the underside of a bracket is smooth or has thousands of minute pores. Note: the illustrations here are not to scale.

BRACKET- OR SKIN-LIKE

With pores
SEE PAGE 211

Wrinkled or smooth underneath
SEE PAGE 228

Skin-like, growing flat or crust-like
SEE PAGE 232

CLUB-SHAPED

Smooth or hairy
SEE PAGE 240

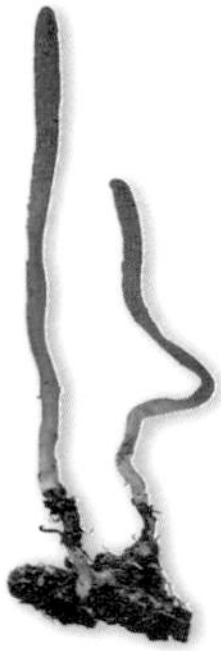

With pimples or a dusty surface
SEE PAGE 244

Phallus-like
SEE PAGE 246

ROUNDED

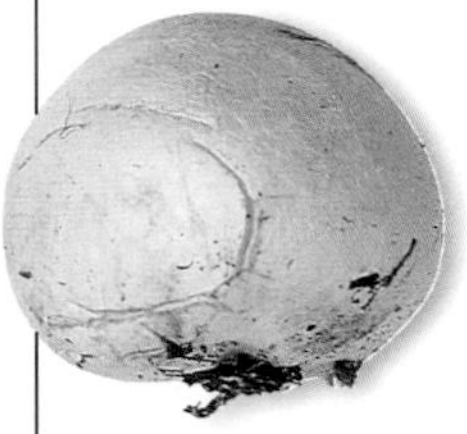

Above ground
SEE PAGE 253

Below ground
SEE PAGE 258

CUP- TO DISC-SHAPED

Without "eggs"
SEE PAGE 264

Cup-shaped containing "eggs"
SEE PAGE 274

CAP & STEM FUNGI WITH DECURRENT GILLS

Fungi that have caps and stems, with gills under the caps, are called agarics. This section consists of agarics with "decurrent" gills – gills that run down the stem. Chanterelles with gill-like, decurrent veins are included here.

• *decurrent gills run down stem*

FUNNEL-SHAPED WITH FIBROUS FLESH

T HIS SUBSECTION features agarics with funnel-shaped to depressed caps. They also have distinctly fibrous flesh, unlike the crumbly flesh of milk-caps (see pp.43–55) or russules (see pp.120–31). The combination of fibrous flesh and funnel-shaped caps can also be found in distantly related families.

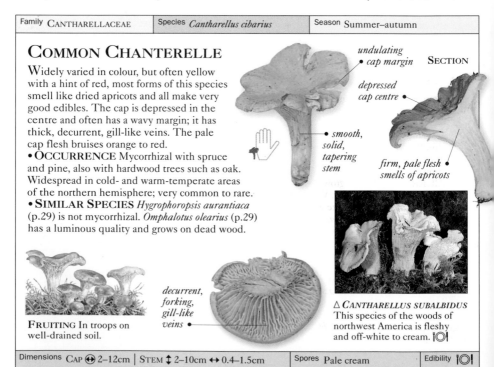

Family CANTHARELLACEAE	Species *Cantharellus cibarius*	Season Summer–autumn

COMMON CHANTERELLE

Widely varied in colour, but often yellow with a hint of red, most forms of this species smell like dried apricots and all make very good edibles. The cap is depressed in the centre and often has a wavy margin; it has thick, decurrent, gill-like veins. The pale cap flesh bruises orange to red.
• **OCCURRENCE** Mycorrhizal with spruce and pine, also with hardwood trees such as oak. Widespread in cold- and warm-temperate areas of the northern hemisphere; very common to rare.
• **SIMILAR SPECIES** *Hygrophoropsis aurantiaca* (p.29) is not mycorrhizal. *Omphalotus olearius* (p.29) has a luminous quality and grows on dead wood.

undulating • cap margin SECTION

depressed cap centre •

• smooth, solid, tapering stem

firm, pale flesh • smells of apricots

FRUITING In troops on well-drained soil.

decurrent, forking, gill-like veins •

△ *CANTHARELLUS SUBALBIDUS*
This species of the woods of northwest America is fleshy and off-white to cream. |O|

Dimensions CAP ⊕ 2–12cm	STEM ↕ 2–10cm ↔ 0.4–1.5cm	Spores Pale cream	Edibility |O|

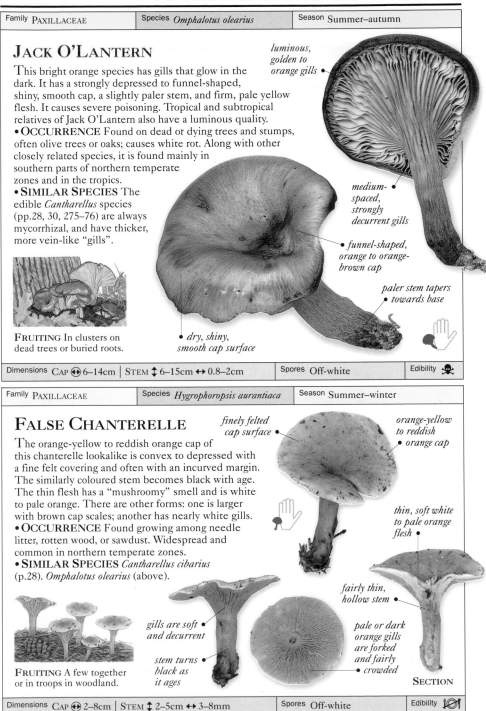

| Family PAXILLACEAE | Species *Omphalotus olearius* | Season Summer–autumn |

JACK O'LANTERN

This bright orange species has gills that glow in the dark. It has a strongly depressed to funnel-shaped, shiny, smooth cap, a slightly paler stem, and firm, pale yellow flesh. It causes severe poisoning. Tropical and subtropical relatives of Jack O'Lantern also have a luminous quality.
• OCCURRENCE Found on dead or dying trees and stumps, often olive trees or oaks; causes white rot. Along with other closely related species, it is found mainly in southern parts of northern temperate zones and in the tropics.
• SIMILAR SPECIES The edible *Cantharellus* species (pp.28, 30, 275–76) are always mycorrhizal, and have thicker, more vein-like "gills".

luminous, golden to orange gills

medium-spaced, strongly decurrent gills

funnel-shaped, orange to orange-brown cap

paler stem tapers towards base

FRUITING In clusters on dead trees or buried roots.

dry, shiny, smooth cap surface

| Dimensions CAP ⊕ 6–14cm | STEM ↕ 6–15cm ↔ 0.8–2cm | Spores Off-white | Edibility 💀 |

| Family PAXILLACEAE | Species *Hygrophoropsis aurantiaca* | Season Summer–winter |

FALSE CHANTERELLE

The orange-yellow to reddish orange cap of this chanterelle lookalike is convex to depressed with a fine felt covering and often with an incurved margin. The similarly coloured stem becomes black with age. The thin flesh has a "mushroomy" smell and is white to pale orange. There are other forms: one is larger with brown cap scales; another has nearly white gills.
• OCCURRENCE Found growing among needle litter, rotten wood, or sawdust. Widespread and common in northern temperate zones.
• SIMILAR SPECIES *Cantharellus cibarius* (p.28). *Omphalotus olearius* (above).

finely felted cap surface

orange-yellow to reddish orange cap

thin, soft white to pale orange flesh

fairly thin, hollow stem

gills are soft and decurrent

stem turns black as it ages

pale or dark orange gills are forked and fairly crowded

FRUITING A few together or in troops in woodland.

SECTION

| Dimensions CAP ⊕ 2–8cm | STEM ↕ 2–5cm ↔ 3–8mm | Spores Off-white | Edibility 🍴 |

| Family CANTHARELLACEAE | Species *Cantharellus cinnabarinus* | Season Summer–autumn |

CINNABAR CHANTERELLE

This very brightly coloured species has a broadly convex cap that becomes funnel-shaped with a distinctly incurved and wavy margin as it matures. The cap emerges cinnabar-red and ages to pink-red. The pink to red stem is fairly short. The decurrent, pink, gill-like veins are forked with thick edges. The edible, fibrous flesh is fairly thin and red to off-white in the cap, thicker and white in the stem.
• **OCCURRENCE** Mycorrhizal especially with oak trees, often appearing in moss. Widespread and common in eastern North America.
• **SIMILAR SPECIES** *Hygrocybe cantharellus* has comparatively sharp-edged, unforked gills.

incurved, wavy cap margin

decurrent, thick-edged, forked "gills"

cinnabar-red cap matures pink-red

cap surface is matted and fibrillose

convex cap ages to funnel-shaped

FRUITING Appears in great troops of conspicuous fruitbodies on soil along paths in woodland.

| Dimensions CAP ⊕ 1–4cm | STEM ↕ 1.5–4cm ↔ 0.3–1cm | Spores Pinkish cream | Edibility |O| |

| Family CANTHARELLACEAE | Species *Cantharellus tubaeformis* | Season Autumn–winter |

TRUMPET CHANTERELLE

This species has a domed cap when young, which becomes funnel-shaped with a wavy margin with age. The cap is in shades of brown; the stem is chrome-yellow, fading to dull yellow in mature specimens. It has gill-like veins. Its thin flesh tastes bitter and has an aromatic smell. The dull colouring makes it fairly difficult to find, but when discovered it is normally abundant, enabling large quantities to be gathered for eating.
• **OCCURRENCE** Mycorrhizal with both hard- and softwood trees, especially in older spruce forests and plantations. Widespread throughout northern temperate zones.
• **SIMILAR SPECIES** *Cantharellus lutescens* (p.275) lacks veins beneath.

wavy, irregular cap margin

funnel-shaped mature cap

more or less hollow stem

pale grey veins are decurrent

SECTION

chrome-yellow stem fades to dull yellow

cap occurs in shades of brown

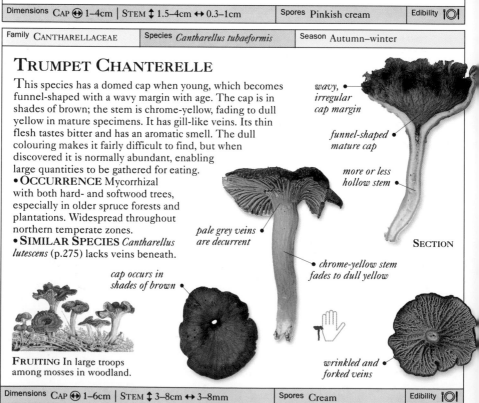

FRUITING In large troops among mosses in woodland.

wrinkled and forked veins

| Dimensions CAP ⊕ 1–6cm | STEM ↕ 3–8cm ↔ 3–8mm | Spores Cream | Edibility |O| |

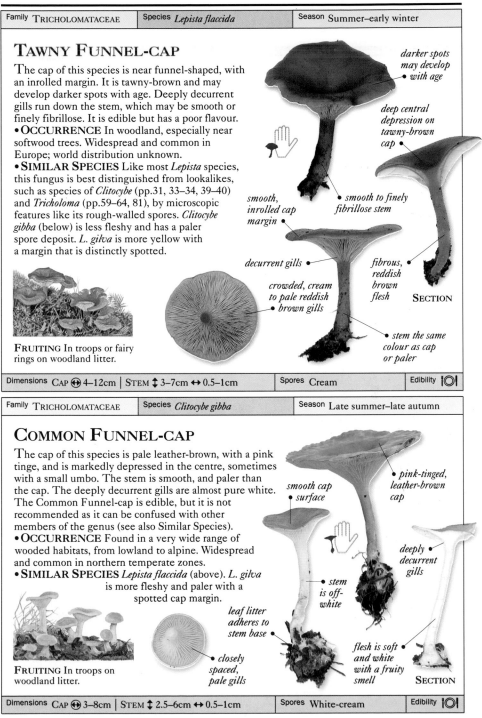

| Family TRICHOLOMATACEAE | Species *Lepista flaccida* | Season Summer–early winter |

TAWNY FUNNEL-CAP

The cap of this species is near funnel-shaped, with an inrolled margin. It is tawny-brown and may develop darker spots with age. Deeply decurrent gills run down the stem, which may be smooth or finely fibrillose. It is edible but has a poor flavour.
• OCCURRENCE In woodland, especially near softwood trees. Widespread and common in Europe; world distribution unknown.
• SIMILAR SPECIES Like most *Lepista* species, this fungus is best distinguished from lookalikes, such as species of *Clitocybe* (pp.31, 33–34, 39–40) and *Tricholoma* (pp.59–64, 81), by microscopic features like its rough-walled spores. *Clitocybe gibba* (below) is less fleshy and has a paler spore deposit. *L. gilva* is more yellow with a margin that is distinctly spotted.

darker spots may develop with age

deep central depression on tawny-brown cap

smooth to finely fibrillose stem

smooth, inrolled cap margin

decurrent gills

crowded, cream to pale reddish brown gills

fibrous, reddish brown flesh

SECTION

stem the same colour as cap or paler

FRUITING In troops or fairy rings on woodland litter.

| Dimensions CAP ⊕ 4–12cm | STEM ‡ 3–7cm ↔ 0.5–1cm | Spores Cream | Edibility |O| |

| Family TRICHOLOMATACEAE | Species *Clitocybe gibba* | Season Late summer–late autumn |

COMMON FUNNEL-CAP

The cap of this species is pale leather-brown, with a pink tinge, and is markedly depressed in the centre, sometimes with a small umbo. The stem is smooth, and paler than the cap. The deeply decurrent gills are almost pure white. The Common Funnel-cap is edible, but it is not recommended as it can be confused with other members of the genus (see also Similar Species).
• OCCURRENCE Found in a very wide range of wooded habitats, from lowland to alpine. Widespread and common in northern temperate zones.
• SIMILAR SPECIES *Lepista flaccida* (above). *L. gilva* is more fleshy and paler with a spotted cap margin.

pink-tinged, leather-brown cap

smooth cap surface

deeply decurrent gills

stem is off-white

leaf litter adheres to stem base

flesh is soft and white with a fruity smell

closely spaced, pale gills

SECTION

FRUITING In troops on woodland litter.

| Dimensions CAP ⊕ 3–8cm | STEM ‡ 2.5–6cm ↔ 0.5–1cm | Spores White-cream | Edibility |O| |

| Family TRICHOLOMATACEAE | Species *Pseudoclitocybe cyathiformis* | Season Late autumn–early winter |

THE GOBLET

This very distinctive species has a strongly funnel-shaped cap, very dark coloration, and a tall stem. The cap dries from dark grey-brown to pale greyish leather-brown and has an inrolled margin. The flesh is aromatic and mild tasting; although edible, it is not recommended. The genus *Pseudoclitocybe* differs from *Clitocybe* (pp.31, 33–34, 39–40) in that the spores produce a blue reaction in iodine reagents (amyloid).
• **OCCURRENCE** In woodland, parkland, and hedgerows, on litter in tall grass, or on very decayed hardwood trunks. Widespread in northern temperate zones; quite common.
• **SIMILAR SPECIES** Other *Pseudoclitocybe* species, on the whole smaller and paler, are often found in more open habitats. *Omphalina* species (p.36) are smaller.

gills are strongly decurrent

smooth, deeply funnel-shaped cap

inrolled cap margin

dark grey-brown cap dries to pale greyish leather-brown

longitudinal striations on stem

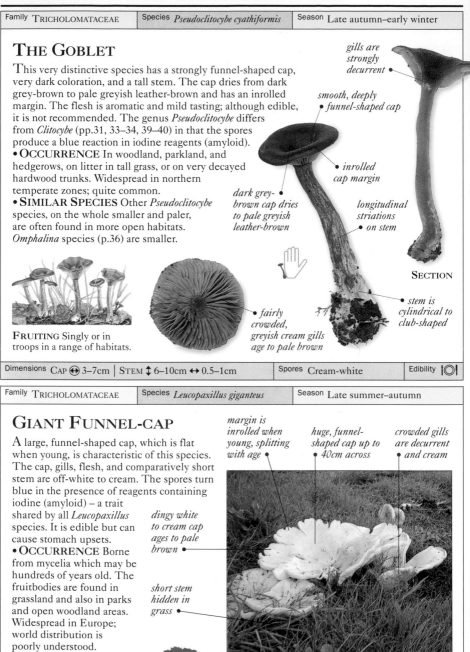

SECTION

stem is cylindrical to club-shaped

fairly crowded, greyish cream gills age to pale brown

FRUITING Singly or in troops in a range of habitats.

| Dimensions CAP ⊕ 3–7cm | STEM ↕ 6–10cm ↔ 0.5–1cm | Spores Cream-white | Edibility |O| |

| Family TRICHOLOMATACEAE | Species *Leucopaxillus giganteus* | Season Late summer–autumn |

GIANT FUNNEL-CAP

A large, funnel-shaped cap, which is flat when young, is characteristic of this species. The cap, gills, flesh, and comparatively short stem are off-white to cream. The spores turn blue in the presence of reagents containing iodine (amyloid) – a trait shared by all *Leucopaxillus* species. It is edible but can cause stomach upsets.
• **OCCURRENCE** Borne from mycelia which may be hundreds of years old. The fruitbodies are found in grassland and also in parks and open woodland areas. Widespread in Europe; world distribution is poorly understood.
• **SIMILAR SPECIES** *Clitocybe geotropa* (p.33) has a longer stem.

margin is inrolled when young, splitting with age

huge, funnel-shaped cap up to 40cm across

crowded gills are decurrent and cream

dingy white to cream cap ages to pale brown

short stem hidden in grass

FRUITING Appears in fairy rings, which may be huge, mostly on nutrient-rich grassland.

| Dimensions CAP ⊕ 12–40cm | STEM ↕ 4–8cm ↔ 2–4cm | Spores Whitish cream | Edibility |O| |

Family TRICHOLOMATACEAE	Species *Clitocybe geotropa*	Season Autumn–early winter

RICKSTONE FUNNEL-CAP

A funnel-shaped, fairly fleshy cap with a central umbo, a tall stem, pale leather-brown colouring, and a tendency to grow in fairy rings make this edible species remarkably easy to identify. This is unusual for the *Clitocybe* genus, which is generally ridden with identification problems.

• **OCCURRENCE** Mostly occurs in woodland. In some parts it is found growing mainly under hardwood trees, but it also thrives in certain types of softwood woodland. Widespread and common in Europe, although not in cooler regions; worldwide distribution is poorly understood.

• **SIMILAR SPECIES** *Clitocybe nebularis* (p.40), often found in similar woodland habitats, is much greyer and has a bun-shaped cap. *Leucopaxillus giganteus* (p.32) has a shorter stem and mostly fruits in nutrient-rich grassland.

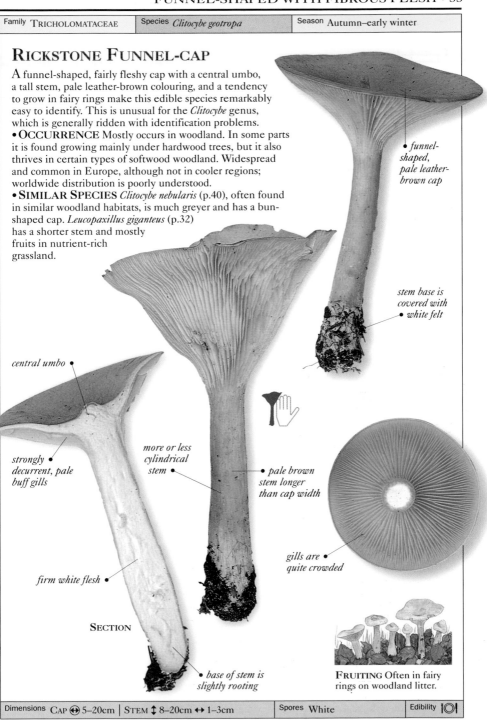

• *funnel-shaped, pale leather-brown cap*

stem base is covered with • *white felt*

central umbo •

strongly • *decurrent, pale buff gills*

more or less cylindrical stem •

• *pale brown stem longer than cap width*

firm white flesh •

SECTION

• *base of stem is slightly rooting*

gills are • *quite crowded*

FRUITING Often in fairy rings on woodland litter.

| Dimensions CAP ⊕ 5–20cm \| STEM ↕ 8–20cm ↔ 1–3cm | Spores White | Edibility |O| |

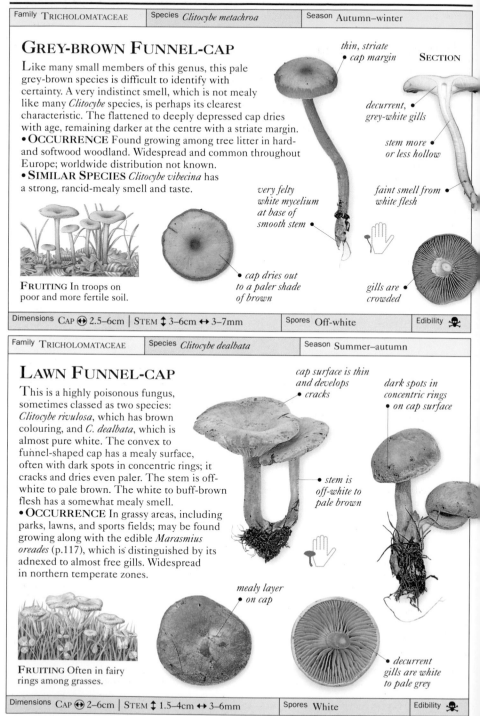

| Family TRICHOLOMATACEAE | Species *Clitocybe metachroa* | Season Autumn–winter |

GREY-BROWN FUNNEL-CAP

Like many small members of this genus, this pale grey-brown species is difficult to identify with certainty. A very indistinct smell, which is not mealy like many *Clitocybe* species, is perhaps its clearest characteristic. The flattened to deeply depressed cap dries with age, remaining darker at the centre with a striate margin.
• **OCCURRENCE** Found growing among tree litter in hard- and softwood woodland. Widespread and common throughout Europe; worldwide distribution not known.
• **SIMILAR SPECIES** *Clitocybe vibecina* has a strong, rancid-mealy smell and taste.

SECTION

thin, striate cap margin

decurrent, grey-white gills

stem more or less hollow

faint smell from white flesh

very felty white mycelium at base of smooth stem

cap dries out to a paler shade of brown

gills are crowded

FRUITING In troops on poor and more fertile soil.

| Dimensions CAP ⊕ 2.5–6cm | STEM ↕ 3–6cm ↔ 3–7mm | Spores Off-white | Edibility ☠ |

| Family TRICHOLOMATACEAE | Species *Clitocybe dealbata* | Season Summer–autumn |

LAWN FUNNEL-CAP

This is a highly poisonous fungus, sometimes classed as two species: *Clitocybe rivulosa*, which has brown colouring, and *C. dealbata*, which is almost pure white. The convex to funnel-shaped cap has a mealy surface, often with dark spots in concentric rings; it cracks and dries even paler. The stem is off-white to pale brown. The white to buff-brown flesh has a somewhat mealy smell.
• **OCCURRENCE** In grassy areas, including parks, lawns, and sports fields; may be found growing along with the edible *Marasmius oreades* (p.117), which is distinguished by its adnexed to almost free gills. Widespread in northern temperate zones.

cap surface is thin and develops cracks

dark spots in concentric rings on cap surface

stem is off-white to pale brown

mealy layer on cap

decurrent gills are white to pale grey

FRUITING Often in fairy rings among grasses.

| Dimensions CAP ⊕ 2–6cm | STEM ↕ 1.5–4cm ↔ 3–6mm | Spores White | Edibility ☠ |

Family PAXILLACEAE	Species *Paxillus involutus*	Season Summer–autumn

BROWN ROLL-RIM

SECTION

A strongly inrolled, yellow- to red-brown cap, with a downy margin and slightly depressed centre, are particularly clear indicators of this very common poisonous species. So are the soft, crowded yellow gills which stain brown where touched and which are removable with a knife tip. Coloured like the cap, the stem is short and felty; the flesh is pale yellow to pale brown and darkens on cutting.

• OCCURRENCE Mycorrhizal mostly with softwood trees and birch, in woodland, parks, and gardens. Widespread and common in northern temperate zones.

• SIMILAR SPECIES *Paxillus filamentosus* has a less incurved margin, yellow flesh, and occurs under alder.

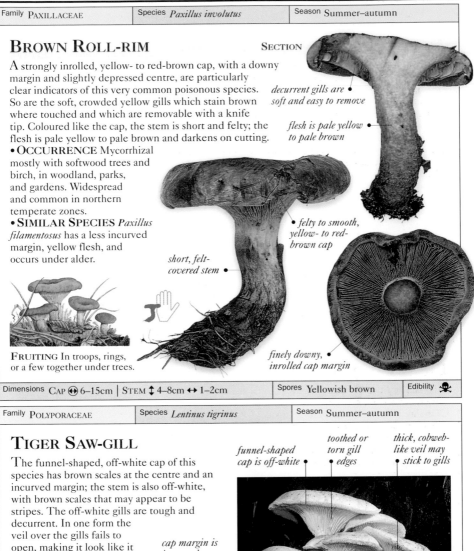

decurrent gills are soft and easy to remove

flesh is pale yellow to pale brown

felty to smooth, yellow- to red-brown cap

short, felt-covered stem •

finely downy, inrolled cap margin

FRUITING In troops, rings, or a few together under trees.

Dimensions CAP ⊕ 6–15cm	STEM ↕ 4–8cm ↔ 1–2cm	Spores Yellowish brown	Edibility ☠

Family POLYPORACEAE	Species *Lentinus tigrinus*	Season Summer–autumn

TIGER SAW-GILL

The funnel-shaped, off-white cap of this species has brown scales at the centre and an incurved margin; the stem is also off-white, with brown scales that may appear to be stripes. The off-white gills are tough and decurrent. In one form the veil over the gills fails to open, making it look like it is parasitized by a mould.

• OCCURRENCE On hardwood trees, in which it causes a white rot. Widespread and common in Europe and also in eastern North America.

• SIMILAR SPECIES *Lentinus lepideus* typically appears singly or in small clusters on softwood, and produces a crumbly brown rot.

funnel-shaped cap is off-white •

toothed or torn gill edges

thick, cobweb-like veil may stick to gills

cap margin is incurved •

scales in stripes on off-white stem •

FRUITING In clusters on old branches or logs, particularly of poplar and willow, often near water.

Dimensions CAP ⊕ 1–10cm	STEM ↕ 1.5–7.5cm ↔ 0.5–1cm	Spores White	Edibility ⬢

| Family TRICHOLOMATACEAE | Species *Omphalina umbellifera* | Season Spring–late autumn |

TURF NAVEL-CAP

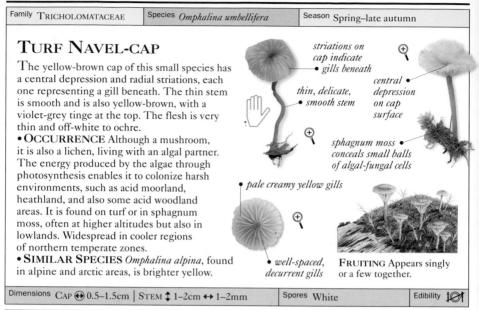

The yellow-brown cap of this small species has a central depression and radial striations, each one representing a gill beneath. The thin stem is smooth and is also yellow-brown, with a violet-grey tinge at the top. The flesh is very thin and off-white to ochre.

• **OCCURRENCE** Although a mushroom, it is also a lichen, living with an algal partner. The energy produced by the algae through photosynthesis enables it to colonize harsh environments, such as acid moorland, heathland, and also some acid woodland areas. It is found on turf or in sphagnum moss, often at higher altitudes but also in lowlands. Widespread in cooler regions of northern temperate zones.

• **SIMILAR SPECIES** *Omphalina alpina*, found in alpine and arctic areas, is brighter yellow.

striations on cap indicate gills beneath

thin, delicate, smooth stem

central depression on cap surface

sphagnum moss conceals small balls of algal-fungal cells

pale creamy yellow gills

well-spaced, decurrent gills

FRUITING Appears singly or a few together.

| Dimensions CAP ⊕ 0.5–1.5cm │ STEM ↕ 1–2cm ↔ 1–2mm | Spores White | Edibility |

| Family TRICHOLOMATACEAE | Species *Rickenella fibula* | Season Summer–autumn |

ORANGE NAVEL-CAP

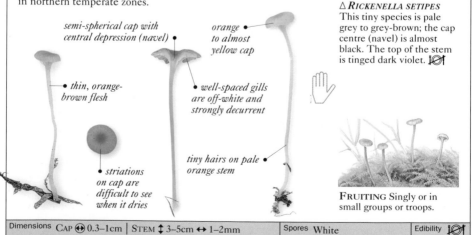

Orange to pale yellow in colour, this species is tiny, with a semi-spherical cap that is centrally depressed and has radial striations, which fade as it dries. The stem is long and thin, and the gills are strongly decurrent. A hand lens reveals fine hairs all over the fruitbody. This and *Rickenella setipes* (inset, right) are the two most common species in the genus. *Rickenella* species have been classified under *Mycena*, *Omphalina*, and *Gerronema*.

• **OCCURRENCE** Parasitic on moss in a range of grassy habitats; a typical lawn mushroom. Widespread and common in northern temperate zones.

△ *RICKENELLA SETIPES*
This tiny species is pale grey to grey-brown; the cap centre (navel) is almost black. The top of the stem is tinged dark violet.

semi-spherical cap with central depression (navel)

orange to almost yellow cap

thin, orange-brown flesh

well-spaced gills are off-white and strongly decurrent

striations on cap are difficult to see when it dries

tiny hairs on pale orange stem

FRUITING Singly or in small groups or troops.

| Dimensions CAP ⊕ 0.3–1cm │ STEM ↕ 3–5cm ↔ 1–2mm | Spores White | Edibility |

WITH CONVEX CAP AND FIBROUS FLESH

THE SPECIES here have semi-spherical, convex, or umbonate caps and fibrous flesh. Unlike the species on pp.28–36, the caps very rarely develop a central depression. Those on pp.43–55 may have caps of a similar shape but they are distinguished by their crumbly, cheese-like flesh.

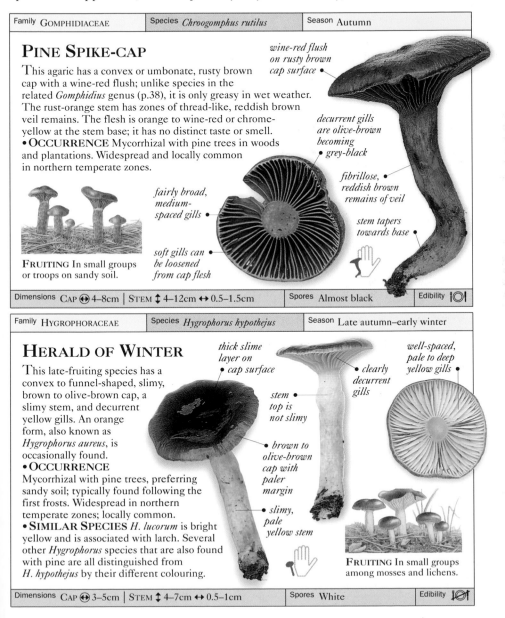

Family GOMPHIDIACEAE	Species *Chroogomphus rutilus*	Season Autumn

PINE SPIKE-CAP

This agaric has a convex or umbonate, rusty brown cap with a wine-red flush; unlike species in the related *Gomphidius* genus (p.38), it is only greasy in wet weather. The rust-orange stem has zones of thread-like, reddish brown veil remains. The flesh is orange to wine-red or chrome-yellow at the stem base; it has no distinct taste or smell.
• OCCURRENCE Mycorrhizal with pine trees in woods and plantations. Widespread and locally common in northern temperate zones.

wine-red flush on rusty brown cap surface

decurrent gills are olive-brown becoming grey-black

fibrillose, reddish brown remains of veil

fairly broad, medium-spaced gills

stem tapers towards base

soft gills can be loosened from cap flesh

FRUITING In small groups or troops on sandy soil.

Dimensions CAP ⊕ 4–8cm	STEM ↕ 4–12cm ↔ 0.5–1.5cm	Spores Almost black	Edibility

Family HYGROPHORACEAE	Species *Hygrophorus hypothejus*	Season Late autumn–early winter

HERALD OF WINTER

This late-fruiting species has a convex to funnel-shaped, slimy, brown to olive-brown cap, a slimy stem, and decurrent yellow gills. An orange form, also known as *Hygrophorus aureus*, is occasionally found.
• OCCURRENCE Mycorrhizal with pine trees, preferring sandy soil; typically found following the first frosts. Widespread in northern temperate zones; locally common.
• SIMILAR SPECIES *H. lucorum* is bright yellow and is associated with larch. Several other *Hygrophorus* species that are also found with pine are all distinguished from *H. hypothejus* by their different colouring.

thick slime layer on cap surface

well-spaced, pale to deep yellow gills

clearly decurrent gills

stem top is not slimy

brown to olive-brown cap with paler margin

slimy, pale yellow stem

FRUITING In small groups among mosses and lichens.

Dimensions CAP ⊕ 3–5cm	STEM ↕ 4–7cm ↔ 0.5–1cm	Spores White	Edibility

Family GOMPHIDIACEAE	Species *Gomphidius roseus*	Season Late summer–autumn

ROSY SPIKE-CAP

This unmistakable species has a coral-red cap that is convex with an inrolled margin when young, becoming flattened with age. The stem is spindle-shaped and bears the remains of the slimy, colourless veil, which is often stained black by the falling spores. The flesh is off-white with a coral-red tint and has no distinctive smell or taste. It is edible but not recommended, due to its rarity.
• **OCCURRENCE** Under pine trees on sandy soil, among mosses, lichens, and pine litter. Widespread in northern temperate zones.

△ *GOMPHIDIUS GLUTINOSUS*
This grey-brown species is covered in a colourless, slimy veil. The stem has an indistinct ring zone, often stained black by spores, and its base is lemon-yellow. Mycorrhizal with spruce. ¡○¡

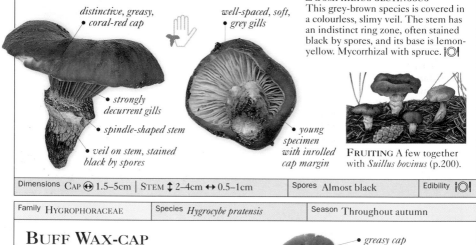

distinctive, greasy,
• *coral-red cap*

well-spaced, soft,
• *grey gills*

• *strongly decurrent gills*

• *spindle-shaped stem*

• *veil on stem, stained black by spores*

young • *specimen with inrolled cap margin*

FRUITING A few together with *Suillus bovinus* (p.200).

Dimensions CAP ⊕ 1.5–5cm | STEM ↕ 2–4cm ↔ 0.5–1cm	Spores Almost black	Edibility ¡○¡

Family HYGROPHORACEAE	Species *Hygrocybe pratensis*	Season Throughout autumn

BUFF WAX-CAP

This orange species has a fleshy, dry to greasy, convex cap that flattens with age. It has a wavy margin and sometimes a central umbo. The faintly striated stem is paler than the cap and may taper towards the base. A popular edible, with fairly solid, buff flesh, it has a "mushroomy" smell and pleasant taste. Along with *Hygrocybe virginea* (p.39), it is often classified in the genera *Camarophyllus* or *Cuphophyllus*.
• **OCCURRENCE** Found in unimproved grassland, rarely in damp woodland. Widespread and fairly common in northern temperate zones.
• **SIMILAR SPECIES** *Hygrophorus nemoreus* has a dry cap and grows in oak woodland.

• *greasy cap*

• *decurrent gills are paler than cap surface*

• *dry stem with fine, longitudinal fibres*

stem may taper • *towards base*

widely spaced, thick, waxy gills •

• *cap colour is uniform orange or slightly frosted with white*

FRUITING In groups or rings with moss and grass.

Dimensions CAP ⊕ 2.5–6cm | STEM ↕ 2.5–6cm ↔ 0.5–1.5cm	Spores White	Edibility ¡○¡

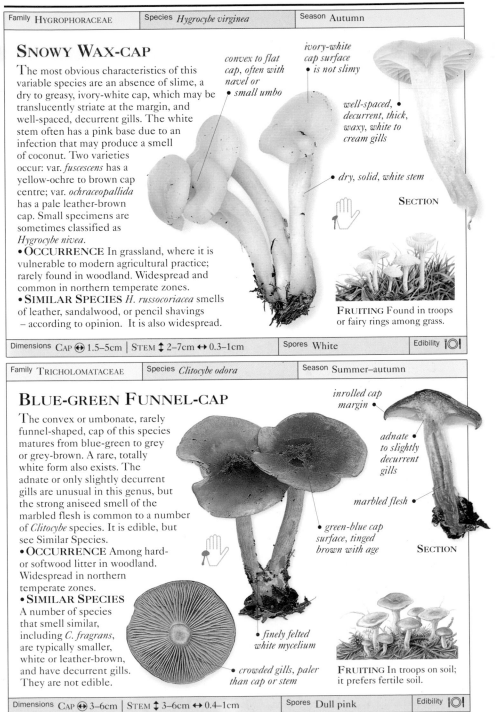

| Family HYGROPHORACEAE | Species *Hygrocybe virginea* | Season Autumn |

SNOWY WAX-CAP

The most obvious characteristics of this variable species are an absence of slime, a dry to greasy, ivory-white cap, which may be translucently striate at the margin, and well-spaced, decurrent gills. The white stem often has a pink base due to an infection that may produce a smell of coconut. Two varieties occur: var. *fuscescens* has a yellow-ochre to brown cap centre; var. *ochraceopallida* has a pale leather-brown cap. Small specimens are sometimes classified as *Hygrocybe nivea*.

• **OCCURRENCE** In grassland, where it is vulnerable to modern agricultural practice; rarely found in woodland. Widespread and common in northern temperate zones.

• **SIMILAR SPECIES** *H. russocoriacea* smells of leather, sandalwood, or pencil shavings – according to opinion. It is also widespread.

convex to flat cap, often with navel or small umbo

ivory-white cap surface is not slimy

well-spaced, decurrent, thick, waxy, white to cream gills

dry, solid, white stem

SECTION

FRUITING Found in troops or fairy rings among grass.

| Dimensions CAP ⊕ 1.5–5cm | STEM ↕ 2–7cm ↔ 0.3–1cm | Spores White | Edibility |

| Family TRICHOLOMATACEAE | Species *Clitocybe odora* | Season Summer–autumn |

BLUE-GREEN FUNNEL-CAP

The convex or umbonate, rarely funnel-shaped, cap of this species matures from blue-green to grey or grey-brown. A rare, totally white form also exists. The adnate or only slightly decurrent gills are unusual in this genus, but the strong aniseed smell of the marbled flesh is common to a number of *Clitocybe* species. It is edible, but see Similar Species.

• **OCCURRENCE** Among hard- or softwood litter in woodland. Widespread in northern temperate zones.

• **SIMILAR SPECIES** A number of species that smell similar, including *C. fragrans*, are typically smaller, white or leather-brown, and have decurrent gills. They are not edible.

inrolled cap margin

adnate to slightly decurrent gills

marbled flesh

green-blue cap surface, tinged brown with age

SECTION

finely felted white mycelium

crowded gills, paler than cap or stem

FRUITING In troops on soil; it prefers fertile soil.

| Dimensions CAP ⊕ 3–6cm | STEM ↕ 3–6cm ↔ 0.4–1cm | Spores Dull pink | Edibility |

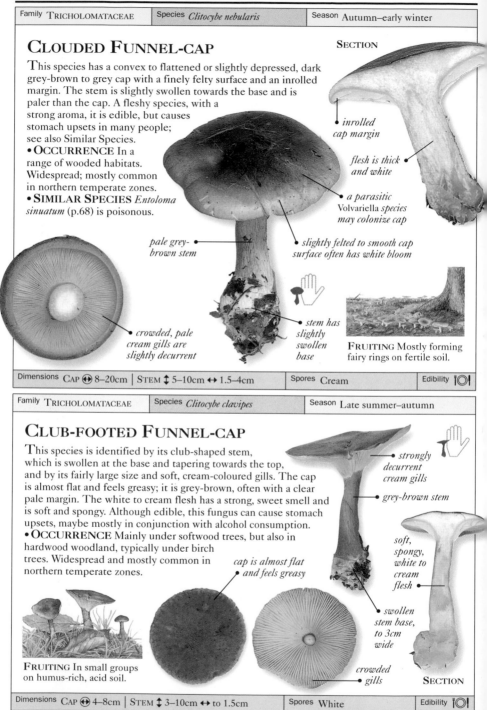

| Family TRICHOLOMATACEAE | Species *Clitocybe nebularis* | Season Autumn–early winter |

CLOUDED FUNNEL-CAP

This species has a convex to flattened or slightly depressed, dark grey-brown to grey cap with a finely felty surface and an inrolled margin. The stem is slightly swollen towards the base and is paler than the cap. A fleshy species, with a strong aroma, it is edible, but causes stomach upsets in many people; see also Similar Species.
• OCCURRENCE In a range of wooded habitats. Widespread; mostly common in northern temperate zones.
• SIMILAR SPECIES *Entoloma sinuatum* (p.68) is poisonous.

SECTION

• inrolled cap margin

flesh is thick • and white

• a parasitic Volvariella *species* may colonize cap

pale grey- • brown stem

• slightly felted to smooth cap surface often has white bloom

• stem has slightly swollen base

• crowded, pale cream gills are slightly decurrent

FRUITING Mostly forming fairy rings on fertile soil.

| Dimensions CAP ⊕ 8–20cm \| STEM ↕ 5–10cm ↔ 1.5–4cm | Spores Cream | Edibility |

| Family TRICHOLOMATACEAE | Species *Clitocybe clavipes* | Season Late summer–autumn |

CLUB-FOOTED FUNNEL-CAP

This species is identified by its club-shaped stem, which is swollen at the base and tapering towards the top, and by its fairly large size and soft, cream-coloured gills. The cap is almost flat and feels greasy; it is grey-brown, often with a clear pale margin. The white to cream flesh has a strong, sweet smell and is soft and spongy. Although edible, this fungus can cause stomach upsets, maybe mostly in conjunction with alcohol consumption.
• OCCURRENCE Mainly under softwood trees, but also in hardwood woodland, typically under birch trees. Widespread and mostly common in northern temperate zones.

• strongly decurrent cream gills

• grey-brown stem

soft, spongy, white to cream flesh

cap is almost flat • and feels greasy

• swollen stem base, to 3cm wide

FRUITING In small groups on humus-rich, acid soil.

crowded • gills

SECTION

| Dimensions CAP ⊕ 4–8cm \| STEM ↕ 3–10cm ↔ to 1.5cm | Spores White | Edibility |

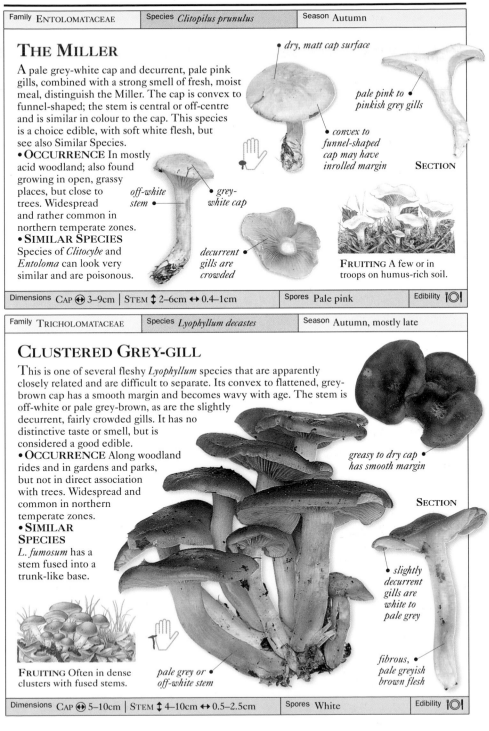

Family ENTOMATACEAE	Species *Clitopilus prunulus*	Season Autumn

THE MILLER

A pale grey-white cap and decurrent, pale pink gills, combined with a strong smell of fresh, moist meal, distinguish the Miller. The cap is convex to funnel-shaped; the stem is central or off-centre and is similar in colour to the cap. This species is a choice edible, with soft white flesh, but see also Similar Species.

• OCCURRENCE In mostly acid woodland; also found growing in open, grassy places, but close to trees. Widespread and rather common in northern temperate zones.

• SIMILAR SPECIES Species of *Clitocybe* and *Entoloma* can look very similar and are poisonous.

dry, matt cap surface

pale pink to pinkish grey gills

convex to funnel-shaped cap may have inrolled margin

SECTION

off-white stem

grey-white cap

decurrent gills are crowded

FRUITING A few or in troops on humus-rich soil.

Dimensions CAP ⊕ 3–9cm	STEM ↕ 2–6cm ↔ 0.4–1cm	Spores Pale pink	Edibility

Family TRICHOLOMATACEAE	Species *Lyophyllum decastes*	Season Autumn, mostly late

CLUSTERED GREY-GILL

This is one of several fleshy *Lyophyllum* species that are apparently closely related and are difficult to separate. Its convex to flattened, grey-brown cap has a smooth margin and becomes wavy with age. The stem is off-white or pale grey-brown, as are the slightly decurrent, fairly crowded gills. It has no distinctive taste or smell, but is considered a good edible.

• OCCURRENCE Along woodland rides and in gardens and parks, but not in direct association with trees. Widespread and common in northern temperate zones.

• SIMILAR SPECIES *L. fumosum* has a stem fused into a trunk-like base.

greasy to dry cap has smooth margin

SECTION

slightly decurrent gills are white to pale grey

fibrous, pale greyish brown flesh

FRUITING Often in dense clusters with fused stems.

pale grey or off-white stem

Dimensions CAP ⊕ 5–10cm	STEM ↕ 4–10cm ↔ 0.5–2.5cm	Spores White	Edibility

Family TRICHOLOMATACEAE	Species *Lyophyllum connatum*	Season Autumn

WHITE GREY-GILL

The cap of this white fungus is convex, often with a wavy margin, and the stem tapers towards the base. The rather crowded, white to pale grey gills are slightly decurrent; they stain violet when in contact with solid or dissolved iron salt ($FeSO_4$). The flesh is white and also stains violet with $FeSO_4$.
• OCCURRENCE Mostly on disturbed soil on woodland verges. Widespread in northern temperate zones, including alpine areas.
• SIMILAR SPECIES Some of the white *Clitocybe* species are fairly similar in appearance. They are distinguished by their lack of staining with $FeSO_4$.

convex cap with wavy margin •

decurrent, pale • grey to white gills

FRUITING Singly or in clusters of fruitbodies on road verges in woodland.

Dimensions CAP ⊕ 3–10cm │ STEM ↕ 5–12cm ↔ 0.5–1.5cm	Spores White	Edibility ☠

Family TRICHOLOMATACEAE	Species *Armillaria tabescens*	Season Autumn

RINGLESS HONEY FUNGUS

The convex to flat or depressed, dry, yellowish brown cap of this species has erect brown scales at the centre. The stem is fibrous and off-white and is often fused with many others at its base. Black mycelial strands are present on the substrate. Its off-white flesh is edible after careful cooking.
• OCCURRENCE Attached to roots or near trees. Rare in warmer parts of Europe but widespread and common in eastern North America.
• SIMILAR SPECIES *Armillaria mellea* (p.80) has a stem ring. *Clitocybe* species (pp.31, 33–4, 39–40) lack the cap scales and the black mycelial strands.

erect brown scales at cap centre •

fibrous, off- • white stem

FRUITING In clusters on the ground near trees such as oaks; it kills the host tree.

Dimensions CAP ⊕ 2.5–10cm │ STEM ↕ 7.5–20cm ↔ 0.5–1.5cm	Spores Pale cream	Edibility ⦿

Family BOLETACEAE	Species *Phylloporus rhodoxanthus*	Season Summer–autumn

GILLED BOLETE

This species has a dry, reddish brown cap. Its stem is red to reddish yellow. This is a gilled bolete, but it may produce a tube layer and is more closely related to pored boletes, such as *Boletus pascuus* (p.192), than to agarics. The gills are easily separated from the yellow to red-tinged flesh.
• OCCURRENCE Mycorrhizal with oak; also found under conifers. Widespread and common in northern temperate zones, except the far north.
• SIMILAR SPECIES *Phylloporus leucomycelinus* has a white mycelium at the base.

convex to flat or depressed cap •

bright yellow gills may bruise green or blue •

decurrent • gills with interlinking veins

FRUITING Singly or scattered in small groups or troops.

Dimensions CAP ⊕ 2.5–7.5cm │ STEM ↕ 4.5–10cm ↔ 0.5–1cm	Spores Ochre-yellow	Edibility ⦿

CRUMBLY FLESH EXUDING MILK

BELONGING EXCLUSIVELY to the genus *Lactarius*, all species in this subsection have slightly decurrent gills and variable cap shapes, and almost all exude a white or coloured fluid from cut or broken flesh. This "milk" may change colour rapidly on exposure and is a good identification feature; the best way to see this is by testing one or two drops on a white handkerchief.

Family RUSSULACEAE	Species *Lactarius piperatus*	Season Summer–early autumn

PEPPERY MILK-CAP

This large, crumbly-fleshed species has an off-white fruitbody, very crowded gills, and an almost smooth cap that is depressed in the centre. Although the white milk, which dries olive-green, has a very peppery taste, this species can be made edible by salting followed by marinating, or by prolonged frying, which removes the acrid flavour.

• **OCCURRENCE** Mycorrhizal with both hard- and softwood trees in woodland on well-drained soil. Widespread and rather common in northern temperate zones.

• **SIMILAR SPECIES** The milk of *Lactarius glaucescens* dries greyish blue-green. Some relatives, such as *L. vellereus* (p.44), can be distinguished by their felted caps and more widely spaced, often green-tinged gills.

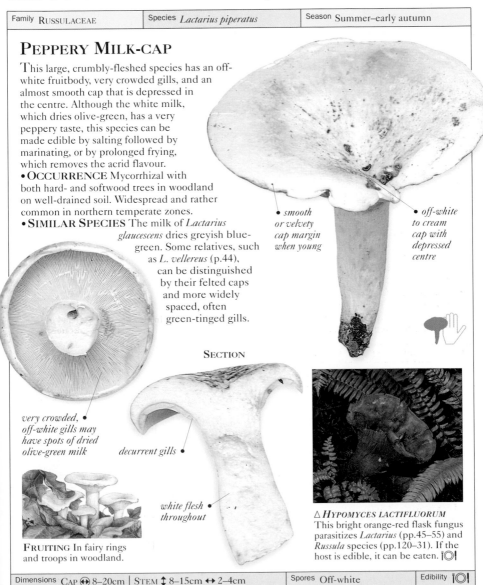

• *smooth or velvety cap margin when young*

• *off-white to cream cap with depressed centre*

SECTION

very crowded, • off-white gills may have spots of dried olive-green milk

decurrent gills •

white flesh • throughout

FRUITING In fairy rings and troops in woodland.

△ *HYPOMYCES LACTIFLUORUM*
This bright orange-red flask fungus parasitizes *Lactarius* (pp.45–55) and *Russula* species (pp.120–31). If the host is edible, it can be eaten. 🍴

Dimensions CAP ⊕ 8–20cm | STEM ↕ 8–15cm ↔ 2–4cm	Spores Off-white	Edibility 🍴

Family RUSSULACEAE	Species *Lactarius vellereus*	Season Autumn

FLEECY MILK-CAP

The white to cream cap of this very large species is densely felted and has a clear central depression. Its cream gills are fairly crowded, and it has a comparatively short, tapered stem. The white milk from its crumbly white flesh is copious and dries to brown on the gills; it does not stain with potassium hydroxide (KOH).

• OCCURRENCE Mycorrhizal with hardwood trees, such as beech, but also found with various softwoods. Exact range unknown but widespread in northern temperate zones.

• SIMILAR SPECIES The milk in *Lactarius bertillonii* stains yellow then orange with KOH and has a hot taste. *L. piperatus* (p.43) is distinguished by more crowded gills, a longer stem, and a smooth cap.

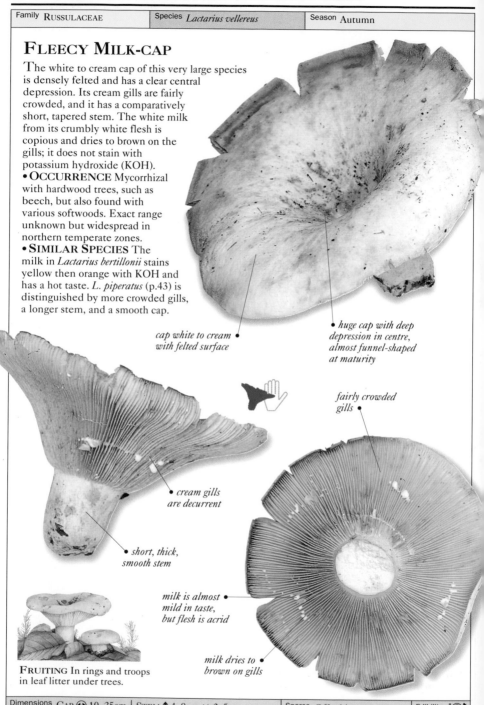

cap white to cream • with felted surface

• huge cap with deep depression in centre, almost funnel-shaped at maturity

fairly crowded gills •

• cream gills are decurrent

• short, thick, smooth stem

milk is almost • mild in taste, but flesh is acrid

milk dries to • brown on gills

FRUITING In rings and troops in leaf litter under trees.

Dimensions CAP ⊕ 10–25cm	STEM ↕ 4–8cm ↔ 2–5cm	Spores Off-white	Edibility

| Family RUSSULACEAE | Species *Lactarius controversus* | Season Autumn |

WILLOW MILK-CAP

Salmon-pink gills distinguish this fungus from other *Lactarius* species. It is off-white, with faint grey or pink zoning on the convex to depressed cap, which has an inrolled margin. The short stem is white or flushed pink to grey; the crumbly flesh exudes copious white milk, which does not change colour as it dries.
• **OCCURRENCE** Mycorrhizal with both willow and poplar, in woods and sand dunes. Widespread in northern temperate zones, but not very common.

sticky cap is covered with debris

slightly decurrent gills

short, often tapered stem

white or pinkish white flesh yields white milk

SECTION

forked and crowded, salmon-pink gills

FRUITING Singly or in fairy rings or troops.

| Dimensions CAP ⊕ 7–20cm | STEM ↕ 2–7cm ↔ 1.5–4cm | Spores Off-white | Edibility |

| Family RUSSULACEAE | Species *Lactarius torminosus* | Season Summer–autumn |

WOOLLY MILK-CAP

This species has a strongly depressed cap with a shaggy surface and an inrolled margin. The crowded, off-white to pale pink gills are slightly decurrent. Its crumbly white flesh produces very hot-tasting white milk, pale yellow on a white handkerchief, which does not change colour as it dries. It is edible after salting and pickling.
• **OCCURRENCE** Mycorrhizal with birch trees and often found in open, grassy sites. Widespread and common in parts of northern temperate zones.
• **SIMILAR SPECIES** *Lactarius pubescens* is paler and has a less shaggy cap and fainter zones. *L. scoticus* is also pale, and is smaller.

cap with zones in shades of orange and orange-brown

depressed cap centre

FRUITING In rings and troops on damp ground.

shaggy cap surface, especially at the inrolled margin

short, smooth, club-shaped stem, hollowing with age

SECTION

| Dimensions CAP ⊕ 5–15cm | STEM ↕ 3–6cm ↔ 1–3cm | Spores Pale yellowish cream | Edibility |

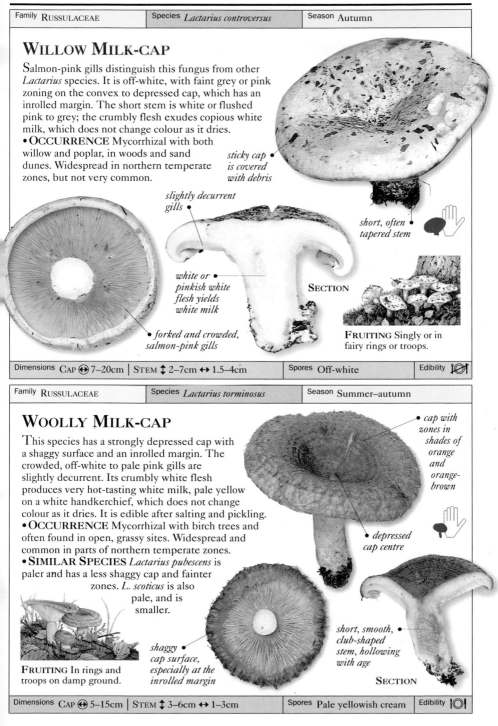

Family RUSSULACEAE	Species *Lactarius deliciosus*	Season Late summer–autumn

DELICIOUS MILK-CAP

This brownish orange species has a depressed cap with faint concentric zones and an inrolled margin; its short stem is covered with orange depressions. It has thick, crumbly, pale yellow flesh yielding carrot-orange milk, which does not change colour. A choice edible, it has the harmless, if slightly alarming, effect of making urine turn red.

• **OCCURRENCE** Mycorrhizal with pine trees, often on sandy, alkaline soil. Widespread in northern temperate zones, but distribution unclear.

• **SIMILAR SPECIES** *Lactarius deterrimus* (inset, below left). *L. hemicyaneus* has blue flesh and milk in the cap. It grows under fir trees (*Abies*). *L. salmonicolor*, which grows with firs, is larger. *L. semisanguifluus* (inset, below right).

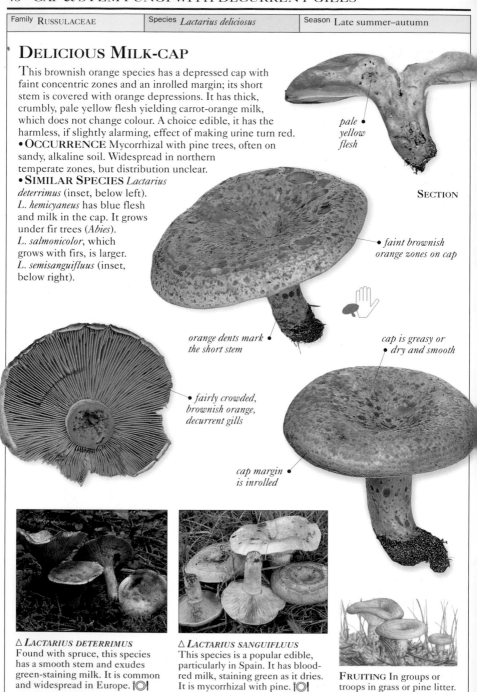

pale • yellow flesh

SECTION

• faint brownish orange zones on cap

orange dents mark • the short stem

cap is greasy or • dry and smooth

• fairly crowded, brownish orange, decurrent gills

cap margin • is inrolled

△ *LACTARIUS DETERRIMUS*
Found with spruce, this species has a smooth stem and exudes green-staining milk. It is common and widespread in Europe. |○|

△ *LACTARIUS SANGUIFLUUS*
This species is a popular edible, particularly in Spain. It has blood-red milk, staining green as it dries. It is mycorrhizal with pine. |○|

FRUITING In groups or troops in grass or pine litter.

| Dimensions CAP ⊕ 5–15cm | STEM ↕ 3–7cm ↔ 1–3cm | Spores Off-white | Edibility |○| |

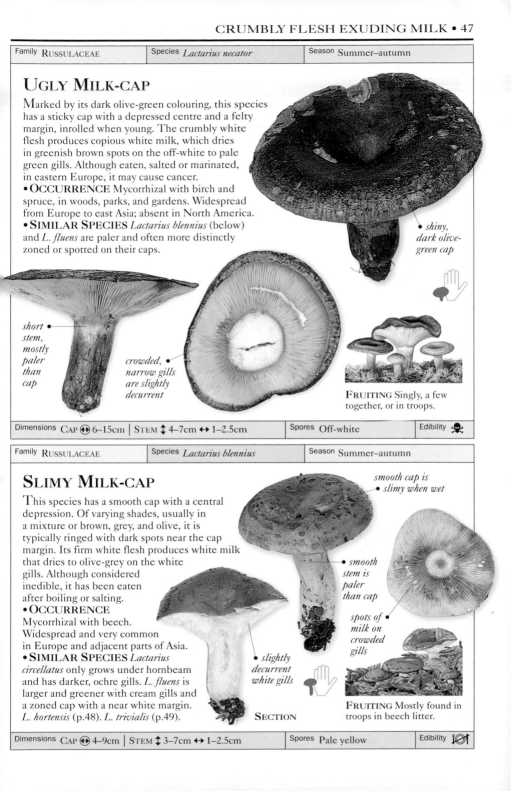

| Family RUSSULACEAE | Species *Lactarius necator* | Season Summer–autumn |

UGLY MILK-CAP

Marked by its dark olive-green colouring, this species has a sticky cap with a depressed centre and a felty margin, inrolled when young. The crumbly white flesh produces copious white milk, which dries in greenish brown spots on the off-white to pale green gills. Although eaten, salted or marinated, in eastern Europe, it may cause cancer.
• **OCCURRENCE** Mycorrhizal with birch and spruce, in woods, parks, and gardens. Widespread from Europe to east Asia; absent in North America.
• **SIMILAR SPECIES** *Lactarius blennius* (below) and *L. fluens* are paler and often more distinctly zoned or spotted on their caps.

• *shiny, dark olive-green cap*

short stem, mostly paler than cap •

crowded, narrow gills are slightly decurrent •

FRUITING Singly, a few together, or in troops.

| Dimensions CAP ⊕ 6–15cm | STEM ↕ 4–7cm ↔ 1–2.5cm | Spores Off-white | Edibility ☠ |

| Family RUSSULACEAE | Species *Lactarius blennius* | Season Summer–autumn |

SLIMY MILK-CAP

This species has a smooth cap with a central depression. Of varying shades, usually in a mixture or brown, grey, and olive, it is typically ringed with dark spots near the cap margin. Its firm white flesh produces white milk that dries to olive-grey on the white gills. Although considered inedible, it has been eaten after boiling or salting.
• **OCCURRENCE** Mycorrhizal with beech. Widespread and very common in Europe and adjacent parts of Asia.
• **SIMILAR SPECIES** *Lactarius circellatus* only grows under hornbeam and has darker, ochre gills. *L. fluens* is larger and greener with cream gills and a zoned cap with a near white margin. *L. hortensis* (p.48). *L. trivialis* (p.49).

smooth cap is • *slimy when wet*

• *smooth stem is paler than cap*

spots of milk on crowded gills •

• *slightly decurrent white gills*

SECTION

FRUITING Mostly found in troops in beech litter.

| Dimensions CAP ⊕ 4–9cm | STEM ↕ 3–7cm ↔ 1–2.5cm | Spores Pale yellow | Edibility |

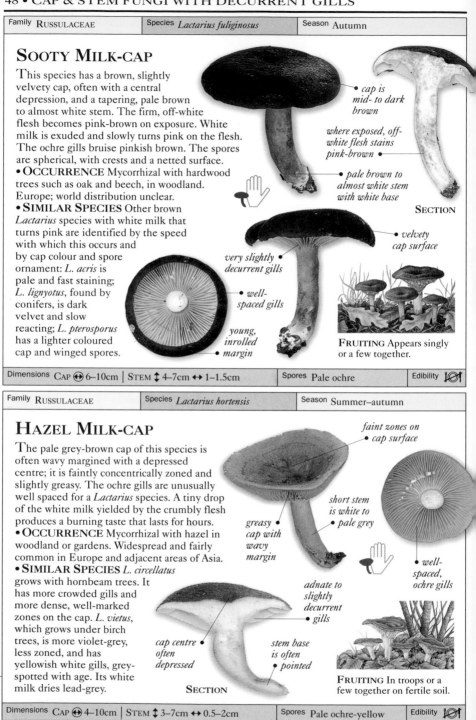

Family RUSSULACEAE	Species *Lactarius fuliginosus*	Season Autumn

SOOTY MILK-CAP

This species has a brown, slightly velvety cap, often with a central depression, and a tapering, pale brown to almost white stem. The firm, off-white flesh becomes pink-brown on exposure. White milk is exuded and slowly turns pink on the flesh. The ochre gills bruise pinkish brown. The spores are spherical, with crests and a netted surface.

• **OCCURRENCE** Mycorrhizal with hardwood trees such as oak and beech, in woodland. Europe; world distribution unclear.

• **SIMILAR SPECIES** Other brown *Lactarius* species with white milk that turns pink are identified by the speed with which this occurs and by cap colour and spore ornament: *L. acris* is pale and fast staining; *L. lignyotus*, found by conifers, is dark velvet and slow reacting; *L. pterosporus* has a lighter coloured cap and winged spores.

cap is mid- to dark brown

where exposed, off-white flesh stains pink-brown

pale brown to almost white stem with white base

SECTION

velvety cap surface

very slightly decurrent gills

well-spaced gills

young, inrolled margin

FRUITING Appears singly or a few together.

Dimensions CAP ⊕ 6–10cm | STEM ↕ 4–7cm ↔ 1–1.5cm	Spores Pale ochre	Edibility

Family RUSSULACEAE	Species *Lactarius hortensis*	Season Summer–autumn

HAZEL MILK-CAP

The pale grey-brown cap of this species is often wavy margined with a depressed centre; it is faintly concentrically zoned and slightly greasy. The ochre gills are unusually well spaced for a *Lactarius* species. A tiny drop of the white milk yielded by the crumbly flesh produces a burning taste that lasts for hours.

• **OCCURRENCE** Mycorrhizal with hazel in woodland or gardens. Widespread and fairly common in Europe and adjacent areas of Asia.

• **SIMILAR SPECIES** *L. circellatus* grows with hornbeam trees. It has more crowded gills and more dense, well-marked zones on the cap. *L. vietus*, which grows under birch trees, is more violet-grey, less zoned, and has yellowish white gills, grey-spotted with age. Its white milk dries lead-grey.

faint zones on cap surface

short stem is white to pale grey

greasy cap with wavy margin

well-spaced, ochre gills

adnate to slightly decurrent gills

cap centre often depressed

stem base is often pointed

SECTION

FRUITING In troops or a few together on fertile soil.

Dimensions CAP ⊕ 4–10cm | STEM ↕ 3–7cm ↔ 0.5–2cm	Spores Pale ochre-yellow	Edibility

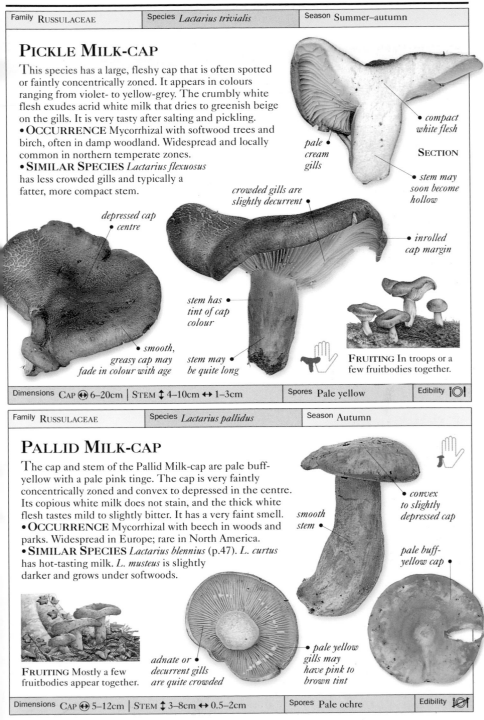

| Family RUSSULACEAE | Species *Lactarius trivialis* | Season Summer–autumn |

PICKLE MILK-CAP

This species has a large, fleshy cap that is often spotted or faintly concentrically zoned. It appears in colours ranging from violet- to yellow-grey. The crumbly white flesh exudes acrid white milk that dries to greenish beige on the gills. It is very tasty after salting and pickling.
• OCCURRENCE Mycorrhizal with softwood trees and birch, often in damp woodland. Widespread and locally common in northern temperate zones.
• SIMILAR SPECIES *Lactarius flexuosus* has less crowded gills and typically a fatter, more compact stem.

compact white flesh

pale • cream gills

SECTION

stem may soon become hollow

depressed cap centre •

crowded gills are slightly decurrent •

• inrolled cap margin

stem has • tint of cap colour

• smooth, greasy cap may fade in colour with age

stem may • be quite long

FRUITING In troops or a few fruitbodies together.

| Dimensions CAP ⊕ 6–20cm | STEM ↕ 4–10cm ↔ 1–3cm | Spores Pale yellow | Edibility |

| Family RUSSULACEAE | Species *Lactarius pallidus* | Season Autumn |

PALLID MILK-CAP

The cap and stem of the Pallid Milk-cap are pale buff-yellow with a pale pink tinge. The cap is very faintly concentrically zoned and convex to depressed in the centre. Its copious white milk does not stain, and the thick white flesh tastes mild to slightly bitter. It has a very faint smell.
• OCCURRENCE Mycorrhizal with beech in woods and parks. Widespread in Europe; rare in North America.
• SIMILAR SPECIES *Lactarius blennius* (p.47). *L. curtus* has hot-tasting milk. *L. musteus* is slightly darker and grows under softwoods.

• convex to slightly depressed cap

smooth stem •

pale buff-yellow cap •

FRUITING Mostly a few fruitbodies appear together.

adnate or • decurrent gills are quite crowded

• pale yellow gills may have pink to brown tint

| Dimensions CAP ⊕ 5–12cm | STEM ↕ 3–8cm ↔ 0.5–2cm | Spores Pale ochre | Edibility |

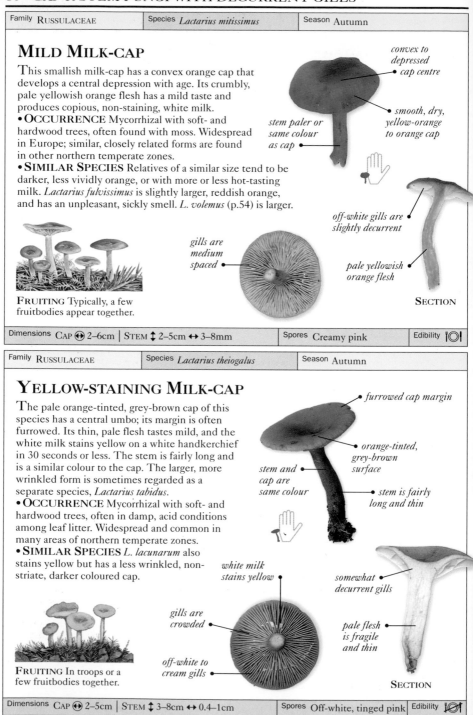

| Family RUSSULACEAE | Species *Lactarius mitissimus* | Season Autumn |

MILD MILK-CAP

This smallish milk-cap has a convex orange cap that develops a central depression with age. Its crumbly, pale yellowish orange flesh has a mild taste and produces copious, non-staining, white milk.
• **OCCURRENCE** Mycorrhizal with soft- and hardwood trees, often found with moss. Widespread in Europe; similar, closely related forms are found in other northern temperate zones.
• **SIMILAR SPECIES** Relatives of a similar size tend to be darker, less vividly orange, or with more or less hot-tasting milk. *Lactarius fulvissimus* is slightly larger, reddish orange, and has an unpleasant, sickly smell. *L. volemus* (p.54) is larger.

convex to depressed cap centre

smooth, dry, yellow-orange to orange cap

stem paler or same colour as cap

off-white gills are slightly decurrent

pale yellowish orange flesh

SECTION

gills are medium spaced

FRUITING Typically, a few fruitbodies appear together.

| Dimensions CAP ⊕ 2–6cm | STEM ↕ 2–5cm ↔ 3–8mm | Spores Creamy pink | Edibility |

| Family RUSSULACEAE | Species *Lactarius theiogalus* | Season Autumn |

YELLOW-STAINING MILK-CAP

The pale orange-tinted, grey-brown cap of this species has a central umbo; its margin is often furrowed. Its thin, pale flesh tastes mild, and the white milk stains yellow on a white handkerchief in 30 seconds or less. The stem is fairly long and is a similar colour to the cap. The larger, more wrinkled form is sometimes regarded as a separate species, *Lactarius tabidus*.
• **OCCURRENCE** Mycorrhizal with soft- and hardwood trees, often in damp, acid conditions among leaf litter. Widespread and common in many areas of northern temperate zones.
• **SIMILAR SPECIES** *L. lacunarum* also stains yellow but has a less wrinkled, non-striate, darker coloured cap.

furrowed cap margin

orange-tinted, grey-brown surface

stem and cap are same colour

stem is fairly long and thin

white milk stains yellow

somewhat decurrent gills

pale flesh is fragile and thin

gills are crowded

off-white to cream gills

FRUITING In troops or a few fruitbodies together.

SECTION

| Dimensions CAP ⊕ 2–5cm | STEM ↕ 3–8cm ↔ 0.4–1cm | Spores Off-white, tinged pink | Edibility |

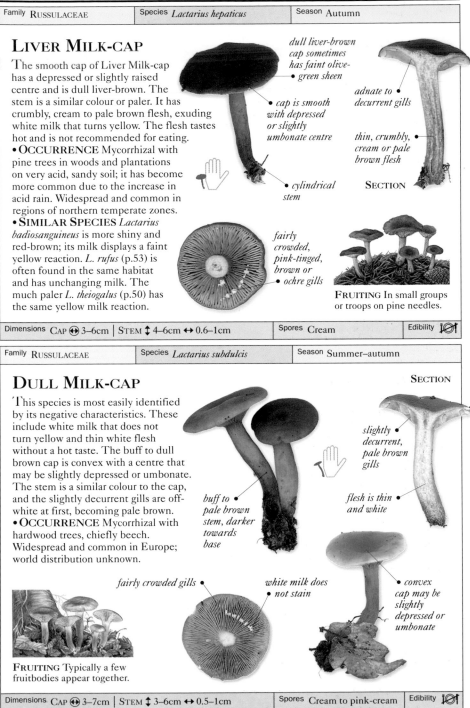

Family RUSSULACEAE	Species *Lactarius hepaticus*	Season Autumn

LIVER MILK-CAP

The smooth cap of Liver Milk-cap has a depressed or slightly raised centre and is dull liver-brown. The stem is a similar colour or paler. It has crumbly, cream to pale brown flesh, exuding white milk that turns yellow. The flesh tastes hot and is not recommended for eating.

• **OCCURRENCE** Mycorrhizal with pine trees in woods and plantations on very acid, sandy soil; it has become more common due to the increase in acid rain. Widespread and common in regions of northern temperate zones.

• **SIMILAR SPECIES** *Lactarius badiosanguineus* is more shiny and red-brown; its milk displays a faint yellow reaction. *L. rufus* (p.53) is often found in the same habitat and has unchanging milk. The much paler *L. theiogalus* (p.50) has the same yellow milk reaction.

dull liver-brown cap sometimes has faint olive-green sheen

cap is smooth with depressed or slightly umbonate centre

adnate to decurrent gills

thin, crumbly, cream or pale brown flesh

cylindrical stem

SECTION

fairly crowded, pink-tinged, brown or ochre gills

FRUITING In small groups or troops on pine needles.

Dimensions CAP ⊕ 3–6cm	STEM ↕ 4–6cm ↔ 0.6–1cm	Spores Cream	Edibility

Family RUSSULACEAE	Species *Lactarius subdulcis*	Season Summer–autumn

DULL MILK-CAP

SECTION

This species is most easily identified by its negative characteristics. These include white milk that does not turn yellow and thin white flesh without a hot taste. The buff to dull brown cap is convex with a centre that may be slightly depressed or umbonate. The stem is a similar colour to the cap, and the slightly decurrent gills are off-white at first, becoming pale brown.

• **OCCURRENCE** Mycorrhizal with hardwood trees, chiefly beech. Widespread and common in Europe; world distribution unknown.

slightly decurrent, pale brown gills

flesh is thin and white

buff to pale brown stem, darker towards base

fairly crowded gills

white milk does not stain

convex cap may be slightly depressed or umbonate

FRUITING Typically a few fruitbodies appear together.

Dimensions CAP ⊕ 3–7cm	STEM ↕ 3–6cm ↔ 0.5–1cm	Spores Cream to pink-cream	Edibility

Family RUSSULACEAE	Species *Lactarius hygrophoroides*	Season Summer–autumn

DISTANT-GILLED MILK-CAP

This orange-brown species has a convex to flat or depressed cap without any zoning. Both the cap and the stem have a dry surface. The crumbly flesh is white and exudes abundant, unchanging white milk, which has a mild taste.
• **OCCURRENCE**
Mycorrhizal, especially with oak trees in woodland areas. Widespread and common in eastern North America; not found in Europe.
• **SIMILAR SPECIES**
Lactarius corrugis has a reddish brown cap with a wrinkled margin, ochre gills, and milk that stains brown. *L. volemus* (p.54). Both are also choice edibles, and all three species can be found growing in the same area at the same time of the year.

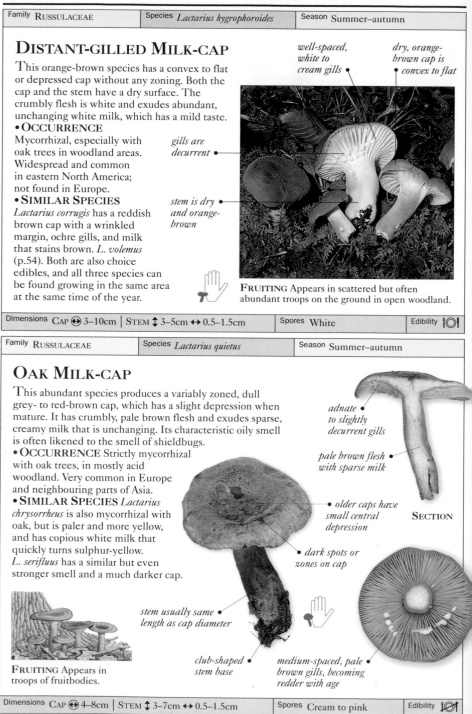

well-spaced, white to cream gills

dry, orange-brown cap is convex to flat

gills are decurrent

stem is dry and orange-brown

FRUITING Appears in scattered but often abundant troops on the ground in open woodland.

Dimensions CAP ⊕ 3–10cm │ STEM ↕ 3–5cm ↔ 0.5–1.5cm	Spores White	Edibility ❘◎❘

Family RUSSULACEAE	Species *Lactarius quietus*	Season Summer–autumn

OAK MILK-CAP

This abundant species produces a variably zoned, dull grey- to red-brown cap, which has a slight depression when mature. It has crumbly, pale brown flesh and exudes sparse, creamy milk that is unchanging. Its characteristic oily smell is often likened to the smell of shieldbugs.
• **OCCURRENCE** Strictly mycorrhizal with oak trees, in mostly acid woodland. Very common in Europe and neighbouring parts of Asia.
• **SIMILAR SPECIES** *Lactarius chrysorrheus* is also mycorrhizal with oak, but is paler and more yellow, and has copious white milk that quickly turns sulphur-yellow. *L. serifluus* has a similar but even stronger smell and a much darker cap.

adnate to slightly decurrent gills

pale brown flesh with sparse milk

older caps have small central depression

SECTION

dark spots or zones on cap

FRUITING Appears in troops of fruitbodies.

stem usually same length as cap diameter

club-shaped stem base

medium-spaced, pale brown gills, becoming redder with age

Dimensions CAP ⊕ 4–8cm │ STEM ↕ 3–7cm ↔ 0.5–1.5cm	Spores Cream to pink	Edibility ❘◎❘

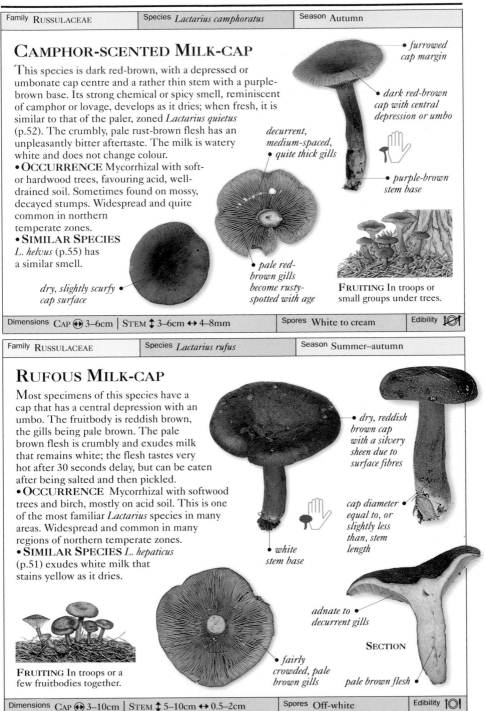

| Family RUSSULACEAE | Species *Lactarius camphoratus* | Season Autumn |

CAMPHOR-SCENTED MILK-CAP

This species is dark red-brown, with a depressed or umbonate cap centre and a rather thin stem with a purple-brown base. Its strong chemical or spicy smell, reminiscent of camphor or lovage, develops as it dries; when fresh, it is similar to that of the paler, zoned *Lactarius quietus* (p.52). The crumbly, pale rust-brown flesh has an unpleasantly bitter aftertaste. The milk is watery white and does not change colour.
• OCCURRENCE Mycorrhizal with soft- or hardwood trees, favouring acid, well-drained soil. Sometimes found on mossy, decayed stumps. Widespread and quite common in northern temperate zones.
• SIMILAR SPECIES *L. helvus* (p.55) has a similar smell.

furrowed cap margin

dark red-brown cap with central depression or umbo

decurrent, medium-spaced, quite thick gills

purple-brown stem base

dry, slightly scurfy cap surface

pale red-brown gills become rusty-spotted with age

FRUITING In troops or small groups under trees.

| Dimensions CAP ⊕ 3–6cm | STEM ↕ 3–6cm ↔ 4–8mm | Spores White to cream | Edibility |

| Family RUSSULACEAE | Species *Lactarius rufus* | Season Summer–autumn |

RUFOUS MILK-CAP

Most specimens of this species have a cap that has a central depression with an umbo. The fruitbody is reddish brown, the gills being pale brown. The pale brown flesh is crumbly and exudes milk that remains white; the flesh tastes very hot after 30 seconds delay, but can be eaten after being salted and then pickled.
• OCCURRENCE Mycorrhizal with softwood trees and birch, mostly on acid soil. This is one of the most familiar *Lactarius* species in many areas. Widespread and common in many regions of northern temperate zones.
• SIMILAR SPECIES *L. hepaticus* (p.51) exudes white milk that stains yellow as it dries.

dry, reddish brown cap with a silvery sheen due to surface fibres

cap diameter equal to, or slightly less than, stem length

white stem base

adnate to decurrent gills

SECTION

pale brown flesh

FRUITING In troops or a few fruitbodies together.

fairly crowded, pale brown gills

| Dimensions CAP ⊕ 3–10cm | STEM ↕ 5–10cm ↔ 0.5–2cm | Spores Off-white | Edibility |

Family RUSSULACEAE	Species *Lactarius glyciosmus*	Season Summer–autumn

COCONUT-SCENTED MILK-CAP

A smell like freshly baked coconut biscuits exudes from this species, which has subtle, grey to ochre colouring, with pink-tinged, pale cream gills. The cap may have a central depression and an upward-flaring margin. The thin white flesh produces sparse amounts of mild- or slightly acrid-tasting white milk that does not stain on exposure to air.
• **OCCURRENCE** Mycorrhizal with birch, often in damp places. Widespread and common in many areas of northern temperate zones.
• **SIMILAR SPECIES** *Lactarius mammosus* is rarer and has the same coconut fragrance but is much darker and grows under softwoods.

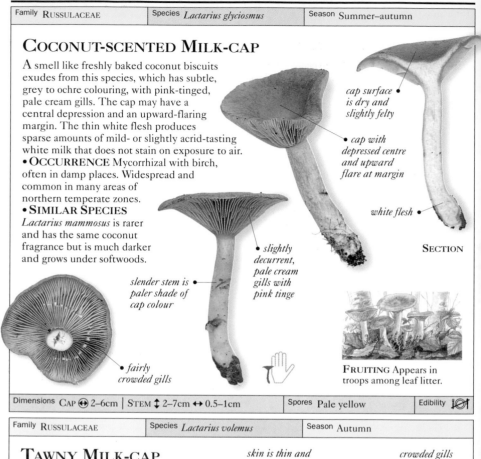

cap surface is dry and slightly felty •

• cap with depressed centre and upward flare at margin

white flesh •

SECTION

• slightly decurrent, pale cream gills with pink tinge

slender stem is • paler shade of cap colour

• fairly crowded gills

FRUITING Appears in troops among leaf litter.

Dimensions CAP ⊕ 2–6cm	STEM ↕ 2–7cm ↔ 0.5–1cm	Spores Pale yellow	Edibility

---

Family RUSSULACEAE	Species *Lactarius volemus*	Season Autumn

TAWNY MILK-CAP

This very fleshy, matt orange *Lactarius* species has a thin, cracking skin on its convex cap and a thick, paler orange stem with a velvety surface. When cut, its off-white flesh produces copious white milk, which stains pale brown, and its distinctive smell is strongly reminiscent of shellfish, especially in mature specimens. Its crowded, slightly decurrent gills are pale golden yellow. It tastes mild.
• **OCCURRENCE** Mycorrhizal, mainly with hardwood trees. Widespread but mostly uncommon in northern temperate zones.
• **SIMILAR SPECIES** *Lactarius mitissimus* (p.50) and its relatives are smaller and do not have the cracking cap skin or velvety stem surface.

skin is thin and cracking on convex, matt orange cap •

crowded gills are slightly • decurrent

thick stem • is pale orange

FRUITING In troops or a few together under hardwoods, more rarely conifers.

Dimensions CAP ⊕ 6–12cm	STEM ↕ 4–12cm ↔ 1–4cm	Spores Off-white	Edibility

Family RUSSULACEAE	Species *Lactarius helvus*	Season Summer–autumn

LIQUORICE MILK-CAP

A strong, spicy smell, similar to curry or the herbs lovage and fenugreek, characterizes this yellow-ochre to grey-brown species. Fairly large, it becomes funnel-shaped, with a central umbo, as it matures. Its crumbly flesh is yellow, white, or pale pink, and its mild-tasting milk is more sparse and watery than in most *Lactarius* species.
• **OCCURRENCE** Mycorrhizal with birch, pine, and spruce trees, often found growing among sphagnum moss. Widespread in northern temperate zones.
• **SIMILAR SPECIES** *L. aquifluus* is very similar in appearance and occurs in North America.

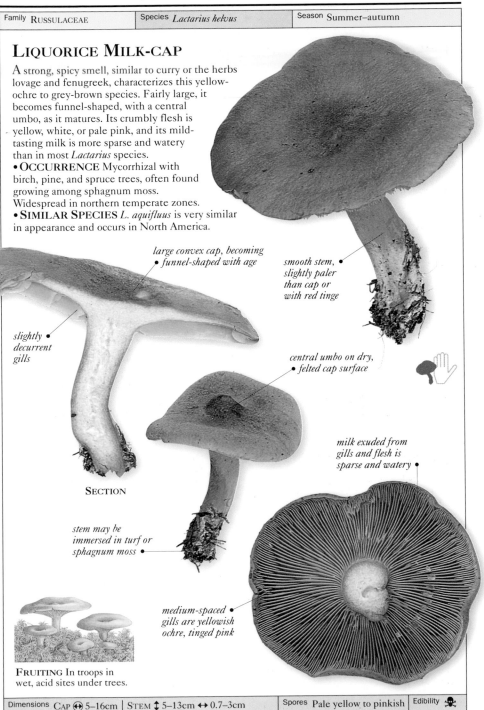

large convex cap, becoming
• funnel-shaped with age

smooth stem,
slightly paler
than cap or
with red tinge

slightly •
decurrent
gills

central umbo on dry,
• felted cap surface

milk exuded from
gills and flesh is
sparse and watery •

SECTION

stem may be
immersed in turf or
sphagnum moss •

medium-spaced •
gills are yellowish
ochre, tinged pink

FRUITING In troops in
wet, acid sites under trees.

Dimensions CAP ⊕ 5–16cm | STEM ↕ 5–13cm ↔ 0.7–3cm	Spores Pale yellow to pinkish	Edibility

CAP & STEM FUNGI WITH ADNEXED TO ADNATE GILLS

This section consists of agarics in which the gill attachment to the stem varies from very narrow (adnexed) to very broad (broadly adnate). Some gills have a sharp indentation close to the stem; this is known as a notch (see p.15). The gill edge may be straight or curved (sinuate).

gills adnate

gills adnexed

FLESHY WITH NO OBVIOUS VEIL

THIS SUBSECTION features agarics with fruitbodies that are fleshy but which, unlike other fleshy species, do not have obvious veil remains either on the cap, the cap margin, or the stem. It includes the blewits and most of the mycorrhizal knight-caps, as well as a range of other groups.

Family HYGROPHORACEAE	Species *Hygrocybe punicea*	Season Autumn

CRIMSON WAX-CAP

This large, fleshy fungus has a broadly conical to almost flat, slightly moist, crimson-red cap and pale crimson-red to orange gills. The yellow stem is red flushed with a dry surface and a covering of fine, longitudinal fibres. Its taste and smell are unremarkable. It should not be eaten. (see Occurrence).

• **OCCURRENCE**
Unimproved grassland, always with other species of *Hygrocybe*, *Geoglossum*, and *Clavulinopsis*. Widespread but local, and in some places threatened with extinction, in northern temperate zones.

• **SIMILAR SPECIES** *H. coccinea* (p.105). *H. splendidissima* is brighter vermilion-red with a dry cap and a sweet, sickly smell. It is also declining in numbers.

SECTION — well-spaced, thick, waxy gills

gills are adnexed

moist, crimson-red cap surface darkens to grey with age

white, yellow, or pale red flesh

FRUITING Appears in small groups or troops.

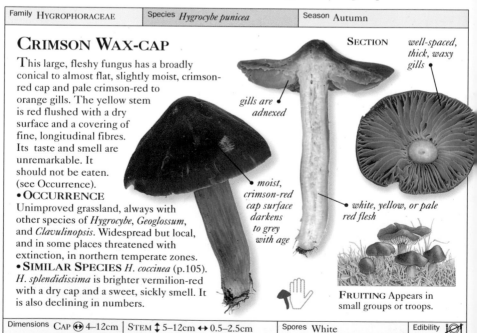

Dimensions CAP ⊕ 4–12cm	STEM ↕ 5–12cm ↔ 0.5–2.5cm	Spores White	Edibility

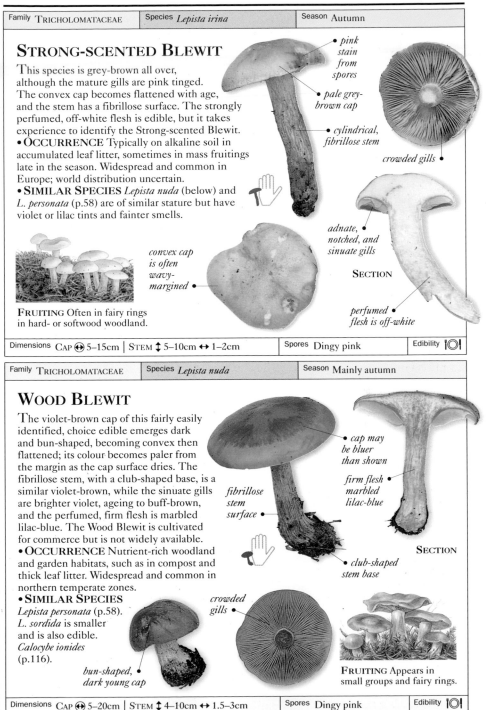

| Family TRICHOLOMATACEAE | Species *Lepista irina* | Season Autumn |

STRONG-SCENTED BLEWIT

This species is grey-brown all over, although the mature gills are pink tinged. The convex cap becomes flattened with age, and the stem has a fibrillose surface. The strongly perfumed, off-white flesh is edible, but it takes experience to identify the Strong-scented Blewit.

• OCCURRENCE Typically on alkaline soil in accumulated leaf litter, sometimes in mass fruitings late in the season. Widespread and common in Europe; world distribution uncertain.

• SIMILAR SPECIES *Lepista nuda* (below) and *L. personata* (p.58) are of similar stature but have violet or lilac tints and fainter smells.

pink stain from spores

pale grey-brown cap

cylindrical, fibrillose stem

crowded gills

adnate, notched, and sinuate gills

SECTION

convex cap is often wavy-margined

FRUITING Often in fairy rings in hard- or softwood woodland.

perfumed flesh is off-white

| Dimensions CAP ⊕ 5–15cm | STEM ↕ 5–10cm ↔ 1–2cm | Spores Dingy pink | Edibility |

| Family TRICHOLOMATACEAE | Species *Lepista nuda* | Season Mainly autumn |

WOOD BLEWIT

The violet-brown cap of this fairly easily identified, choice edible emerges dark and bun-shaped, becoming convex then flattened; its colour becomes paler from the margin as the cap surface dries. The fibrillose stem, with a club-shaped base, is a similar violet-brown, while the sinuate gills are brighter violet, ageing to buff-brown, and the perfumed, firm flesh is marbled lilac-blue. The Wood Blewit is cultivated for commerce but is not widely available.

• OCCURRENCE Nutrient-rich woodland and garden habitats, such as in compost and thick leaf litter. Widespread and common in northern temperate zones.

• SIMILAR SPECIES *Lepista personata* (p.58). *L. sordida* is smaller and is also edible. *Calocybe ionides* (p.116).

cap may be bluer than shown

firm flesh marbled lilac-blue

fibrillose stem surface

SECTION

club-shaped stem base

crowded gills

bun-shaped, dark young cap

FRUITING Appears in small groups and fairy rings.

| Dimensions CAP ⊕ 5–20cm | STEM ↕ 4–10cm ↔ 1.5–3cm | Spores Dingy pink | Edibility |

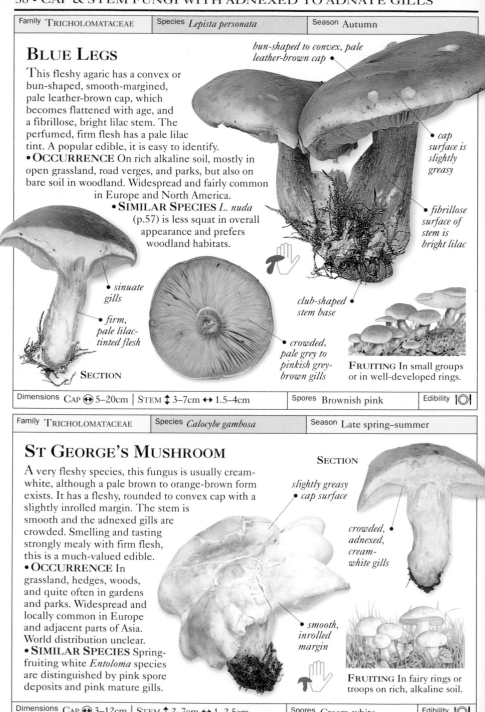

| Family | TRICHOLOMATACEAE | Species | *Lepista personata* | Season | Autumn |

BLUE LEGS

bun-shaped to convex, pale leather-brown cap •

This fleshy agaric has a convex or bun-shaped, smooth-margined, pale leather-brown cap, which becomes flattened with age, and a fibrillose, bright lilac stem. The perfumed, firm flesh has a pale lilac tint. A popular edible, it is easy to identify.

• **OCCURRENCE** On rich alkaline soil, mostly in open grassland, road verges, and parks, but also on bare soil in woodland. Widespread and fairly common in Europe and North America.

• **SIMILAR SPECIES** *L. nuda* (p.57) is less squat in overall appearance and prefers woodland habitats.

• cap surface is slightly greasy

• fibrillose surface of stem is bright lilac

• sinuate gills

• firm, pale lilac-tinted flesh

SECTION

club-shaped • stem base

• crowded, pale grey to pinkish grey-brown gills

FRUITING In small groups or in well-developed rings.

| Dimensions | CAP ⊕ 5–20cm | STEM ↕ 3–7cm ↔ 1.5–4cm | Spores | Brownish pink | Edibility |

| Family | TRICHOLOMATACEAE | Species | *Calocybe gambosa* | Season | Late spring–summer |

ST GEORGE'S MUSHROOM

SECTION

A very fleshy species, this fungus is usually cream-white, although a pale brown to orange-brown form exists. It has a fleshy, rounded to convex cap with a slightly inrolled margin. The stem is smooth and the adnexed gills are crowded. Smelling and tasting strongly mealy with firm flesh, this is a much-valued edible.

• **OCCURRENCE** In grassland, hedges, woods, and quite often in gardens and parks. Widespread and locally common in Europe and adjacent parts of Asia. World distribution unclear.

• **SIMILAR SPECIES** Spring-fruiting white *Entoloma* species are distinguished by pink spore deposits and pink mature gills.

slightly greasy • cap surface

crowded, • adnexed, cream-white gills

• smooth, inrolled margin

FRUITING In fairy rings or troops on rich, alkaline soil.

| Dimensions | CAP ⊕ 3–12cm | STEM ↕ 2–7cm ↔ 1–2.5cm | Spores | Cream-white | Edibility |

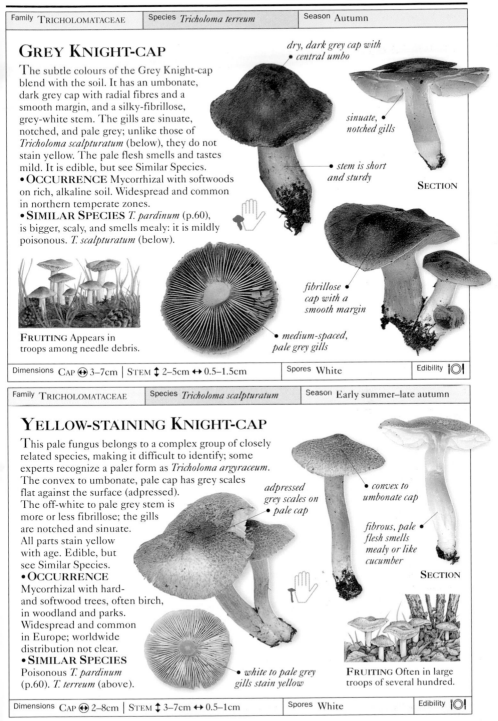

| Family TRICHOLOMATACEAE | Species *Tricholoma terreum* | Season Autumn |

GREY KNIGHT-CAP

The subtle colours of the Grey Knight-cap blend with the soil. It has an umbonate, dark grey cap with radial fibres and a smooth margin, and a silky-fibrillose, grey-white stem. The gills are sinuate, notched, and pale grey; unlike those of *Tricholoma sculpturatum* (below), they do not stain yellow. The pale flesh smells and tastes mild. It is edible, but see Similar Species.
• **OCCURRENCE** Mycorrhizal with softwoods on rich, alkaline soil. Widespread and common in northern temperate zones.
• **SIMILAR SPECIES** *T. pardinum* (p.60), is bigger, scaly, and smells mealy: it is mildly poisonous. *T. sculpturatum* (below).

dry, dark grey cap with central umbo

sinuate, notched gills

stem is short and sturdy

SECTION

fibrillose cap with a smooth margin

FRUITING Appears in troops among needle debris.

medium-spaced, pale grey gills

| Dimensions CAP ⊕ 3–7cm | STEM ↕ 2–5cm ↔ 0.5–1.5cm | Spores White | Edibility |

| Family TRICHOLOMATACEAE | Species *Tricholoma sculpturatum* | Season Early summer–late autumn |

YELLOW-STAINING KNIGHT-CAP

This pale fungus belongs to a complex group of closely related species, making it difficult to identify; some experts recognize a paler form as *Tricholoma argyraceum*. The convex to umbonate, pale cap has grey scales flat against the surface (adpressed). The off-white to pale grey stem is more or less fibrillose; the gills are notched and sinuate. All parts stain yellow with age. Edible, but see Similar Species.
• **OCCURRENCE** Mycorrhizal with hard- and softwood trees, often birch, in woodland and parks. Widespread and common in Europe; worldwide distribution not clear.
• **SIMILAR SPECIES** Poisonous *T. pardinum* (p.60). *T. terreum* (above).

adpressed grey scales on pale cap

convex to umbonate cap

fibrous, pale flesh smells mealy or like cucumber

SECTION

white to pale grey gills stain yellow

FRUITING Often in large troops of several hundred.

| Dimensions CAP ⊕ 2–8cm | STEM ↕ 3–7cm ↔ 0.5–1cm | Spores White | Edibility |

| Family | TRICHOLOMATACEAE | Species | *Tricholoma atrosquamosum* | Season | Autumn–late autumn |

DARK-SCALED KNIGHT-CAP

This species has a convex or umbonate, pale grey cap, with radially arranged, upturned, dark, thread-like, fibrous scales and an inrolled margin. The pale stem is covered with black scales, and the flesh is pale and fibrous with a spicy fragrance like *Pelargonium* (geranium). It can be hard to identify (see Similar Species), so eating it is not recommended.
• OCCURRENCE Mycorrhizal with soft- and hardwood trees. Widespread but local in Europe; world distribution not clear.
• SIMILAR SPECIES *Tricholoma orirubens* stains green and pink. *T. pardinum* (inset, right) is poisonous. *T. squarrulosum* is even more scaly.

sinuate, • notched, pale grey gills stain black at or near edge

SECTION

gills are • medium spaced

• pale flesh smells of spice

• club-shaped stem base

FRUITING Singly or in small groups on alkaline soil.

dark radial • fibres and scales on pale grey cap surface

• hair-like black scales on stem

△ **TRICHOLOMA PARDINUM**
This species has a black-scaly cap and flesh that smells and tastes mealy. It occurs with both hard- and softwoods. ☠

| Dimensions | CAP ⊕ 3–12cm | STEM ↕ 4–8cm ↔ 0.5–1.5cm | Spores | White | Edibility |

| Family | TRICHOLOMATACEAE | Species | *Tricholoma sciodes* | Season | Autumn |

FLECK-GILL KNIGHT-CAP

This species has an off-white cap partially concealed by dark scales flattened against the surface (adpressed); it has a fairly prominent umbo. The gills have distinctive black spots, and the more or less cylindrical, pale stem is clad in hair-like grey scales; both may be pink flushed. It has earthy-smelling, sharp-tasting flesh, and is inedible.
• OCCURRENCE Mycorrhizal with hardwood trees, often beech, on fertile soil. Widespread and common in Europe, except the boreal-arctic; world distribution not clear.
• SIMILAR SPECIES *Tricholoma orirubens* stains green and pink. *T. virgatum*, found in rich softwood forests, is silvery grey and conical.

• adpressed dark scales on off-white cap surface

• umbo in cap centre

fairly crowded, sinuate, • notched gills

pale grey gills have dark edges •

fibrous, • pale flesh with earthy smell

FRUITING A few specimens together in leaf litter.

SECTION

| Dimensions | CAP ⊕ 4–8cm | STEM ↕ 4–10cm ↔ 1–2cm | Spores | White | Edibility |

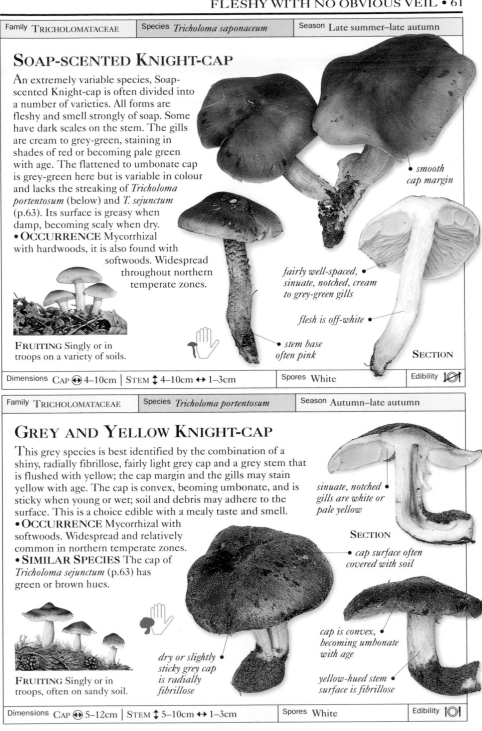

| Family TRICHOLOMATACEAE | Species *Tricholoma saponaceum* | Season Late summer–late autumn |

SOAP-SCENTED KNIGHT-CAP

An extremely variable species, Soap-scented Knight-cap is often divided into a number of varieties. All forms are fleshy and smell strongly of soap. Some have dark scales on the stem. The gills are cream to grey-green, staining in shades of red or becoming pale green with age. The flattened to umbonate cap is grey-green here but is variable in colour and lacks the streaking of *Tricholoma portentosum* (below) and *T. sejunctum* (p.63). Its surface is greasy when damp, becoming scaly when dry.
• **OCCURRENCE** Mycorrhizal with hardwoods, it is also found with softwoods. Widespread throughout northern temperate zones.

smooth cap margin •

fairly well-spaced, • sinuate, notched, cream to grey-green gills

flesh is off-white •

FRUITING Singly or in troops on a variety of soils.

• stem base often pink

SECTION

| Dimensions CAP ⊕ 4–10cm | STEM ↕ 4–10cm ↔ 1–3cm | Spores White | Edibility |

| Family TRICHOLOMATACEAE | Species *Tricholoma portentosum* | Season Autumn–late autumn |

GREY AND YELLOW KNIGHT-CAP

This grey species is best identified by the combination of a shiny, radially fibrillose, fairly light grey cap and a grey stem that is flushed with yellow; the cap margin and the gills may stain yellow with age. The cap is convex, beoming umbonate, and is sticky when young or wet; soil and debris may adhere to the surface. This is a choice edible with a mealy taste and smell.
• **OCCURRENCE** Mycorrhizal with softwoods. Widespread and relatively common in northern temperate zones.
• **SIMILAR SPECIES** The cap of *Tricholoma sejunctum* (p.63) has green or brown hues.

sinuate, notched • gills are white or pale yellow

SECTION

• cap surface often covered with soil

cap is convex, • becoming umbonate with age

FRUITING Singly or in troops, often on sandy soil.

dry or slightly • sticky grey cap is radially fibrillose

yellow-hued stem • surface is fibrillose

| Dimensions CAP ⊕ 5–12cm | STEM ↕ 5–10cm ↔ 1–3cm | Spores White | Edibility |

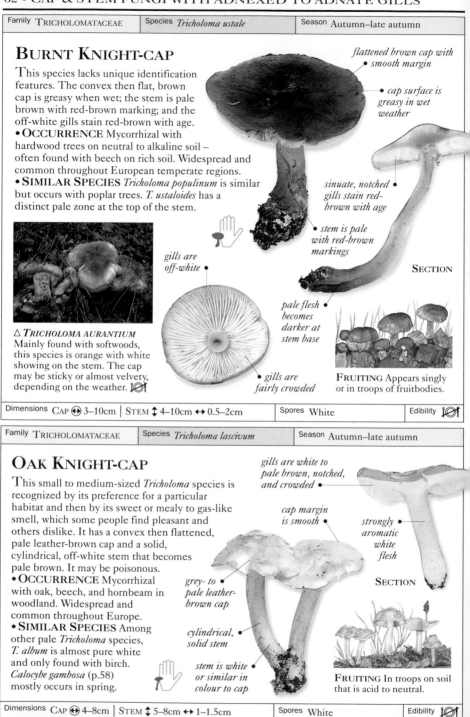

| Family TRICHOLOMATACEAE | Species *Tricholoma ustale* | Season Autumn–late autumn |

BURNT KNIGHT-CAP

This species lacks unique identification features. The convex then flat, brown cap is greasy when wet; the stem is pale brown with red-brown marking; and the off-white gills stain red-brown with age.
• **OCCURRENCE** Mycorrhizal with hardwood trees on neutral to alkaline soil – often found with beech on rich soil. Widespread and common throughout European temperate regions.
• **SIMILAR SPECIES** *Tricholoma populinum* is similar but occurs with poplar trees. *T. ustaloides* has a distinct pale zone at the top of the stem.

flattened brown cap with • smooth margin

• cap surface is greasy in wet weather

sinuate, notched • gills stain red-brown with age

• stem is pale with red-brown markings

gills are off-white •

SECTION

△ *TRICHOLOMA AURANTIUM*
Mainly found with softwoods, this species is orange with white showing on the stem. The cap may be sticky or almost velvety, depending on the weather.

pale flesh • becomes darker at stem base

• gills are fairly crowded

FRUITING Appears singly or in troops of fruitbodies.

| Dimensions CAP ⊕ 3–10cm | STEM ↕ 4–10cm ↔ 0.5–2cm | Spores White | Edibility |

| Family TRICHOLOMATACEAE | Species *Tricholoma lascivum* | Season Autumn–late autumn |

OAK KNIGHT-CAP

This small to medium-sized *Tricholoma* species is recognized by its preference for a particular habitat and then by its sweet or mealy to gas-like smell, which some people find pleasant and others dislike. It has a convex then flattened, pale leather-brown cap and a solid, cylindrical, off-white stem that becomes pale brown. It may be poisonous.
• **OCCURRENCE** Mycorrhizal with oak, beech, and hornbeam in woodland. Widespread and common throughout Europe.
• **SIMILAR SPECIES** Among other pale *Tricholoma* species, *T. album* is almost pure white and only found with birch. *Calocybe gambosa* (p.58) mostly occurs in spring.

gills are white to pale brown, notched, and crowded •

cap margin is smooth •

strongly • aromatic white flesh

SECTION

grey- to pale leather-brown cap

cylindrical, solid stem •

stem is white • or similar in colour to cap

FRUITING In troops on soil that is acid to neutral.

| Dimensions CAP ⊕ 4–8cm | STEM ↕ 5–8cm ↔ 1–1.5cm | Spores White | Edibility |

Family TRICHOLOMATACEAE	Species *Tricholoma sejunctum*	Season Autumn

DECEIVING KNIGHT-CAP

The green or brown cap of this species is moist and domed, flattening with age. Its surface has dark fibrils and is greasy in wet weather. The white stem develops yellow flushes with age, and the flesh is off-white, tinted yellow under the cap skin. It is edible, but can cause nausea; see also Similar Species.
• **OCCURRENCE** Mycorrhizal with hardwoods, such as beech, and softwoods. It is found in woodland or plantations, usually on acid soil; the beech form occurs on alkaline soil. Widespread throughout northern temperate regions.
• **SIMILAR SPECIES** *Tricholoma portentosum* (p.61). Poisonous *Amanita phalloides* (p.151) is distinguished by its volva, stem ring, and free gills.

• *pale brown cap with radiating, dark fibrils*

• *pointed stem base*

cap surface is greasy when wet

• *cap is domed, flattening with age*

sinuate, notched, white to cream gills •

firm, off-white flesh

SECTION

FRUITING Appears in small groups or troops.

white stem develops yellow flushes with age

Dimensions CAP ⊕ 5–10cm | STEM ↕ 5–8cm ↔ 1–1.5cm	Spores White	Edibility |◯|

Family TRICHOLOMATACEAE	Species *Tricholoma auratum*	Season Autumn–early winter

SANDY KNIGHT-CAP

There are several forms of this species, which is also known as *Tricholoma equestre*. They are all yellow, with an expanded convex cap and pale yellow stem, but differ in fruitbody size, being slender or more robust depending on where they are growing. The flesh is a whitish yellow and has a faint to fairly strong mealy smell, differing in the various forms and strongest in the form associated with pine (shown here). It is a choice edible, but the *Pinus* form can be difficult to clean as it becomes ingrained with grit.
• **OCCURRENCE** Mycorrizal: robust forms occur in pine woods; slender forms are mostly found under spruce and aspen. Widespread and fairly common throughout northern temperate zones.

medium-spaced, sinuate, notched gills •

expanded-convex, yellow-brown cap •

dirt sticks to cap and stem •

pale yellow stem •

gills are bright yellow •

FRUITING In troops; different forms are found with pine, on sandy soil, or with spruce or aspen.

Dimensions CAP ⊕ 5–14cm | STEM ↕ 5–10cm ↔ 1.5–2.5cm	Spores White	Edibility |◯|

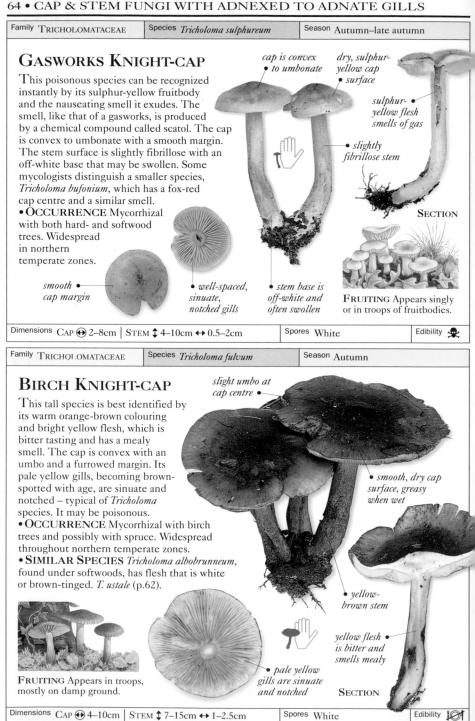

Family TRICHOLOMATACEAE	Species *Tricholoma sulphureum*	Season Autumn–late autumn

GASWORKS KNIGHT-CAP

This poisonous species can be recognized instantly by its sulphur-yellow fruitbody and the nauseating smell it exudes. The smell, like that of a gasworks, is produced by a chemical compound called scatol. The cap is convex to umbonate with a smooth margin. The stem surface is slightly fibrillose with an off-white base that may be swollen. Some mycologists distinguish a smaller species, *Tricholoma bufonium*, which has a fox-red cap centre and a similar smell.

• OCCURRENCE Mycorrhizal with both hard- and softwood trees. Widespread in northern temperate zones.

cap is convex to umbonate

dry, sulphur-yellow cap surface

sulphur-yellow flesh smells of gas

slightly fibrillose stem

SECTION

smooth cap margin

well-spaced, sinuate, notched gills

stem base is off-white and often swollen

FRUITING Appears singly or in troops of fruitbodies.

Dimensions CAP ⊕ 2–8cm | STEM ↕ 4–10cm ↔ 0.5–2cm	Spores White	Edibility ☠

Family TRICHOLOMATACEAE	Species *Tricholoma fulvum*	Season Autumn

BIRCH KNIGHT-CAP

This tall species is best identified by its warm orange-brown colouring and bright yellow flesh, which is bitter tasting and has a mealy smell. The cap is convex with an umbo and a furrowed margin. Its pale yellow gills, becoming brown-spotted with age, are sinuate and notched – typical of *Tricholoma* species. It may be poisonous.

• OCCURRENCE Mycorrhizal with birch trees and possibly with spruce. Widespread throughout northern temperate zones.

• SIMILAR SPECIES *Tricholoma albobrunneum*, found under softwoods, has flesh that is white or brown-tinged. *T. ustale* (p.62).

slight umbo at cap centre

smooth, dry cap surface, greasy when wet

yellow-brown stem

yellow flesh is bitter and smells mealy

FRUITING Appears in troops, mostly on damp ground.

pale yellow gills are sinuate and notched

SECTION

Dimensions CAP ⊕ 4–10cm | STEM ↕ 7–15cm ↔ 1–2.5cm	Spores White	Edibility ⊘

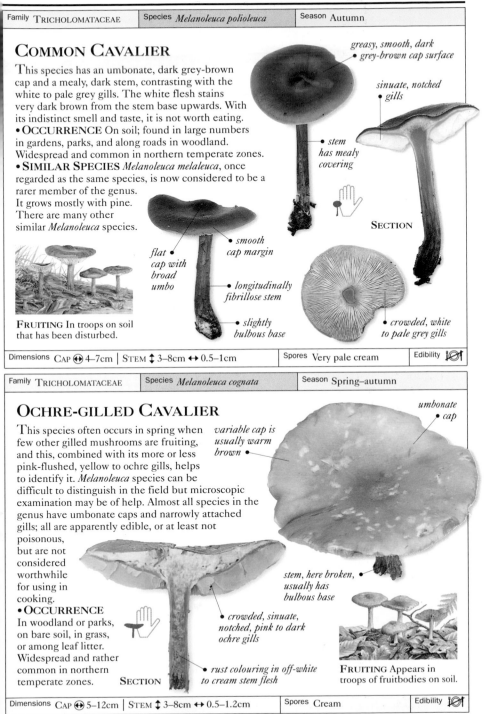

Family TRICHOLOMATACEAE	Species *Melanoleuca polioleuca*	Season Autumn

COMMON CAVALIER

This species has an umbonate, dark grey-brown cap and a mealy, dark stem, contrasting with the white to pale grey gills. The white flesh stains very dark brown from the stem base upwards. With its indistinct smell and taste, it is not worth eating.

• **OCCURRENCE** On soil; found in large numbers in gardens, parks, and along roads in woodland. Widespread and common in northern temperate zones.

• **SIMILAR SPECIES** *Melanoleuca melaleuca*, once regarded as the same species, is now considered to be a rarer member of the genus. It grows mostly with pine. There are many other similar *Melanoleuca* species.

greasy, smooth, dark grey-brown cap surface

sinuate, notched gills

stem has mealy covering

SECTION

flat cap with broad umbo

smooth cap margin

longitudinally fibrillose stem

slightly bulbous base

crowded, white to pale grey gills

FRUITING In troops on soil that has been disturbed.

Dimensions CAP ⊕ 4–7cm	STEM ↕ 3–8cm ↔ 0.5–1cm	Spores Very pale cream	Edibility

Family TRICHOLOMATACEAE	Species *Melanoleuca cognata*	Season Spring–autumn

OCHRE-GILLED CAVALIER

This species often occurs in spring when few other gilled mushrooms are fruiting, and this, combined with its more or less pink-flushed, yellow to ochre gills, helps to identify it. *Melanoleuca* species can be difficult to distinguish in the field but microscopic examination may be of help. Almost all species in the genus have umbonate caps and narrowly attached gills; all are apparently edible, or at least not poisonous, but are not considered worthwhile for using in cooking.

• **OCCURRENCE** In woodland or parks, on bare soil, in grass, or among leaf litter. Widespread and rather common in northern temperate zones.

umbonate cap

variable cap is usually warm brown

stem, here broken, usually has bulbous base

crowded, sinuate, notched, pink to dark ochre gills

rust colouring in off-white to cream stem flesh

SECTION

FRUITING Appears in troops of fruitbodies on soil.

Dimensions CAP ⊕ 5–12cm	STEM ↕ 3–8cm ↔ 0.5–1.2cm	Spores Cream	Edibility

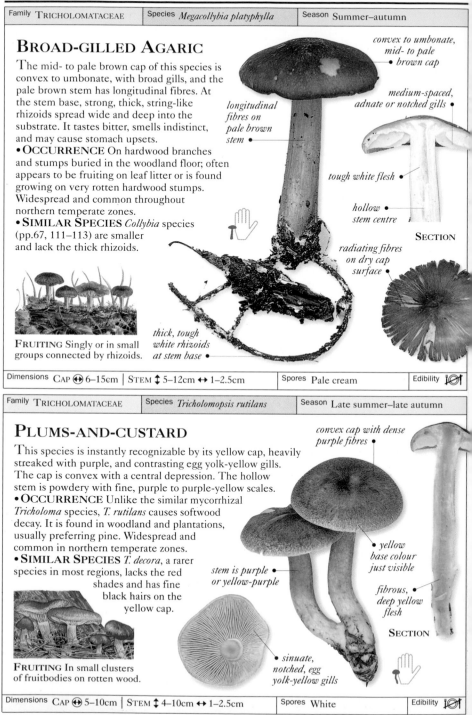

| Family TRICHOLOMATACEAE | Species *Megacollybia platyphylla* | Season Summer–autumn |

BROAD-GILLED AGARIC

The mid- to pale brown cap of this species is convex to umbonate, with broad gills, and the pale brown stem has longitudinal fibres. At the stem base, strong, thick, string-like rhizoids spread wide and deep into the substrate. It tastes bitter, smells indistinct, and may cause stomach upsets.
• **OCCURRENCE** On hardwood branches and stumps buried in the woodland floor; often appears to be fruiting on leaf litter or is found growing on very rotten hardwood stumps. Widespread and common throughout northern temperate zones.
• **SIMILAR SPECIES** *Collybia* species (pp.67, 111–113) are smaller and lack the thick rhizoids.

convex to umbonate, mid- to pale brown cap

medium-spaced, adnate or notched gills

longitudinal fibres on pale brown stem

tough white flesh

hollow stem centre

SECTION

radiating fibres on dry cap surface

FRUITING Singly or in small groups connected by rhizoids.

thick, tough white rhizoids at stem base

| Dimensions CAP ⊕ 6–15cm | STEM ↕ 5–12cm ↔ 1–2.5cm | Spores Pale cream | Edibility |

| Family TRICHOLOMATACEAE | Species *Tricholomopsis rutilans* | Season Late summer–late autumn |

PLUMS-AND-CUSTARD

This species is instantly recognizable by its yellow cap, heavily streaked with purple, and contrasting egg yolk-yellow gills. The cap is convex with a central depression. The hollow stem is powdery with fine, purple to purple-yellow scales.
• **OCCURRENCE** Unlike the similar mycorrhizal *Tricholoma* species, *T. rutilans* causes softwood decay. It is found in woodland and plantations, usually preferring pine. Widespread and common in northern temperate zones.
• **SIMILAR SPECIES** *T. decora*, a rarer species in most regions, lacks the red shades and has fine black hairs on the yellow cap.

convex cap with dense purple fibres

yellow base colour just visible

stem is purple or yellow-purple

fibrous, deep yellow flesh

SECTION

FRUITING In small clusters of fruitbodies on rotten wood.

sinuate, notched, egg yolk-yellow gills

| Dimensions CAP ⊕ 5–10cm | STEM ↕ 4–10cm ↔ 1–2.5cm | Spores White | Edibility |

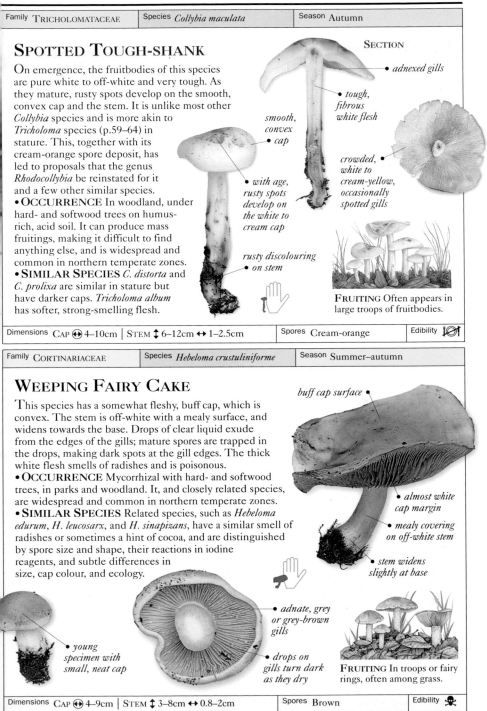

Family TRICHOLOMATACEAE	Species *Collybia maculata*	Season Autumn

SPOTTED TOUGH-SHANK

On emergence, the fruitbodies of this species are pure white to off-white and very tough. As they mature, rusty spots develop on the smooth, convex cap and the stem. It is unlike most other *Collybia* species and is more akin to *Tricholoma* species (p.59–64) in stature. This, together with its cream-orange spore deposit, has led to proposals that the genus *Rhodocollybia* be reinstated for it and a few other similar species.
• **OCCURRENCE** In woodland, under hard- and softwood trees on humus-rich, acid soil. It can produce mass fruitings, making it difficult to find anything else, and is widespread and common in northern temperate zones.
• **SIMILAR SPECIES** *C. distorta* and *C. prolixa* are similar in stature but have darker caps. *Tricholoma album* has softer, strong-smelling flesh.

SECTION
• *adnexed gills*
• *tough, fibrous white flesh*

smooth, convex cap

crowded, white to cream-yellow, occasionally spotted gills

• *with age, rusty spots develop on the white to cream cap*

rusty discolouring on stem

FRUITING Often appears in large troops of fruitbodies.

Dimensions CAP ⊕ 4–10cm	STEM ↕ 6–12cm ↔ 1–2.5cm	Spores Cream-orange	Edibility

Family CORTINARIACEAE	Species *Hebeloma crustuliniforme*	Season Summer–autumn

WEEPING FAIRY CAKE

This species has a somewhat fleshy, buff cap, which is convex. The stem is off-white with a mealy surface, and widens towards the base. Drops of clear liquid exude from the edges of the gills; mature spores are trapped in the drops, making dark spots at the gill edges. The thick white flesh smells of radishes and is poisonous.
• **OCCURRENCE** Mycorrhizal with hard- and softwood trees, in parks and woodland. It, and closely related species, are widespread and common in northern temperate zones.
• **SIMILAR SPECIES** Related species, such as *Hebeloma edurum*, *H. leucosarx*, and *H. sinapizans*, have a similar smell of radishes or sometimes a hint of cocoa, and are distinguished by spore size and shape, their reactions in iodine reagents, and subtle differences in size, cap colour, and ecology.

buff cap surface •

• *almost white cap margin*

• *mealy covering on off-white stem*

• *stem widens slightly at base*

• *young specimen with small, neat cap*

• *adnate, grey or grey-brown gills*

• *drops on gills turn dark as they dry*

FRUITING In troops or fairy rings, often among grass.

Dimensions CAP ⊕ 4–9cm	STEM ↕ 3–8cm ↔ 0.8–2cm	Spores Brown	Edibility ☠

Family ENTOLOMATACEAE	Species *Entoloma sinuatum*	Season Autumn

LEAD POISONER

A convex, pale grey-brown to ochre-cream cap with medium-spaced, sinuate, notched, pale yellow young gills, which become the typical *Entoloma*-pink with age, are good indicators of Lead Poisoner, which also has a white to greyish cream stem and a mealy to nauseating smell. It is important to get to know this *Lepista* lookalike as it is responsible for a high percentage of fungus poisonings.
• **OCCURRENCE** In mature hardwood woodland, often on clay soil. Widespread but local in Europe. Replaced by a close relative in North America and East Asia.
• **SIMILAR SPECIES** Both *Lepista irina* (p.57) and *Clitocybe nebularis* are superficially similar.

sinuate, notched, medium-spaced gills

cap is pale grey-brown to ochre-cream

convex cap with central umbo

FRUITING Appears in small groups often under hardwood trees, such as oak or beech, in woods.

Dimensions CAP ⊕ 8–20cm | STEM ↕ 10–18cm ↔ 2–4cm	Spores Pale pink	Edibility ☠

Family ENTOLOMATACEAE	Species *Entoloma rhodopolium*	Season Autumn–late autumn

WOODLAND PINK-GILL

This very varied species is difficult to identify. The grey or grey-brown cap is convex with an umbo, or slightly depressed. The grey stem is often long and slender with pale grey to pale brown flesh. It is either odourless or smells nitrous. The nitrous-smelling form is slender and was once considered a separate species, *Entoloma nidorosum*. All forms are poisonous.
• **OCCURRENCE** In hardwood woodland, especially beech woods, on rich soil. Widespread and locally common in northern temperate zones; world distribution unclear.
• **SIMILAR SPECIES** A number of similar species differ subtly in colouring and various microscopic characteristics.

fairly broad, thick, sinuate, notched gills

cap margin may have radial striations

soft, pale grey to pale brown flesh **SECTION**

slender, silky grey stem with longitudinal fibres

crowded, whitish grey then pink gills

△ *ENTOLOMA CLYPEATUM*
This spring-fruiting Pink-gill has a grey-brown cap, a brown-tinged, white stem, and sinuate, notched, pale grey gills ageing to pink. |◎|

FRUITING Appears in troops among leaf litter.

Dimensions CAP ⊕ 4–12cm | STEM ↕ 6–15cm ↔ 0.5–2cm	Spores Dirty pink	Edibility ☠

| Family ENTOLOMATACEAE | Species *Entoloma porphyrophaeum* | Season Summer–autumn |

PORPHYRY PINK-GILL

Grey-purple colouring and a tall stature, along with a grassland habitat, make this species easily recognizable. The cap is umbonate, becoming conical with age. It has white flesh, with no distinctive smell, and may be poisonous.
• OCCURRENCE In unimproved grassland, often associated with Hygrophoraceae and Clavariaceae; also in alpine areas and shrubby or coppiced woods. Widespread although uncommon in Europe: it has suffered from the farming practice of using commercial fertilizer on pastures. World distribution unclear.

FRUITING Singly or in small groups of fruitbodies.

cap margin is inrolled •

cap is smoothly • fibrillose

SECTION

pale stem • may be yellow-tinged towards base

fairly crowded gills are sinuate and notched, or free

• fibrillose stem surface

solid • white flesh

| Dimensions CAP ⊕ 4–8cm | STEM ↕ 7–14cm ↔ 0.5–2cm | Spores Pale pink | Edibility 🍴 |

WITH COBWEB-LIKE VEIL

SPECIES OF *CORTINARIUS*, which are featured in this subsection, are highly variable in size and shape. However, they all have a partial veil, looking like a fine spider's web, which protects the young gills. They also have rusty brown spore deposits, often seen as a rusty smudge on the veil remains.

| Family CORTINARIACEAE | Species *Cortinarius bolaris* | Season Autumn |

RED-DAPPLED WEB-CAP

Distinctive red scales covering the cap and stem readily identify this species. A fairly short stem makes it look sturdy, and the fleshy cap is broadly convex with remains of the veil visible as fine threads at the margin. Thick, off-white flesh in the cap becomes yellow to orange towards the stem base.
• OCCURRENCE Mycorrhizal with hardwoods, especially oak and birch, on rather acid soil. Widespread and locally quite common in northern temperate zones but absent from some regions.

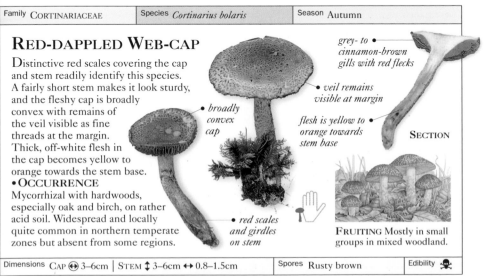

grey- to • cinnamon-brown gills with red flecks

• veil remains visible at margin

• broadly convex cap

flesh is yellow to • orange towards stem base

SECTION

• red scales and girdles on stem

FRUITING Mostly in small groups in mixed woodland.

| Dimensions CAP ⊕ 3–6cm | STEM ↕ 3–6cm ↔ 0.8–1.5cm | Spores Rusty brown | Edibility ☠ |

| Family CORTINARIACEAE | Species *Cortinarius pholideus* | Season Autumn |

SCALY WEB-CAP

A brown-scaled cap and a long stem ringed with brown veil girdles characterize this web-cap. The cap is more or less convex when young, flat with a central umbo when mature. When young, the adnate gills are violet-blue; they age to violet-brown as the spores mature to rusty brown. A faint smell reminiscent of fresh tangerines exudes from the violet-tinged, pale brown flesh.
• OCCURRENCE Typically mycorrhizal with birch, but may also be found with other trees in mixed woodland. It prefers acid soil. Widespread and quite common in northern temperate zones.

FRUITING Appears in small groups on mossy soil.

thin, pointed brown scales on cap

violet to violet-brown gills

fibrous brown girdles on stem

cap is pointed to umbonate

stem is violet at top

solid stem with violet-brown flesh

SECTION

| Dimensions CAP ⊕ 3–8cm | STEM ↕ 5–12cm ↔ 0.5–1cm | Spores Rusty brown | Edibility |

| Family CORTINARIACEAE | Species *Cortinarius semisanguineus* | Season Autumn |

RED-GILLED WEB-CAP

SECTION

The uniform red-brown colouring and blood-red gills are the best aid to identification of this species. It has a convex, olive- to red-brown cap, becoming umbonate with age; the paler stem exhibits thread-like veil remnants. The flesh of the cap is a paler red-brown than that of the stem. The Red-gilled Web-cap is an excellent source of a dye that is used for colouring wool.
• OCCURRENCE Almost exclusively mycorrhizal with softwood trees, it is often abundant under young spruce trees in plantations. Widespread in northern temperate zones.
• SIMILAR SPECIES *Cortinarius phoeniceus* has a redder cap and more distinct red veil girdles around the stem.

FRUITING In troops under softwoods, often in moss.

blood-red gills are fairly crowded

adnate, sinuate gills

stem surface paler than cap

stem flesh darker red-brown than cap flesh

olive- to dark reddish brown cap

convex to umbonate cap

thread-like remnants of veil

△ *CORTINARIUS CINNAMOMEUS*
This close-relative occurs with both hard- and softwoods. It has orange or orange-yellow young gills ageing cinnamon-brown. ☠

| Dimensions CAP ⊕ 2–7cm | STEM ↕ 4–10cm ↔ 0.5–1cm | Spores Rusty brown | Edibility ☠ |

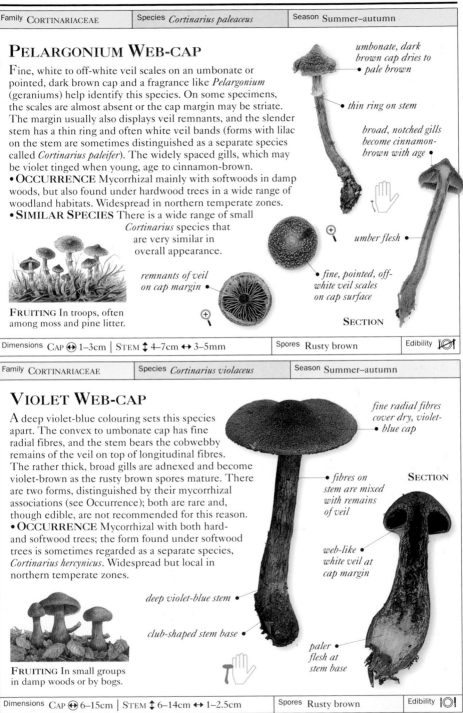

Family CORTINARIACEAE	Species *Cortinarius paleaceus*	Season Summer–autumn

PELARGONIUM WEB-CAP

Fine, white to off-white veil scales on an umbonate or pointed, dark brown cap and a fragrance like *Pelargonium* (geraniums) help identify this species. On some specimens, the scales are almost absent or the cap margin may be striate. The margin usually also displays veil remnants, and the slender stem has a thin ring and often white veil bands (forms with lilac on the stem are sometimes distinguished as a separate species called *Cortinarius paleifer*). The widely spaced gills, which may be violet tinged when young, age to cinnamon-brown.
• OCCURRENCE Mycorrhizal mainly with softwoods in damp woods, but also found under hardwood trees in a wide range of woodland habitats. Widespread in northern temperate zones.
• SIMILAR SPECIES There is a wide range of small *Cortinarius* species that are very similar in overall appearance.

umbonate, dark brown cap dries to • pale brown

thin ring on stem •

broad, notched gills become cinnamon-brown with age •

umber flesh •

remnants of veil on cap margin •

fine, pointed, off-white veil scales on cap surface

FRUITING In troops, often among moss and pine litter.

SECTION

Dimensions CAP ⊕ 1–3cm	STEM ↕ 4–7cm ↔ 3–5mm	Spores Rusty brown	Edibility

Family CORTINARIACEAE	Species *Cortinarius violaceus*	Season Summer–autumn

VIOLET WEB-CAP

A deep violet-blue colouring sets this species apart. The convex to umbonate cap has fine radial fibres, and the stem bears the cobwebby remains of the veil on top of longitudinal fibres. The rather thick, broad gills are adnexed and become violet-brown as the rusty brown spores mature. There are two forms, distinguished by their mycorrhizal associations (see Occurrence); both are rare and, though edible, are not recommended for this reason.
• OCCURRENCE Mycorrhizal with both hard- and softwood trees; the form found under softwood trees is sometimes regarded as a separate species, *Cortinarius hercynicus*. Widespread but local in northern temperate zones.

fine radial fibres cover dry, violet-blue cap

fibres on stem are mixed with remains of veil

SECTION

web-like • white veil at cap margin

deep violet-blue stem •

club-shaped stem base •

paler • flesh at stem base

FRUITING In small groups in damp woods or by bogs.

Dimensions CAP ⊕ 6–15cm	STEM ↕ 6–14cm ↔ 1–2.5cm	Spores Rusty brown	Edibility

Family CORTINARIACEAE	Species *Cortinarius armillatus*	Season Summer–autumn

RED-BANDED WEB-CAP

This web-cap has a large, thick-fleshed, convex, orange-brown cap, the surface of which is covered with fine fibres. The tall, sturdy stem is girdled with prominent cinnamon-red veil remains. The cap margin also bears the remains of the veil.
• **OCCURRENCE** Mycorrhizal with birch and possibly other trees, in damp woodland and boggy areas. Widespread and rather common in northern temperate zones.
• **SIMILAR SPECIES** *Cortinarius paragaudis* is slightly smaller, with stem girdles of a more dirty red. It is associated with softwood trees.

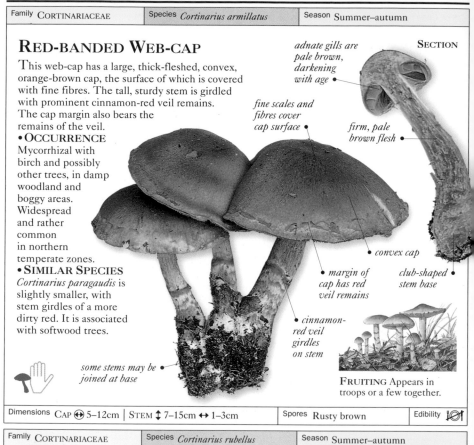

SECTION

adnate gills are pale brown, darkening with age •

fine scales and fibres cover cap surface •

firm, pale brown flesh •

• convex cap

• margin of cap has red veil remains

club-shaped • stem base

• cinnamon-red veil girdles on stem

some stems may be • joined at base

FRUITING Appears in troops or a few together.

Dimensions CAP ⊕ 5–12cm | STEM ↕ 7–15cm ↔ 1–3cm	Spores Rusty brown	Edibility

Family CORTINARIACEAE	Species *Cortinarius rubellus*	Season Summer–autumn

FOXY-ORANGE WEB-CAP

This deadly poisonous web-cap, which smells of radishes, is reddish orange with a pointed, umbonate cap, which is covered with fibrils. The cylindrical to club-shaped, orange-brown stem has pale yellow to ochre bands indicating the veil remnants. The medium-spaced, adnexed to adnate gills are pale ochre-brown, darkening to deep rust-brown with age.
• **OCCURRENCE** Mycorrhizal, mostly with softwood trees, on acid soil. Widespread and locally common in Europe and parts of Asia.
• **SIMILAR SPECIES** *Cortinarius limonius*, also poisonous, has more vivid orange colouring. *C. orellanus* (p.73) has a less conical cap and grows by hardwoods.

pointed, umbonate cap with fibrils •

pale veil girdles on orange-brown stem •

stem base is up to 2cm wide •

FRUITING Appears singly or in troops of fruitbodies on acid soil.

Dimensions CAP ⊕ 3–8cm | STEM ↕ 5–11cm ↔ 0.8–1.5cm	Spores Rusty brown	Edibility ☠

Family CORTINARIACEAE	Species *Cortinarius orellanus*	Season Autumn

COFFIN WEB-CAP

This deadly poisonous species has an umbonate to flattened, red-brown cap with a strongly fibrillose surface. The thick, adnexed to adnate gills are rusty yellow and well spaced, while the cylindrical stem is pale yellow-brown. The stem also bears darker, thread-like traces of the universal veil but it has no girdles, unlike *Cortinarius rubellus* (p.72). Ingestion of the Coffin Web-cap causes severe kidney damage; the symptoms typically appear a long time after it has been consumed.
• **OCCURRENCE** Mostly associated with hardwood trees, such as oak, on acid soils. Widespread in warm-temperate parts of Europe but absent from North America.

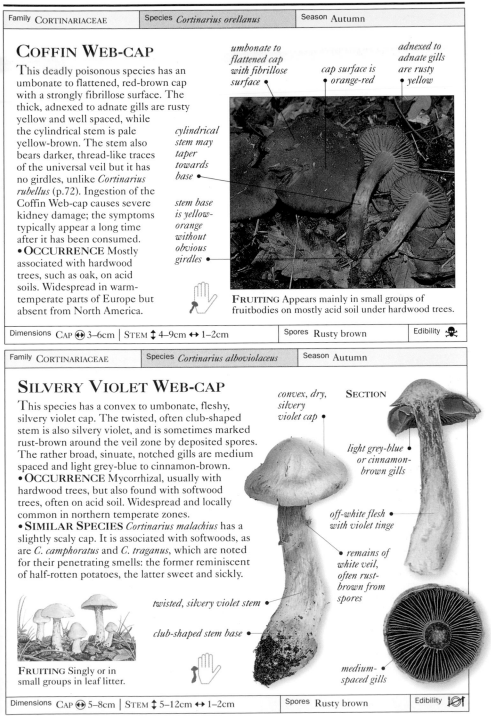

umbonate to flattened cap with fibrillose surface

cap surface is orange-red

adnexed to adnate gills are rusty yellow

cylindrical stem may taper towards base

stem base is yellow-orange without obvious girdles

FRUITING Appears mainly in small groups of fruitbodies on mostly acid soil under hardwood trees.

Dimensions CAP ⊕ 3–6cm | STEM ↕ 4–9cm ↔ 1–2cm	Spores Rusty brown	Edibility 💀

Family CORTINARIACEAE	Species *Cortinarius alboviolaceus*	Season Autumn

SILVERY VIOLET WEB-CAP

This species has a convex to umbonate, fleshy, silvery violet cap. The twisted, often club-shaped stem is also silvery violet, and is sometimes marked rust-brown around the veil zone by deposited spores. The rather broad, sinuate, notched gills are medium spaced and light grey-blue to cinnamon-brown.
• **OCCURRENCE** Mycorrhizal, usually with hardwood trees, but also found with softwood trees, often on acid soil. Widespread and locally common in northern temperate zones.
• **SIMILAR SPECIES** *Cortinarius malachius* has a slightly scaly cap. It is associated with softwoods, as are *C. camphoratus* and *C. traganus*, which are noted for their penetrating smells: the former reminiscent of half-rotten potatoes, the latter sweet and sickly.

convex, dry, silvery violet cap

SECTION

light grey-blue or cinnamon-brown gills

off-white flesh with violet tinge

remains of white veil, often rust-brown from spores

twisted, silvery violet stem

club-shaped stem base

FRUITING Singly or in small groups in leaf litter.

medium-spaced gills

Dimensions CAP ⊕ 5–8cm | STEM ↕ 5–12cm ↔ 1–2cm	Spores Rusty brown	Edibility 🚫🍴

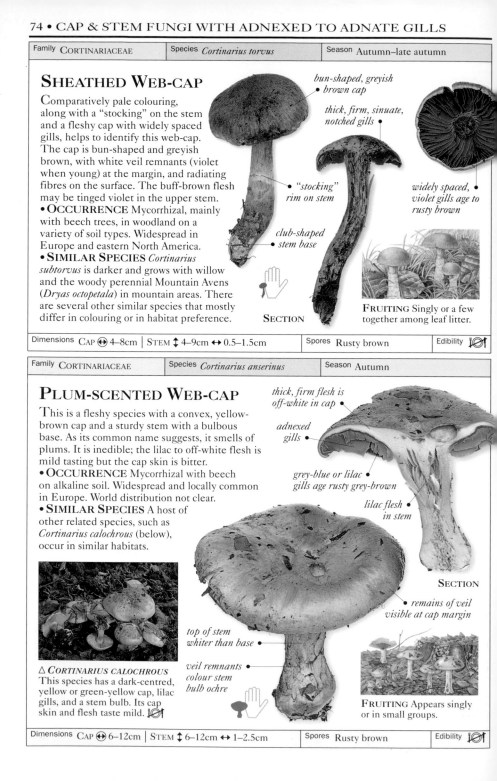

| Family CORTINARIACEAE | Species *Cortinarius torvus* | Season Autumn–late autumn |

SHEATHED WEB-CAP

Comparatively pale colouring, along with a "stocking" on the stem and a fleshy cap with widely spaced gills, helps to identify this web-cap. The cap is bun-shaped and greyish brown, with white veil remnants (violet when young) at the margin, and radiating fibres on the surface. The buff-brown flesh may be tinged violet in the upper stem.
• OCCURRENCE Mycorrhizal, mainly with beech trees, in woodland on a variety of soil types. Widespread in Europe and eastern North America.
• SIMILAR SPECIES *Cortinarius subtorvus* is darker and grows with willow and the woody perennial Mountain Avens (*Dryas octopetala*) in mountain areas. There are several other similar species that mostly differ in colouring or in habitat preference.

bun-shaped, greyish brown cap

thick, firm, sinuate, notched gills

"stocking" rim on stem

widely spaced, violet gills age to rusty brown

club-shaped stem base

SECTION

FRUITING Singly or a few together among leaf litter.

| Dimensions CAP ⊕ 4–8cm | STEM ↕ 4–9cm ↔ 0.5–1.5cm | Spores Rusty brown | Edibility |

| Family CORTINARIACEAE | Species *Cortinarius anserinus* | Season Autumn |

PLUM-SCENTED WEB-CAP

This is a fleshy species with a convex, yellow-brown cap and a sturdy stem with a bulbous base. As its common name suggests, it smells of plums. It is inedible; the lilac to off-white flesh is mild tasting but the cap skin is bitter.
• OCCURRENCE Mycorrhizal with beech on alkaline soil. Widespread and locally common in Europe. World distribution not clear.
• SIMILAR SPECIES A host of other related species, such as *Cortinarius calochrous* (below), occur in similar habitats.

thick, firm flesh is off-white in cap

adnexed gills

grey-blue or lilac gills age rusty grey-brown

lilac flesh in stem

SECTION

remains of veil visible at cap margin

△ CORTINARIUS CALOCHROUS
This species has a dark-centred, yellow or green-yellow cap, lilac gills, and a stem bulb. Its cap skin and flesh taste mild.

top of stem whiter than base

veil remnants colour stem bulb ochre

FRUITING Appears singly or in small groups.

| Dimensions CAP ⊕ 6–12cm | STEM ↕ 6–12cm ↔ 1–2.5cm | Spores Rusty brown | Edibility |

Family CORTINARIACEAE	Species *Cortinarius triumphans*	Season Summer–autumn

YELLOW-GIRDLED WEB-CAP

This impressive species has a greasy, convex, orange-yellow cap, often with veil remnants at the margin, and prominent yellow veil girdles on the sturdy stem. The thick, yellow-cream flesh tastes bitter and has a faint, pleasant smell.
• **OCCURRENCE** Mycorrhizal with birch, in woods and on damp lawns in gardens and parks. Widespread but local in Europe and parts of Asia; reported in northeastern North America.
• **SIMILAR SPECIES** *Cortinarius cliduchus* has a darker cap and grows on alkaline soil among hardwood trees. *C. olidus* has a darker cap and a brown-olive veil. It smells strongly earthy and is not found with birch. *C. saginus* has a redder cap and is found growing among pines.

greasy, convex cap is orange-yellow

notched, grey to blue-white gills

veil girdles are yellow, stained brown by falling spores

sturdy, pale yellow stem, pointed at base

FRUITING In troops in grass under birch trees.

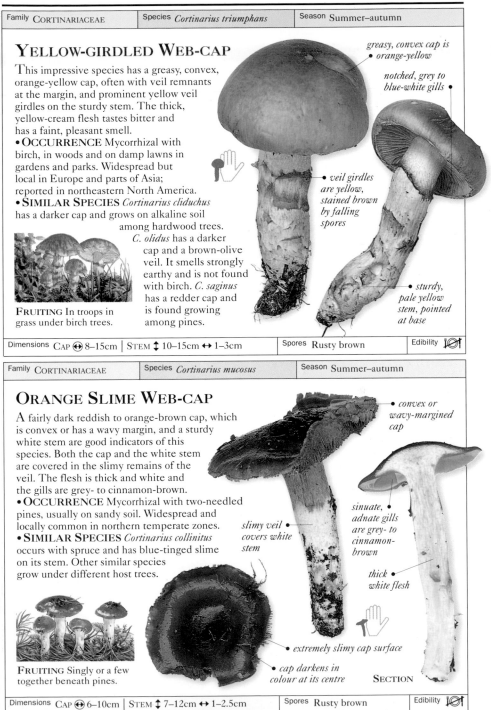

Dimensions CAP ⊕ 8–15cm | STEM ↕ 10–15cm ↔ 1–3cm	Spores Rusty brown	Edibility

Family CORTINARIACEAE	Species *Cortinarius mucosus*	Season Summer–autumn

ORANGE SLIME WEB-CAP

A fairly dark reddish to orange-brown cap, which is convex or has a wavy margin, and a sturdy white stem are good indicators of this species. Both the cap and the white stem are covered in the slimy remains of the veil. The flesh is thick and white and the gills are grey- to cinnamon-brown.
• **OCCURRENCE** Mycorrhizal with two-needled pines, usually on sandy soil. Widespread and locally common in northern temperate zones.
• **SIMILAR SPECIES** *Cortinarius collinitus* occurs with spruce and has blue-tinged slime on its stem. Other similar species grow under different host trees.

convex or wavy-margined cap

sinuate, adnate gills are grey- to cinnamon-brown

slimy veil covers white stem

thick white flesh

extremely slimy cap surface

cap darkens in colour at its centre

SECTION

FRUITING Singly or a few together beneath pines.

Dimensions CAP ⊕ 6–10cm | STEM ↕ 7–12cm ↔ 1–2.5cm	Spores Rusty brown	Edibility

| Family CORTINARIACEAE | Species *Cortinarius sodagnitus* | Season Autumn |

BITTER LILAC WEB-CAP

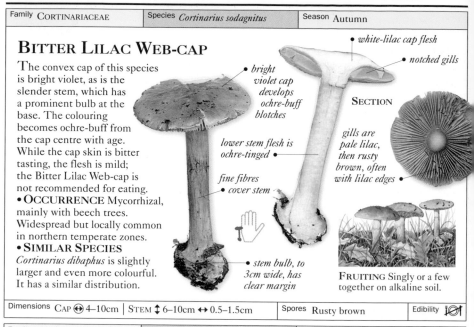

The convex cap of this species
is bright violet, as is the
slender stem, which has
a prominent bulb at the
base. The colouring
becomes ochre-buff from
the cap centre with age.
While the cap skin is bitter
tasting, the flesh is mild;
the Bitter Lilac Web-cap is
not recommended for eating.
• **OCCURRENCE** Mycorrhizal,
mainly with beech trees.
Widespread but locally common
in northern temperate zones.
• **SIMILAR SPECIES**
Cortinarius dibaphus is slightly
larger and even more colourful.
It has a similar distribution.

• *white-lilac cap flesh*

• *notched gills*

bright violet cap develops ochre-buff blotches

SECTION

lower stem flesh is ochre-tinged •

gills are pale lilac, then rusty brown, often with lilac edges •

fine fibres cover stem •

• *stem bulb, to 3cm wide, has clear margin*

FRUITING Singly or a few together on alkaline soil.

| Dimensions CAP ⊕ 4–10cm | STEM ↕ 6–10cm ↔ 0.5–1.5cm | Spores Rusty brown | Edibility |

| Family CORTINARIACEAE | Species *Cortinarius rufoolivaceus* | Season Autumn |

RED AND OLIVE WEB-CAP

This large species, belonging to the subgenus *Phlegmacium*,
is identified by a unique colour combination: its convex to
umbonate cap is rich copper with rhubarb-pink or olive-green
at the margin. The typically long, slender, but bulbous stem
is many coloured; the gills can be tinged olive-green or lilac.
The white flesh is purple-tinged in the cap and upper stem.
• **OCCURRENCE** Mycorrhizal, especially with beech and
oak trees. Widespread but local in Europe;
world distribution unknown.
• **SIMILAR SPECIES** Several
other subgenus *Phlegmacium*
species have olive colouring,
including *Cortinarius
atrovirens*, which has a fleshy,
dark olive cap, a sulphur-
yellow stem, and olive to
rusty brown gills.

△ *CORTINARIUS CAERULESCENS*
This fleshy species has a grey-
blue cap and stem with white
veil patches and purple gills.
It ages to yellow-ochre.

SECTION

FRUITING In small groups
in leaf litter on alkaline soil.

smooth, greasy cap

stem bulb to 3cm wide •

adnexed, sinuate gills •

veil remains stained rust-brown •

flesh at stem base is rusty brown •

| Dimensions CAP ⊕ 6–10cm | STEM ↕ 7–12cm ↔ 1.5–2cm | Spores Rusty brown | Edibility |

| Family CORTINARIACEAE | Species *Cortinarius splendens* | Season Autumn |

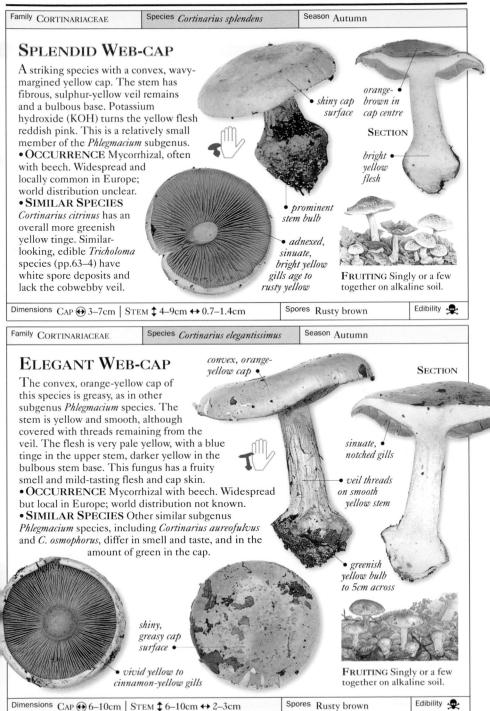

SPLENDID WEB-CAP

A striking species with a convex, wavy-
margined yellow cap. The stem has
fibrous, sulphur-yellow veil remains
and a bulbous base. Potassium
hydroxide (KOH) turns the yellow flesh
reddish pink. This is a relatively small
member of the *Phlegmacium* subgenus.
• **OCCURRENCE** Mycorrhizal, often
with beech. Widespread and
locally common in Europe;
world distribution unclear.
• **SIMILAR SPECIES**
Cortinarius citrinus has an
overall more greenish
yellow tinge. Similar-
looking, edible *Tricholoma*
species (pp.63–4) have
white spore deposits and
lack the cobwebby veil.

shiny cap surface •

orange-brown in cap centre •

SECTION

bright yellow flesh •

• *prominent stem bulb*

• *adnexed, sinuate, bright yellow gills age to rusty yellow*

FRUITING Singly or a few
together on alkaline soil.

| Dimensions CAP ⊕ 3–7cm | STEM ↕ 4–9cm ↔ 0.7–1.4cm | Spores Rusty brown | Edibility ☠ |

| Family CORTINARIACEAE | Species *Cortinarius elegantissimus* | Season Autumn |

ELEGANT WEB-CAP

The convex, orange-yellow cap of
this species is greasy, as in other
subgenus *Phlegmacium* species. The
stem is yellow and smooth, although
covered with threads remaining from the
veil. The flesh is very pale yellow, with a blue
tinge in the upper stem, darker yellow in the
bulbous stem base. This fungus has a fruity
smell and mild-tasting flesh and cap skin.
• **OCCURRENCE** Mycorrhizal with beech. Widespread
but local in Europe; world distribution not known.
• **SIMILAR SPECIES** Other similar subgenus
Phlegmacium species, including *Cortinarius aureofulvus*
and *C. osmophorus*, differ in smell and taste, and in the
amount of green in the cap.

convex, orange-yellow cap •

SECTION

sinuate, notched gills

• *veil threads on smooth yellow stem*

• *greenish yellow bulb to 5cm across*

shiny, greasy cap surface •

• *vivid yellow to cinnamon-yellow gills*

FRUITING Singly or a few
together on alkaline soil.

| Dimensions CAP ⊕ 6–10cm | STEM ↕ 6–10cm ↔ 2–3cm | Spores Rusty brown | Edibility ☠ |

WITH STEM RING OR RING ZONE

T HE FUNGI in this subsection have a veil that protects the young gills. As the cap expands to its mature size, the veil, or part of it, remains attached to the stem, either as a distinct ring around the stem or as a fibrillose zone. (See also pp.69–77 for species that have cobweb-like veil remains.) Both the rings and the zones are often stained by falling spores so that the true veil colour can be difficult to see on mature specimens. Agarics from the mainly white-spored Tricholomataceae, and families with coloured spores, including Strophariaceae, Cortinariaceae, and Coprinaceae, are featured here.

Family STROPHARIACEAE	Species *Pholiota aurivellus*	Season Autumn, rarely spring

GOLDEN SCALE-HEAD

The convex to broadly umbonate, slimy, bright yellow cap of this species has a striking pattern of dark rust-brown veil scales, and its inrolled margin also bears veil remnants. The stem is also slimy and scaly. The inedible but pleasant-smelling flesh is very pale in the cap, darker in the stem.
• OCCURRENCE Typically found growing high in living but damaged hardwood trees, for example where branches have been broken. It has a preference for beech trees, although it is also found on lime and willow. Widespread in northern temperate zones.
• SIMILAR SPECIES *Pholiota jahnii* has more up-turned, black-tipped cap scales, and smaller spores (5.5 x 3.5µm compared to 9 x 5.5µm for *L. aurivellus*). *P. limonella* also has smaller spores (7 x 4.5µm).

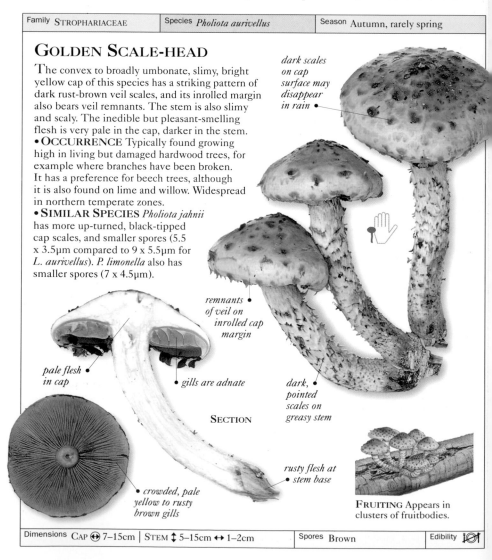

dark scales on cap surface may disappear in rain •

remnants • of veil on inrolled cap margin

pale flesh • in cap

• gills are adnate

dark, • pointed scales on greasy stem

SECTION

• crowded, pale yellow to rusty brown gills

rusty flesh at • stem base

FRUITING Appears in clusters of fruitbodies.

Dimensions CAP ⊕ 7–15cm	STEM ↕ 5–15cm ↔ 1–2cm	Spores Brown	Edibility

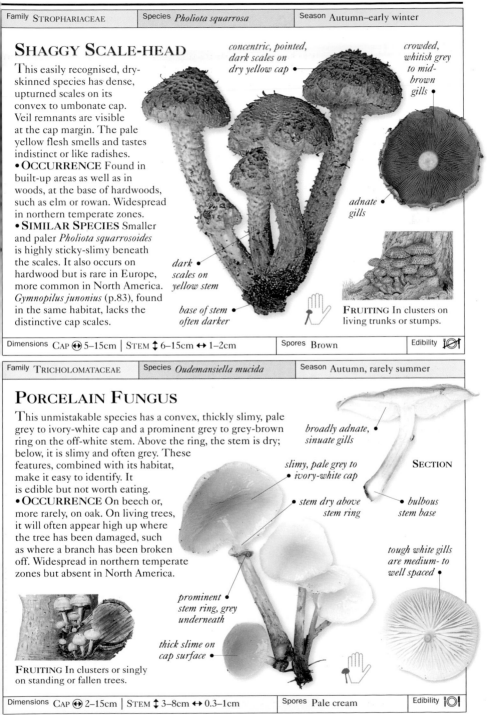

| Family STROPHARIACEAE | Species *Pholiota squarrosa* | Season Autumn–early winter |

SHAGGY SCALE-HEAD

concentric, pointed, dark scales on dry yellow cap •

crowded, whitish grey to mid-brown gills •

This easily recognised, dry-skinned species has dense, upturned scales on its convex to umbonate cap. Veil remnants are visible at the cap margin. The pale yellow flesh smells and tastes indistinct or like radishes.
• **OCCURRENCE** Found in built-up areas as well as in woods, at the base of hardwoods, such as elm or rowan. Widespread in northern temperate zones.
• **SIMILAR SPECIES** Smaller and paler *Pholiota squarrosoides* is highly sticky-slimy beneath the scales. It also occurs on hardwood but is rare in Europe, more common in North America. *Gymnopilus junonius* (p.83), found in the same habitat, lacks the distinctive cap scales.

adnate • gills

dark • scales on yellow stem

base of stem • often darker

FRUITING In clusters on living trunks or stumps.

| Dimensions CAP ⊕ 5–15cm | STEM ↕ 6–15cm ↔ 1–2cm | Spores Brown | Edibility |

| Family TRICHOLOMATACEAE | Species *Oudemansiella mucida* | Season Autumn, rarely summer |

PORCELAIN FUNGUS

This unmistakable species has a convex, thickly slimy, pale grey to ivory-white cap and a prominent grey to grey-brown ring on the off-white stem. Above the ring, the stem is dry; below, it is slimy and often grey. These features, combined with its habitat, make it easy to identify. It is edible but not worth eating.
• **OCCURRENCE** On beech or, more rarely, on oak. On living trees, it will often appear high up where the tree has been damaged, such as where a branch has been broken off. Widespread in northern temperate zones but absent in North America.

broadly adnate, • sinuate gills

slimy, pale grey to • ivory-white cap

SECTION

stem dry above stem ring

• bulbous stem base

tough white gills are medium- to well spaced •

prominent • stem ring, grey underneath

thick slime on • cap surface

FRUITING In clusters or singly on standing or fallen trees.

| Dimensions CAP ⊕ 2–15cm | STEM ↕ 3–8cm ↔ 0.3–1cm | Spores Pale cream | Edibility |

| Family TRICHOLOMATACEAE | Species *Armillaria mellea* | Season Autumn |

HONEY FUNGUS

This large agaric has a convex, flattened, or wavy, olive-tinged, pale yellow-brown cap with a darker centre and sparse pale scales. The pale ochre-yellow stem is slender, long, and pointed, with a yellow-margined white ring; groups of stems are firmly united at their bases. The well-spaced, adnate gills begin white and become pink-brown, often with some dark spotting, with age. Although *Armillaria mellea* once included a range of species with similar features, these have now been reclassified separately (see *A. cepistipes*, below). It is edible, with thick white flesh, but can cause stomach upsets.
• **OCCURRENCE** Found in woodland areas, mainly with beech, often on fallen stumps. Widespread but local in northern temperate zones.

slender, pale ochre-yellow stem is long and tapers to point

centre of cap is darker brown than edge

pale yellow-brown cap with ochre tinges

stems joined in groups at their bases

white ring has yellow margin

cap is convex, flattened, or wavy

FRUITING Almost always found growing in dense tufts with stems joined at the base.

| Dimensions CAP ⊕ 3–10cm | STEM ↕ 8–10cm ↔ 1–2cm | Spores White | Edibility |

| Family TRICHOLOMATACEAE | Species *Armillaria cepistipes* | Season Autumn |

FINE-SCALY HONEY FUNGUS

SECTION

This species has a sturdy, fibrous stem, with a pendent, thin, white to pale grey ring, and a convex to umbonate, tawny to ochre cap with sparse, fibrous scales. The adnate gills are pale yellow to pale tan and well spaced. A range of similar species, now classified separately, were once grouped with this under *Armillaria mellea* (above). It is edible, but may cause stomach upsets.
• **OCCURRENCE** Mostly with dead or dying hardwoods, but also on softwoods, in woods, parks, and gardens. Widespread; common in northern temperate zones.
• **SIMILAR SPECIES** The young cap of *A. gallica* has a pale centre, and the stem ring is white to yellow. *A. ostoyae* has a thicker stem, turning brown from the base, a big, brown-edged ring, and coarser cap scales.

fine, pointed, dark scales on tawny-ochre cap

thin white to pale grey stem ring is pendent and short-lived

thick white flesh

swollen stem base

FRUITING Clustered, or scattered, on and by hardwood.

| Dimensions CAP ⊕ 3–12cm | STEM ↕ 4–12cm ↔ 1–3cm | Spores White | Edibility |

Family TRICHOLOMATACEAE	Species *Tricholoma caligatum*	Season Late summer–autumn

BROWN MATSUTAKE

The convex to flat cap of this species has a brown-scaled, dry surface. The slender stem is white above the flaring ring and has brown veil zones and patches below. The flesh is white. The name actually encompasses a widespread complex of very similar mushrooms, which range from spicy-fragrant, choice edibles with a nutty flavour, to forms that smell bad and are unpalatable.
• OCCURRENCE The true species is found under Atlas Cedar (*Cedrus atlantica*) in southern Europe and North Africa. Other forms occur under softwoods in northern Europe. In eastern North America, they are found under hardwoods, in the Pacific northwest with softwoods. Widespread in northern North America.

cap surface is pale cream under the brown scales •

convex to flat cap with a dry surface •

crowded gills are sinuate, notched, each with a tooth

stem is white above ring •

stem sheathed by flaring white ring •

brown zones and patches below ring

FRUITING Singly or a few fruitbodies together under hard- and softwood trees.

Dimensions CAP ⊕ 5–12.5cm | STEM ↕ 5–10cm ↔ 2–3cm	Spores White	Edibility ¡○¡

Family TRICHOLOMATACEAE	Species *Tricholoma magnivelare*	Season Late summer–autumn

WHITE MATSUTAKE

This choice edible, with firm white flesh, has a distinctive smell of cinnamon and pine. Its convex white cap has an inrolled margin and is tacky when moist. It becomes flat with age and develops yellow to rusty brown scales and spots. A flaring ring sheaths the stem, which is white above the ring, ageing light brown below it.
• OCCURRENCE Under softwoods. Widespread and common across northern North America and in the south in the Rocky Mountains; most common on the Pacific northwest coast.
• SIMILAR SPECIES *Amanita* species such as *A. smithiana* (p.148) lack the spicy smell and have free gills. They also have loose veil patches on their caps.

cottony, thread-like veil remains at cap margin •

ring on stem is prominent and flaring •

white gills stain pinkish brown with age •

crowded, notched gills •

cap is white with light brown scales •

FRUITING Appear singly or in groups of a few fruit-bodies together under softwood trees.

Dimensions CAP ⊕ 5–20cm | STEM ↕ 5–15cm ↔ 2–4cm	Spores White	Edibility ¡○¡

| Family CORTINARIACEAE | Species *Hebeloma radicosum* | Season Autumn |

ROOTING FAIRY CAKE

The convex, cream to pale yellow-brown cap of this large *Hebeloma* species is covered with distinct brown scales that lie flat against its surface (adpressed). The similarly scaly stem has a "root" that goes deep underground. The prominent stem ring is unusual in this genus. The flesh, which is white and firm, has a very strong smell of marzipan or bitter almonds and a bitter taste, both of which also help in the identification of the species.

• OCCURRENCE Mycorrhizal with trees, but also associated with underground voles' nests and latrines, in well-drained soil in hardwood woodland. Widespread in northern temperate zones but not common anywhere.

• SIMILAR SPECIES Some smaller, non-scaly *Hebeloma* species, including *H. pallidoluctuosum*, have sweet smells. *Pholiota* species (pp.78–9, 91–2) are similar in appearance, but none smell of marzipan and all are associated with dead wood.

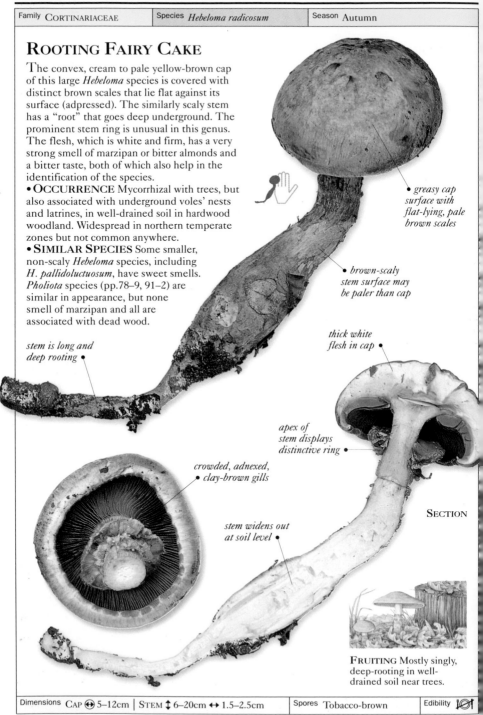

greasy cap surface with flat-lying, pale brown scales

brown-scaly stem surface may be paler than cap

stem is long and deep rooting

thick white flesh in cap

apex of stem displays distinctive ring

crowded, adnexed, clay-brown gills

stem widens out at soil level

SECTION

FRUITING Mostly singly, deep-rooting in well-drained soil near trees.

| Dimensions CAP ⊕ 5–12cm | STEM ↕ 6–20cm ↔ 1.5–2.5cm | Spores Tobacco-brown | Edibility |

| Family TRICHOLOMATACEAE | Species *Phaeolepiota aurea* | Season Summer–autumn |

GOLDEN CAP

This large, golden yellow agaric, which smells of bitter almonds, has a convex cap with a fringed margin and granular surface, and a flaring stem ring beneath which the stem is very wrinkled. The adnexed gills are crowded and off-white, becoming russet-brown. It is sometimes classified within the Cortinariaceae family due to its ochre-brown spore deposit. It is reported as edible, but may cause stomach upsets.

• **OCCURRENCE** In woodland areas along rides or in other disturbed sites, often with nettles; it prefers rich soil. Widespread and locally common in northern temperate zones.

• **SIMILAR SPECIES** *Gymnopilus junonius* (below) occurs on rotting wood and has a streaked cap and stem.

golden yellow cap surface is granular •

cap margin • is fringed with veil remains

large, flaring • stem ring is stained ochre-brown by falling spores

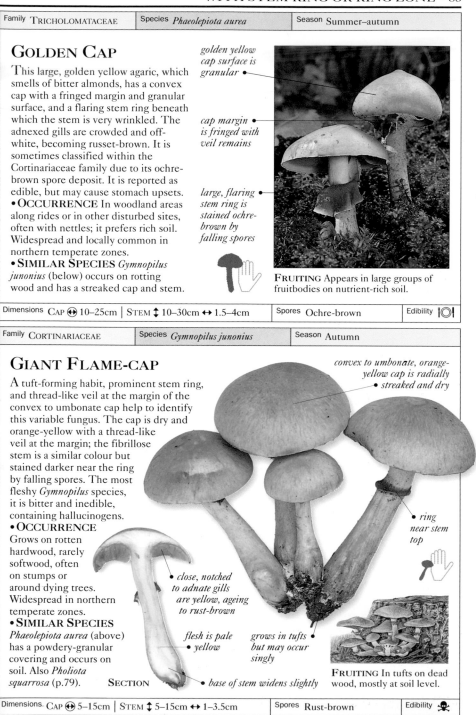

FRUITING Appears in large groups of fruitbodies on nutrient-rich soil.

| Dimensions CAP ⊕ 10–25cm | STEM ↕ 10–30cm ↔ 1.5–4cm | Spores Ochre-brown | Edibility ¡◎¡ |

| Family CORTINARIACEAE | Species *Gymnopilus junonius* | Season Autumn |

GIANT FLAME-CAP

A tuft-forming habit, prominent stem ring, and thread-like veil at the margin of the convex to umbonate cap help to identify this variable fungus. The cap is dry and orange-yellow with a thread-like veil at the margin; the fibrillose stem is a similar colour but stained darker near the ring by falling spores. The most fleshy *Gymnopilus* species, it is bitter and inedible, containing hallucinogens.

• **OCCURRENCE** Grows on rotten hardwood, rarely softwood, often on stumps or around dying trees. Widespread in northern temperate zones.

• **SIMILAR SPECIES** *Phaeolepiota aurea* (above) has a powdery-granular covering and occurs on soil. Also *Pholiota squarrosa* (p.79). **SECTION**

convex to umbonate, orange-yellow cap is radially • streaked and dry

• ring near stem top

close, notched to adnate gills are yellow, ageing to rust-brown

flesh is pale • yellow

grows in tufts • but may occur singly

• base of stem widens slightly

FRUITING In tufts on dead wood, mostly at soil level.

| Dimensions CAP ⊕ 5–15cm | STEM ↕ 5–15cm ↔ 1–3.5cm | Spores Rust-brown | Edibility ☠ |

Family STROPHARIACEAE	Species *Psilocybe cubensis*	Season All year

SAN ISIDRO LIBERTY-CAP

This large *Psilocybe* species has a bell-shaped to umbonate, sticky, yellow-brown cap, the surface of which may be covered with small white scales – the remains of the veil. The stem is off-white with a pendent ring that soon becomes black from falling spores. The white to cream flesh bruises blue. The fairly crowded, adnate gills are purple-brown with white edges when mature. It is a dangerous hallucinogen.
• **OCCURRENCE** In subtropical to tropical grassland, where animals graze. Widespread and common in Caribbean and Gulf coastal areas of North America and elsewhere in the tropics. It has been introduced into Europe, where it can be cultivated.
• **SIMILAR SPECIES** *Panaeolus semiovatus* (p.95) does not stain blue.

dark purple-brown gills with white edge

bell-shaped to umbonate cap

white veil scales on surface

off-white stem with pendent ring

FRUITING Appears singly or in small groups on cow and horse dung in grassland.

Dimensions CAP ⊕ 2–12cm	STEM ↕ 5–15cm ↔ 0.5–1.2cm	Spores Dark purple-brown	Edibility ☠

Family STROPHARIACEAE	Species *Psilocybe squamosa*	Season Autumn–late autumn

SCALY-STALKED PSILOCYBE

Short-lived, concentric cap scales and a distinctive stem ring characterize this comparatively large *Psilocybe* species. The bell-shaped to umbonate cap is yellowish white with white-edged, grey or purple-brown to almost black gills; the stem is scaly and off-white, turning yellow-brown with age. It is not edible; the pale brown flesh has a slight aroma and a mild to slightly bitter taste.
• **OCCURRENCE** In woodland, emerging from buried or half-buried hardwood debris, woodchippings, or sawdust. Widespread and fairly common in northern temperate zones.
• **SIMILAR SPECIES** *Stropharia* species (pp.88–90) differ in microscopic features.

bell-shaped to umbonate cap

white-edged, grey or purple-brown to almost black gills

pendent, furrowed stem ring, stained by spores

broad, adnate to slightly decurrent gills

long, slender stem is quite sturdy

scaly, off-white stem ages to brown towards base

SECTION

pale brown flesh, darker towards base

FRUITING Appears singly or in small groups.

Dimensions CAP ⊕ 2–5cm	STEM ↕ 10–15cm ↔ 3–5mm	Spores Purple-brown	Edibility 🍴

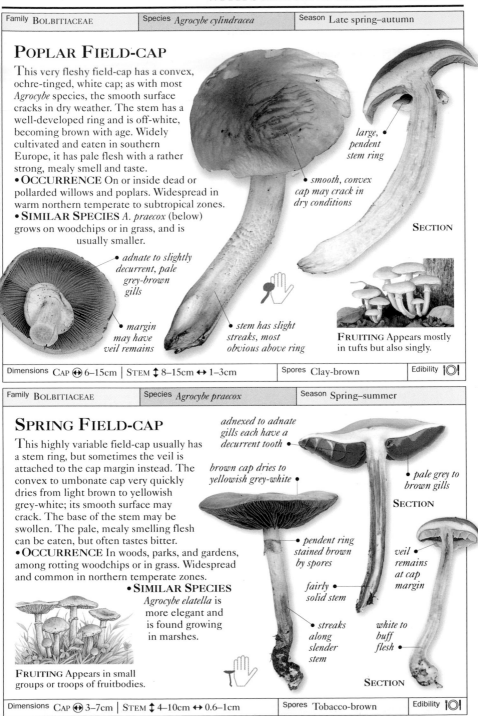

| Family BOLBITIACEAE | Species *Agrocybe cylindracea* | Season Late spring–autumn |

POPLAR FIELD-CAP

This very fleshy field-cap has a convex, ochre-tinged, white cap; as with most *Agrocybe* species, the smooth surface cracks in dry weather. The stem has a well-developed ring and is off-white, becoming brown with age. Widely cultivated and eaten in southern Europe, it has pale flesh with a rather strong, mealy smell and taste.
• **OCCURRENCE** On or inside dead or pollarded willows and poplars. Widespread in warm northern temperate to subtropical zones.
• **SIMILAR SPECIES** *A. praecox* (below) grows on woodchips or in grass, and is usually smaller.

large, pendent stem ring

smooth, convex cap may crack in dry conditions

SECTION

adnate to slightly decurrent, pale grey-brown gills

margin may have veil remains

stem has slight streaks, most obvious above ring

FRUITING Appears mostly in tufts but also singly.

| Dimensions CAP ⊕ 6–15cm | STEM ↕ 8–15cm ↔ 1–3cm | Spores Clay-brown | Edibility |

| Family BOLBITIACEAE | Species *Agrocybe praecox* | Season Spring–summer |

SPRING FIELD-CAP

This highly variable field-cap usually has a stem ring, but sometimes the veil is attached to the cap margin instead. The convex to umbonate cap very quickly dries from light brown to yellowish grey-white; its smooth surface may crack. The base of the stem may be swollen. The pale, mealy smelling flesh can be eaten, but often tastes bitter.
• **OCCURRENCE** In woods, parks, and gardens, among rotting woodchips or in grass. Widespread and common in northern temperate zones.
• **SIMILAR SPECIES** *Agrocybe elatella* is more elegant and is found growing in marshes.

adnexed to adnate gills each have a decurrent tooth

brown cap dries to yellowish grey-white

pale grey to brown gills

SECTION

pendent ring stained brown by spores

veil remains at cap margin

fairly solid stem

streaks along slender stem

white to buff flesh

SECTION

FRUITING Appears in small groups or troops of fruitbodies.

| Dimensions CAP ⊕ 3–7cm | STEM ↕ 4–10cm ↔ 0.6–1cm | Spores Tobacco-brown | Edibility |

Family STROPHARIACEAE	Species *Hypholoma capnoides*	Season All year

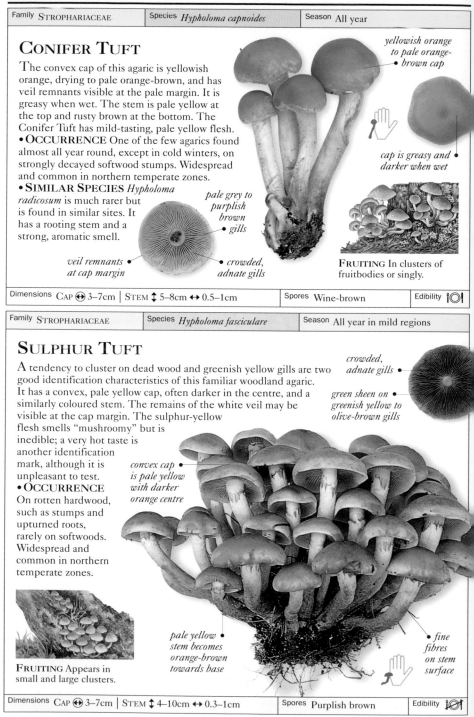

CONIFER TUFT

The convex cap of this agaric is yellowish orange, drying to pale orange-brown, and has veil remnants visible at the pale margin. It is greasy when wet. The stem is pale yellow at the top and rusty brown at the bottom. The Conifer Tuft has mild-tasting, pale yellow flesh.
• OCCURRENCE One of the few agarics found almost all year round, except in cold winters, on strongly decayed softwood stumps. Widespread and common in northern temperate zones.
• SIMILAR SPECIES *Hypholoma radicosum* is much rarer but is found in similar sites. It has a rooting stem and a strong, aromatic smell.

yellowish orange to pale orange-brown cap

cap is greasy and darker when wet

pale grey to purplish brown gills

veil remnants at cap margin

crowded, adnate gills

FRUITING In clusters of fruitbodies or singly.

Dimensions CAP ⊕ 3–7cm | STEM ↕ 5–8cm ↔ 0.5–1cm	Spores Wine-brown	Edibility

Family STROPHARIACEAE	Species *Hypholoma fasciculare*	Season All year in mild regions

SULPHUR TUFT

A tendency to cluster on dead wood and greenish yellow gills are two good identification characteristics of this familiar woodland agaric. It has a convex, pale yellow cap, often darker in the centre, and a similarly coloured stem. The remains of the white veil may be visible at the cap margin. The sulphur-yellow flesh smells "mushroomy" but is inedible; a very hot taste is another identification mark, although it is unpleasant to test.
• OCCURRENCE On rotten hardwood, such as stumps and upturned roots, rarely on softwoods. Widespread and common in northern temperate zones.

crowded, adnate gills

green sheen on greenish yellow to olive-brown gills

convex cap is pale yellow with darker orange centre

pale yellow stem becomes orange-brown towards base

fine fibres on stem surface

FRUITING Appears in small and large clusters.

Dimensions CAP ⊕ 3–7cm | STEM ↕ 4–10cm ↔ 0.3–1cm	Spores Purplish brown	Edibility

| Family STROPHARIACEAE | Species *Hypholoma sublateritium* | Season Autumn–late autumn |

BRICK TUFT

This large species is best identified by its size, the lack of green in the gills, and the distinct brick-red cap colour. The cap is convex and the stem fibrous and pale yellow at the top, reddish brown at the base. The yellow to reddish brown flesh has a pleasant odour but it tastes unpleasantly bitter.

• **OCCURRENCE** On hardwood stumps or roots, in woodland or parks. Widespread in northern temperate zones.

• **SIMILAR SPECIES** A range of much smaller, more elegant species such as *Hypholoma udum* and *H. elongatum* occur in boggy places, sometimes in sphagnum moss. *H. marginata* occurs in large troops on needle beds or on softwood remains.

smooth, brick-red cap

fairly crowded, adnate gills are white-grey to olive-brown

fibrous surface of sturdy stem

SECTION

young cap margin with white veil, stained black by spores

stem base is reddish brown

FRUITING Appears in clusters of fruitbodies.

| Dimensions CAP ⊕ 5–10cm \| STEM ↕ 5–10cm ↔ 0.5–1.5cm | Spores Purplish brown | Edibility |

| Family CORTINARIACEAE | Species *Rozites caperatus* | Season Summer–autumn |

GYPSY

Egg-shaped on emerging, the cap of this species becomes convex to umbonate with age. It is yellow-brown with a furrowed or wrinkled surface, and with remnants of the white to pale violet veil in the centre. The smooth stem is prominently marked by a narrow, sheathing ring.

• **OCCURRENCE** Mycorrhizal and most commonly found with softwood trees, but also occurs with hardwoods, often beech. Widespread in some areas of northern temperate zones but absent in others.

• **SIMILAR SPECIES** *Cortinarius* species (pp.69–77) are related, but have no true stem rings and have rust-brown spores.

umbonate to convex cap is yellow-brown

edges of gills are toothed

ring on stem is narrow and sheathing

solid, fibrous stem flesh

SECTION

centre of cap bears pale veil remnants

FRUITING Appears in troops or small groups on acid soil.

surface of cap has furrows or wrinkles

gills are medium spaced and adnexed

| Dimensions CAP ⊕ 5–12cm \| STEM ↕ 5–15cm ↔ 1–2cm | Spores Pale brown | Edibility |

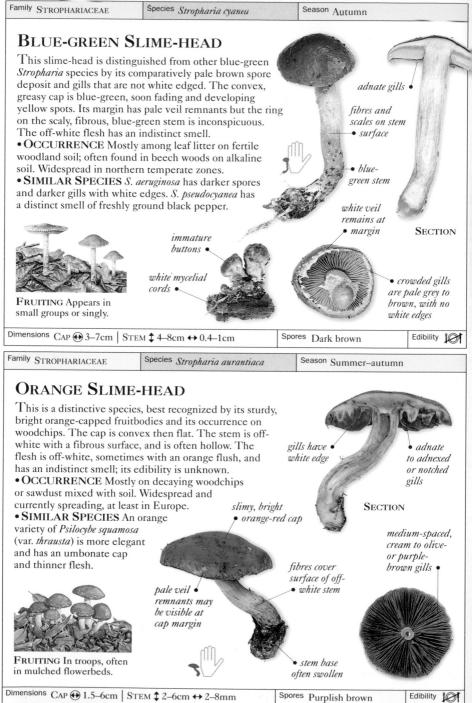

| Family STROPHARIACEAE | Species *Stropharia cyanea* | Season Autumn |

BLUE-GREEN SLIME-HEAD

This slime-head is distinguished from other blue-green *Stropharia* species by its comparatively pale spore deposit and gills that are not white edged. The convex, greasy cap is blue-green, soon fading and developing yellow spots. Its margin has pale veil remnants but the ring on the scaly, fibrous, blue-green stem is inconspicuous. The off-white flesh has an indistinct smell.
• **OCCURRENCE** Mostly among leaf litter on fertile woodland soil; often found in beech woods on alkaline soil. Widespread in northern temperate zones.
• **SIMILAR SPECIES** *S. aeruginosa* has darker spores and darker gills with white edges. *S. pseudocyanea* has a distinct smell of freshly ground black pepper.

adnate gills

fibres and scales on stem surface

blue-green stem

white veil remains at margin

SECTION

immature buttons

white mycelial cords

crowded gills are pale grey to brown, with no white edges

FRUITING Appears in small groups or singly.

| Dimensions CAP ⊕ 3–7cm | STEM ↕ 4–8cm ↔ 0.4–1cm | Spores Dark brown | Edibility |

| Family STROPHARIACEAE | Species *Stropharia aurantiaca* | Season Summer–autumn |

ORANGE SLIME-HEAD

This is a distinctive species, best recognized by its sturdy, bright orange-capped fruitbodies and its occurrence on woodchips. The cap is convex then flat. The stem is off-white with a fibrous surface, and is often hollow. The flesh is off-white, sometimes with an orange flush, and has an indistinct smell; its edibility is unknown.
• **OCCURRENCE** Mostly on decaying woodchips or sawdust mixed with soil. Widespread and currently spreading, at least in Europe.
• **SIMILAR SPECIES** An orange variety of *Psilocybe squamosa* (var. *thrausta*) is more elegant and has an umbonate cap and thinner flesh.

gills have white edge

adnate to adnexed or notched gills

SECTION

slimy, bright orange-red cap

medium-spaced, cream to olive- or purple-brown gills

fibres cover surface of off-white stem

pale veil remnants may be visible at cap margin

stem base often swollen

FRUITING In troops, often in mulched flowerbeds.

| Dimensions CAP ⊕ 1.5–6cm | STEM ↕ 2–6cm ↔ 2–8mm | Spores Purplish brown | Edibility |

| Family STROPHARIACEAE | Species *Stropharia rugoso-annulata* | Season Spring and autumn |

BURGUNDY SLIME-HEAD

The smooth, dry cap of this species is red to tan, depending on its exposure to light. It is bell-shaped, becoming convex to flat with age. The off-white stem has a ring with dark lines above and cog-like structures below. The stem base is widened or bulbous and has a conspicuous, cord-like white mycelium. The flesh is white and tastes good if eaten when young.
• **OCCURRENCE** In woodchip mulch. Widespread in southern Europe, rare further north; also found in North America.
• **SIMILAR SPECIES** *Stropharia aurantiaca* (p.88) is smaller and more bright orange-red. *Agaricus* species (pp.156–163) have free gills.

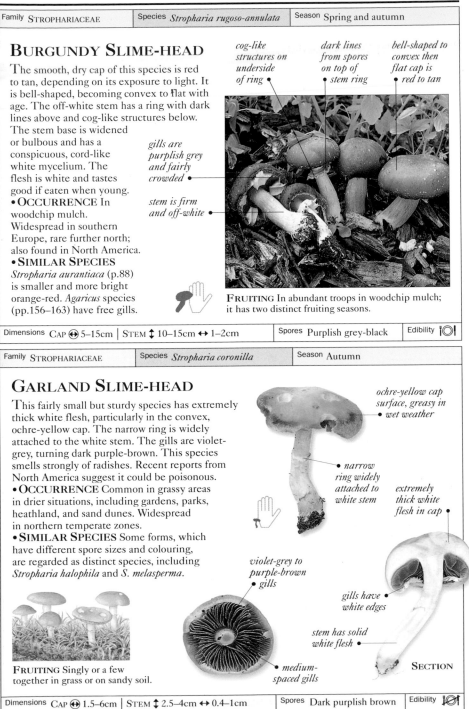

cog-like structures on underside of ring •

dark lines from spores on top of • stem ring

bell-shaped to convex then flat cap is • red to tan

gills are purplish grey and fairly crowded •

stem is firm and off-white •

FRUITING In abundant troops in woodchip mulch; it has two distinct fruiting seasons.

| Dimensions CAP ⊕ 5–15cm | STEM ↕ 10–15cm ↔ 1–2cm | Spores Purplish grey-black | Edibility |

| Family STROPHARIACEAE | Species *Stropharia coronilla* | Season Autumn |

GARLAND SLIME-HEAD

This fairly small but sturdy species has extremely thick white flesh, particularly in the convex, ochre-yellow cap. The narrow ring is widely attached to the white stem. The gills are violet-grey, turning dark purple-brown. This species smells strongly of radishes. Recent reports from North America suggest it could be poisonous.
• **OCCURRENCE** Common in grassy areas in drier situations, including gardens, parks, heathland, and sand dunes. Widespread in northern temperate zones.
• **SIMILAR SPECIES** Some forms, which have different spore sizes and colouring, are regarded as distinct species, including *Stropharia halophila* and *S. melasperma*.

ochre-yellow cap surface, greasy in • wet weather

• narrow ring widely attached to white stem

extremely thick white flesh in cap •

violet-grey to purple-brown • gills

gills have • white edges

stem has solid white flesh •

SECTION

FRUITING Singly or a few together in grass or on sandy soil.

• medium-spaced gills

| Dimensions CAP ⊕ 1.5–6cm | STEM ↕ 2.5–4cm ↔ 0.4–1cm | Spores Dark purplish brown | Edibility |

Family STROPHARIACEAE	Species *Stropharia semiglobata*	Season Late spring–autumn

DUNG SLIME-HEAD

This elegant, variably sized species has a smooth, often hemispherical, light yellow cap and a long, slender, slimy, off-white stem. In common with many of its close relatives, its cap is greasy when wet and it has a tiny, often inconspicuous stem ring, which is frequently stained black by deposited spores. The inedible, thin, pale flesh has a mealy smell.
• **OCCURRENCE** In grassland and pastures on old horse, cow, and sheep manure. A range of fungi fruit on herbivore dung at different stages of decay. Widespread in northern temperate zones and elsewhere.
• **SIMILAR SPECIES** *Stropharia umbonatescens* has a pimple or umbo at the cap centre and basidia with only 2 spores; those of *S. semiglobata* have 4.

smooth cap surface, greasy in wet weather

SECTION

convex or hemispherical cap

white edge on olive-grey gills

broad, adnate, medium-spaced gills

hollow stem

long, slender stem

stem base slightly swollen

FRUITING Appears in small groups on dung.

Dimensions CAP ⊕ 0.5–4cm	STEM ↕ 2–8cm ↔ 2–5mm	Spores Brownish black	Edibility

Family STROPHARIACEAE	Species *Kuehneromyces mutabilis*	Season Almost all year

TWO-TONED WOOD-TUFT

This species has an umbonate, honey-brown to leathery yellow cap, which dries from the centre, producing a marked two-tone effect. Paler than the cap, the stem has a distinct ring, often stained ochre-brown by falling spores; below the ring, the stem is covered with pointed scales. This is a choice edible, but see Similar Species.
• **OCCURRENCE** On rotten hardwood and, rarely, softwood, in woods and parks. Widespread and common in northern temperate zones.
• **SIMILAR SPECIES** A group of poisonous *Galerina* species are similar: *G. unicolor* (p.91) and *G. marginata* have fibres and no scales below the stem ring.

two-toned cap dries from centre

broadly adnate to decurrent gills

medium-spaced, pale to rusty brown gills

stem above ring is pale and smooth

pale brown, aromatic flesh

SECTION

stem is dark and scaly below ring

FRUITING In dense troops of individual clusters.

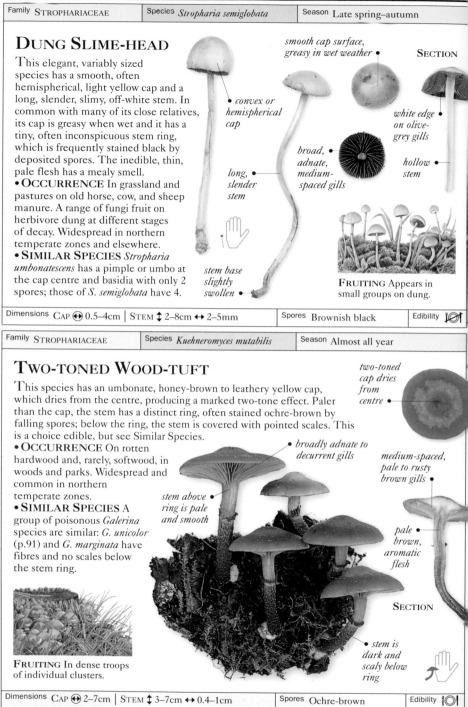

Dimensions CAP ⊕ 2–7cm	STEM ↕ 3–7cm ↔ 0.4–1cm	Spores Ochre-brown	Edibility

Family CORTINARIACEAE	Species *Galerina unicolor*	Season Summer–winter

WOOD-LOVING PIXIE-CAP

more or less wavy • cap margin

pale grey to rust-brown gills •

The convex to broadly umbonate, wavy-margined cap of this species is rich brown; it changes colour to pale yellow-brown as it dries. The off-white to basally brown stem has a ring towards the top and is fibrous below. The narrow gills are adnate to slightly decurrent and are medium spaced. *Galerina* species need careful identification; there are seven others that can cause severe poisoning.

distinct ring, • below which stem is fibrous

• **OCCURRENCE** On dead and rotten stumps and trunks, often on moss and leaf litter in damp, boggy hardwood woodland. Widespread in northern temperate zones.
• **SIMILAR SPECIES** Edible *Kuehneromyces mutabilis* (p.90) is similar, but has scales, rather than fibres below the stem ring.

• stems may be joined

FRUITING Mostly appears in dense swarms.

Dimensions CAP ⊕ 1–5cm	STEM ↕ 3–7cm ↔ 3–7mm	Spores Rust-brown	Edibility ☠

Family STROPHARIACEAE	Species *Pholiota alnicola*	Season Autumn

ALDER SCALE-HEAD

greasy cap surface, often with rusty • brown spots

adnate to slightly decurrent, straw-yellow to rust-brown gills •

A yellow cap – or yellow with some green intermixed – and a densely tufted habit are two distinguishing features of this species. A scaly cap is typical of the genus, but in this and some other members, the scales are not very conspicuous and are usually seen more clearly in young specimens as veil scales at the cap margin. The wavy stem is almost smooth, more fibrous at the base. The pale flesh has a pleasant smell and a mild taste.

SECTION

• stem yellow towards top

• medium-spaced gills

• stem dry to touch

• **OCCURRENCE** On dead or dying hardwoods, such as alder and birch, rarely on softwoods; often in damp sites. Exact distribution unknown but widespread in northern temperate zones.
• **SIMILAR SPECIES** Three forms of *Pholiota alnicola* are sometimes classified separately: *P. salicicola* grows on willow and tastes bitter; *P. flavida* and *P. pinicola* grow on softwood trees.

stem rusty brown towards base •

FRUITING Appears in clusters of fruitbodies.

Dimensions CAP ⊕ 3–7cm	STEM ↕ 8–15cm ↔ 0.6–1cm	Spores Brown	Edibility

Family STROPHARIACEAE	Species *Pholiota gummosa*	Season Autumn–late autumn

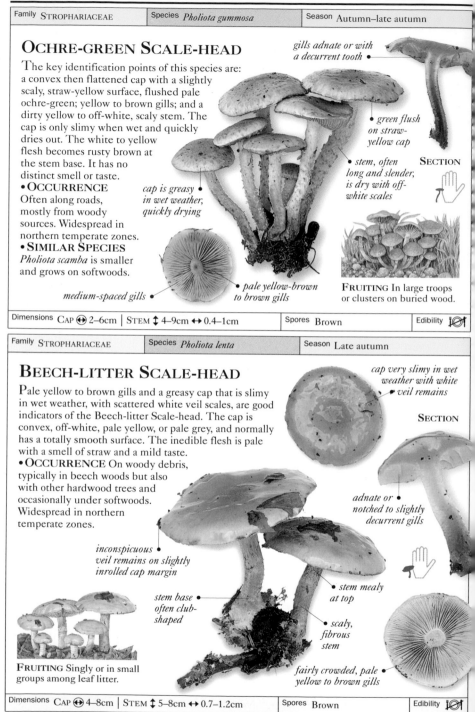

OCHRE-GREEN SCALE-HEAD

The key identification points of this species are:
a convex then flattened cap with a slightly
scaly, straw-yellow surface, flushed pale
ochre-green; yellow to brown gills; and a
dirty yellow to off-white, scaly stem. The
cap is only slimy when wet and quickly
dries out. The white to yellow
flesh becomes rusty brown at
the stem base. It has no
distinct smell or taste.
• **OCCURRENCE**
Often along roads,
mostly from woody
sources. Widespread in
northern temperate zones.
• **SIMILAR SPECIES**
Pholiota scamba is smaller
and grows on softwoods.

gills adnate or with a decurrent tooth •

• green flush on straw-yellow cap

• stem, often long and slender, is dry with off-white scales

SECTION

cap is greasy • in wet weather, quickly drying

medium-spaced gills •

• pale yellow-brown to brown gills

FRUITING In large troops
or clusters on buried wood.

| Dimensions CAP ⊕ 2–6cm | STEM ↕ 4–9cm ↔ 0.4–1cm | Spores Brown | Edibility |

Family STROPHARIACEAE	Species *Pholiota lenta*	Season Late autumn

BEECH-LITTER SCALE-HEAD

Pale yellow to brown gills and a greasy cap that is slimy
in wet weather, with scattered white veil scales, are good
indicators of the Beech-litter Scale-head. The cap is
convex, off-white, pale yellow, or pale grey, and normally
has a totally smooth surface. The inedible flesh is pale
with a smell of straw and a mild taste.
• **OCCURRENCE** On woody debris,
typically in beech woods but also
with other hardwood trees and
occasionally under softwoods.
Widespread in northern
temperate zones.

cap very slimy in wet weather with white • veil remains

SECTION

adnate or • notched to slightly decurrent gills

inconspicuous • veil remains on slightly inrolled cap margin

stem base • often club-shaped

• stem mealy at top

• scaly, fibrous stem

FRUITING Singly or in small
groups among leaf litter.

fairly crowded, pale • yellow to brown gills

| Dimensions CAP ⊕ 4–8cm | STEM ↕ 5–8cm ↔ 0.7–1.2cm | Spores Brown | Edibility |

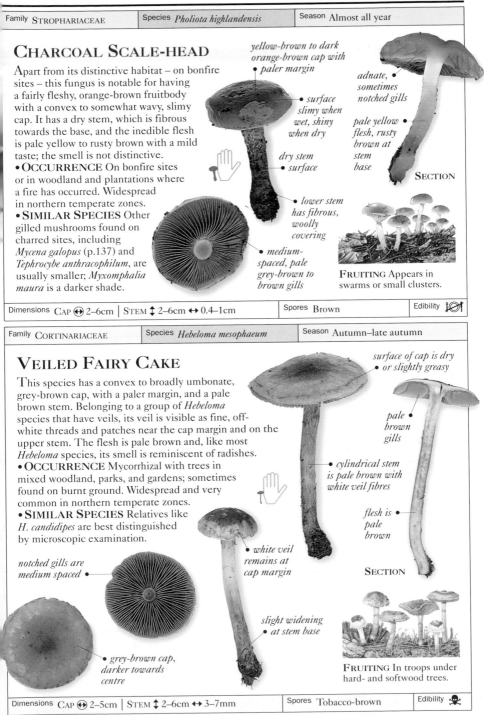

| Family STROPHARIACEAE | Species *Pholiota highlandensis* | Season Almost all year |

CHARCOAL SCALE-HEAD

Apart from its distinctive habitat – on bonfire sites – this fungus is notable for having a fairly fleshy, orange-brown fruitbody with a convex to somewhat wavy, slimy cap. It has a dry stem, which is fibrous towards the base, and the inedible flesh is pale yellow to rusty brown with a mild taste; the smell is not distinctive.
• **OCCURRENCE** On bonfire sites or in woodland and plantations where a fire has occurred. Widespread in northern temperate zones.
• **SIMILAR SPECIES** Other gilled mushrooms found on charred sites, including *Mycena galopus* (p.137) and *Tephrocybe anthracophilum*, are usually smaller; *Myxomphalia maura* is a darker shade.

yellow-brown to dark orange-brown cap with • paler margin

• surface slimy when wet, shiny when dry

dry stem • surface

adnate, • sometimes notched gills

pale yellow • flesh, rusty brown at stem base

SECTION

• lower stem has fibrous, woolly covering

medium- • spaced, pale grey-brown to brown gills

FRUITING Appears in swarms or small clusters.

| Dimensions CAP ⊕ 2–6cm | STEM ↕ 2–6cm ↔ 0.4–1cm | Spores Brown | Edibility 🚫🍴 |

| Family CORTINARIACEAE | Species *Hebeloma mesophaeum* | Season Autumn–late autumn |

VEILED FAIRY CAKE

This species has a convex to broadly umbonate, grey-brown cap, with a paler margin, and a pale brown stem. Belonging to a group of *Hebeloma* species that have veils, its veil is visible as fine, off-white threads and patches near the cap margin and on the upper stem. The flesh is pale brown and, like most *Hebeloma* species, its smell is reminiscent of radishes.
• **OCCURRENCE** Mycorrhizal with trees in mixed woodland, parks, and gardens; sometimes found on burnt ground. Widespread and very common in northern temperate zones.
• **SIMILAR SPECIES** Relatives like *H. candidipes* are best distinguished by microscopic examination.

surface of cap is dry • or slightly greasy

pale • brown gills

• cylindrical stem is pale brown with white veil fibres

flesh is • pale brown

SECTION

notched gills are medium spaced •

white veil • remains at cap margin

slight widening • at stem base

• grey-brown cap, darker towards centre

FRUITING In troops under hard- and softwood trees.

| Dimensions CAP ⊕ 2–5cm | STEM ↕ 2–6cm ↔ 3–7mm | Spores Tobacco-brown | Edibility ☠ |

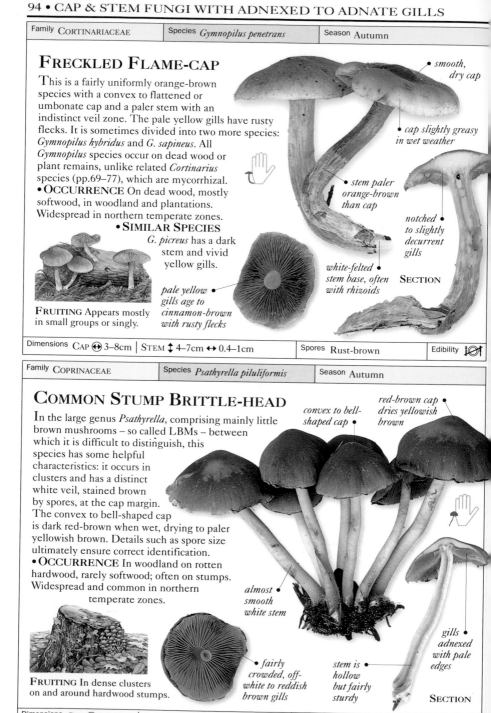

| Family CORTINARIACEAE | Species *Gymnopilus penetrans* | Season Autumn |

FRECKLED FLAME-CAP

This is a fairly uniformly orange-brown species with a convex to flattened or umbonate cap and a paler stem with an indistinct veil zone. The pale yellow gills have rusty flecks. It is sometimes divided into two more species: *Gymnopilus hybridus* and *G. sapineus*. All *Gymnopilus* species occur on dead wood or plant remains, unlike related *Cortinarius* species (pp.69–77), which are mycorrhizal.
• **OCCURRENCE** On dead wood, mostly softwood, in woodland and plantations. Widespread in northern temperate zones.
  • **SIMILAR SPECIES**
G. picreus has a dark stem and vivid yellow gills.

FRUITING Appears mostly in small groups or singly.

• smooth, dry cap

• cap slightly greasy in wet weather

• stem paler orange-brown than cap

notched • to slightly decurrent gills

white-felted • stem base, often with rhizoids   **SECTION**

pale yellow • gills age to cinnamon-brown with rusty flecks

| Dimensions CAP ⊕ 3–8cm | STEM ↕ 4–7cm ↔ 0.4–1cm | Spores Rust-brown | Edibility |

| Family COPRINACEAE | Species *Psathyrella piluliformis* | Season Autumn |

COMMON STUMP BRITTLE-HEAD

In the large genus *Psathyrella*, comprising mainly little brown mushrooms – so called LBMs – between which it is difficult to distinguish, this species has some helpful characteristics: it occurs in clusters and has a distinct white veil, stained brown by spores, at the cap margin. The convex to bell-shaped cap is dark red-brown when wet, drying to paler yellowish brown. Details such as spore size ultimately ensure correct identification.
• **OCCURRENCE** In woodland on rotten hardwood, rarely softwood; often on stumps. Widespread and common in northern temperate zones.

FRUITING In dense clusters on and around hardwood stumps.

convex to bell-shaped cap •

red-brown cap • dries yellowish brown

almost • smooth white stem

fairly • crowded, off-white to reddish brown gills

stem is • hollow but fairly sturdy

gills • adnexed with pale edges

SECTION

| Dimensions CAP ⊕ 1.5–6cm | STEM ↕ 3–10cm ↔ 3–9mm | Spores Dark purplish brown | Edibility |

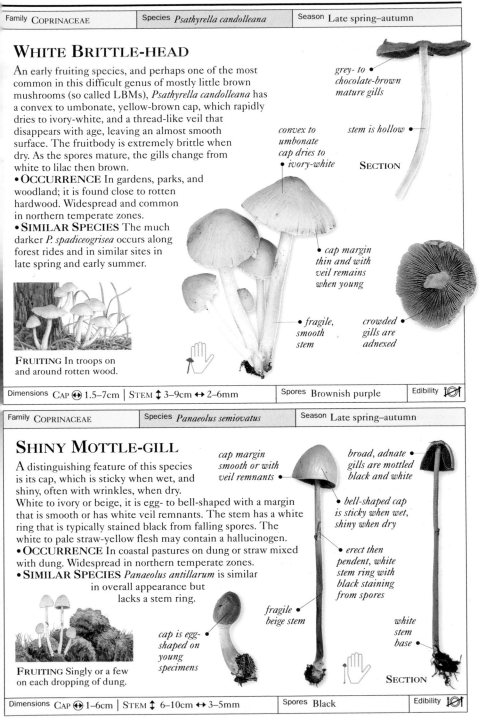

| Family COPRINACEAE | Species *Psathyrella candolleana* | Season Late spring–autumn |

WHITE BRITTLE-HEAD

An early fruiting species, and perhaps one of the most common in this difficult genus of mostly little brown mushrooms (so called LBMs), *Psathyrella candolleana* has a convex to umbonate, yellow-brown cap, which rapidly dries to ivory-white, and a thread-like veil that disappears with age, leaving an almost smooth surface. The fruitbody is extremely brittle when dry. As the spores mature, the gills change from white to lilac then brown.
• OCCURRENCE In gardens, parks, and woodland; it is found close to rotten hardwood. Widespread and common in northern temperate zones.
• SIMILAR SPECIES The much darker *P. spadiceogrisea* occurs along forest rides and in similar sites in late spring and early summer.

grey- to chocolate-brown mature gills

convex to umbonate cap dries to ivory-white

stem is hollow

SECTION

cap margin thin and with veil remains when young

fragile, smooth stem

crowded gills are adnexed

FRUITING In troops on and around rotten wood.

| Dimensions CAP ⊕ 1.5–7cm | STEM ↕ 3–9cm ↔ 2–6mm | Spores Brownish purple | Edibility |

| Family COPRINACEAE | Species *Panaeolus semiovatus* | Season Late spring–autumn |

SHINY MOTTLE-GILL

A distinguishing feature of this species is its cap, which is sticky when wet, and shiny, often with wrinkles, when dry. White to ivory or beige, it is egg- to bell-shaped with a margin that is smooth or has white veil remnants. The stem has a white ring that is typically stained black from falling spores. The white to pale straw-yellow flesh may contain a hallucinogen.
• OCCURRENCE In coastal pastures on dung or straw mixed with dung. Widespread in northern temperate zones.
• SIMILAR SPECIES *Panaeolus antillarum* is similar in overall appearance but lacks a stem ring.

cap margin smooth or with veil remnants

broad, adnate gills are mottled black and white

bell-shaped cap is sticky when wet, shiny when dry

erect then pendent, white stem ring with black staining from spores

fragile beige stem

white stem base

cap is egg-shaped on young specimens

FRUITING Singly or a few on each dropping of dung.

SECTION

| Dimensions CAP ⊕ 1–6cm | STEM ↕ 6–10cm ↔ 3–5mm | Spores Black | Edibility |

Family BOLBITIACEAE	Species *Conocybe arrhenii*	Season Late summer–late autumn

RINGED CONE-CAP

This is one of the most common members of a subgroup of *Conocybe* species often called *Pholiotina*. Members are so similar that they are best distinguished by their spores. They have scaly veil remnants at the cap margin or a stem ring. The ring tends to be loose and is easily lost. The gills are fairly crowded and adnexed, often with a white margin. All members are suspected to be poisonous.
• **OCCURRENCE** Typically on nutrient-rich soil in disturbed sites. Often occurs with other *Conocybe* species and with species of *Lepiota* and *Psathyrella*. Widespread in Asia and Europe; world distribution not clear.
• **SIMILAR SPECIES** *C. blattaria* and *C. percincta* have 2-spored basidia; those of *C. arrhenii* are 4-spored.

cap is striate at margin when moist

cuff-like white ring is striate on top

stem is pale brown at base, becoming paler towards top

cap is initially brick-red at centre, drying pale ochre

FRUITING Often singly or just a few fruitbodies, along roads and beside paths.

Dimensions CAP ⊕ 1–3cm │ STEM ↕ 1.5–5cm ↔ 1.5–3mm	Spores Rusty brown	Edibility ☠

Family TRICHOLOMATACEAE	Species *Cystoderma terrei*	Season Autumn

CINNABAR POWDER-CAP

A convex to umbonate, brick-red cap, with a mealy surface and a club-shaped stem with red scales on the lower part, are the main features of this species. It has fairly crowded, adnexed, pale gills. When examined with a hand lens, the gills can be seen to be fimbriate. A microscope reveals cystidia (special sterile cells) on the edges of the gills.
• **OCCURRENCE** In all kinds of woodland areas and in plantations on humus-rich, acid soil. The world distribution of this species is not fully understood, but it is widespread in Europe and also occurs in Japan.
• **SIMILAR SPECIES** There are several similar *Cystoderma* species found in similar habitats. *C. granulosum* has more dirty, rusty brown colouring. Close relative *C. adnatifolium* lacks cystidia and is brighter in colour.

edges of pale gills are fimbriate (visible through hand lens)

pale pink to orange flesh

SECTION

mealy, brick-red cap surface

convex to umbonate cap

stem is swollen at base

small red scales on lower stem

FRUITING Appears singly or a few together.

Dimensions CAP ⊕ 2–8cm │ STEM ↕ 3–7cm ↔ 4–8mm	Spores Off-white	Edibility 🍴

| Family TRICHOLOMATACEAE | Species *Cystoderma amianthinum* | Season Autumn |

SAFFRON POWDER-CAP

This bright ochre-yellow species has a bell-shaped to flat cap with a mealy surface and a fringed margin. Below the short-lived ring, the stem surface is mealy or granular. The crowded, adnexed gills are white becoming creamy yellow with age, and the musty-smelling flesh is thin and pale yellow. The identity of *Cystoderma* species is best confirmed by microscopic comparison of spore size: those of *C. amianthinum* are 6 x 3µm on average.
• **OCCURRENCE** In varied sites – in moss in woodland, with willow, or with grasses or bracken. Widespread and common in northern temperate zones.
• **SIMILAR SPECIES** *C. jasonis* is darker with a coarser cap surface; its spores are larger (7 x 4µm). Other similar species are distinguished by more robust, permanent stem rings or the presence of lilac colouring at the stem top.

mealy or granular surface below stem ring

ochre-yellow cap has fringe at margin

bell-shaped to flat cap with mealy surface

FRUITING Appears singly or a few fruitbodies together among mosses in damp, acid woodland.

| Dimensions CAP ⊕ 1–4cm | STEM ↕ 2.5–6cm ↔ 3–7mm | Spores Off-white | Edibility |

| Family TRICHOLOMATACEAE | Species *Cystoderma carcharias* | Season Autumn–late autumn |

PINK-GREY POWDER-CAP

Besides the pinkish grey colour of both cap and stem, this species is characterized by a prominent, cuff-like, pink-grey stem ring. The surfaces of the cap and stem are powdery, as in other members of the genus *Cystoderma*. The adnexed gills are white and medium spaced. The white flesh has an unpleasant, rancid smell.
• **OCCURRENCE** Hard- and softwood woodland and on heathland. Widespread in parts of northern temperate zones but not as commonly found in most places as *C. amianthinum* (above).
• **SIMILAR SPECIES** *C. ambrosii* has fruitbodies that are almost pure white and become slightly brown with age. The fruitbodies of *C. fallax* are yellow-brown.

centre of pinkish grey cap is umbonate

distinctive, cuff-like stem ring

white gills are adnexed and medium spaced

cap has fringed margin

stem is pinkish grey and powdery, particularly below ring

FRUITING Typically in small groups or singly, always on acid soil and humus among leaf litter and moss.

| Dimensions CAP ⊕ 2–5cm | STEM ↕ 4–8cm ↔ 2–7mm | Spores Off-white | Edibility |

WITH FIBROUS CAP AND DARK SPORES

T HIS SUBSECTION comprises agarics that, in addition to having adnate to adnexed gills (see p.56), have a cap with a distinctly fibrous or scaly surface. The spore deposits of all the species featured here are in various shades of brown, although not rust-coloured (see pp.69–77 for species with rusty brown spores). The species that belong in this subsection are members of the genera *Inocybe* and *Lacrymaria*; some have veils, others do not. Those *Inocybe* species that lack veils have very fine hairs covering the entire stems. A hand lens is needed in order to see these hairs, which are called cystidia.

Family CORTINARIACEAE	Species *Inocybe haemacta*	Season Autumn

GREEN AND PINK FIBRE-CAP

The fruitbodies of this species have green tones, rare in this usually dull-coloured genus. The convex to umbonate, grey- to greenish brown cap has a fibrous or scaly centre. Both the cap and the pale grey flesh become redder with age. The greenish grey stem is fibrous towards the base and has a mealy covering at the top, which is paler in colour. The Green and Pink Fibre-cap smells similar to urine or a stable.
• OCCURRENCE Mycorrhizal with hardwood trees on rich soil, in parks and woods or on road verges. Widespread but local to rare in Europe; world distribution unknown.
• SIMILAR SPECIES *Inocybe corydalina*, which has a cider-like smell, may have green hues on the cap.

grey- or greenish brown • cap reddens with age

• convex or umbonate cap

greenish grey stem, • paler at top

adnexed, grey to grey-brown gills become pinker then • brown with age

paler flesh visible • beneath fibres

• meal covers upper stem

• fibrous or scaly cap centre

flesh ages from • pale grey to redder hue

SECTION

gills are fairly crowded •

FRUITING Appears singly or a few together.

Dimensions CAP ⊕ 3–6.5cm | STEM ↕ 2–8cm ↔ 4–6mm	Spores Tobacco-brown	Edibility ☠

| Family CORTINARIACEAE | Species *Inocybe erubescens* | Season Spring–autumn |

REDDISH FIBRE-CAP

The early appearance of this fleshy species, which is known to be involved in poisonings (see Similar Species), is a noteworthy characteristic, as is the fact that the fruitbody stains red when older or if handled. It has a bell-shaped to broadly conical or umbonate cap, the surface of which has distinct radial fibres, common to the genus. The fairly squat stem, which is rarely longer than the diameter of the cap, is sturdy, and its surface is covered in meal.

• **OCCURRENCE** Mycorrhizal with trees such as beech and lime, on clay or alkaline soil. Widespread but local in Europe and parts of Asia.

• **SIMILAR SPECIES** It has been mistaken for edible fungi, such as *Calocybe gambosa* (p.58). *Inocybe pudica* stains red, but has more slender, whiter fruitbodies.

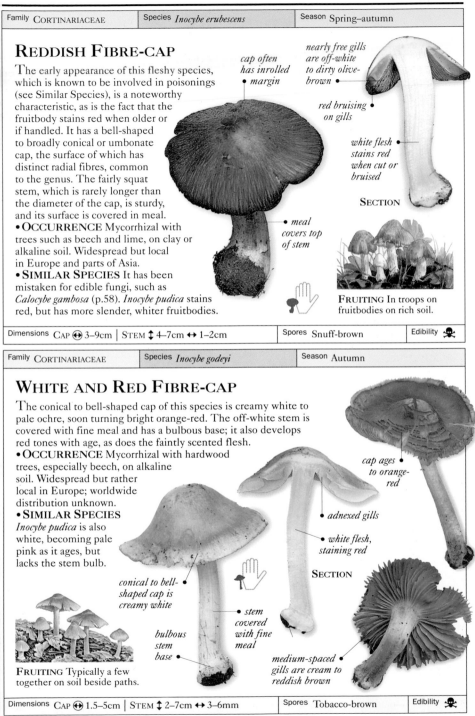

cap often has inrolled margin

nearly free gills are off-white to dirty olive-brown

red bruising on gills

white flesh stains red when cut or bruised

SECTION

meal covers top of stem

FRUITING In troops on fruitbodies on rich soil.

| Dimensions CAP ⊕ 3–9cm | STEM ↕ 4–7cm ↔ 1–2cm | Spores Snuff-brown | Edibility ☠ |

| Family CORTINARIACEAE | Species *Inocybe godeyi* | Season Autumn |

WHITE AND RED FIBRE-CAP

The conical to bell-shaped cap of this species is creamy white to pale ochre, soon turning bright orange-red. The off-white stem is covered with fine meal and has a bulbous base; it also develops red tones with age, as does the faintly scented flesh.

• **OCCURRENCE** Mycorrhizal with hardwood trees, especially beech, on alkaline soil. Widespread but rather local in Europe; worldwide distribution unknown.

• **SIMILAR SPECIES** *Inocybe pudica* is also white, becoming pale pink as it ages, but lacks the stem bulb.

cap ages to orange-red

adnexed gills

white flesh, staining red

SECTION

conical to bell-shaped cap is creamy white

stem covered with fine meal

bulbous stem base

medium-spaced gills are cream to reddish brown

FRUITING Typically a few together on soil beside paths.

| Dimensions CAP ⊕ 1.5–5cm | STEM ↕ 2–7cm ↔ 3–6mm | Spores Tobacco-brown | Edibility ☠ |

Family CORTINARIACEAE	Species *Inocybe geophylla*	Season Autumn

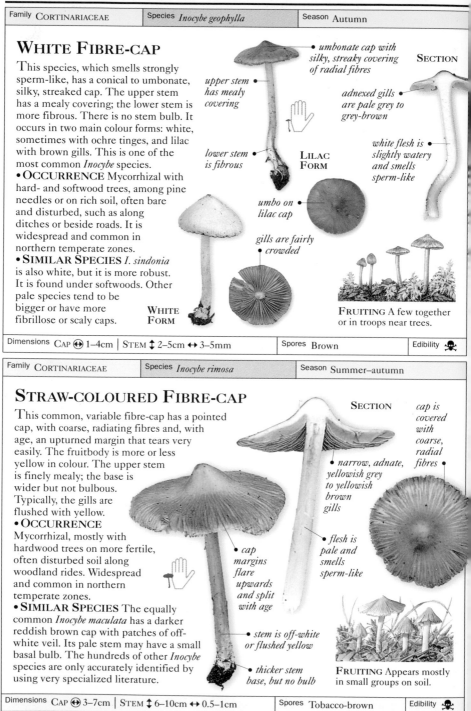

WHITE FIBRE-CAP

This species, which smells strongly sperm-like, has a conical to umbonate, silky, streaked cap. The upper stem has a mealy covering; the lower stem is more fibrous. There is no stem bulb. It occurs in two main colour forms: white, sometimes with ochre tinges, and lilac with brown gills. This is one of the most common *Inocybe* species.
• OCCURRENCE Mycorrhizal with hard- and softwood trees, among pine needles or on rich soil, often bare and disturbed, such as along ditches or beside roads. It is widespread and common in northern temperate zones.
• SIMILAR SPECIES *I. sindonia* is also white, but it is more robust. It is found under softwoods. Other pale species tend to be bigger or have more fibrillose or scaly caps.

umbonate cap with silky, streaky covering of radial fibres

SECTION

upper stem has mealy covering

adnexed gills are pale grey to grey-brown

lower stem is fibrous

LILAC FORM

white flesh is slightly watery and smells sperm-like

umbo on lilac cap

gills are fairly crowded

WHITE FORM

FRUITING A few together or in troops near trees.

Dimensions CAP ⊕ 1–4cm │ STEM ↕ 2–5cm ↔ 3–5mm	Spores Brown	Edibility ☠

Family CORTINARIACEAE	Species *Inocybe rimosa*	Season Summer–autumn

STRAW-COLOURED FIBRE-CAP

This common, variable fibre-cap has a pointed cap, with coarse, radiating fibres and, with age, an upturned margin that tears very easily. The fruitbody is more or less yellow in colour. The upper stem is finely mealy; the base is wider but not bulbous. Typically, the gills are flushed with yellow.
• OCCURRENCE Mycorrhizal, mostly with hardwood trees on more fertile, often disturbed soil along woodland rides. Widespread and common in northern temperate zones.
• SIMILAR SPECIES The equally common *Inocybe maculata* has a darker reddish brown cap with patches of off-white veil. Its pale stem may have a small basal bulb. The hundreds of other *Inocybe* species are only accurately identified by using very specialized literature.

SECTION

cap is covered with coarse, radial fibres

narrow, adnate, yellowish grey to yellowish brown gills

flesh is pale and smells sperm-like

cap margins flare upwards and split with age

stem is off-white or flushed yellow

thicker stem base, but no bulb

FRUITING Appears mostly in small groups on soil.

Dimensions CAP ⊕ 3–7cm │ STEM ↕ 6–10cm ↔ 0.5–1cm	Spores Tobacco-brown	Edibility ☠

| Family CORTINARIACEAE | Species *Inocybe griseolilacina* | Season Autumn |

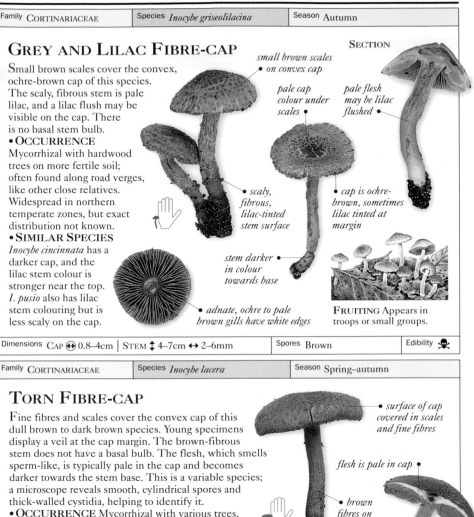

GREY AND LILAC FIBRE-CAP

Small brown scales cover the convex, ochre-brown cap of this species. The scaly, fibrous stem is pale lilac, and a lilac flush may be visible on the cap. There is no basal stem bulb.

• **OCCURRENCE** Mycorrhizal with hardwood trees on more fertile soil; often found along road verges, like other close relatives. Widespread in northern temperate zones, but exact distribution not known.

• **SIMILAR SPECIES** *Inocybe cincinnata* has a darker cap, and the lilac stem colour is stronger near the top. *I. pusio* also has lilac stem colouring but is less scaly on the cap.

SECTION

small brown scales • on convex cap

pale cap colour under scales •

pale flesh may be lilac flushed •

• scaly, fibrous, lilac-tinted stem surface

• cap is ochre-brown, sometimes lilac tinted at margin

stem darker • in colour towards base

• adnate, ochre to pale brown gills have white edges

FRUITING Appears in troops or small groups.

| Dimensions CAP ⊕ 0.8–4cm │ STEM ↕ 4–7cm ↔ 2–6mm | Spores Brown | Edibility ☠ |

| Family CORTINARIACEAE | Species *Inocybe lacera* | Season Spring–autumn |

TORN FIBRE-CAP

Fine fibres and scales cover the convex cap of this dull brown to dark brown species. Young specimens display a veil at the cap margin. The brown-fibrous stem does not have a basal bulb. The flesh, which smells sperm-like, is typically pale in the cap and becomes darker towards the stem base. This is a variable species; a microscope reveals smooth, cylindrical spores and thick-walled cystidia, helping to identify it.

• **OCCURRENCE** Mycorrhizal with various trees, including willow and softwoods. Widespread and common in northern temperate zones.

• **SIMILAR SPECIES** *Inocybe lanuginosa* has a more woolly stem and spores with nodules.

• surface of cap covered in scales and fine fibres

flesh is pale in cap •

• brown fibres on stem surface

flesh is dark in stem base •

SECTION

• convex, dull to dark brown cap

• adnexed gills are grey-brown with white edges

FRUITING A few together or in troops, often on poor soil.

| Dimensions CAP ⊕ 1–4.5cm │ STEM ↕ 2.5–6cm ↔ 2–6mm | Spores Tobacco-brown | Edibility ☠ |

Family CORTINARIACEAE	Species *Inocybe asterospora*	Season Autumn

STAR-SPORED FIBRE-CAP

A distinctive, flattened bulb at the base of a slender, meal-covered stem, and a slightly umbonate, pale cap thickly covered with radiating, coarse, dark red-brown fibres characterize this species. Microscopic examination reveals star-shaped spores: the spores of *Inocybe* species are usually either smooth or have nodules; a star-shape is an extreme form of the latter type.
• **OCCURRENCE** Mycorrhizal with hardwood trees, especially hazel or beech, often growing on bare soil. Widespread in northern temperate zones, but its status is unknown in many regions.
• **SIMILAR SPECIES** *I. margaritispora* has star-shaped spores but a paler, more yellow cap. *I. napipes* has a less marked bulb, is smaller, and has ordinary noduled spores.

slightly umbonate cap is • pale beneath fibres

pale cap flesh, • darker in stem

radiating, coarse, dark red-brown • fibres on cap

• flattened, rimmed bulb at stem base

SECTION

• adnexed, tobacco-brown gills

• stem mealy along its length

FRUITING Appears singly or a few fruitbodies together.

Dimensions CAP ⊕ 3–7cm	STEM ↕ 4–9cm ↔ 0.5–1.2cm	Spores Tobacco-brown	Edibility ☠

Family COPRINACEAE	Species *Lacrymaria velutina*	Season Autumn

WEEPING WIDOW

The convex or umbonate cap of this species is brownish grey to ochre with a felted surface. The similarly coloured stem is fibrillose and fragile. Grey becoming black, the gills are well spaced and adnate. Milk-like drops can be seen along the gill edges when they are young – hence the common name; these droplets fill with spores and dry as black spots.
• **OCCURRENCE** Saprotrophic; on nutrient-rich, disturbed soil. Widespread in northern temperate zones.
• **SIMILAR SPECIES** There are several similar species, including *Lacrymaria glareosa* and *L. pyrotricha*. These are distinguished by their size and cap colour and by spore characteristics.

striations at slightly wavy cap margin •

cap is convex or with an • umbo

brownish grey to ochre cap • is felted

gills are grey with droplets at the edge •

well-spaced, • adnate gills

FRUITING Appears in large troops of fruitbodies along roads and paths, often near nettles.

Dimensions CAP ⊕ 2–10cm	STEM ↕ 4–12cm ↔ 0.5–2cm	Spores Black	Edibility ⚭

MEDIUM-SIZED WITH SMOOTH CAP

I N THIS SUBSECTION, species with adnate, adnexed, or notched gills (see pp.15 and 56) have been grouped together according to their size and cap characteristics. Medium-sized refers to the fruitbodies, which have caps that are typically in the range 1.5–6cm in diameter. The smooth surface of the caps is one of the most readily visible characteristics. The colour of the spore deposits of species featured here varies widely from white, which is common to *Hygrocybe* species, through cream, found in species of *Collybia*, to pink, produced by *Entoloma* species, and black, which occurs in many *Psathyrella* species.

Family HYGROPHORACEAE	Species *Hygrocybe calyptraeformis*	Season Throughout autumn

PINK WAX-CAP

The elegant and fragile, dusky pink fruitbodies of this rare species are quite unmistakable. Each has a cap that begins conical and opens out fully as it matures, eventually splitting radially. The stem is very brittle and is difficult to pull out of the substrate. It has mild-tasting, pale pink to white flesh, but is not recommended for eating due to concern about its conservation and the fact that its edibility is not very well documented.
• **OCCURRENCE** Long-established areas of grassland where commercial fertilizers have not been applied, often on alkaline soil. Widespread throughout Europe, including on islands of the North Atlantic.
• **SIMILAR SPECIES** *Hygrocybe citrinovirens* is similar in shape but is yellow-green and orange; it is also rare. Other *Hygrocybe* species have conical caps but *H. calyptraeformis* and *H. citrinovirens* are the only ones that split so widely. *H. conica* (p.104) blackens with age. *H. spadicea* has a dark cap and yellow gills. It does not blacken.

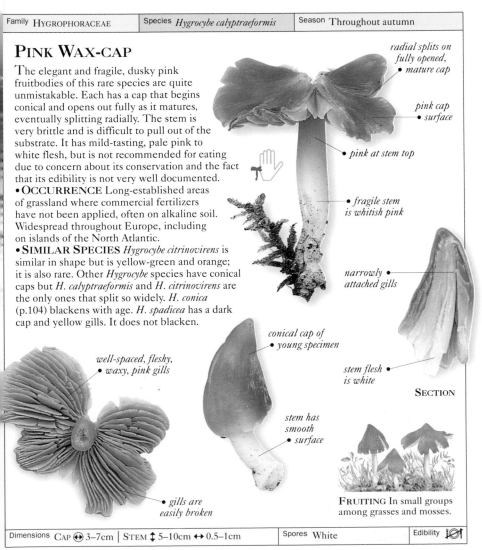

radial splits on fully opened, • mature cap

pink cap • surface

• pink at stem top

• fragile stem is whitish pink

narrowly • attached gills

well-spaced, fleshy, • waxy, pink gills

conical cap of • young specimen

stem flesh • is white

SECTION

stem has smooth • surface

• gills are easily broken

FRUITING In small groups among grasses and mosses.

Dimensions CAP ⊕ 3–7cm | STEM ↕ 5–10cm ↔ 0.5–1cm	Spores White	Edibility

| Family HYGROPHORACEAE | Species *Hygrocybe conica* | Season Summer–late autumn |

BLACKENING WAX-CAP

The more or less conical cap of this variable fungus is dry and fibrillose; the stem is yellow to red with longitudinal lines. This species occurs in a wide variety of colours, sizes, and shapes and, among *Hygrocybe* species, it probably has the broadest range of habitats (leading some mycologists to suggest it is a range of species and varieties). It goes black with age or when handled. It may be slightly poisonous.

• OCCURRENCE In grassy areas, except those that have been heavily fertilized. Widespread and common in northern temperate zones.

• SIMILAR SPECIES *H. persistens* often has a more shiny cap and does not stain black.

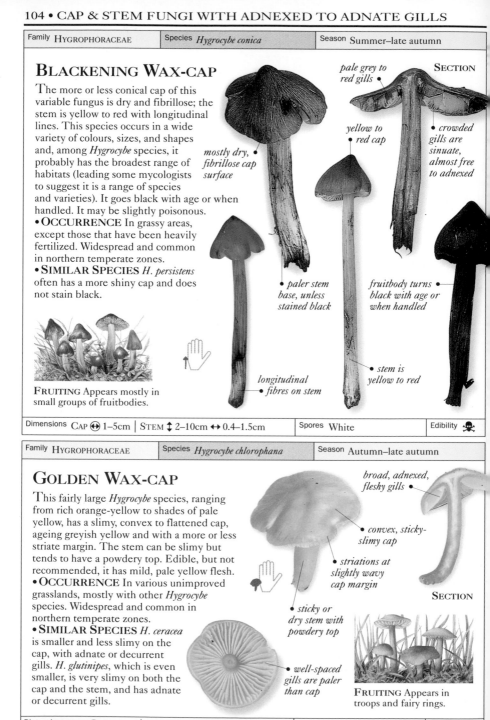

pale grey to red gills

SECTION

yellow to red cap

crowded gills are sinuate, almost free to adnexed

mostly dry, fibrillose cap surface

paler stem base, unless stained black

fruitbody turns black with age or when handled

stem is yellow to red

longitudinal fibres on stem

FRUITING Appears mostly in small groups of fruitbodies.

| Dimensions CAP ⊕ 1–5cm | STEM ↕ 2–10cm ↔ 0.4–1.5cm | Spores White | Edibility ☠ |

| Family HYGROPHORACEAE | Species *Hygrocybe chlorophana* | Season Autumn–late autumn |

GOLDEN WAX-CAP

This fairly large *Hygrocybe* species, ranging from rich orange-yellow to shades of pale yellow, has a slimy, convex to flattened cap, ageing greyish yellow and with a more or less striate margin. The stem can be slimy but tends to have a powdery top. Edible, but not recommended, it has mild, pale yellow flesh.

• OCCURRENCE In various unimproved grasslands, mostly with other *Hygrocybe* species. Widespread and common in northern temperate zones.

• SIMILAR SPECIES *H. ceracea* is smaller and less slimy on the cap, with adnate or decurrent gills. *H. glutinipes*, which is even smaller, is very slimy on both the cap and the stem, and has adnate or decurrent gills.

broad, adnexed, fleshy gills

convex, sticky-slimy cap

striations at slightly wavy cap margin

SECTION

sticky or dry stem with powdery top

well-spaced gills are paler than cap

FRUITING Appears in troops and fairy rings.

| Dimensions CAP ⊕ 1.5–7cm | STEM ↕ 2.5–10cm ↔ 3–8mm | Spores White | Edibility ☺ |

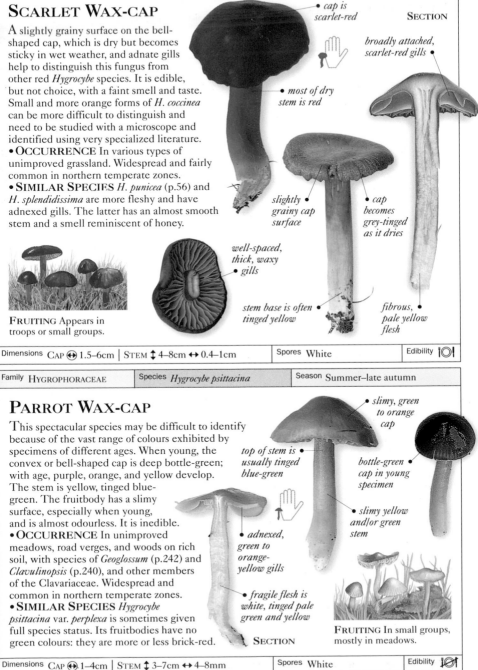

| Family HYGROPHORACEAE | Species *Hygrocybe coccinea* | Season Late summer–late autumn |

SCARLET WAX-CAP

A slightly grainy surface on the bell-shaped cap, which is dry but becomes sticky in wet weather, and adnate gills help to distinguish this fungus from other red *Hygrocybe* species. It is edible, but not choice, with a faint smell and taste. Small and more orange forms of *H. coccinea* can be more difficult to distinguish and need to be studied with a microscope and identified using very specialized literature.

• **OCCURRENCE** In various types of unimproved grassland. Widespread and fairly common in northern temperate zones.

• **SIMILAR SPECIES** *H. punicea* (p.56) and *H. splendidissima* are more fleshy and have adnexed gills. The latter has an almost smooth stem and a smell reminiscent of honey.

SECTION

• *cap is scarlet-red*

broadly attached, scarlet-red gills •

• *most of dry stem is red*

slightly grainy cap surface

• *cap becomes grey-tinged as it dries*

well-spaced, thick, waxy gills •

stem base is often tinged yellow

fibrous, pale yellow flesh •

FRUITING Appears in troops or small groups.

| Dimensions CAP ⊕ 1.5–6cm │ STEM ↕ 4–8cm ↔ 0.4–1cm | Spores White | Edibility ¦◎¦ |

| Family HYGROPHORACEAE | Species *Hygrocybe psittacina* | Season Summer–late autumn |

PARROT WAX-CAP

This spectacular species may be difficult to identify because of the vast range of colours exhibited by specimens of different ages. When young, the convex or bell-shaped cap is deep bottle-green; with age, purple, orange, and yellow develop. The stem is yellow, tinged blue-green. The fruitbody has a slimy surface, especially when young, and is almost odourless. It is inedible.

• **OCCURRENCE** In unimproved meadows, road verges, and woods on rich soil, with species of *Geoglossum* (p.242) and *Clavulinopsis* (p.240), and other members of the Clavariaceae. Widespread and common in northern temperate zones.

• **SIMILAR SPECIES** *Hygrocybe psittacina* var. *perplexa* is sometimes given full species status. Its fruitbodies have no green colours: they are more or less brick-red.

• *slimy, green to orange cap*

top of stem is usually tinged blue-green

bottle-green cap in young specimen

• *slimy yellow and/or green stem*

• *adnexed, green to orange-yellow gills*

• *fragile flesh is white, tinged pale green and yellow*

SECTION

FRUITING In small groups, mostly in meadows.

| Dimensions CAP ⊕ 1–4cm │ STEM ↕ 3–7cm ↔ 4–8mm | Spores White | Edibility ⬤¦ |

| Family HYGROPHORACEAE | Species *Hygrophorus eburneus* | Season Autumn–early winter |

SATIN WAX-CAP

The convex to flattened, sparkling white cap of the Satin Wax-cap drips with slime in wet weather. The stem is also slimy and white. Both stain slightly yellow with age. The gills are thick and waxy, and the white flesh smells pleasantly aromatic but it is not worth eating.
• **OCCURRENCE** Mycorrhizal with beech trees on fertile soil. Widespread in northern temperate regions where beech grows. Worldwide distribution unclear.
• **SIMILAR SPECIES** *Hygrophorus discoxanthus* stains deep orange.

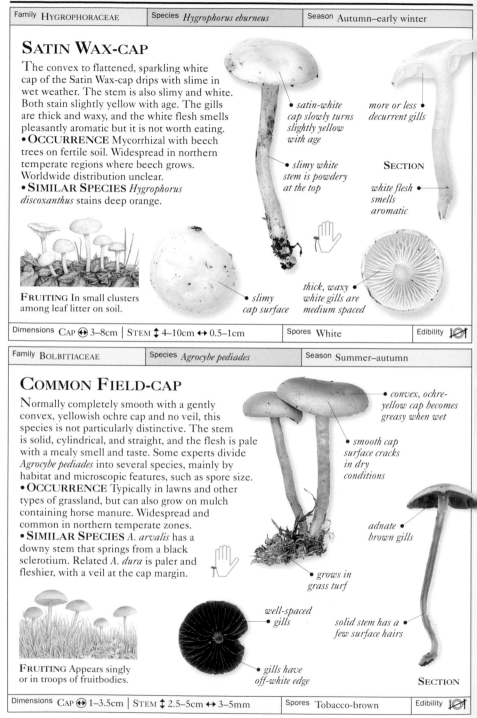

satin-white cap slowly turns slightly yellow with age

more or less decurrent gills

slimy white stem is powdery at the top

SECTION

white flesh smells aromatic

FRUITING In small clusters among leaf litter on soil.

slimy cap surface

thick, waxy white gills are medium spaced

| Dimensions CAP ⊕ 3–8cm | STEM ↕ 4–10cm ↔ 0.5–1cm | Spores White | Edibility |

| Family BOLBITIACEAE | Species *Agrocybe pediades* | Season Summer–autumn |

COMMON FIELD-CAP

Normally completely smooth with a gently convex, yellowish ochre cap and no veil, this species is not particularly distinctive. The stem is solid, cylindrical, and straight, and the flesh is pale with a mealy smell and taste. Some experts divide *Agrocybe pediades* into several species, mainly by habitat and microscopic features, such as spore size.
• **OCCURRENCE** Typically in lawns and other types of grassland, but can also grow on mulch containing horse manure. Widespread and common in northern temperate zones.
• **SIMILAR SPECIES** *A. arvalis* has a downy stem that springs from a black sclerotium. Related *A. dura* is paler and fleshier, with a veil at the cap margin.

convex, ochre-yellow cap becomes greasy when wet

smooth cap surface cracks in dry conditions

adnate brown gills

grows in grass turf

FRUITING Appears singly or in troops of fruitbodies.

well-spaced gills

gills have off-white edge

solid stem has a few surface hairs

SECTION

| Dimensions CAP ⊕ 1–3.5cm | STEM ↕ 2.5–5cm ↔ 3–5mm | Spores Tobacco-brown | Edibility |

| Family COPRINACEAE | Species *Panaeolus papilionaceus* | Season Summer–late autumn |

FRINGED MOTTLE-GILL

Triangular veil remnants at the cap margin are characteristic of this mottle-gill. The cap is convex or bell-shaped and varies from dark grey to brownish grey; older specimens may have pale caps contrasting with the dark brown stems. Marbled gills caused by uneven ripening of the spores are typical of *Panaeolus* species. The flesh is dark brown in the stem, paler in the cap, and has no distinct smell. A form with a strongly veined cap was previously regarded as a separate species: *P. retirugis*. Due to conflicting reports on toxicity, this species should not be eaten.
• **OCCURRENCE** On old dung or in manured, grazed fields. Widespread in northern temperate zones and elsewhere.

convex or bell-shaped, smooth cap

SECTION

triangular veil remnants just visible at cap margin

broad, adnate gills are mottled black and grey

rather fragile stem is grey to dark brown

stem is hollow

medium-spaced, nearly black gills with white edges

FRUITING Singly or a few together on or near manure.

pale brownish grey cap indicates an older specimen

| Dimensions CAP ⊕ 1–4cm | STEM ↕ 4–10cm ↔ 2–3mm | Spores Black | Edibility ☠ |

| Family STROPHARIACEAE | Species *Psilocybe cyanescens* | Season Autumn–early winter |

BLUE-RIMMED LIBERTY-CAP

This hallucinogenic agaric has a flattened cap with a wavy margin; reddish buff at first, it dries to creamy ochre and develops dark blue discoloration when handled. It becomes greasy in wet weather. The off-white to grey stem, which also stains blue, has no ring. Several stems are frequently joined at the base. The white flesh has a faint mealy smell.
• **OCCURRENCE** Mostly in disturbed sites, such as a flowerbed mulch that contains woodchippings (especially softwood chippings). Widespread but rather local, in northern temperate zones.
• **SIMILAR SPECIES** *Psilocybe caerulipes* has spores that are ellipsoid; those of *P. cyanescens* are flattened ellipsoid. *Hypholoma myosotis* does not stain.

adnate to slightly decurrent gills

SECTION

pale flesh and stem surface stain blue

cap margin may be wavy and upturned when old

fairly well-spaced gills

blue most obvious at cap margin

silky, fibrillose, off-white to grey stem

FRUITING In troops or clusters in disturbed sites.

gills are whitish grey to dark purplish brown with white edges

| Dimensions CAP ⊕ 2–4cm | STEM ↕ 3–6cm ↔ 3–8mm | Spores Dark purplish brown | Edibility ☠ |

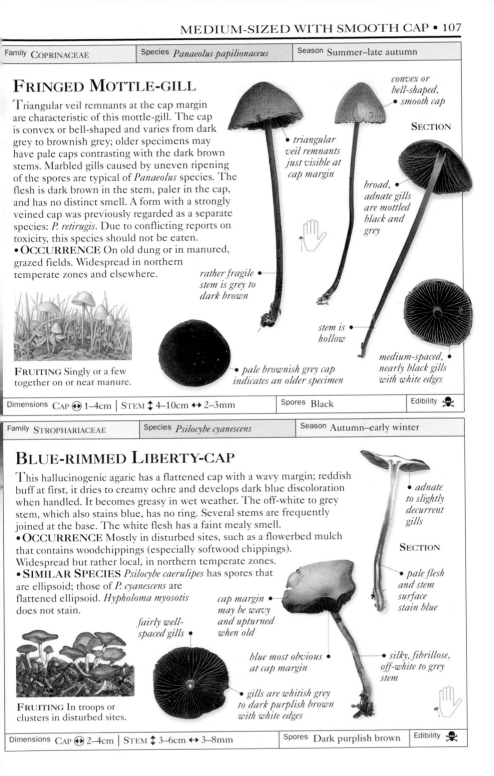

Family TRICHOLOMATACEAE	Species *Macrocystidia cucumis*	Season Late summer–autumn

CUCUMBER-SCENTED TOADSTOOL

This agaric has a strong, rancid smell, reminiscent of cucumbers or pickled herrings. Another feature is the dark brown or orange-brown cap with a pale yellow margin and velvety surface. The fairly tough stem is also densely velvety; it is dark at the base and paler towards the top. The dark rusty ochre spore deposit is unusual within the family.

• **OCCURRENCE** In gardens or parks, or along woodland ditches and roads, on rich soil mixed with leaf litter or sawdust. Widespread but rather local in northern temperate zones; widespread in Europe but more local in North America.

adnexed gills are pale cream to pale reddish brown

fine down on cap surface, which may be striated

SECTION

yellow cap margin

cap may be convex, conical, or bell-shaped

fairly crowded, medium to very broad gills

black to dark brown stem base

FRUITING A few fruitbodies together or in troops.

Dimensions CAP ⊕ 0.5–5cm | STEM ↕ 3–7cm ↔ 2–5mm	Spores Rusty ochre or off-white	Edibility

Family COPRINACEAE	Species *Psathyrella multipedata*	Season Autumn

TUFTED BRITTLE-HEAD

The bell-shaped to conical, grey- or red-brown cap of this cluster-forming species has striations halfway to the centre. It dries to pale yellow-brown and has no obvious veil. Clusters of up to 80 smooth white stems are joined at the base and extend, root-like, deep into the soil. This is among the very few *Psathyrella* species with clear identification features, distinguishing it from most other little brown mushrooms (LBMs).

• **OCCURRENCE** On rich, loamy or clay soil, often in urban areas such as at roadsides and in city parks. Widespread in Europe. Worldwide distribution not clear.

• **SIMILAR SPECIES** *P. piluliformis* (p.94). Other tufted agarics in open areas include *Lyophyllum decastes* (p.41) and other species of *Lyophyllum* (p.132), which all have white spore deposits.

moist, grey- or red-brown cap, striated at margin

hollow stems

SECTION

pale grey to dark purple-brown gills are white edged

FRUITING Always in tight clusters, rooted deeply in turf.

smooth cap dries from centre to pale yellow-brown

crowded, narrow, adnexed gills

Dimensions CAP ⊕ 0.8–4cm | STEM ↕ 8–14cm ↔ 2–4mm	Spores Brownish black	Edibility

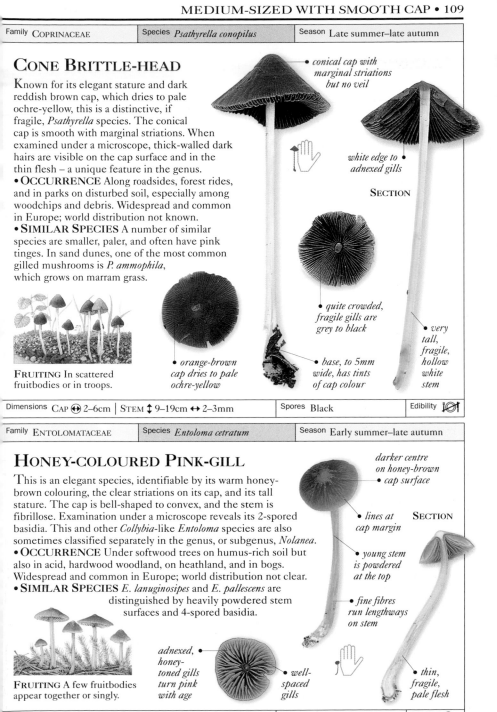

Family COPRINACEAE	Species *Psathyrella conopilus*	Season Late summer–late autumn

CONE BRITTLE-HEAD

Known for its elegant stature and dark reddish brown cap, which dries to pale ochre-yellow, this is a distinctive, if fragile, *Psathyrella* species. The conical cap is smooth with marginal striations. When examined under a microscope, thick-walled dark hairs are visible on the cap surface and in the thin flesh – a unique feature in the genus.
• OCCURRENCE Along roadsides, forest rides, and in parks on disturbed soil, especially among woodchips and debris. Widespread and common in Europe; world distribution not known.
• SIMILAR SPECIES A number of similar species are smaller, paler, and often have pink tinges. In sand dunes, one of the most common gilled mushrooms is *P. ammophila*, which grows on marram grass.

conical cap with marginal striations but no veil

white edge to adnexed gills

SECTION

quite crowded, fragile gills are grey to black

very tall, fragile, hollow white stem

FRUITING In scattered fruitbodies or in troops.

orange-brown cap dries to pale ochre-yellow

base, to 5mm wide, has tints of cap colour

Dimensions CAP ⊕ 2–6cm │ STEM ↕ 9–19cm ↔ 2–3mm	Spores Black	Edibility 🍴

Family ENTOLOMATACEAE	Species *Entoloma cetratum*	Season Early summer–late autumn

HONEY-COLOURED PINK-GILL

This is an elegant species, identifiable by its warm honey-brown colouring, the clear striations on its cap, and its tall stature. The cap is bell-shaped to convex, and the stem is fibrillose. Examination under a microscope reveals its 2-spored basidia. This and other *Collybia*-like *Entoloma* species are also sometimes classified separately in the genus, or subgenus, *Nolanea*.
• OCCURRENCE Under softwood trees on humus-rich soil but also in acid, hardwood woodland, on heathland, and in bogs. Widespread and common in Europe; world distribution not clear.
• SIMILAR SPECIES *E. lanuginosipes* and *E. pallescens* are distinguished by heavily powdered stem surfaces and 4-spored basidia.

darker centre on honey-brown cap surface

lines at cap margin   SECTION

young stem is powdered at the top

fine fibres run lengthways on stem

FRUITING A few fruitbodies appear together or singly.

adnexed, honey-toned gills turn pink with age

well-spaced gills

thin, fragile, pale flesh

Dimensions CAP ⊕ 0.5–3cm │ STEM ↕ 5–8cm ↔ 2–4mm	Spores Pale pink	Edibility ☠

Family ENTOLOMATACEAE	Species *Entoloma conferendum*	Season Spring–late autumn

STAR-SPORED PINK-GILL

Despite an elegant stature and a strongly fibrillose, silvery stem, this species is not easy to distinguish. A microscope reveals its key identification feature: star-shaped spores. The reddish brown to grey-brown cap tends to be conical, ageing to convex or umbonate; darker striations on the surface fade as it dries to pale grey-brown. The crowded gills are adnate, and the pale flesh smells and tastes mealy.

• **OCCURRENCE** Mostly in grassy places in parks and sports grounds but also in grass or moss in open woods. Widespread and common in northern temperate zones.

• **SIMILAR SPECIES** There are several *Entoloma* species that are similar in appearance, such as *E. cetratum* (p.109), which is warmer honey-brown, and *E. sericeum* (inset, right). All have spores that are angular and not star-shaped.

cap dries from reddish brown or grey-brown to pale grey-brown

△ *ENTOLOMA SERICEUM*
Short-stemmed, with a dark sepia-brown to horn-grey cap, this common European species has a very strong rancid-mealy smell. The spores are angular, but not star-shaped. ☣

pale grey then pink-tinged gills

margin has darker striations when moist

young cap is conical

fine silvery fibres on elegant stem

stem slightly swollen and paler at base

FRUITING Appears singly or in small groups.

Dimensions CAP ⊕ 2–4cm	STEM ↕ 3–6cm ↔ 3–7mm	Spores Pale pink	Edibility ☠

Family ENTOLOMATACEAE	Species *Entoloma nitidum*	Season Autumn

STEEL-BLUE PINK-GILL

This is among the very few blue *Entoloma* species that are quite large and fleshy. It is very dark grey-blue with a convex to umbonate, smooth to fibrillose cap and a slender, twisted stem. The well-spaced, adnate gills are white, becoming pale pink with age. The white cap flesh has a blue tinge near the skin, and has a faint smell. This species should not be eaten.

• **OCCURRENCE** Among moss in damp, acid softwood woodland or plantations. Widespread but mostly in northern Europe and adjacent parts of Asia; world distribution unknown.

• **SIMILAR SPECIES** *E. bloxamii* is more fleshy and prefers alkaline grassland. *E. euchroum* is smaller, more blue, and grows on hardwood.

dark grey-blue cap is smooth to fibrillose

cap is convex to umbonate

well-spaced, white gills age to pink

slender, twisted stem is dark grey-blue

FRUITING Appears singly or in small groups of fruitbodies in damp woodland.

Dimensions CAP ⊕ 1–2.5cm	STEM ↕ 2–6cm ↔ 2–4mm	Spores Pale pink	Edibility ⍚

Family TRICHOLOMATACEAE	Species *Collybia fusipes*	Season Summer–autumn

SPINDLE-SHANK

A clustered habit and deeply rooting stems, with twisted fibres along their length, are distinctive features of this species; a digging tool is necessary to get the entire stem out of the ground. The reddish brown cap varies in shape from convex to umbonate or irregular. The fox-brown stem, paler at the top, is very tough, with pale, fibrous flesh that is mild in taste and indistinct in smell.
• OCCURRENCE A weak parasite, it is found attached to buried roots, mainly of old oak trees, in parks and also ancient woodland. Fairly common and widespread in the oak regions of Europe.

convex, reddish brown cap often has dark spots and darkens when wet

surface of cap is smooth and greasy

adnexed, notched to slightly decurrent gills are toothed

SECTION

pale, fibrous flesh

long portion of stem in soil

fairly well-spaced, thick gills are cream with rust-brown spots

FRUITING In clusters on oak roots, rarely on beech.

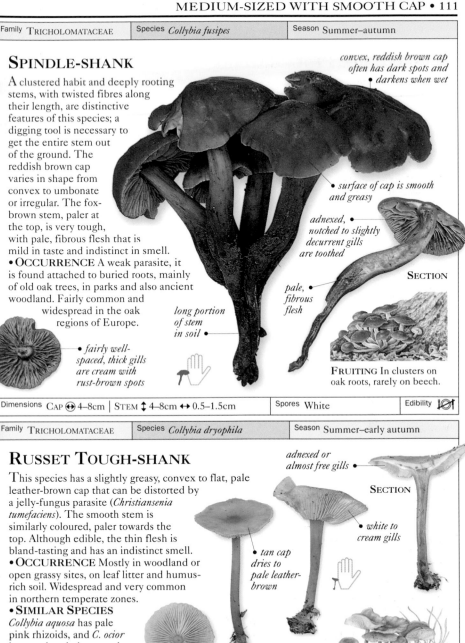

Dimensions CAP ⊕ 4–8cm	STEM ↕ 4–8cm ↔ 0.5–1.5cm	Spores White	Edibility

Family TRICHOLOMATACEAE	Species *Collybia dryophila*	Season Summer–early autumn

RUSSET TOUGH-SHANK

This species has a slightly greasy, convex to flat, pale leather-brown cap that can be distorted by a jelly-fungus parasite (*Christiansenia tumefaciens*). The smooth stem is similarly coloured, paler towards the top. Although edible, the thin flesh is bland-tasting and has an indistinct smell.
• OCCURRENCE Mostly in woodland or open grassy sites, on leaf litter and humus-rich soil. Widespread and very common in northern temperate zones.
• SIMILAR SPECIES
Collybia aquosa has pale pink rhizoids, and *C. ocior* has a rather dark cap and pale yellow gills. Both are mostly late spring to summer fruiting. *Marasmius oreades* (p.117) fruits in rings in grass.

adnexed or almost free gills

SECTION

white to cream gills

tan cap dries to pale leather-brown

crowded, fairly broad gills

stem base with white rhizoids

FRUITING In troops on leaf litter and humus.

Dimensions CAP ⊕ 2–6cm	STEM ↕ 3.5–7cm ↔ 3–5mm	Spores Cream	Edibility

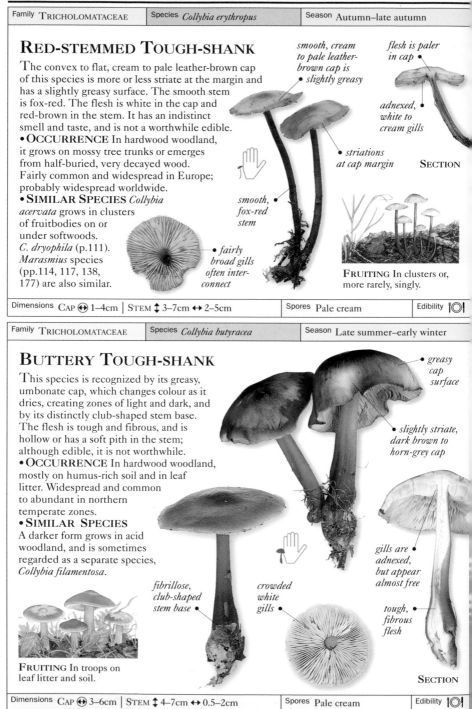

| Family TRICHOLOMATACEAE | Species *Collybia erythropus* | Season Autumn–late autumn |

RED-STEMMED TOUGH-SHANK

The convex to flat, cream to pale leather-brown cap of this species is more or less striate at the margin and has a slightly greasy surface. The smooth stem is fox-red. The flesh is white in the cap and red-brown in the stem. It has an indistinct smell and taste, and is not a worthwhile edible.
• **OCCURRENCE** In hardwood woodland, it grows on mossy tree trunks or emerges from half-buried, very decayed wood. Fairly common and widespread in Europe; probably widespread worldwide.
• **SIMILAR SPECIES** *Collybia acervata* grows in clusters of fruitbodies on or under softwoods. *C. dryophila* (p.111). *Marasmius* species (pp.114, 117, 138, 177) are also similar.

smooth, cream to pale leather-brown cap is slightly greasy

flesh is paler in cap

adnexed, white to cream gills

striations at cap margin

SECTION

smooth, fox-red stem

fairly broad gills often inter-connect

FRUITING In clusters or, more rarely, singly.

| Dimensions CAP ⊕ 1–4cm | STEM ↕ 3–7cm ↔ 2–5cm | Spores Pale cream | Edibility |

| Family TRICHOLOMATACEAE | Species *Collybia butyracea* | Season Late summer–early winter |

BUTTERY TOUGH-SHANK

This species is recognized by its greasy, umbonate cap, which changes colour as it dries, creating zones of light and dark, and by its distinctly club-shaped stem base. The flesh is tough and fibrous, and is hollow or has a soft pith in the stem; although edible, it is not worthwhile.
• **OCCURRENCE** In hardwood woodland, mostly on humus-rich soil and in leaf litter. Widespread and common to abundant in northern temperate zones.
• **SIMILAR SPECIES** A darker form grows in acid woodland, and is sometimes regarded as a separate species, *Collybia filamentosa*.

greasy cap surface

slightly striate, dark brown to horn-grey cap

gills are adnexed, but appear almost free

tough, fibrous flesh

fibrillose, club-shaped stem base

crowded white gills

SECTION

FRUITING In troops on leaf litter and soil.

| Dimensions CAP ⊕ 3–6cm | STEM ↕ 4–7cm ↔ 0.5–2cm | Spores Pale cream | Edibility |

| Family TRICHOLOMATACEAE | Species *Collybia confluens* | Season Autumn |

TUFTED TOUGH-SHANK

Producing dense tufts of
fruitbodies, this species has a
tall, slender stem clothed in
grey-white felt, and a rounded,
very pale greyish white cap,
smaller than those of most
Collybia species. It has a faint,
pleasantly aromatic smell and
taste but it is not considered worth
eating, as it has little flesh.
• OCCURRENCE In hard- and
softwood woodland, on thick leaf
litter; probably more common on
rich, fertile soil. Widespread in
northern temperate zones.
• SIMILAR SPECIES *C. acervata*
also grows in clusters, but
it has reddish colouring,
stems with felt on the
lower half only, and is
always associated with
softwood trees.

adnexed gills •

• *dry, smooth, very pale grey-white cap*

dense, grey-white felt on • *entire stem*

flesh is • *off-white to pale brown*

• *stem is dark brown on over-mature specimens*

SECTION

• *crowded, narrow, white to cream gills*

FRUITING In dense tufts, sometimes in fairy rings.

| Dimensions CAP ⊕ 1–3cm | STEM ↕ 5–9cm ↔ 3–7mm | Spores Pale cream | Edibility |

| Family TRICHOLOMATACEAE | Species *Collybia peronata* | Season Autumn–late autumn |

WOOD WOOLLY-FOOT

The leather-brown cap of this fungus is bell-shaped
to almost flat, and has radial but irregular, dark brown
streaks. Its main distinguishing features are its stem
and its taste: the pale yellow stem is covered with felty
yellow fibres at the base, becoming downy towards the
top, and the inedible, strongly acrid-tasting flesh is
white to sulphur-yellow, tough, and fibrous. Also
useful in identification are its fairly well-spaced gills.
• OCCURRENCE In soft- and hardwood woodland,
on leaf litter. Widespread in northern temperate zones;
very common in Europe, rare in North America.
• SIMILAR SPECIES Both *Collybia
alcalivirens* and *C. fuscopurpurea* have
darker caps and stem felt that is not
yellow. They both
have a mild taste.

fairly well-spaced, narrow, tough gills •

thick, felt-like covering on lower stem, which is often curved • *and foot-like*

adnexed • *or almost free, tan gills*

white to • *sulphur-yellow flesh*

FRUITING In troops or small
clusters of fruitbodies.

• *dry cap is leather-brown with darker streaks*

SECTION

| Dimensions CAP ⊕ 2.5–6cm | STEM ↕ 4–8cm ↔ 3–5mm | Spores Pale cream | Edibility |

Family TRICHOLOMATACEAE	Species *Marasmius alliaceus*	Season Late summer–autumn

WOOD GARLIC MUMMY-CAP

A pungent smell, reminiscent of rancid garlic, a fairly pale leather-brown cap, and an almost smooth black stem identify this large *Marasmius* species. The cap is convex or umbonate, and its surface may have darker striations, either at the margin, or rarely almost to the centre. They disappear with age. Despite the very rancid taste, some people use it as a garlic substitute in cooking.
• OCCURRENCE On buried branches or trunks in beech woodland. Widespread in the beech regions of Europe and adjacent parts of Asia.
• SIMILAR SPECIES *M. scorodonius* is smaller and paler but with a similar smell. It often occurs in grassland.

dark striations in pale leather-brown cap

adnexed gills

hollow stem

dry, smooth cap surface

nearly black stem is pale brown at top

SECTION

stem smooth to slightly downy

fairly crowded, off-white to tan gills

fibrillose stem base

FRUITING Solitary or in troops in beech woodland.

DWARF FORM

Dimensions CAP ⊕ 1.5–4cm │ STEM ↕ 7–15cm ↔ 3–6mm	Spores Off-white	Edibility 🍽

Family TRICHOLOMATACEAE	Species *Flammulina velutipes*	Season Late autumn–spring

VELVET-SHANK

The orange-brown cap and velvety, dark brown stem make this species easy to identify. It is one of the very few agarics that survive frosts. The gills are adnexed, crowded, and white to pale yellow. The thin, pale yellow flesh has a mild flavour; in Japan, it is cultivated for cooking.
• OCCURRENCE On living but sickly hardwood trees, especially willow or poplar; on weakened sites, such as where a branch has broken. More rarely found on softwoods. Widespread and rather common in northern temperate zones.
• SIMILAR SPECIES *Flammulina fennae* and *F. ononidis* are rarer and have different habitats.

tough, solid stem

velvety brown stem

SYZYGITES MEGALOCARPUS △
A grey-white species, parasitic on a range of agarics, including *Flammulina*. 🍽

smooth, orange-brown cap surface, greasy when wet

pale yellow cap margin

FRUITING In dense clumps of fruitbodies.

Dimensions CAP ⊕ 1–6cm │ STEM ↕ 2–7cm ↔ 0.3–1cm	Spores White	Edibility 🍽

Family HYDNANGIACEAE	Species *Laccaria amethystina*	Season Autumn

AMETHYST DECEIVER

When young, this very common species is easily identified by its amethyst colouring, combined with thick gills; the colouring fades with age, making older specimens difficult to distinguish from the redder *Laccaria* species. The dry, slightly felted cap has an inconspicuous navel and pale striations at the margin. Its well-spaced, thick gills are typical of the genus; microscopic examination reveals spiny spores (9.5µm in diameter). It is edible, without a strong taste or smell, but contains a high concentration of arsenic.

• **OCCURRENCE** Mycorrhizal with a range of trees, including beech and softwoods. Widespread and abundant to local in northern temperate zones.

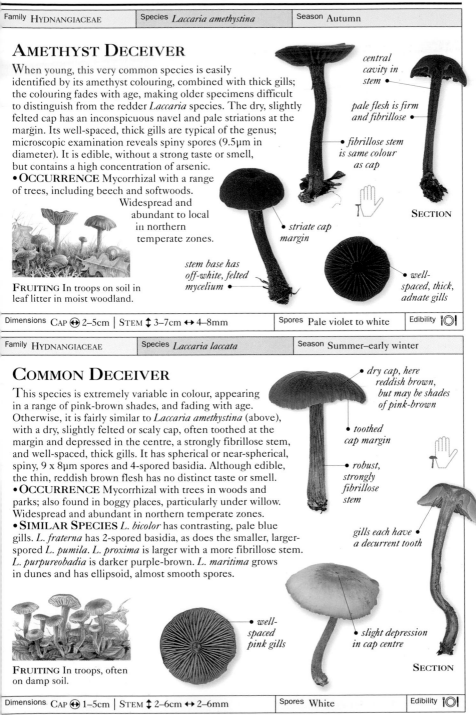

central cavity in stem

pale flesh is firm and fibrillose

fibrillose stem is same colour as cap

SECTION

striate cap margin

stem base has off-white, felted mycelium

well-spaced, thick, adnate gills

FRUITING In troops on soil in leaf litter in moist woodland.

Dimensions CAP ⊕ 2–5cm | STEM ↕ 3–7cm ↔ 4–8mm	Spores Pale violet to white	Edibility

Family HYDNANGIACEAE	Species *Laccaria laccata*	Season Summer–early winter

COMMON DECEIVER

This species is extremely variable in colour, appearing in a range of pink-brown shades, and fading with age. Otherwise, it is fairly similar to *Laccaria amethystina* (above), with a dry, slightly felted or scaly cap, often toothed at the margin and depressed in the centre, a strongly fibrillose stem, and well-spaced, thick gills. It has spherical or near-spherical, spiny, 9 x 8µm spores and 4-spored basidia. Although edible, the thin, reddish brown flesh has no distinct taste or smell.

• **OCCURRENCE** Mycorrhizal with trees in woods and parks; also found in boggy places, particularly under willow. Widespread and abundant in northern temperate zones.

• **SIMILAR SPECIES** *L. bicolor* has contrasting, pale blue gills. *L. fraterna* has 2-spored basidia, as does the smaller, larger-spored *L. pumila*. *L. proxima* is larger with a more fibrillose stem. *L. purpureobadia* is darker purple-brown. *L. maritima* grows in dunes and has ellipsoid, almost smooth spores.

dry cap, here reddish brown, but may be shades of pink-brown

toothed cap margin

robust, strongly fibrillose stem

gills each have a decurrent tooth

well-spaced pink gills

slight depression in cap centre

SECTION

FRUITING In troops, often on damp soil.

Dimensions CAP ⊕ 1–5cm | STEM ↕ 2–6cm ↔ 2–6mm	Spores White	Edibility

Family TRICHOLOMATACEAE	Species *Calocybe carnea*	Season Mid–late autumn

PINK FAIR-HEAD

This species is easily identified by its pink cap and stem, contrasting with its crowded, sinuate, notched white gills, although, favouring a grassland habitat, it can be difficult to spot. Indistinct in smell and taste, it is considered to be edible, but is so small that it is not really worth the effort.
• **OCCURRENCE** Grassland, including fertilized agricultural grassland, and lawns. Widespread in northern temperate zones; rather common.
• **SIMILAR SPECIES** *Calocybe persicolor*, possibly the same species, is said to be duller and to have a hairy stem base, often joined in clusters. *C. obscurissima* is even duller and grows on alkaline soil in woodland. *Entoloma rosea* is a brighter shade with a pink spore deposit.

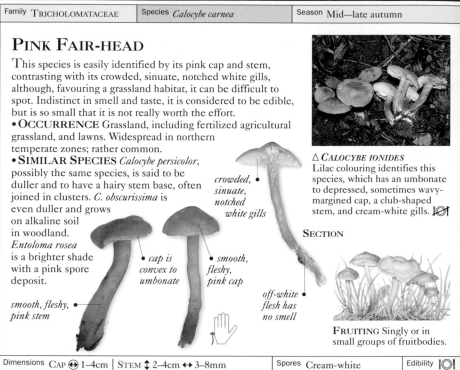

crowded, •
sinuate,
notched
white gills

△ **CALOCYBE IONIDES**
Lilac colouring identifies this species, which has an umbonate to depressed, sometimes wavy-margined cap, a club-shaped stem, and cream-white gills.

SECTION

• cap is
convex to
umbonate

• smooth,
fleshy,
pink cap

smooth, fleshy, •
pink stem

off-white •
flesh has
no smell

FRUITING Singly or in small groups of fruitbodies.

Dimensions CAP ⊕ 1–4cm | STEM ↕ 2–4cm ↔ 3–8mm	Spores Cream-white	Edibility

Family TRICHOLOMATACEAE	Species *Mycena galericulata*	Season Summer–early winter

COMMON BONNET

Two distinguishing features of this common but difficult to identify agaric are its unusual toughness in comparison with other *Mycena* species, and a noticeable tendency for the gills to take on a pale pink hue with age. The cap varies from bell-shaped to convex and may be yellow-brown or grey-brown. The similarly coloured stem is hollow but very tough and can be twisted without breaking. The flesh has a mealy, rancid smell, and a similar taste.
• **OCCURRENCE** In woodland on the trunks, stumps, and fallen branches of various types of hardwood trees. Widespread and common in northern temperate zones, extending south.

dry cap surface, •
greasy when wet

• bell-
shaped,
umbonate to
convex cap

extremely •
tough stem

tough, •
adnexed
gills, often
interveined
or forked

FRUITING Appears in tufts and troops of fruitbodies.

pale brown cap
often has furrows
and wrinkles •

• medium-spaced,
white to grey gills
age to pale pink

SECTION

Dimensions CAP ⊕ 1–6cm | STEM ↕ 3–8cm ↔ 2–7mm	Spores Pale cream	Edibility

Family TRICHOLOMATACEAE	Species *Marasmius oreades*	Season Early summer–mid-autumn

FAIRY RING CHAMPIGNON

Producing characteristic rings in turf, this species has a bell-shaped to convex cap, which becomes flatter with a broad umbo with age; it emerges tan and dries to pale leather-brown from the centre. The off-white to pale buff stem is tough and solid. It is pleasant tasting, with a smell reminiscent of bitter almonds, but see Similar Species before eating.
• **OCCURRENCE** In grassland, including lawns. Widespread and common in northern temperate zones.
• **SIMILAR SPECIES**
The poisonous *Clitocybe dealbata* (p.34) is found in the same grassland type habitat. It is distinguished by its decurrent gills.

cap surface dries to • pale leather-brown

adnexed or • almost free gills

creamy white • to leather-brown flesh

moist cap surface is tan •

SECTION

off-white stem • top is finely velvety or powdery

• well-spaced, cream to pale leather-brown gills

FRUITING Appears in fairy rings among grasses.

Dimensions CAP ⊕ 1–5cm | STEM ↕ 3–6cm ↔ 3–7mm	Spores Off-white	Edibility

Family TRICHOLOMATACEAE	Species *Oudemansiella radicata*	Season Summer–late autumn

ROOTING SHANK

This species has an umbonate to flattened, greasy, grey- to yellow-brown cap and a twisted, furrowed stem, which is white at the top, brown towards the base. The stem extends 5–15cm into the soil and the buried woody substrate, with the same amount above ground. This, and some more velvety species, all lacking stem rings, are sometimes placed in the genus *Xerula*.
• **OCCURRENCE** In parks and woods, by trees and stumps. Widespread in northern temperate zones; common in some regions; world distribution unclear.
• **SIMILAR SPECIES** *Oudemansiella pudens* and *O. caussei* have dry caps and strongly velvety stems.

adnate gills, each with a decurrent tooth •

• greasy, veined cap surface

• pale grey-brown stem, with white upper part

tough, • off-white flesh

medium-spaced, pale cream gills, often • with brown edges

twisted, • furrowed stem

SECTION

FRUITING Appears singly or in scattered groups.

Dimensions CAP ⊕ 3–10cm | STEM ↕ 5–15cm ↔ 0.5–1cm	Spores Pale cream	Edibility

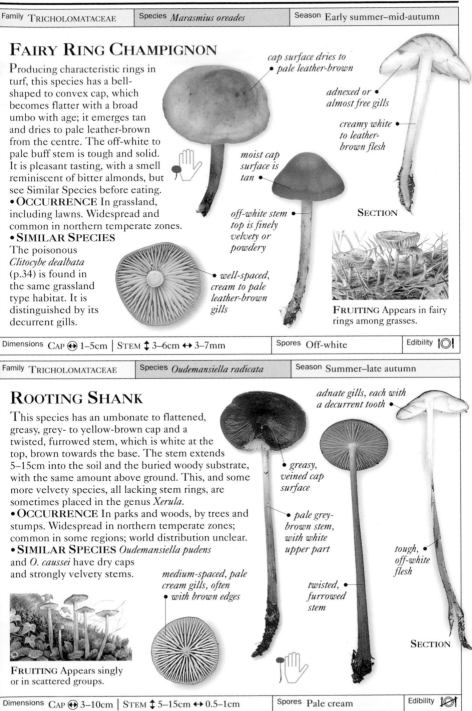

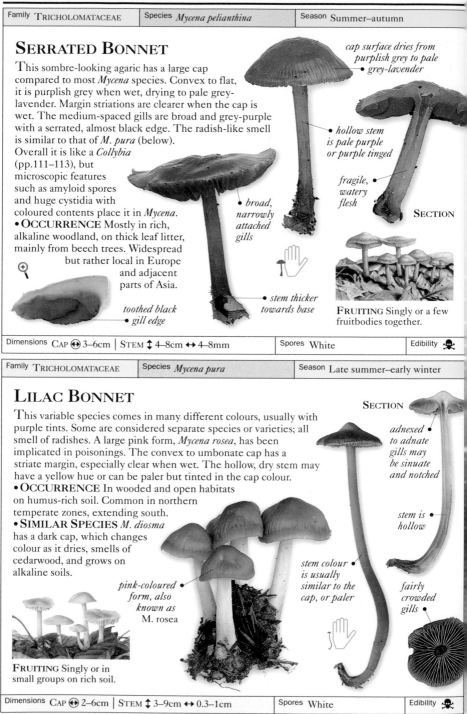

Family TRICHOLOMATACEAE	Species *Mycena pelianthina*	Season Summer–autumn

SERRATED BONNET

This sombre-looking agaric has a large cap compared to most *Mycena* species. Convex to flat, it is purplish grey when wet, drying to pale grey-lavender. Margin striations are clearer when the cap is wet. The medium-spaced gills are broad and grey-purple with a serrated, almost black edge. The radish-like smell is similar to that of *M. pura* (below). Overall it is like a *Collybia* (pp.111–113), but microscopic features such as amyloid spores and huge cystidia with coloured contents place it in *Mycena*.

• **OCCURRENCE** Mostly in rich, alkaline woodland, on thick leaf litter, mainly from beech trees. Widespread but rather local in Europe and adjacent parts of Asia.

cap surface dries from purplish grey to pale grey-lavender

hollow stem is pale purple or purple tinged

fragile, watery flesh

SECTION

broad, narrowly attached gills

toothed black gill edge

stem thicker towards base

FRUITING Singly or a few fruitbodies together.

Dimensions CAP ⊕ 3–6cm │ STEM ↕ 4–8cm ↔ 4–8mm	Spores White	Edibility ☠

Family TRICHOLOMATACEAE	Species *Mycena pura*	Season Late summer–early winter

LILAC BONNET

This variable species comes in many different colours, usually with purple tints. Some are considered separate species or varieties; all smell of radishes. A large pink form, *Mycena rosea*, has been implicated in poisonings. The convex to umbonate cap has a striate margin, especially clear when wet. The hollow, dry stem may have a yellow hue or can be paler but tinted in the cap colour.

• **OCCURRENCE** In wooded and open habitats on humus-rich soil. Common in northern temperate zones, extending south.

• **SIMILAR SPECIES** *M. diosma* has a dark cap, which changes colour as it dries, smells of cedarwood, and grows on alkaline soils.

SECTION

adnexed to adnate gills may be sinuate and notched

stem is hollow

pink-coloured form, also known as M. rosea

stem colour is usually similar to the cap, or paler

fairly crowded gills

FRUITING Singly or in small groups on rich soil.

Dimensions CAP ⊕ 2–6cm │ STEM ↕ 3–9cm ↔ 0.3–1cm	Spores White	Edibility ☠

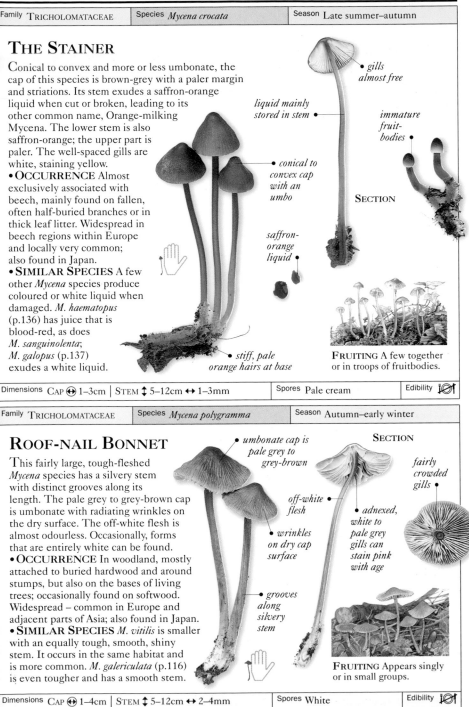

Family TRICHOLOMATACEAE	Species *Mycena crocata*	Season Late summer–autumn

THE STAINER

Conical to convex and more or less umbonate, the cap of this species is brown-grey with a paler margin and striations. Its stem exudes a saffron-orange liquid when cut or broken, leading to its other common name, Orange-milking Mycena. The lower stem is also saffron-orange; the upper part is paler. The well-spaced gills are white, staining yellow.

• **OCCURRENCE** Almost exclusively associated with beech, mainly found on fallen, often half-buried branches or in thick leaf litter. Widespread in beech regions within Europe and locally very common; also found in Japan.

• **SIMILAR SPECIES** A few other *Mycena* species produce coloured or white liquid when damaged. *M. haematopus* (p.136) has juice that is blood-red, as does *M. sanguinolenta*; *M. galopus* (p.137) exudes a white liquid.

gills almost free

liquid mainly stored in stem

immature fruit-bodies

conical to convex cap with an umbo

SECTION

saffron-orange liquid

stiff, pale orange hairs at base

FRUITING A few together or in troops of fruitbodies.

Dimensions CAP ⊕ 1–3cm | STEM ↕ 5–12cm ↔ 1–3mm	Spores Pale cream	Edibility

Family TRICHOLOMATACEAE	Species *Mycena polygramma*	Season Autumn–early winter

ROOF-NAIL BONNET

This fairly large, tough-fleshed *Mycena* species has a silvery stem with distinct grooves along its length. The pale grey to grey-brown cap is umbonate with radiating wrinkles on the dry surface. The off-white flesh is almost odourless. Occasionally, forms that are entirely white can be found.

• **OCCURRENCE** In woodland, mostly attached to buried hardwood and around stumps, but also on the bases of living trees; occasionally found on softwood. Widespread – common in Europe and adjacent parts of Asia; also found in Japan.

• **SIMILAR SPECIES** *M. vitilis* is smaller with an equally tough, smooth, shiny stem. It occurs in the same habitat and is more common. *M. galericulata* (p.116) is even tougher and has a smooth stem.

umbonate cap is pale grey to grey-brown

SECTION

fairly crowded gills

off-white flesh

adnexed, white to pale grey gills can stain pink with age

wrinkles on dry cap surface

grooves along silvery stem

FRUITING Appears singly or in small groups.

Dimensions CAP ⊕ 1–4cm | STEM ↕ 5–12cm ↔ 2–4mm	Spores White	Edibility

WITH CRUMBLY FLESH

THE SPECIES FEATURED in this subsection all belong to the genus *Russula*, and all have adnexed to adnate gills and crumbly flesh. The crumbly flesh is created by round tissue cells that are grouped in "nests" in the flesh. Russules are very similar in appearance to the milk-caps (*Lactarius*, pp.43–55), which also have flesh that is crumbly. However, milk-caps exude a milk-like liquid when cut and tend to have decurrent gills. Most *Russula* species have brighter-coloured fruitbodies than those of the milk-caps.

All *Russula* species form mycorrhizal relationships (see pp.18–19) with trees or, in a few cases, with shrubs and herbaceous plants. As a rule, mild-tasting russules are edible, while those that taste hot are considered poisonous.

Family RUSSULACEAE	Species *Russula delica*	Season Summer–autumn

MILK-WHITE RUSSULE

This is a large species, with a funnel-shaped cap, stout stem, and firm white flesh. Soil and leaf litter often stick to it, hiding its creamy white colouring. The gills are white and may have a turquoise sheen; they are usually quite well spaced.
• **OCCURRENCE** Mycorrhizal with hard- and softwood trees on well-drained soil. Reaching the tree line in alpine areas, it is widespread and common in many parts of northern temperate zones.
• **SIMILAR SPECIES** *Russula chloroides* has more crowded gills, often with a stronger turquoise sheen and often also a turquoise zone around the stem top. *Lactarius vellereus* (p.44) is usually larger with a felted cap surface and white milk.

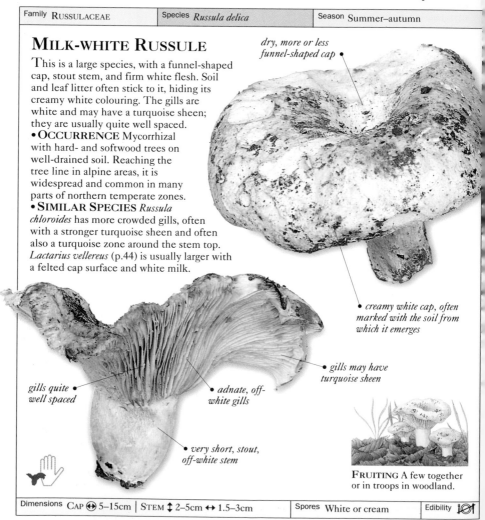

dry, more or less funnel-shaped cap

• *creamy white cap, often marked with the soil from which it emerges*

• *gills may have turquoise sheen*

gills quite well spaced •

• *adnate, off-white gills*

• *very short, stout, off-white stem*

FRUITING A few together or in troops in woodland.

Dimensions CAP ⊕ 5–15cm │ STEM ↕ 2–5cm ↔ 1.5–3cm	Spores White or cream	Edibility

| Family RUSSULACEAE | Species *Russula foetens* | Season Summer–autumn |

FOETID RUSSULE

This rancid-smelling species has a fleshy, convex, orange-brown cap that is greasy to the touch and has a grooved margin. Its white stem, stained brown at the base, is short and almost barrel-shaped. The crumbly, very hot-tasting flesh is off-white and may be stained brown.

• **OCCURRENCE** Mycorrhizal with both soft- and hardwood trees in woodland. Widespread and common in many areas of northern temperate zones.

• **SIMILAR SPECIES** *Russula laurocerasi* smells of bitter almonds. *R. illota* has a rancid, slightly almondy smell and dark gill edges. The flesh of *R. subfoetens* stains yellow with potassium hydroxide (KOH). (*R. foetens* has no reaction.)

surface of cap is greasy, particularly in wet weather

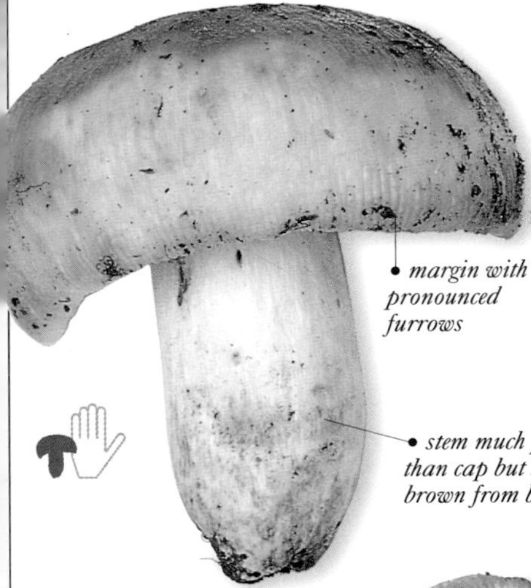

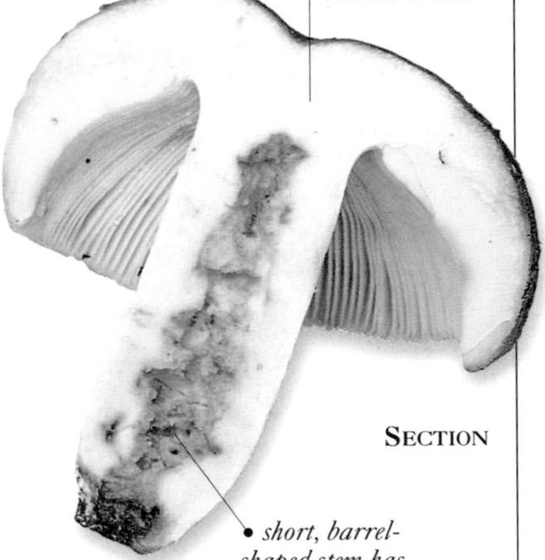

flesh off-white or stained brown

margin with pronounced furrows

stem much paler than cap but stains brown from base

SECTION

fragile, adnexed, white to cream gills, often stained brown

short, barrel-shaped stem has chambers within

crowded gills

FRUITING Singly or in troops in woodland sites.

| Dimensions CAP ⊕ 8–15cm | STEM ↕ 6–12cm ↔ 1.5–3cm | Spores Cream | Edibility |

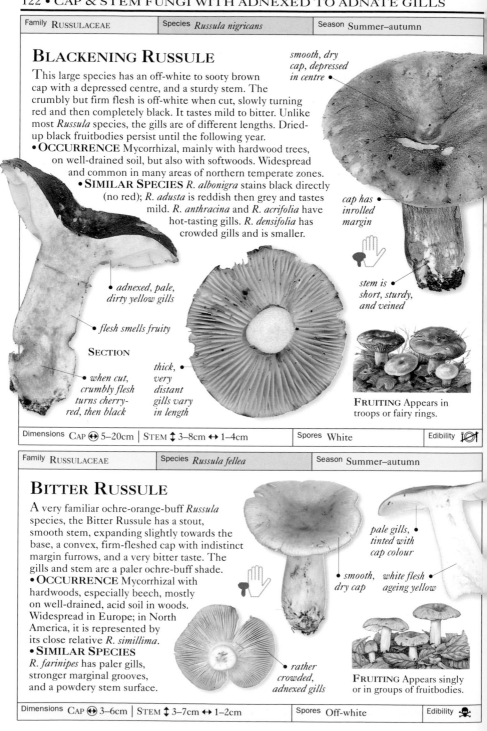

Family RUSSULACEAE	Species *Russula nigricans*	Season Summer–autumn

BLACKENING RUSSULE

This large species has an off-white to sooty brown cap with a depressed centre, and a sturdy stem. The crumbly but firm flesh is off-white when cut, slowly turning red and then completely black. It tastes mild to bitter. Unlike most *Russula* species, the gills are of different lengths. Dried-up black fruitbodies persist until the following year.

• **OCCURRENCE** Mycorrhizal, mainly with hardwood trees, on well-drained soil, but also with softwoods. Widespread and common in many areas of northern temperate zones.

• **SIMILAR SPECIES** *R. albonigra* stains black directly (no red); *R. adusta* is reddish then grey and tastes mild. *R. anthracina* and *R. acrifolia* have hot-tasting gills. *R. densifolia* has crowded gills and is smaller.

smooth, dry cap, depressed in centre •

cap has • inrolled margin

stem is • short, sturdy, and veined

• adnexed, pale, dirty yellow gills

• flesh smells fruity

SECTION

• when cut, crumbly flesh turns cherry-red, then black

thick, very distant gills vary in length

FRUITING Appears in troops or fairy rings.

Dimensions CAP ⊕ 5–20cm	STEM ↕ 3–8cm ↔ 1–4cm	Spores White	Edibility

Family RUSSULACEAE	Species *Russula fellea*	Season Summer–autumn

BITTER RUSSULE

A very familiar ochre-orange-buff *Russula* species, the Bitter Russule has a stout, smooth stem, expanding slightly towards the base, a convex, firm-fleshed cap with indistinct margin furrows, and a very bitter taste. The gills and stem are a paler ochre-buff shade.

• **OCCURRENCE** Mycorrhizal with hardwoods, especially beech, mostly on well-drained, acid soil in woods. Widespread in Europe; in North America, it is represented by its close relative *R. simillima*.

• **SIMILAR SPECIES** *R. farinipes* has paler gills, stronger marginal grooves, and a powdery stem surface.

pale gills, • tinted with cap colour

• smooth, dry cap

white flesh • ageing yellow

• rather crowded, adnexed gills

FRUITING Appears singly or in groups of fruitbodies.

Dimensions CAP ⊕ 3–6cm	STEM ↕ 3–7cm ↔ 1–2cm	Spores Off-white	Edibility ☠

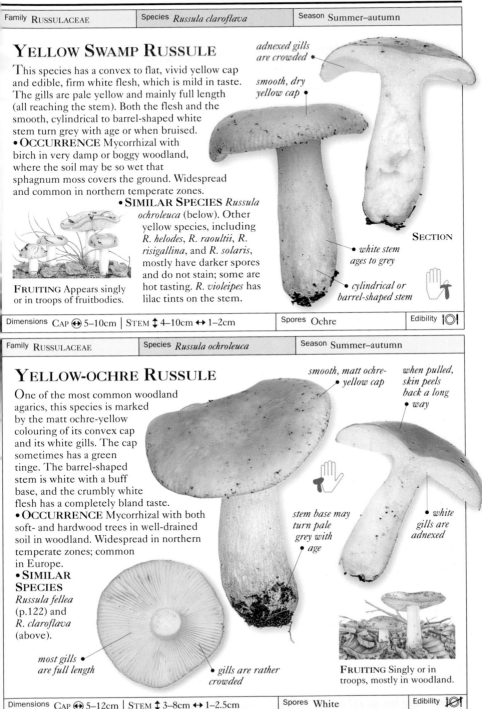

| Family RUSSULACEAE | Species *Russula claroflava* | Season Summer–autumn |

YELLOW SWAMP RUSSULE

This species has a convex to flat, vivid yellow cap and edible, firm white flesh, which is mild in taste. The gills are pale yellow and mainly full length (all reaching the stem). Both the flesh and the smooth, cylindrical to barrel-shaped white stem turn grey with age or when bruised.
• **OCCURRENCE** Mycorrhizal with birch in very damp or boggy woodland, where the soil may be so wet that sphagnum moss covers the ground. Widespread and common in northern temperate zones.
• **SIMILAR SPECIES** *Russula ochroleuca* (below). Other yellow species, including *R. helodes, R. raoultii, R. risigallina,* and *R. solaris,* mostly have darker spores and do not stain; some are hot tasting. *R. violeipes* has lilac tints on the stem.

adnexed gills are crowded

smooth, dry yellow cap

SECTION

white stem ages to grey

cylindrical or barrel-shaped stem

FRUITING Appears singly or in troops of fruitbodies.

| Dimensions CAP ⊕ 5–10cm | STEM ↕ 4–10cm ↔ 1–2cm | Spores Ochre | Edibility |

| Family RUSSULACEAE | Species *Russula ochroleuca* | Season Summer–autumn |

YELLOW-OCHRE RUSSULE

One of the most common woodland agarics, this species is marked by the matt ochre-yellow colouring of its convex cap and its white gills. The cap sometimes has a green tinge. The barrel-shaped stem is white with a buff base, and the crumbly white flesh has a completely bland taste.
• **OCCURRENCE** Mycorrhizal with both soft- and hardwood trees in well-drained soil in woodland. Widespread in northern temperate zones; common in Europe.
• **SIMILAR SPECIES** *Russula fellea* (p.122) and *R. claroflava* (above).

smooth, matt ochre-yellow cap

when pulled, skin peels back a long way

stem base may turn pale grey with age

white gills are adnexed

most gills are full length

gills are rather crowded

FRUITING Singly or in troops, mostly in woodland.

| Dimensions CAP ⊕ 5–12cm | STEM ↕ 3–8cm ↔ 1–2.5cm | Spores White | Edibility |

| Family RUSSULACEAE | Species *Russula cyanoxantha* | Season Summer–autumn |

CHARCOAL BURNER

This large species has a convex to flat or depressed, green to wine-red cap, off-white gills, and a chunky, off-white stem. The flesh is firm though brittle and, unlike many other *Russula* species, the gills are not crumbly, but feel oily to the touch. It is a highly valued edible and can be eaten raw.

• **OCCURRENCE**
Mycorrhizal with hardwoods, especially beech trees, but also with softwoods; it prefers acid soil. Widespread and common in parts of northern temperate zones.

• **SIMILAR SPECIES**
Russula integra and *R. vinosa* (see insets, below).

cap may be green to wine-red, or a • mixture of both

cap is smooth and slightly greasy •

• chunky stem is off-white

• crowded, adnexed, off-white gills

gills • are pliable and feel oily

SECTION

• firm but brittle flesh is pleasant tasting and can be eaten raw

FRUITING Singly or in troops in well-drained woodland.

△ **RUSSULA VINOSA**
This species, found with pine, has a variably brown-spotted, wine-red cap. The pleasant-tasting flesh and the white stem turn grey when cut or with age. The crowded, adnexed gills are cream, tinged grey with age. |⊙|

△ **RUSSULA INTEGRA**
Distinguished by a yellow-buff spore deposit, this softwood species varies in colour. It has thick, well-spaced, almost free gills. The stem is white, ageing brown spotted. The firm white flesh tastes of almonds. |⊙|

| Dimensions CAP ⊕ 5–15cm | STEM ↕ 5–10cm ↔ 1–3cm | Spores White | Edibility |⊙| |

Family RUSSULACEAE	Species *Russula vesca*	Season Summer–autumn

BARE-TOOTHED RUSSULE

This distinctive species owes its common name to the white gills that are clearly visible at the cap margin. The flattened-convex to depressed cap is pale wine-red, mixed with brown, and rust-brown spots mark the pointed, off-white stem. The edible, firm white flesh has a nutty taste. It can be eaten raw.

• OCCURRENCE Mycorrhizal with soft- and hardwood trees in well-drained woodland. Widespread in northern temperate zones; common in Europe.

wine-red or brown wine-red cap, sometimes paler

almost all gills reach stem

firm white flesh • SECTION

exposed gills at margin

gills are white, brittle, and fairly crowded

rust-brown spots at stem base

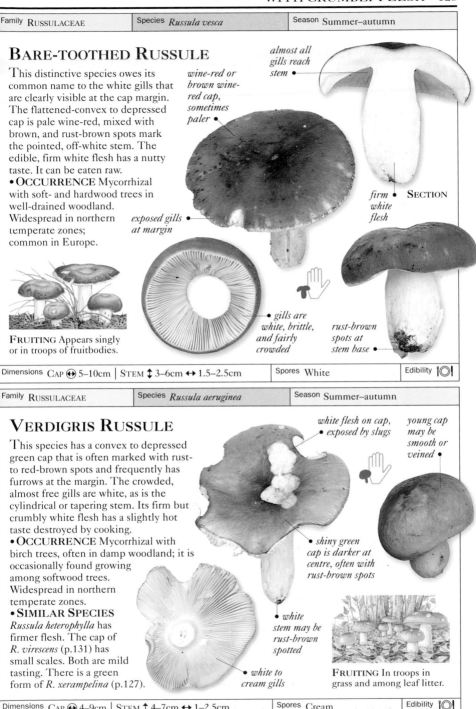

FRUITING Appears singly or in troops of fruitbodies.

Dimensions CAP ⊕ 5–10cm	STEM ↕ 3–6cm ↔ 1.5–2.5cm	Spores White	Edibility

Family RUSSULACEAE	Species *Russula aeruginea*	Season Summer–autumn

VERDIGRIS RUSSULE

This species has a convex to depressed green cap that is often marked with rust- to red-brown spots and frequently has furrows at the margin. The crowded, almost free gills are white, as is the cylindrical or tapering stem. Its firm but crumbly white flesh has a slightly hot taste destroyed by cooking.

• OCCURRENCE Mycorrhizal with birch trees, often in damp woodland; it is occasionally found growing among softwood trees. Widespread in northern temperate zones.

• SIMILAR SPECIES *Russula heterophylla* has firmer flesh. The cap of *R. virescens* (p.131) has small scales. Both are mild tasting. There is a green form of *R. xerampelina* (p.127).

white flesh on cap, exposed by slugs

young cap may be smooth or veined

shiny green cap is darker at centre, often with rust-brown spots

white stem may be rust-brown spotted

white to cream gills

FRUITING In troops in grass and among leaf litter.

Dimensions CAP ⊕ 4–9cm	STEM ↕ 4–7cm ↔ 1–2.5cm	Spores Cream	Edibility

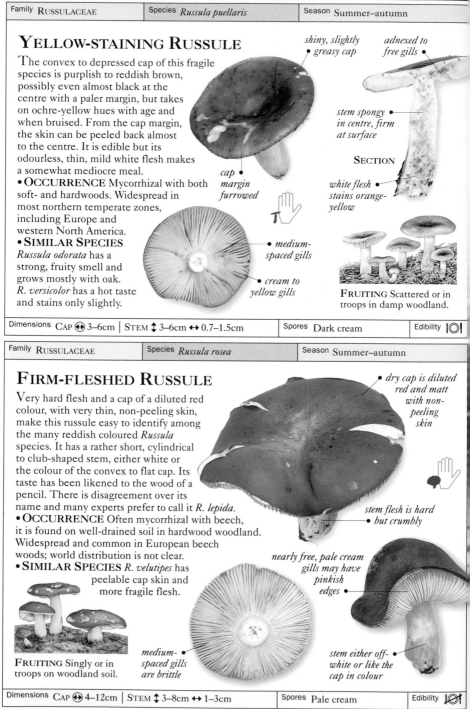

Family RUSSULACEAE	Species *Russula puellaris*	Season Summer–autumn

YELLOW-STAINING RUSSULE

The convex to depressed cap of this fragile species is purplish to reddish brown, possibly even almost black at the centre with a paler margin, but takes on ochre-yellow hues with age and when bruised. From the cap margin, the skin can be peeled back almost to the centre. It is edible but its odourless, thin, mild white flesh makes a somewhat mediocre meal.

• OCCURRENCE Mycorrhizal with both soft- and hardwoods. Widespread in most northern temperate zones, including Europe and western North America.

• SIMILAR SPECIES *Russula odorata* has a strong, fruity smell and grows mostly with oak. *R. versicolor* has a hot taste and stains only slightly.

shiny, slightly greasy cap

adnexed to free gills •

stem spongy in centre, firm at surface

SECTION

cap margin furrowed

white flesh stains orange-yellow

• medium-spaced gills

• cream to yellow gills

FRUITING Scattered or in troops in damp woodland.

Dimensions CAP ⊕ 3–6cm	STEM ↕ 3–6cm ↔ 0.7–1.5cm	Spores Dark cream	Edibility

Family RUSSULACEAE	Species *Russula rosea*	Season Summer–autumn

FIRM-FLESHED RUSSULE

Very hard flesh and a cap of a diluted red colour, with very thin, non-peeling skin, make this russule easy to identify among the many reddish coloured *Russula* species. It has a rather short, cylindrical to club-shaped stem, either white or the colour of the convex to flat cap. Its taste has been likened to the wood of a pencil. There is disagreement over its name and many experts prefer to call it *R. lepida*.

• OCCURRENCE Often mycorrhizal with beech, it is found on well-drained soil in hardwood woodland. Widespread and common in European beech woods; world distribution is not clear.

• SIMILAR SPECIES *R. velutipes* has peelable cap skin and more fragile flesh.

• dry cap is diluted red and matt with non-peeling skin

stem flesh is hard • but crumbly

nearly free, pale cream gills may have pinkish edges •

FRUITING Singly or in troops on woodland soil.

medium-spaced gills are brittle

stem either off-white or like the cap in colour

Dimensions CAP ⊕ 4–12cm	STEM ↕ 3–8cm ↔ 1–3cm	Spores Pale cream	Edibility

Family RUSSULACEAE	Species *Russula turci*	Season Summer–autumn

IODOFORM-SCENTED RUSSULE

This species has a cap with a depressed centre and a smooth margin, which may have a fine dust-like coating. It is coloured in shades of wine-red, sometimes mixed with green, black, or orange. A distinct smell of iodoform, especially at the base of the club-shaped stem, along with a pale ochre spore deposit, helps to identify it. The crumbly white flesh has a mild taste.

• OCCURRENCE Mycorrhizal with pine trees (mainly two-needled species) and possibly also with spruce. Widespread in Europe and also found across northern North America.

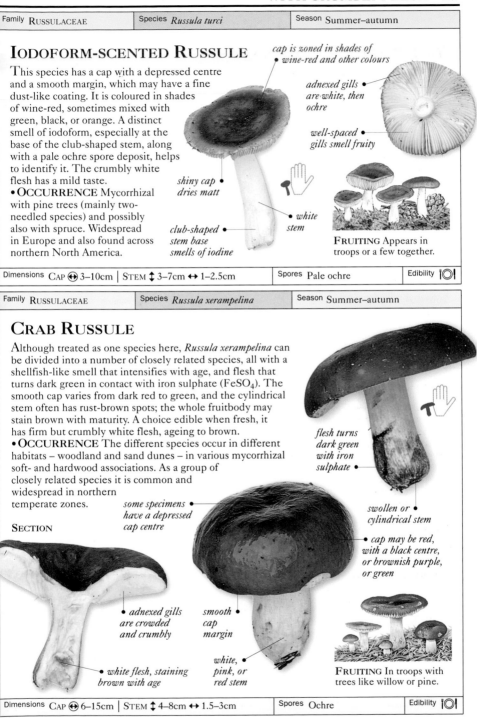

cap is zoned in shades of wine-red and other colours

adnexed gills are white, then ochre

well-spaced gills smell fruity

shiny cap dries matt

club-shaped stem base smells of iodine

white stem

FRUITING Appears in troops or a few together.

| Dimensions CAP ⊕ 3–10cm | STEM ↕ 3–7cm ↔ 1–2.5cm | Spores Pale ochre | Edibility |

Family RUSSULACEAE	Species *Russula xerampelina*	Season Summer–autumn

CRAB RUSSULE

Although treated as one species here, *Russula xerampelina* can be divided into a number of closely related species, all with a shellfish-like smell that intensifies with age, and flesh that turns dark green in contact with iron sulphate ($FeSO_4$). The smooth cap varies from dark red to green, and the cylindrical stem often has rust-brown spots; the whole fruitbody may stain brown with maturity. A choice edible when fresh, it has firm but crumbly white flesh, ageing to brown.

• OCCURRENCE The different species occur in different habitats – woodland and sand dunes – in various mycorrhizal soft- and hardwood associations. As a group of closely related species it is common and widespread in northern temperate zones.

SECTION

flesh turns dark green with iron sulphate

swollen or cylindrical stem

cap may be red, with a black centre, or brownish purple, or green

some specimens have a depressed cap centre

smooth cap margin

adnexed gills are crowded and crumbly

white flesh, staining brown with age

white, pink, or red stem

FRUITING In troops with trees like willow or pine.

| Dimensions CAP ⊕ 6–15cm | STEM ↕ 4–8cm ↔ 1.5–3cm | Spores Ochre | Edibility |

| Family RUSSULACEAE | Species *Russula paludosa* | Season Summer–autumn |

TALL RUSSULE

Taller than most, this large, attractive *Russula* species has a convex to depressed, orange-red cap, with yellow discoloration in the centre and a slightly sticky surface when damp. The crowded, adnexed gills are pale golden yellow. Both the gill edges and the cap margin are often red. The cylindrical to narrowly club-shaped stem is white, flushed pink, and turns slightly grey with age. It is good to eat, with firm, crumbly, mild-tasting flesh, but see Similar Species.
• **OCCURRENCE** Mycorrhizal with softwoods, especially pine. Widespread and locally common in northern temperate zones.
• **SIMILAR SPECIES** The poisonous and hot-tasting *R. emetica* (below) has no yellow colouring on the cap.

cap surface is slightly sticky when wet

crowded, pale golden yellow gills

cap discolors to yellow in centre

cap margin may be red

white stem is flushed pink, grey with age

FRUITING Appears in troops, or fruitbodies are scattered, typically on sandy soil.

| Dimensions CAP ⊕ 8–16cm | STEM ↕ 10–15cm ↔ 1–3cm | Spores Pale ochre | Edibility |

| Family RUSSULACEAE | Species *Russula emetica* | Season Summer–autumn |

THE SICKENER

This species has a convex to slightly depressed, scarlet-red cap, the surface of which is smooth and often shiny, becoming sticky when wet. Its white stem is club-shaped with a scurfy skin. The crumbly, odourless white flesh has a very hot taste, which soon alerts an unwary eater, but in any case it is not highly poisonous.
• **OCCURRENCE** Mycorrhizal, mainly with softwood trees in damp sites. Widespread and common in northern temperate zones.
• **SIMILAR SPECIES** *Russula betularum* is smaller, ages to white, and occurs in bogs under birch trees. *R. fageticola* usually grows under beech trees and also tastes hot. *Amanita muscaria* (p.146) has veil patches on the cap, and a stem ring and bulb.

convex to slightly depressed, smooth and often shiny, scarlet-red cap

slightly scurfy, club-shaped stem

faintly furrowed margin

medium-spaced gills

adnexed to free, white to pale cream gills

FRUITING In troops or singly in damp sites under softwoods.

| Dimensions CAP ⊕ 3–8cm | STEM ↕ 5–8cm ↔ 1–2cm | Spores White | Edibility ☠ |

| Family RUSSULACEAE | Species *Russula mairei* | Season Summer–autumn |

BEECHWOOD SICKENER

The smooth, matt, strongly scarlet-red cap of this species is convex to flat, and is sticky when wet. The slightly club-shaped, off-white stem has a smooth surface. Its crumbly flesh is firm and white and smells slightly of coconut or honey.
• OCCURRENCE Mycorrhizal with beech trees in woodland areas. Widespread and common in the beechwood regions of Europe and adjacent parts of Asia.
• SIMILAR SPECIES *Russula emetica* (p.128). *R. velenovskyi*, which is edible, is smaller, and typically occurs near birch.

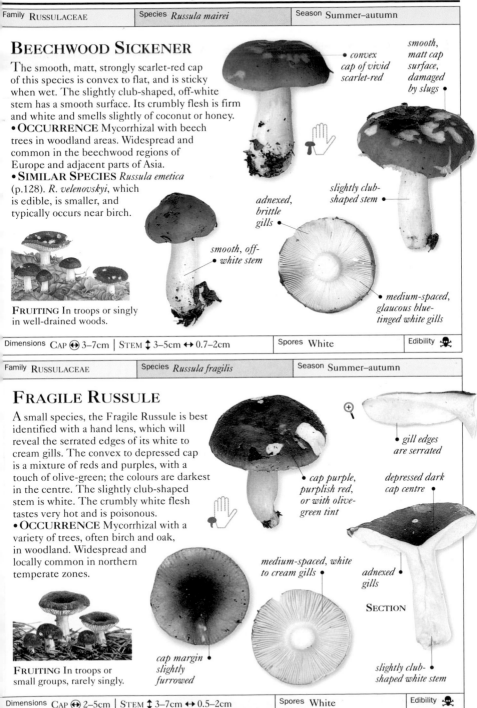

convex cap of vivid scarlet-red

smooth, matt cap surface, damaged by slugs

slightly club-shaped stem

adnexed, brittle gills

smooth, off-white stem

medium-spaced, glaucous blue-tinged white gills

FRUITING In troops or singly in well-drained woods.

| Dimensions CAP ⊕ 3–7cm | STEM ↕ 3–5cm ↔ 0.7–2cm | Spores White | Edibility ☠ |

| Family RUSSULACEAE | Species *Russula fragilis* | Season Summer–autumn |

FRAGILE RUSSULE

A small species, the Fragile Russule is best identified with a hand lens, which will reveal the serrated edges of its white to cream gills. The convex to depressed cap is a mixture of reds and purples, with a touch of olive-green; the colours are darkest in the centre. The slightly club-shaped stem is white. The crumbly white flesh tastes very hot and is poisonous.
• OCCURRENCE Mycorrhizal with a variety of trees, often birch and oak, in woodland. Widespread and locally common in northern temperate zones.

gill edges are serrated

cap purple, purplish red, or with olive-green tint

depressed dark cap centre

medium-spaced, white to cream gills

adnexed gills

SECTION

FRUITING In troops or small groups, rarely singly.

cap margin slightly furrowed

slightly club-shaped white stem

| Dimensions CAP ⊕ 2–5cm | STEM ↕ 3–7cm ↔ 0.5–2cm | Spores White | Edibility ☠ |

Family RUSSULACEAE	Species *Russula sanguinaria*	Season Summer–autumn

BLOOD-RED RUSSULE

This slightly poisonous species has a convex to depressed, blood-red cap and a red-streaked stem that turns greyish pink with age. It has crumbly white flesh and can be identified by its moderately hot taste and the pale ochre colour of its spore deposit.

• OCCURRENCE Mycorrhizal with softwood trees, mostly pine. Widespread in northern temperate zones.

• SIMILAR SPECIES *Russula helodes* has a lighter stem that turns a more distinct grey with age; tends to be found in sphagnum moss.

gills may be slightly decurrent

cap with thin, blood-red skin

cylindrical to tapering stem

SECTION

crumbly white flesh

crowded gills

stem is streaked blood-red, and ages to greyish pink

fragile, cream to ochre gills

FRUITING Appears singly or in troops on acid soil.

Dimensions CAP ⊕ 5–10cm	STEM ↕ 4–7cm ↔ 1–2cm	Spores Pale ochre	Edibility ☠

Family RUSSULACEAE	Species *Russula undulata*	Season Summer–autumn

BLACKISH-PURPLE RUSSULE

This rather fleshy species has a convex cap, the usually depressed centre of which is almost black; the rest of the cap surface is purple or violet, often spotted yellow. The cap colour contrasts strongly with the white to cream stem and gills. The stem is fairly short and club-shaped, and the gills are crowded and adnexed. The white to grey flesh is slightly hot tasting and inedible.

• OCCURRENCE Mycorrhizal with oak trees, rarely found with other trees. Widespread in northern temperate zones.

• SIMILAR SPECIES *Russula brunneoviolacea* has a darker spore deposit, as does *R. romellii*.

centre of cap is almost black

purple or violet cap may have yellow spots

short, white to cream stem

adnexed gills are white to cream and crowded

FRUITING In troops beneath oak trees, mostly on acid soil, in woodland sites.

Dimensions CAP ⊕ 4–10cm	STEM ↕ 3–6cm ↔ 1–2.5cm	Spores White	Edibility 🍴

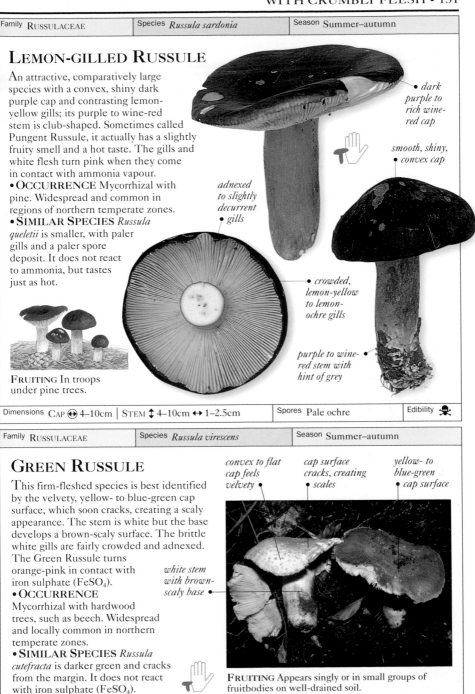

Family RUSSULACEAE	Species *Russula sardonia*	Season Summer–autumn

LEMON-GILLED RUSSULE

An attractive, comparatively large
species with a convex, shiny dark
purple cap and contrasting lemon-
yellow gills; its purple to wine-red
stem is club-shaped. Sometimes called
Pungent Russule, it actually has a slightly
fruity smell and a hot taste. The gills and
white flesh turn pink when they come
in contact with ammonia vapour.
•**OCCURRENCE** Mycorrhizal with
pine. Widespread and common in
regions of northern temperate zones.
•**SIMILAR SPECIES** *Russula
queletii* is smaller, with paler
gills and a paler spore
deposit. It does not react
to ammonia, but tastes
just as hot.

FRUITING In troops
under pine trees.

*dark
purple to
rich wine-
red cap*

*smooth, shiny,
convex cap*

*adnexed
to slightly
decurrent
gills*

*crowded,
lemon-yellow
to lemon-
ochre gills*

*purple to wine-
red stem with
hint of grey*

Dimensions CAP ⊕ 4–10cm | STEM ↕ 4–10cm ↔ 1–2.5cm	Spores Pale ochre	Edibility ☠

Family RUSSULACEAE	Species *Russula virescens*	Season Summer–autumn

GREEN RUSSULE

This firm-fleshed species is best identified
by the velvety, yellow- to blue-green cap
surface, which soon cracks, creating a scaly
appearance. The stem is white but the base
develops a brown-scaly surface. The brittle
white gills are fairly crowded and adnexed.
The Green Russule turns
orange-pink in contact with
iron sulphate ($FeSO_4$).
•**OCCURRENCE**
Mycorrhizal with hardwood
trees, such as beech. Widespread
and locally common in northern
temperate zones.
•**SIMILAR SPECIES** *Russula
cutefracta* is darker green and cracks
from the margin. It does not react
with iron sulphate ($FeSO_4$).

*convex to flat
cap feels
velvety*

*cap surface
cracks, creating
scales*

*yellow- to
blue-green
cap surface*

*white stem
with brown-
scaly base*

FRUITING Appears singly or in small groups of
fruitbodies on well-drained soil.

Dimensions CAP ⊕ 4–10cm | STEM ↕ 4–8cm ↔ 1–3cm	Spores White	Edibility ⦿

VERY SMALL WITH SMOOTH CAP

T HERE ARE A GREAT MANY very small agarics with smooth caps, and they belong to a very wide range of genera and families, although, in this book, it is the small, white-spored members of the Tricholomataceae that predominate. Species included here may have a fine bloom on the cap but never have distinct hairs, coarse fibres, or scales (see pp.142–144).

Family TRICHOLOMATACEAE	Species *Lyophyllum palustre*	Season Summer–autumn

SPHAGNUM GREYLING

On a thin, pale grey-brown stem, the greyish brown cap of this species is convex, expanding to flat or slightly depressed. The cap surface is striated from the margin to its centre, and it has thin flesh, which smells faintly of meal and is not palatable. The white to pale grey gills are adnexed and medium spaced.
• **OCCURRENCE** Only found growing in boggy situations on sphagnum moss, which it eventually kills. Widespread throughout northern temperate zones.
• **SIMILAR SPECIES** Other species found with sphagnum moss, such as *Galerina paludosa*, *G. tibiicystis*, *Omphalina sphagnicola*, and *O. philonotis*, usually have brown spores or decurrent gills.

cap is convex to flat or depressed •

long, rooting stem is grey-brown •

striations from margin to cap centre •

FRUITING Appears in troops of fruitbodies or fairy rings on sphagnum moss in boggy areas.

Dimensions CAP ⊕ 1–3cm	STEM ↕ 4–8cm ↔ 1–3mm	Spores White	Edibility ⦸

Family TRICHOLOMATACEAE	Species *Baeospora myosura*	Season Autumn–late autumn

CONE-CAP

This pale brown member of the small genus *Baeospora* has a flat to slightly umbonate, dry cap and a powder-covered stem. It has a musty smell and indistinct taste. The gills are almost free.
• **OCCURRENCE** In parks and woodland on cones and cone scales from various softwoods, including spruce and pine. Widespread and common in northern temperate zones.
• **SIMILAR SPECIES** *B. myriadophylla* is also pale brown but has brighter, more or less lilac gills. It mainly grows on fallen trunks of softwoods and is rare or absent in most areas. Other fungi that grow on pine cones include *Strobilurus esculentus* (p.133), *Mycena seynei*, which has a striking, pale wine-pink cap and dark red-brown gill edges.

crowded, fairly narrow, pale grey gills

adnexed or free gills •

dry, pale brown cap surface •

SECTION

FRUITING A few on a cone or singly on detached scales.

Dimensions CAP ⊕ 0.5–2cm	STEM ↕ 1–4cm ↔ 1–2mm	Spores White	Edibility ⦸

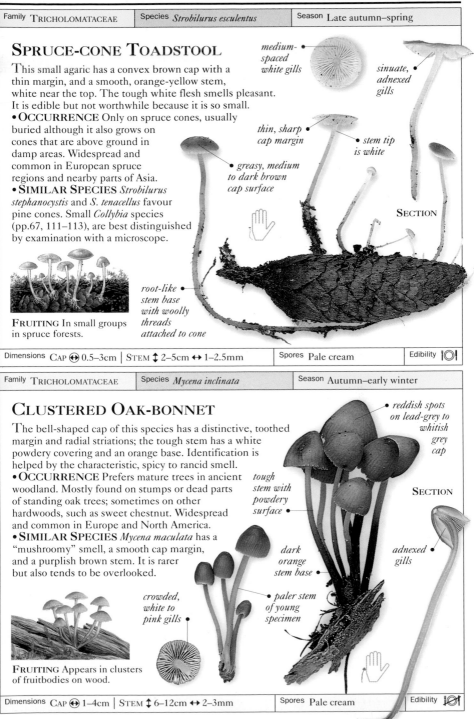

Family TRICHOLOMATACEAE	Species *Strobilurus esculentus*	Season Late autumn–spring

SPRUCE-CONE TOADSTOOL

This small agaric has a convex brown cap with a thin margin, and a smooth, orange-yellow stem, white near the top. The tough white flesh smells pleasant. It is edible but not worthwhile because it is so small.
• **OCCURRENCE** Only on spruce cones, usually buried although it also grows on cones that are above ground in damp areas. Widespread and common in European spruce regions and nearby parts of Asia.
• **SIMILAR SPECIES** *Strobilurus stephanocystis* and *S. tenacellus* favour pine cones. Small *Collybia* species (pp.67, 111–113), are best distinguished by examination with a microscope.

medium-spaced white gills •

sinuate, adnexed gills •

thin, sharp cap margin •

• stem tip is white

• greasy, medium to dark brown cap surface

SECTION

root-like • stem base with woolly threads attached to cone

FRUITING In small groups in spruce forests.

Dimensions CAP ⊕ 0.5–3cm	STEM ↕ 2–5cm ↔ 1–2.5mm	Spores Pale cream	Edibility

Family TRICHOLOMATACEAE	Species *Mycena inclinata*	Season Autumn–early winter

CLUSTERED OAK-BONNET

The bell-shaped cap of this species has a distinctive, toothed margin and radial striations; the tough stem has a white powdery covering and an orange base. Identification is helped by the characteristic, spicy to rancid smell.
• **OCCURRENCE** Prefers mature trees in ancient woodland. Mostly found on stumps or dead parts of standing oak trees; sometimes on other hardwoods, such as sweet chestnut. Widespread and common in Europe and North America.
• **SIMILAR SPECIES** *Mycena maculata* has a "mushroomy" smell, a smooth cap margin, and a purplish brown stem. It is rarer but also tends to be overlooked.

• reddish spots on lead-grey to whitish grey cap

tough stem with powdery surface •

SECTION

dark orange stem base

adnexed • gills

crowded, white to pink gills •

• paler stem of young specimen

FRUITING Appears in clusters of fruitbodies on wood.

Dimensions CAP ⊕ 1–4cm	STEM ↕ 6–12cm ↔ 2–3mm	Spores Pale cream	Edibility

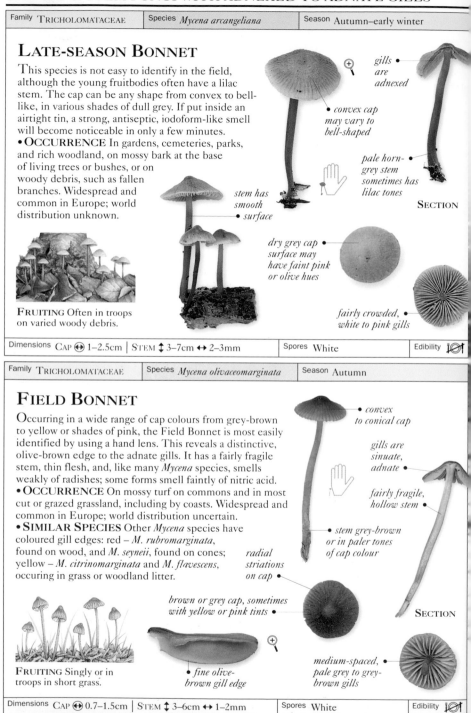

| Family TRICHOLOMATACEAE | Species *Mycena arcangeliana* | Season Autumn–early winter |

LATE-SEASON BONNET

This species is not easy to identify in the field, although the young fruitbodies often have a lilac stem. The cap can be any shape from convex to bell-like, in various shades of dull grey. If put inside an airtight tin, a strong, antiseptic, iodoform-like smell will become noticeable in only a few minutes.

• **OCCURRENCE** In gardens, cemeteries, parks, and rich woodland, on mossy bark at the base of living trees or bushes, or on woody debris, such as fallen branches. Widespread and common in Europe; world distribution unknown.

gills •
are adnexed

• *convex cap may vary to bell-shaped*

pale horn-grey stem sometimes has lilac tones

SECTION

stem has smooth • *surface*

dry grey cap surface may have faint pink or olive hues •

fairly crowded, • *white to pink gills*

FRUITING Often in troops on varied woody debris.

| Dimensions CAP ⊕ 1–2.5cm | STEM ↕ 3–7cm ↔ 2–3mm | Spores White | Edibility |

| Family TRICHOLOMATACEAE | Species *Mycena olivaceomarginata* | Season Autumn |

FIELD BONNET

Occurring in a wide range of cap colours from grey-brown to yellow or shades of pink, the Field Bonnet is most easily identified by using a hand lens. This reveals a distinctive, olive-brown edge to the adnate gills. It has a fairly fragile stem, thin flesh, and, like many *Mycena* species, smells weakly of radishes; some forms smell faintly of nitric acid.

• **OCCURRENCE** On mossy turf on commons and in most cut or grazed grassland, including by coasts. Widespread and common in Europe; world distribution uncertain.

• **SIMILAR SPECIES** Other *Mycena* species have coloured gill edges: red – *M. rubromarginata*, found on wood, and *M. seyneii*, found on cones; yellow – *M. citrinomarginata* and *M. flavescens*, occuring in grass or woodland litter.

• *convex to conical cap*

gills are sinuate, adnate •

fairly fragile, hollow stem •

• *stem grey-brown or in paler tones of cap colour*

radial striations on cap •

SECTION

brown or grey cap, sometimes with yellow or pink tints •

• *fine olive-brown gill edge*

medium-spaced, • *pale grey to grey-brown gills*

FRUITING Singly or in troops in short grass.

| Dimensions CAP ⊕ 0.7–1.5cm | STEM ↕ 3–6cm ↔ 1–2mm | Spores White | Edibility |

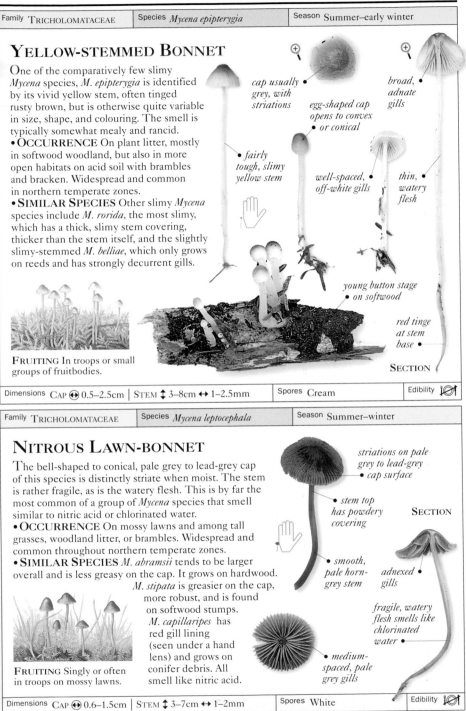

| Family TRICHOLOMATACEAE | Species *Mycena epipterygia* | Season Summer–early winter |

YELLOW-STEMMED BONNET

One of the comparatively few slimy *Mycena* species, *M. epipterygia* is identified by its vivid yellow stem, often tinged rusty brown, but is otherwise quite variable in size, shape, and colouring. The smell is typically somewhat mealy and rancid.
• **OCCURRENCE** On plant litter, mostly in softwood woodland, but also in more open habitats on acid soil with brambles and bracken. Widespread and common in northern temperate zones.
• **SIMILAR SPECIES** Other slimy *Mycena* species include *M. rorida*, the most slimy, which has a thick, slimy stem covering, thicker than the stem itself, and the slightly slimy-stemmed *M. belliae*, which only grows on reeds and has strongly decurrent gills.

cap usually grey, with striations

egg-shaped cap opens to convex or conical

broad, adnate gills

fairly tough, slimy yellow stem

well-spaced, off-white gills

thin, watery flesh

young button stage on softwood

red tinge at stem base

SECTION

FRUITING In troops or small groups of fruitbodies.

| Dimensions CAP ⊕ 0.5–2.5cm | STEM ↕ 3–8cm ↔ 1–2.5mm | Spores Cream | Edibility |

| Family TRICHOLOMATACEAE | Species *Mycena leptocephala* | Season Summer–winter |

NITROUS LAWN-BONNET

The bell-shaped to conical, pale grey to lead-grey cap of this species is distinctly striate when moist. The stem is rather fragile, as is the watery flesh. This is by far the most common of a group of *Mycena* species that smell similar to nitric acid or chlorinated water.
• **OCCURRENCE** On mossy lawns and among tall grasses, woodland litter, or brambles. Widespread and common throughout northern temperate zones.
• **SIMILAR SPECIES** *M. abramsii* tends to be larger overall and is less greasy on the cap. It grows on hardwood. *M. stipata* is greasier on the cap, more robust, and is found on softwood stumps. *M. capillaripes* has red gill lining (seen under a hand lens) and grows on conifer debris. All smell like nitric acid.

striations on pale grey to lead-grey cap surface

stem top has powdery covering

SECTION

smooth, pale horn-grey stem

adnexed gills

fragile, watery flesh smells like chlorinated water

medium-spaced, pale grey gills

FRUITING Singly or often in troops on mossy lawns.

| Dimensions CAP ⊕ 0.6–1.5cm | STEM ↕ 3–7cm ↔ 1–2mm | Spores White | Edibility |

Family TRICHOLOMATACEAE	Species *Mycena filopes*	Season Autumn

IODOFORM BONNET

This species is best identified with the aid of a microscope, which shows its spiny cystidia and other characteristics, and by its combination of fragile stem, grey colouring, and antiseptic, iodoform-like smell. Both cap and stem have a covering of white bloom, and the cap has striations to its centre.
• **OCCURRENCE** Mostly in hardwood woodland, on humus or small pieces of litter, but also beneath softwoods on needle beds. Often found among nettles along woodland paths. Widespread and common in Europe; world distribution unknown.
• **SIMILAR SPECIES** *Mycena arcangeliana* (p.134). *M. metata* tends to have pinkish hues and prefers more acid conditions and softwood woodland. Both smell of iodoform and appear very similar under a microscope.

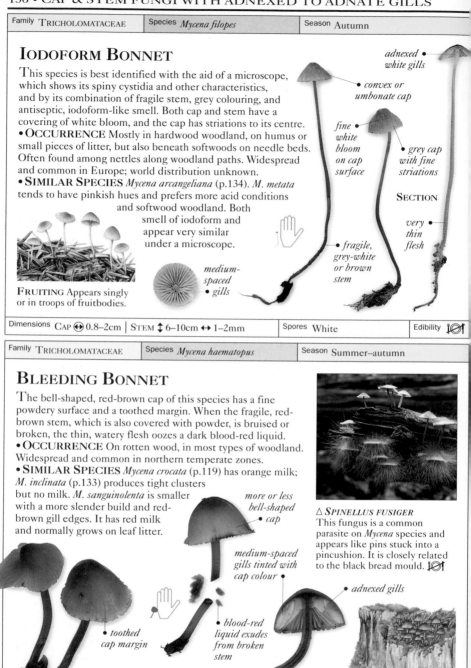

FRUITING Appears singly or in troops of fruitbodies.

adnexed • white gills

• convex or umbonate cap

fine • white bloom on cap surface

• grey cap with fine striations

SECTION

very • thin flesh

• fragile, grey-white or brown stem

medium-spaced • gills

Dimensions CAP ⊕ 0.8–2cm │ STEM ↕ 6–10cm ↔ 1–2mm	Spores White	Edibility

Family TRICHOLOMATACEAE	Species *Mycena haematopus*	Season Summer–autumn

BLEEDING BONNET

The bell-shaped, red-brown cap of this species has a fine powdery surface and a toothed margin. When the fragile, red-brown stem, which is also covered with powder, is bruised or broken, the thin, watery flesh oozes a dark blood-red liquid.
• **OCCURRENCE** On rotten wood, in most types of woodland. Widespread and common in northern temperate zones.
• **SIMILAR SPECIES** *Mycena crocata* (p.119) has orange milk; *M. inclinata* (p.133) produces tight clusters but no milk. *M. sanguinolenta* is smaller with a more slender build and red-brown gill edges. It has red milk and normally grows on leaf litter.

△ ***SPINELLUS FUSIGER***
This fungus is a common parasite on *Mycena* species and appears like pins stuck into a pincushion. It is closely related to the black bread mould.

more or less bell-shaped • cap

medium-spaced gills tinted with cap colour •

• adnexed gills

• toothed cap margin

• blood-red liquid exudes from broken stem

• stems typically joined at base

SECTION

FRUITING In dense clusters of fruitbodies.

Dimensions CAP ⊕ 0.5–3cm │ STEM ↕ 3–7cm ↔ 2–4mm	Spores Whitish cream	Edibility

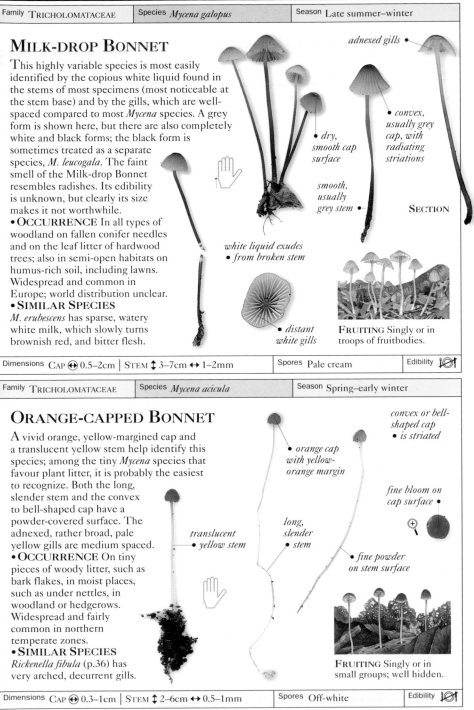

Family TRICHOLOMATACEAE	Species *Mycena galopus*	Season Late summer–winter

MILK-DROP BONNET

This highly variable species is most easily identified by the copious white liquid found in the stems of most specimens (most noticeable at the stem base) and by the gills, which are well-spaced compared to most *Mycena* species. A grey form is shown here, but there are also completely white and black forms; the black form is sometimes treated as a separate species, *M. leucogala*. The faint smell of the Milk-drop Bonnet resembles radishes. Its edibility is unknown, but clearly its size makes it not worthwhile.
• **OCCURRENCE** In all types of woodland on fallen conifer needles and on the leaf litter of hardwood trees; also in semi-open habitats on humus-rich soil, including lawns. Widespread and common in Europe; world distribution unclear.
• **SIMILAR SPECIES**
M. erubescens has sparse, watery white milk, which slowly turns brownish red, and bitter flesh.

adnexed gills •

• convex, usually grey cap, with radiating striations

• dry, smooth cap surface

smooth, usually grey stem •

SECTION

white liquid exudes • from broken stem

• distant white gills

FRUITING Singly or in troops of fruitbodies.

Dimensions CAP ⊕ 0.5–2cm | STEM ↕ 3–7cm ↔ 1–2mm	Spores Pale cream	Edibility

Family TRICHOLOMATACEAE	Species *Mycena acicula*	Season Spring–early winter

ORANGE-CAPPED BONNET

A vivid orange, yellow-margined cap and a translucent yellow stem help identify this species; among the tiny *Mycena* species that favour plant litter, it is probably the easiest to recognize. Both the long, slender stem and the convex to bell-shaped cap have a powder-covered surface. The adnexed, rather broad, pale yellow gills are medium spaced.
• **OCCURRENCE** On tiny pieces of woody litter, such as bark flakes, in moist places, such as under nettles, in woodland or hedgerows. Widespread and fairly common in northern temperate zones.
• **SIMILAR SPECIES**
Rickenella fibula (p.36) has very arched, decurrent gills.

convex or bell-shaped cap • is striated

• orange cap with yellow-orange margin

fine bloom on cap surface •

translucent • yellow stem

long, slender • stem

• fine powder on stem surface

FRUITING Singly or in small groups; well hidden.

Dimensions CAP ⊕ 0.3–1cm | STEM ↕ 2–6cm ↔ 0.5–1mm	Spores Off-white	Edibility

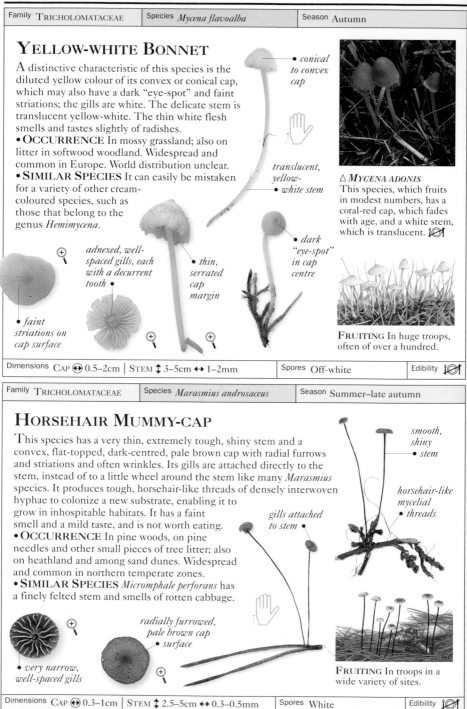

| Family TRICHOLOMATACEAE | Species *Mycena flavoalba* | Season Autumn |

YELLOW-WHITE BONNET

A distinctive characteristic of this species is the diluted yellow colour of its convex or conical cap, which may also have a dark "eye-spot" and faint striations; the gills are white. The delicate stem is translucent yellow-white. The thin white flesh smells and tastes slightly of radishes.
• **OCCURRENCE** In mossy grassland; also on litter in softwood woodland. Widespread and common in Europe. World distribution unclear.
• **SIMILAR SPECIES** It can easily be mistaken for a variety of other cream-coloured species, such as those that belong to the genus *Hemimycena*.

conical to convex cap

translucent, yellow-white stem

△ **MYCENA ADONIS**
This species, which fruits in modest numbers, has a coral-red cap, which fades with age, and a white stem, which is translucent.

adnexed, well-spaced gills, each with a decurrent tooth

thin, serrated cap margin

dark "eye-spot" in cap centre

faint striations on cap surface

FRUITING In huge troops, often of over a hundred.

| Dimensions CAP ⊕ 0.5–2cm | STEM ↕ 3–5cm ↔ 1–2mm | Spores Off-white | Edibility |

| Family TRICHOLOMATACEAE | Species *Marasmius androsaceus* | Season Summer–late autumn |

HORSEHAIR MUMMY-CAP

This species has a very thin, extremely tough, shiny stem and a convex, flat-topped, dark-centred, pale brown cap with radial furrows and striations and often wrinkles. Its gills are attached directly to the stem, instead of to a little wheel around the stem like many *Marasmius* species. It produces tough, horsehair-like threads of densely interwoven hyphae to colonize a new substrate, enabling it to grow in inhospitable habitats. It has a faint smell and a mild taste, and is not worth eating.
• **OCCURRENCE** In pine woods, on pine needles and other small pieces of tree litter; also on heathland and among sand dunes. Widespread and common in northern temperate zones.
• **SIMILAR SPECIES** *Micromphale perforans* has a finely felted stem and smells of rotten cabbage.

smooth, shiny stem

horsehair-like mycelial threads

gills attached to stem

radially furrowed, pale brown cap surface

very narrow, well-spaced gills

FRUITING In troops in a wide variety of sites.

| Dimensions CAP ⊕ 0.3–1cm | STEM ↕ 2.5–5cm ↔ 0.3–0.5mm | Spores White | Edibility |

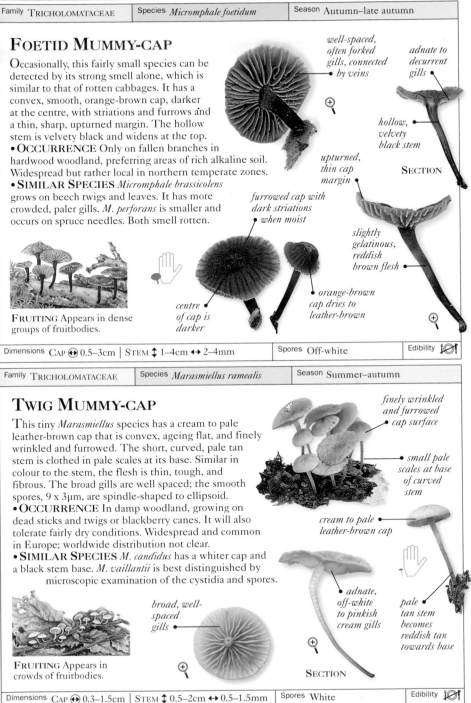

Family TRICHOLOMATACEAE	Species *Micromphale foetidum*	Season Autumn–late autumn

FOETID MUMMY-CAP

Occasionally, this fairly small species can be detected by its strong smell alone, which is similar to that of rotten cabbages. It has a convex, smooth, orange-brown cap, darker at the centre, with striations and furrows and a thin, sharp, upturned margin. The hollow stem is velvety black and widens at the top.
• **OCCURRENCE** Only on fallen branches in hardwood woodland, preferring areas of rich alkaline soil. Widespread but rather local in northern temperate zones.
• **SIMILAR SPECIES** *Micromphale brassicolens* grows on beech twigs and leaves. It has more crowded, paler gills. *M. perforans* is smaller and occurs on spruce needles. Both smell rotten.

well-spaced, often forked gills, connected by veins

adnate to decurrent gills

hollow, velvety black stem

upturned, thin cap margin

SECTION

furrowed cap with dark striations when moist

slightly gelatinous, reddish brown flesh

FRUITING Appears in dense groups of fruitbodies.

centre of cap is darker

orange-brown cap dries to leather-brown

Dimensions CAP ⊕ 0.5–3cm | STEM ↕ 1–4cm ↔ 2–4mm	Spores Off-white	Edibility

Family TRICHOLOMATACEAE	Species *Marasmiellus ramealis*	Season Summer–autumn

TWIG MUMMY-CAP

This tiny *Marasmiellus* species has a cream to pale leather-brown cap that is convex, ageing flat, and finely wrinkled and furrowed. The short, curved, pale tan stem is clothed in pale scales at its base. Similar in colour to the stem, the flesh is thin, tough, and fibrous. The broad gills are well spaced; the smooth spores, 9 x 3µm, are spindle-shaped to ellipsoid.
• **OCCURRENCE** In damp woodland, growing on dead sticks and twigs or blackberry canes. It will also tolerate fairly dry conditions. Widespread and common in Europe; worldwide distribution not clear.
• **SIMILAR SPECIES** *M. candidus* has a whiter cap and a black stem base. *M. vaillantii* is best distinguished by microscopic examination of the cystidia and spores.

finely wrinkled and furrowed cap surface

small pale scales at base of curved stem

cream to pale leather-brown cap

adnate, off-white to pinkish cream gills

pale tan stem becomes reddish tan towards base

FRUITING Appears in crowds of fruitbodies.

broad, well-spaced gills

SECTION

Dimensions CAP ⊕ 0.3–1.5cm | STEM ↕ 0.5–2cm ↔ 0.5–1.5mm	Spores White	Edibility

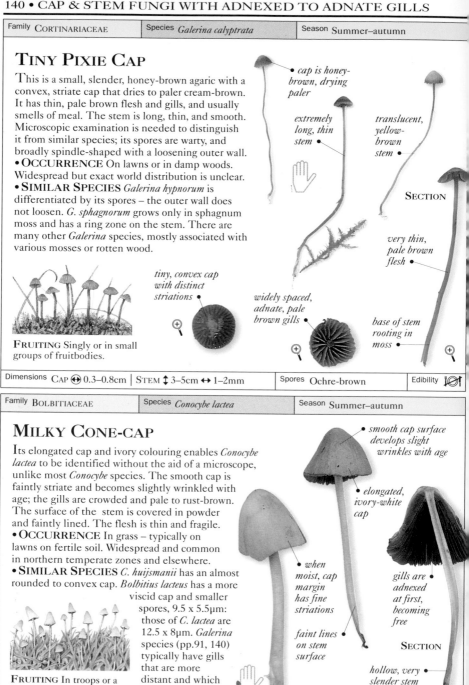

| Family CORTINARIACEAE | Species *Galerina calyptrata* | Season Summer–autumn |

TINY PIXIE CAP

This is a small, slender, honey-brown agaric with a convex, striate cap that dries to paler cream-brown. It has thin, pale brown flesh and gills, and usually smells of meal. The stem is long, thin, and smooth. Microscopic examination is needed to distinguish it from similar species; its spores are warty, and broadly spindle-shaped with a loosening outer wall.
• **OCCURRENCE** On lawns or in damp woods. Widespread but exact world distribution is unclear.
• **SIMILAR SPECIES** *Galerina hypnorum* is differentiated by its spores – the outer wall does not loosen. *G. sphagnorum* grows only in sphagnum moss and has a ring zone on the stem. There are many other *Galerina* species, mostly associated with various mosses or rotten wood.

cap is honey-brown, drying paler

extremely long, thin stem

translucent, yellow-brown stem

SECTION

very thin, pale brown flesh

tiny, convex cap with distinct striations

widely spaced, adnate, pale brown gills

base of stem rooting in moss

FRUITING Singly or in small groups of fruitbodies.

| Dimensions CAP ⊕ 0.3–0.8cm | STEM ↕ 3–5cm ↔ 1–2mm | Spores Ochre-brown | Edibility |

| Family BOLBITIACEAE | Species *Conocybe lactea* | Season Summer–autumn |

MILKY CONE-CAP

Its elongated cap and ivory colouring enables *Conocybe lactea* to be identified without the aid of a microscope, unlike most *Conocybe* species. The smooth cap is faintly striate and becomes slightly wrinkled with age; the gills are crowded and pale to rust-brown. The surface of the stem is covered in powder and faintly lined. The flesh is thin and fragile.
• **OCCURRENCE** In grass – typically on lawns on fertile soil. Widespread and common in northern temperate zones and elsewhere.
• **SIMILAR SPECIES** *C. huijsmanii* has an almost rounded to convex cap. *Bolbitius lacteus* has a more viscid cap and smaller spores, 9.5 x 5.5µm: those of *C. lactea* are 12.5 x 8µm. *Galerina* species (pp.91, 140) typically have gills that are more distant and which are usually adnate.

smooth cap surface develops slight wrinkles with age

elongated, ivory-white cap

when moist, cap margin has fine striations

faint lines on stem surface

gills are adnexed at first, becoming free

SECTION

hollow, very slender stem

FRUITING In troops or a few fruitbodies together.

| Dimensions CAP ⊕ 1–1.5cm | STEM ↕ 5–11cm ↔ 1–3cm | Spores Orange-brown | Edibility |

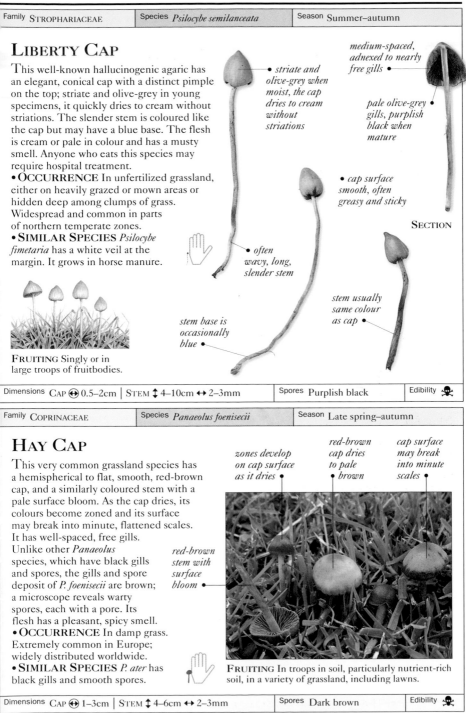

| Family STROPHARIACEAE | Species *Psilocybe semilanceata* | Season Summer–autumn |

LIBERTY CAP

This well-known hallucinogenic agaric has an elegant, conical cap with a distinct pimple on the top; striate and olive-grey in young specimens, it quickly dries to cream without striations. The slender stem is coloured like the cap but may have a blue base. The flesh is cream or pale in colour and has a musty smell. Anyone who eats this species may require hospital treatment.
• **OCCURRENCE** In unfertilized grassland, either on heavily grazed or mown areas or hidden deep among clumps of grass. Widespread and common in parts of northern temperate zones.
• **SIMILAR SPECIES** *Psilocybe fimetaria* has a white veil at the margin. It grows in horse manure.

medium-spaced, adnexed to nearly free gills •

• *striate and olive-grey when moist, the cap dries to cream without striations*

pale olive-grey gills, purplish black when mature •

• *cap surface smooth, often greasy and sticky*

SECTION

• *often wavy, long, slender stem*

stem usually same colour as cap •

stem base is occasionally blue •

FRUITING Singly or in large troops of fruitbodies.

stem base is occasionally blue •

| Dimensions CAP ⊕ 0.5–2cm | STEM ↕ 4–10cm ↔ 2–3mm | Spores Purplish black | Edibility ☠ |

| Family COPRINACEAE | Species *Panaeolus foenisecii* | Season Late spring–autumn |

HAY CAP

This very common grassland species has a hemispherical to flat, smooth, red-brown cap, and a similarly coloured stem with a pale surface bloom. As the cap dries, its colours become zoned and its surface may break into minute, flattened scales. It has well-spaced, free gills.
Unlike other *Panaeolus* species, which have black gills and spores, the gills and spore deposit of *P. foenisecii* are brown; a microscope reveals warty spores, each with a pore. Its flesh has a pleasant, spicy smell.
• **OCCURRENCE** In damp grass. Extremely common in Europe; widely distributed worldwide.
• **SIMILAR SPECIES** *P. ater* has black gills and smooth spores.

zones develop on cap surface as it dries •

red-brown cap dries to pale brown •

cap surface may break into minute scales •

red-brown stem with surface bloom •

FRUITING In troops in soil, particularly nutrient-rich soil, in a variety of grassland, including lawns.

| Dimensions CAP ⊕ 1–3cm | STEM ↕ 4–6cm ↔ 2–3mm | Spores Dark brown | Edibility ☠ |

VERY SMALL, CAP NOT SMOOTH

AGARICS IN THIS SUBSECTION, as in the last (pp.132–141), have very small fruitbodies, but are characterized by their very varied, never smooth, cap surfaces. They too are represented in many different families and genera. Their cap surfaces may be fibrous or scaly, or they can be covered with loose grains, as in *Coprinus disseminatus* (p.143), which also has fine hairs.

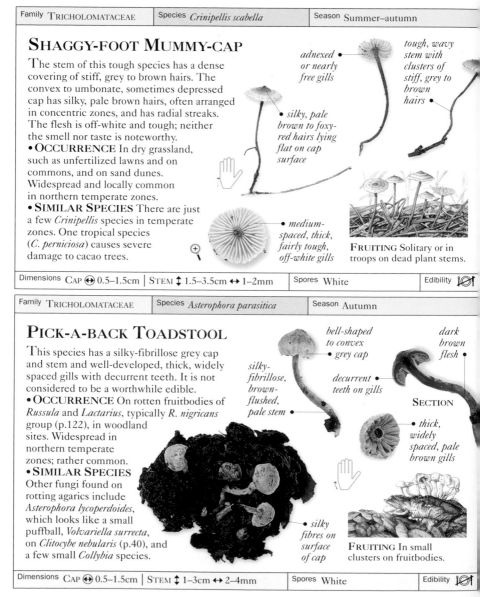

| Family TRICHOLOMATACEAE | Species *Crinipellis scabella* | Season Summer–autumn |

SHAGGY-FOOT MUMMY-CAP

The stem of this tough species has a dense covering of stiff, grey to brown hairs. The convex to umbonate, sometimes depressed cap has silky, pale brown hairs, often arranged in concentric zones, and has radial streaks. The flesh is off-white and tough; neither the smell nor taste is noteworthy.
• **OCCURRENCE** In dry grassland, such as unfertilized lawns and on commons, and on sand dunes. Widespread and locally common in northern temperate zones.
• **SIMILAR SPECIES** There are just a few *Crinipellis* species in temperate zones. One tropical species (*C. perniciosa*) causes severe damage to cacao trees.

adnexed or nearly free gills

silky, pale brown to foxy-red hairs lying flat on cap surface

tough, wavy stem with clusters of stiff, grey to brown hairs

medium-spaced, thick, fairly tough, off-white gills

FRUITING Solitary or in troops on dead plant stems.

| Dimensions CAP ⊕ 0.5–1.5cm │ STEM ↕ 1.5–3.5cm ↔ 1–2mm | Spores White | Edibility |

| Family TRICHOLOMATACEAE | Species *Asterophora parasitica* | Season Autumn |

PICK-A-BACK TOADSTOOL

This species has a silky-fibrillose grey cap and stem and well-developed, thick, widely spaced gills with decurrent teeth. It is not considered to be a worthwhile edible.
• **OCCURRENCE** On rotten fruitbodies of *Russula* and *Lactarius*, typically *R. nigricans* group (p.122), in woodland sites. Widespread in northern temperate zones; rather common.
• **SIMILAR SPECIES** Other fungi found on rotting agarics include *Asterophora lycoperdoides*, which looks like a small puffball, *Volvariella surrecta*, on *Clitocybe nebularis* (p.40), and a few small *Collybia* species.

bell-shaped to convex grey cap

silky-fibrillose, brown-flushed, pale stem

decurrent teeth on gills

dark brown flesh

SECTION

thick, widely spaced, pale brown gills

silky fibres on surface of cap

FRUITING In small clusters on fruitbodies.

| Dimensions CAP ⊕ 0.5–1.5cm │ STEM ↕ 1–3cm ↔ 2–4mm | Spores White | Edibility |

| Family COPRINACEAE | Species *Coprinus disseminatus* | Season Spring–early autumn |

FAIRIES' BONNETS

Cream-white when young, the pleated (parachute-like) cap of this species ages grey, but unlike many *Coprinus* species, produces only a little ink. Fine hairs and grains on the surface are visible through a hand lens. The delicate stem is white, as is the very thin flesh.

• **OCCURRENCE** On and around stumps and dying hardwood trees. Widespread and common in northern temperate zones.

• **SIMILAR SPECIES** *Psathyrella pygmaea* is similar in appearance and habitat, but its cap surface has neither hairs nor grains and is less pleated.

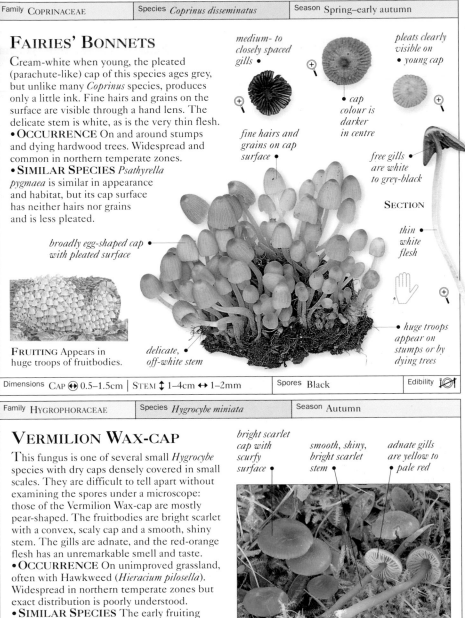

medium- to closely spaced gills •

pleats clearly visible on • young cap

• cap colour is darker in centre

fine hairs and grains on cap surface •

free gills • are white to grey-black

SECTION

thin • white flesh

broadly egg-shaped cap • with pleated surface

FRUITING Appears in huge troops of fruitbodies.

delicate, off-white stem

• huge troops appear on stumps or by dying trees

| Dimensions CAP ⊕ 0.5–1.5cm │ STEM ↕ 1–4cm ↔ 1–2mm | Spores Black | Edibility |

| Family HYGROPHORACEAE | Species *Hygrocybe miniata* | Season Autumn |

VERMILION WAX-CAP

This fungus is one of several small *Hygrocybe* species with dry caps densely covered in small scales. They are difficult to tell apart without examining the spores under a microscope: those of the Vermilion Wax-cap are mostly pear-shaped. The fruitbodies are bright scarlet with a convex, scaly cap and a smooth, shiny stem. The gills are adnate, and the red-orange flesh has an unremarkable smell and taste.

• **OCCURRENCE** On unimproved grassland, often with Hawkweed (*Hieracium pilosella*). Widespread in northern temperate zones but exact distribution is poorly understood.

• **SIMILAR SPECIES** The early fruiting *H. helobia* prefers less acid conditions, smells of garlic, and has spores of a more regular ellipsoid shape. *H. calciphila* also has more regular-shaped spores and tends to occur on alkaline soil.

bright scarlet cap with scurfy surface •

smooth, shiny, bright scarlet stem

adnate gills are yellow to • pale red

FRUITING In troops, mostly on slightly acid soil, in unimproved grass- and heathland.

| Dimensions CAP ⊕ 1–3cm │ STEM ↕ 1–6cm ↔ 2–8mm | Spores White | Edibility |

Family ENTOLOMATACEAE	Species *Entoloma serrulatum*	Season Late summer–autumn

SAW-GILLED BLUE-CAP

The convex, dark blue-black cap surface of the Saw-gilled Blue-cap is dry to the touch with tiny, erect scales and a central, navel-like depression. The stem is a similar colour to the cap. The adnexed, pale blue gills have a serrated, blue-black edge.

• **OCCURRENCE** In grassland, among sparse roadside vegetation, or in sand tips. Widespread in Europe and North America and probably elsewhere.

• **SIMILAR SPECIES** Similar, more or less blue *Entoloma* species with coloured gill edges include *E. caesiocinctum*, with a browner cap, *E. chalybaeum*, with brown-edged, blue gills that are less serrated, and *E. querquedula*, which has an olive-tinged cap.

central depression on dry,
• *blue-black cap surface*

• *cap surface has tiny, erect scales*

thin, bluish white flesh has faint aroma •

gill edge is •
serrated and blue-black

medium-spaced gills are adnexed •

SECTION

pale blue gills turn •
pinkish blue with age

FRUITING In small groups on most types of soil.

Dimensions CAP ⊕ 1–2.5cm	STEM ↕ 2–6cm ↔ 2–4mm	Spores Pale pink	Edibility ☠

Family ENTOLOMATACEAE	Species *Entoloma incanum*	Season Summer–early autumn

GREEN PINK-GILL

The overall colour of this species is green or green-brown, but the flesh discolours to sky-blue when bruised. The cap is convex, with a slightly depressed centre, and the slender stem is hollow. It is probably poisonous, and has a strong smell reminiscent of mice. Although perhaps the most striking of the smaller *Entoloma* species, its colouring camouflages it well in its grassy habitat.

• **OCCURRENCE** On soil in alkaline grassland or grassy verges in woodland. Widespread but uncommon in Europe and North America.

gills are medium spaced •

pale grass-green to greenish golden brown cap •

pale pink gills may be adnate or adnexed

translucent green stem stains blue where bruised •

hollow stem

cap margin is •
often wavy

slight depression in cap centre •

SECTION

striations at cap margin •

FRUITING Appears singly or in troops of fruitbodies among herbaceous plants.

stem base is white and stains blue •

Dimensions CAP ⊕ 1–3cm	STEM ↕ 2–6cm ↔ 2–4mm	Spores Pale pink	Edibility ☠

CAP & STEM FUNGI WITH FREE GILLS

*This section features the few families of agarics –
Amanitaceae, Agaricaceae, and Pluteaceae – in
which all the species have gills that are not attached
to the stem ("free"). Often the stem can be twisted away
from the cap flesh without any damage to the gills.*

• gills not attached to stem (free)

WITH VOLVA AND/OR VEIL SCALES ON CAP

THIS GROUP OF AGARICS comprises species from the genera *Amanita* and *Volvariella*. They are comparatively large and fleshy, and distinct remains of the universal veil persist as a sac-like structure at the stem base (volva) and/or as loose scales on the cap. Some also have a ring around the stem.

Family AMANITACEAE	Species *Amanita caesarea*	Season Autumn

CAESAR'S MUSHROOM

A legend in warm regions, this fungus has a convex to flat, golden orange cap and an orange stem with a very prominent, loose white volva, up to 5cm wide, at the base. The soft gills are crowded and cream to golden yellow. This is a choice edible, but unless it is positively identified by an expert, it should not be eaten (see Similar Species).
• **OCCURRENCE** Mycorrhizal with hardwood trees, such as chestnut and oak, on sandy soil. Widespread but local in warmer parts of northern temperate zones; also in subtropical areas.
• **SIMILAR SPECIES** *Amanita muscaria* (p.146) has a yellow-orange form.

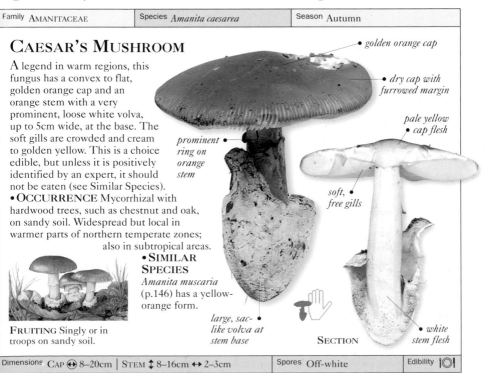

• golden orange cap

• dry cap with furrowed margin

pale yellow • cap flesh

prominent • ring on orange stem

soft, • free gills

large, sac- • like volva at stem base

SECTION

• white stem flesh

FRUITING Singly or in troops on sandy soil.

Dimensions CAP ⊕ 8–20cm	STEM ↕ 8–16cm ↔ 2–3cm	Spores Off-white	Edibility

Family AMANITACEAE	Species *Amanita muscaria*	Season Summer–autumn

FLY AGARIC

This is the classic fairy-tale toadstool. It has a convex to flattened cap with a smooth or faintly grooved margin and white veil scales on the surface. It occurs in several colour forms, including yellow-orange and orange; the brilliant red version is the most familiar. The swollen stem base lacks the loose volva found in other *Amanita* species, such as *A. virosa* (p.150). While the Fly Agaric may not always be fatal if eaten, it is seriously poisonous – eating several fruitbodies can cause very severe symptoms.

• **OCCURRENCE** Mycorrhizal, mostly with birch or spruce, usually on acid soil. Widespread and common in northern temperate zones.

faint grooves • at cap margin

• red, orange, or orange-yellow cap

• white stem with remnants of veil

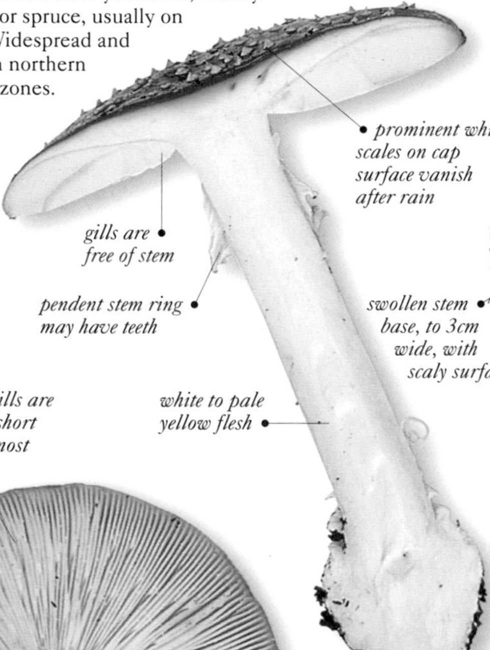

• prominent white scales on cap surface vanish after rain

gills are • free of stem

pendent stem ring • may have teeth

swollen stem • base, to 3cm wide, with scaly surface

full-length gills are mixed with short ones, as in most agarics •

white to pale yellow flesh •

SECTION

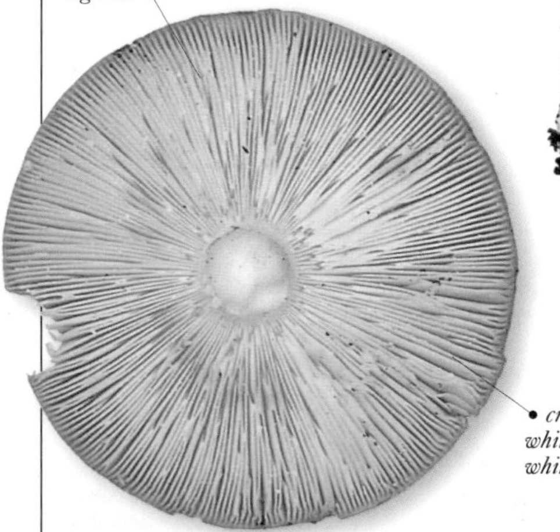

• crowded, white to off-white gills

FRUITING In troops or rings under or near trees.

△ *AMANITA MUSCARIA* VAR. *FORMOSA*
This yellow- to orange-capped variant is common in north-eastern North America. 💀

Dimensions CAP ⊕ 6–15cm | STEM ↕ 8–20cm ↔ 1–2.5cm	Spores Off-white	Edibility 💀

Family AMANITACEAE	Species *Amanita rubescens*	Season Summer–autumn

THE BLUSHER

The convex cap of this species is pinkish brown with grey to pink veil patches. The downy, grey, white, or pink stem bears a prominent pendent ring with furrows on its upper surface; the base is swollen and girdled. Small insects lay eggs in the fruitbodies, and the damaged flesh becomes pink tinged – often the best clue to its identity. It is difficult to recognize so should only be picked for eating by experienced foragers.

• **OCCURRENCE** Mycorrhizal with hardwoods, such as beech, and softwoods. Widespread and common in northern temperate zones.

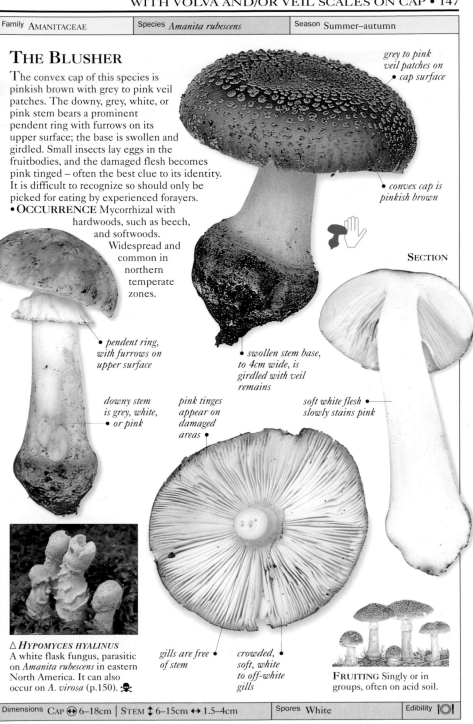

grey to pink
veil patches on
• cap surface

• convex cap is
pinkish brown

SECTION

• pendent ring,
with furrows on
upper surface

• swollen stem base,
to 4cm wide, is
girdled with veil
remains

downy stem
is grey, white,
• or pink

pink tinges
appear on
damaged
areas •

soft white flesh •
slowly stains pink

△ *HYPOMYCES HYALINUS*
A white flask fungus, parasitic on *Amanita rubescens* in eastern North America. It can also occur on *A. virosa* (p.150). ☠

gills are free •
of stem

crowded, •
soft, white
to off-white
gills

FRUITING Singly or in groups, often on acid soil.

| Dimensions CAP ⊕ 6–18cm | STEM ↕ 6–15cm ↔ 1.5–4cm | Spores White | Edibility |

Family AMANITACEAE	Species *Amanita spissa*	Season Summer–autumn

STOUT AGARIC

This species has a convex, usually dark brown cap with a smooth margin and grey veil patches. The ring on its club-shaped stem has grooves on the upper surface. It smells faintly of oil-seed rape. Although the Stout Agaric is edible after cooking, it is not recommended; see Similar Species. *A. excelsa*, which is considered by some mycologists to be a separate species, has a rooting stem, is paler, and has no smell.

• **OCCURRENCE** Mycorrhizal, typically with beech or spruce in woodland. Widespread in northern temperate zones.

• **SIMILAR SPECIES** Poisonous *A. pantherina* (p.149). *A. rubescens* (p.147) has pink tinges.

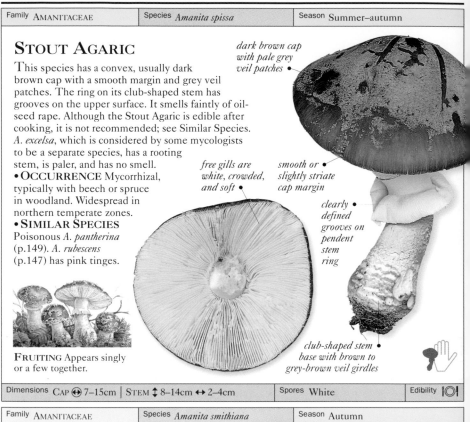

dark brown cap with pale grey veil patches •

free gills are white, crowded, and soft •

smooth or • slightly striate cap margin

clearly • defined grooves on pendent stem ring

FRUITING Appears singly or a few together.

club-shaped stem base with brown to grey-brown veil girdles •

| Dimensions CAP ⊕ 7–15cm \| STEM ↕ 8–14cm ↔ 2–4cm | Spores White | Edibility |

Family AMANITACEAE	Species *Amanita smithiana*	Season Autumn

SMITH'S AGARIC

This species has a convex to flat white cap with conical veil patches. The veil is also visible in shreds around the smooth cap margin. The scaly white stem has a ragged ring and gets larger towards the rooting base, where the basal bulb may be up to 5cm wide. The thick, white, faintly pungent flesh can cause kidney failure or liver disease.

• **OCCURRENCE** Mycorrhizal with softwood trees. Widespread and common in the Pacific Northwest of North America.

• **SIMILAR SPECIES** *Tricholoma magnivelare* (p.81) has a spicy smell and a rooting stem. *Amanita virosa* (p.150) has a smooth cap and is easily distinguished.

veil shreds at smooth cap margin •

crowded, free white gills •

scaly white • stem with ragged ring

FRUITING Singly or in scattered groups under softwood trees in woodland.

| Dimensions CAP ⊕ 5–12.5cm \| STEM ↕ 10–20cm ↔ 1–3cm | Spores White | Edibility ☠ |

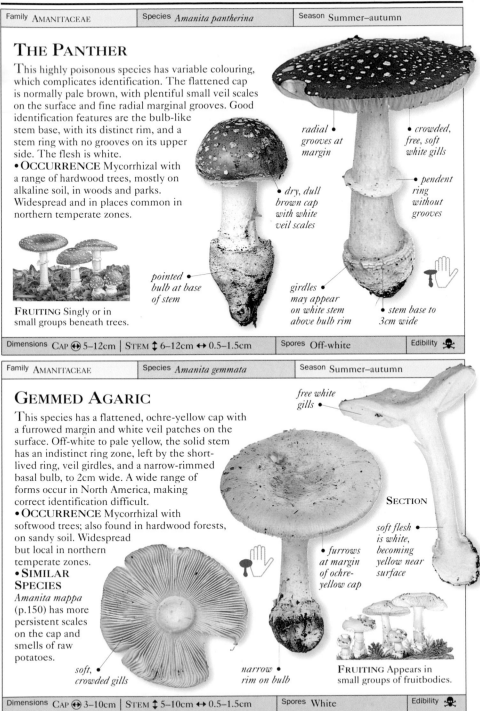

| Family AMANITACEAE | Species *Amanita pantherina* | Season Summer–autumn |

THE PANTHER

This highly poisonous species has variable colouring, which complicates identification. The flattened cap is normally pale brown, with plentiful small veil scales on the surface and fine radial marginal grooves. Good identification features are the bulb-like stem base, with its distinct rim, and a stem ring with no grooves on its upper side. The flesh is white.

• **OCCURRENCE** Mycorrhizal with a range of hardwood trees, mostly on alkaline soil, in woods and parks. Widespread and in places common in northern temperate zones.

radial • grooves at margin

• crowded, free, soft white gills

• dry, dull brown cap with white veil scales

• pendent ring without grooves

FRUITING Singly or in small groups beneath trees.

pointed • bulb at base of stem

girdles may appear on white stem above bulb rim

• stem base to 3cm wide

| Dimensions CAP ⊕ 5–12cm | STEM ↕ 6–12cm ↔ 0.5–1.5cm | Spores Off-white | Edibility ☠ |

| Family AMANITACEAE | Species *Amanita gemmata* | Season Summer–autumn |

GEMMED AGARIC

free white gills •

This species has a flattened, ochre-yellow cap with a furrowed margin and white veil patches on the surface. Off-white to pale yellow, the solid stem has an indistinct ring zone, left by the short-lived ring, veil girdles, and a narrow-rimmed basal bulb, to 2cm wide. A wide range of forms occur in North America, making correct identification difficult.

• **OCCURRENCE** Mycorrhizal with softwood trees; also found in hardwood forests, on sandy soil. Widespread but local in northern temperate zones.

• **SIMILAR SPECIES** *Amanita mappa* (p.150) has more persistent scales on the cap and smells of raw potatoes.

SECTION

soft flesh • is white, becoming yellow near surface

• furrows at margin of ochre-yellow cap

soft, crowded gills

narrow • rim on bulb

FRUITING Appears in small groups of fruitbodies.

| Dimensions CAP ⊕ 3–10cm | STEM ↕ 5–10cm ↔ 0.5–1.5cm | Spores White | Edibility ☠ |

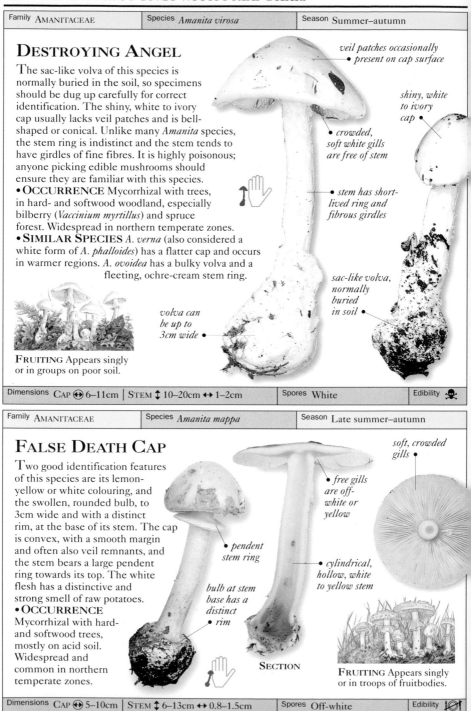

| Family AMANITACEAE | Species *Amanita virosa* | Season Summer–autumn |

DESTROYING ANGEL

The sac-like volva of this species is normally buried in the soil, so specimens should be dug up carefully for correct identification. The shiny, white to ivory cap usually lacks veil patches and is bell-shaped or conical. Unlike many *Amanita* species, the stem ring is indistinct and the stem tends to have girdles of fine fibres. It is highly poisonous; anyone picking edible mushrooms should ensure they are familiar with this species.
• **OCCURRENCE** Mycorrhizal with trees, in hard- and softwood woodland, especially bilberry (*Vaccinium myrtillus*) and spruce forest. Widespread in northern temperate zones.
• **SIMILAR SPECIES** *A. verna* (also considered a white form of *A. phalloides*) has a flatter cap and occurs in warmer regions. *A. ovoidea* has a bulky volva and a fleeting, ochre-cream stem ring.

veil patches occasionally present on cap surface

shiny, white to ivory cap

crowded, soft white gills are free of stem

stem has short-lived ring and fibrous girdles

sac-like volva, normally buried in soil

volva can be up to 3cm wide

FRUITING Appears singly or in groups on poor soil.

| Dimensions CAP ⊕ 6–11cm | STEM ↕ 10–20cm ↔ 1–2cm | Spores White | Edibility ☠ |

| Family AMANITACEAE | Species *Amanita mappa* | Season Late summer–autumn |

FALSE DEATH CAP

Two good identification features of this species are its lemon-yellow or white colouring, and the swollen, rounded bulb, to 3cm wide and with a distinct rim, at the base of its stem. The cap is convex, with a smooth margin and often also veil remnants, and the stem bears a large pendent ring towards its top. The white flesh has a distinctive and strong smell of raw potatoes.
• **OCCURRENCE** Mycorrhizal with hard- and softwood trees, mostly on acid soil. Widespread and common in northern temperate zones.

soft, crowded gills

free gills are off-white or yellow

pendent stem ring

cylindrical, hollow, white to yellow stem

bulb at stem base has a distinct rim

SECTION

FRUITING Appears singly or in troops of fruitbodies.

| Dimensions CAP ⊕ 5–10cm | STEM ↕ 6–13cm ↔ 0.8–1.5cm | Spores Off-white | Edibility ⬤ |

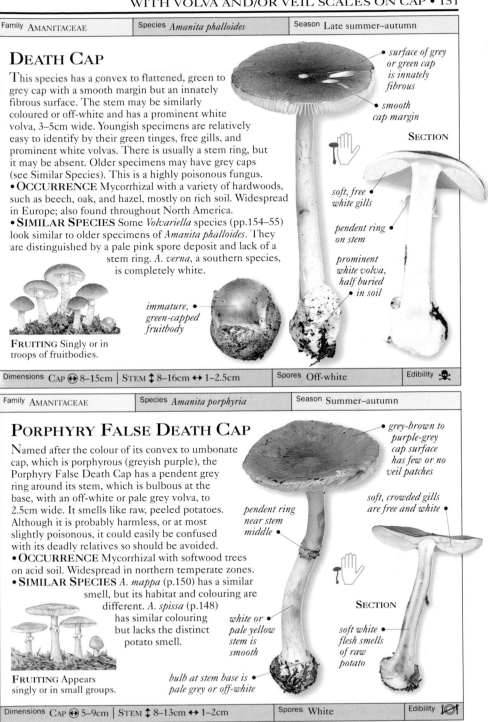

| Family AMANITACEAE | Species *Amanita phalloides* | Season Late summer–autumn |

DEATH CAP

This species has a convex to flattened, green to grey cap with a smooth margin but an innately fibrous surface. The stem may be similarly coloured or off-white and has a prominent white volva, 3–5cm wide. Youngish specimens are relatively easy to identify by their green tinges, free gills, and prominent white volvas. There is usually a stem ring, but it may be absent. Older specimens may have grey caps (see Similar Species). This is a highly poisonous fungus.
• **OCCURRENCE** Mycorrhizal with a variety of hardwoods, such as beech, oak, and hazel, mostly on rich soil. Widespread in Europe; also found throughout North America.
• **SIMILAR SPECIES** Some *Volvariella* species (pp.154–55) look similar to older specimens of *Amanita phalloides*. They are distinguished by a pale pink spore deposit and lack of a stem ring. *A. verna*, a southern species, is completely white.

FRUITING Singly or in troops of fruitbodies.

immature, green-capped fruitbody

surface of grey or green cap is innately fibrous

smooth cap margin

SECTION

soft, free white gills

pendent ring on stem

prominent white volva, half buried in soil

| Dimensions CAP ⊕ 8–15cm | STEM ↕ 8–16cm ↔ 1–2.5cm | Spores Off-white | Edibility ☠ |

| Family AMANITACEAE | Species *Amanita porphyria* | Season Summer–autumn |

PORPHYRY FALSE DEATH CAP

Named after the colour of its convex to umbonate cap, which is porphyrous (greyish purple), the Porphyry False Death Cap has a pendent grey ring around its stem, which is bulbous at the base, with an off-white or pale grey volva, to 2.5cm wide. It smells like raw, peeled potatoes. Although it is probably harmless, or at most slightly poisonous, it could easily be confused with its deadly relatives so should be avoided.
• **OCCURRENCE** Mycorrhizal with softwood trees on acid soil. Widespread in northern temperate zones.
• **SIMILAR SPECIES** *A. mappa* (p.150) has a similar smell, but its habitat and colouring are different. *A. spissa* (p.148) has similar colouring but lacks the distinct potato smell.

FRUITING Appears singly or in small groups.

grey-brown to purple-grey cap surface has few or no veil patches

soft, crowded gills are free and white

pendent ring near stem middle

white or pale yellow stem is smooth

SECTION

soft white flesh smells of raw potato

bulb at stem base is pale grey or off-white

| Dimensions CAP ⊕ 5–9cm | STEM ↕ 8–13cm ↔ 1–2cm | Spores White | Edibility ◑ |

Family AMANITACEAE	Species *Amanita fulva*	Season Summer–autumn

TAWNY GRISETTE

This species has a conical to umbonate, smooth, tawny brown cap and a downy and slightly fibrillose stem in a similar colour. A furrowed cap margin and the absence of a stem ring or girdles indicate that this species belongs to the subgenus *Amanitopsis*. Many *Amanitopsis* species can be difficult to identify: the colour of the volva – off-white to pale brown in this species – is an important characteristic. Although edible, *Amanita fulva* must be cooked thoroughly before being eaten. The soft, watery flesh is off-white. It turns chocolate-brown in contact with phenol.

• **OCCURRENCE** Mycorrhizal with birch trees in woodland areas. Widespread in northern temperate zones.

• **SIMILAR SPECIES** *A. crocea* and *A. vaginata* (both p.153).

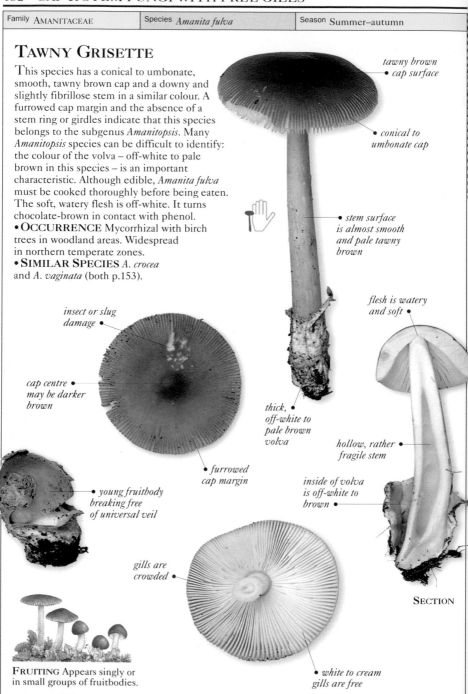

tawny brown cap surface

conical to umbonate cap

stem surface is almost smooth and pale tawny brown

flesh is watery and soft

insect or slug damage

cap centre may be darker brown

thick, off-white to pale brown volva

hollow, rather fragile stem

furrowed cap margin

young fruitbody breaking free of universal veil

inside of volva is off-white to brown

SECTION

gills are crowded

white to cream gills are free

FRUITING Appears singly or in small groups of fruitbodies.

Dimensions CAP ⊕ 3–8cm | STEM ↕ 7–15cm ↔ 0.7–1.2cm	Spores Off-white	Edibility

Family AMANITACEAE	Species *Amanita crocea*	Season Early summer–autumn

ORANGE GRISETTE

This striking species has a convex to umbonate, shiny orange cap, which is smooth with a furrowed margin. The stem, which is without a ring, has thin orange girdles and a prominent, thick white volva. Like *Amanita fulva* (p.152), it belongs to the subgenus *Amanitopsis*. Although both species are often found near birch, *A. crocea* prefers much richer soil. It is edible, with soft, off-white flesh, but must be thoroughly cooked before eating. If harvested for eating, the fruitbodies should be used as soon as possible as they do not keep well.

• **OCCURRENCE** Mycorrhizal with birch trees, and possibly also spruce, beech, and oak, on fairly rich soil in lowland areas and at higher altitudes, near the tree line. Widespread in Europe and North America.

• **SIMILAR SPECIES**
A. fulva (p.152) has off-white flesh turning chocolate-brown in contact with phenol whereas the flesh of *A. crocea* turns dark wine-red. *A. vaginata* (inset, below).

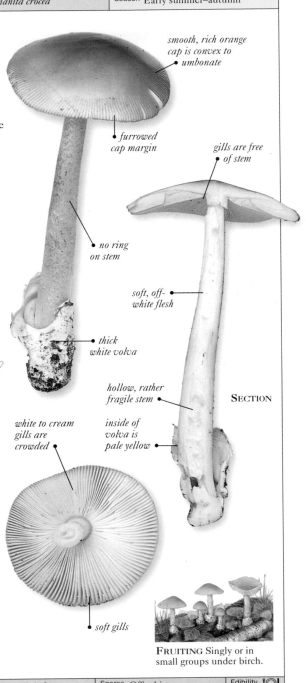

smooth, rich orange cap is convex to umbonate

furrowed cap margin

gills are free of stem

no ring on stem

soft, off-white flesh

thick white volva

hollow, rather fragile stem

SECTION

white to cream gills are crowded

inside of volva is pale yellow

soft gills

△ *AMANITA VAGINATA*
This grey to near white species has a convex to umbonate cap, which is furrowed at the margin. The stem has a mealy surface and a prominent volva, which often develops orange spots when older. It occurs mainly under hardwoods on rich soil. |O|

FRUITING Singly or in small groups under birch.

| Dimensions CAP ⊕ 6–12cm | STEM ↕ 10–20cm ↔ 1–2cm | Spores Off-white | Edibility |O| |

| Family PLUTEACEAE | Species *Volvariella bombycina* | Season Summer–autumn |

SILKY VOLVAR

An easy species to identify, but not so easy to find as it is rare and may be high up in trees, the Silky Volvar has a very large, conical to umbonate, white to pale yellow cap, covered in silky fibres, and a pronounced volva at the base of the white to yellowish cream stem. It has a pleasant smell and is edible, but because of its rarity is not recommended.

• **OCCURRENCE** On standing dead trees (rarely on fallen trunks), on stored timber, or in buildings. Widespread in northern temperate zones, but mostly rather local; also further south.

• **SIMILAR SPECIES** *Volvariella caesiotincta* has a similar habitat but lacks the silky cap surface and is smaller and darker.

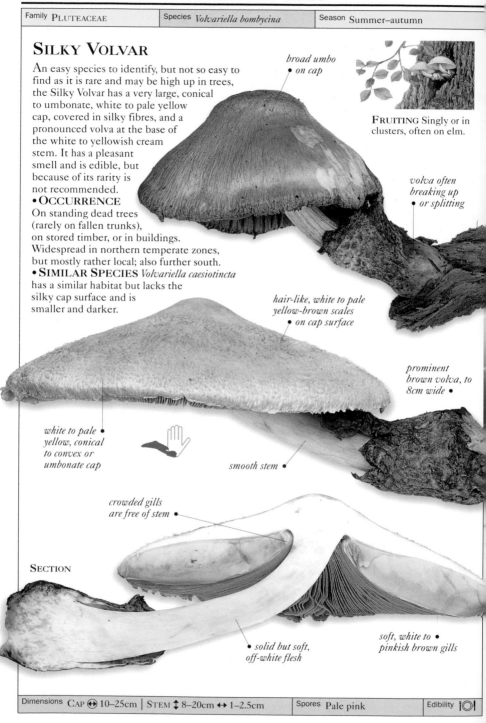

broad umbo on cap

FRUITING Singly or in clusters, often on elm.

volva often breaking up or splitting

hair-like, white to pale yellow-brown scales on cap surface

prominent brown volva, to 8cm wide

white to pale yellow, conical to convex or umbonate cap

smooth stem

crowded gills are free of stem

SECTION

solid but soft, off-white flesh

soft, white to pinkish brown gills

| Dimensions CAP ⊕ 10–25cm | STEM ↕ 8–20cm ↔ 1–2.5cm | Spores Pale pink | Edibility |

Family PLUTEACEAE	Species *Volvariella gloiocephala*	Season Summer–autumn

STUBBLE-FIELD VOLVAR

This is the largest of all the soil-growing *Volvariella* species; it is distinguished further by a smooth, sticky, conical or umbonate cap that ranges between white and mouse-grey in colour. The stem is off-white to dingy grey-yellow with a white to pale grey volva at the base. The off-white flesh tastes like cucumber and may smell of radishes. Once gathered, the fruitbodies soon deteriorate so should be used quickly if picked for eating.

• **OCCURRENCE** On disturbed, nutrient-rich soil, such as in stubble fields, compost beds, bark mulches, or beneath haystacks. Widespread and fairly common in northern temperate zones, extending further south.

• **SIMILAR SPECIES** A close relative, *V. volvacea*, is commercially grown in parts of southeast Asia. It has a shorter stem and a dark grey volva. The caps of young specimens are darker grey-brown in colour.

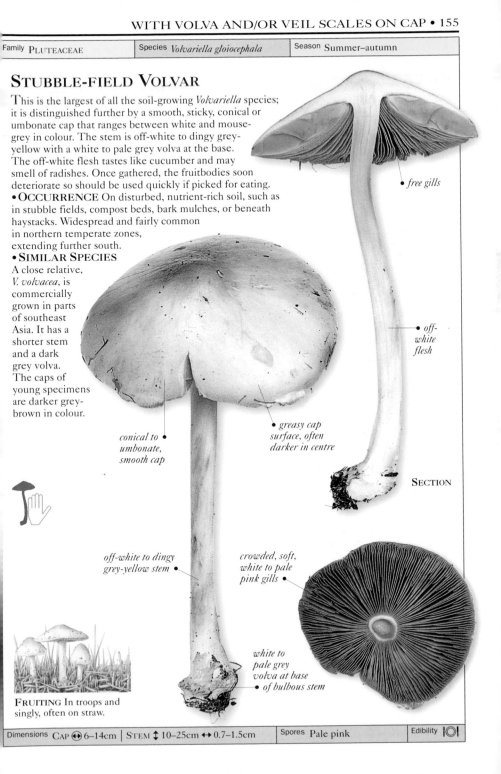

• *free gills*

• *off-white flesh*

conical to umbonate, smooth cap

greasy cap surface, often darker in centre

SECTION

off-white to dingy grey-yellow stem •

crowded, soft, white to pale pink gills •

white to pale grey volva at base of bulbous stem

FRUITING In troops and singly, often on straw.

| Dimensions CAP ⊕ 6–14cm | STEM ↕ 10–25cm ↔ 0.7–1.5cm | Spores Pale pink | Edibility |O| |

WITH STEM RING OR RING ZONE

T HE SPECIES in this subsection have free gills (see p.145) and the remains of the partial veil clearly visible on the stem, either as a ring or a ring zone. The ring varies from large to small and may be persistent or short- lived. Where there is no ring, the are where it would be – the ring zone – i marked by threads or darker marking Most species featured have white o dark brown to black spore deposits and belong to the family Agaricaceae.

Family AGARICACEAE	Species *Agaricus sylvicola*	Season Summer–autumn

WOOD MUSHROOM

This species is a woodland form of *Agaricus arvensis* (p.157), but its stem is more slender, with a usually flat bulb at the base. The cap is convex to expanded, then flat, with a smooth surface that is yellow- or off-white to orange-yellow or pale ochre. Like *A. arvensis*, it smells of almonds and has white flesh that very slowly stains yellow with age or when damaged. Although a choice edible, it should be eaten only in small quantities as it contains cadmium.
• **OCCURRENCE** On rich woodland soil mixed with debris, under soft- and hardwood trees. Widespread and common throughout northern temperate zones.

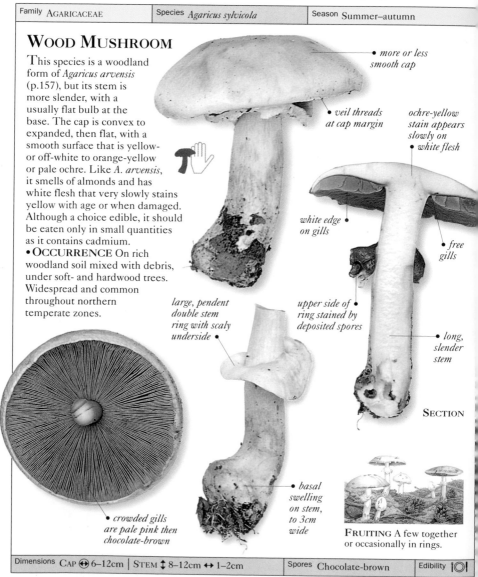

• *more or less smooth cap*

• *veil threads at cap margin*

ochre-yellow stain appears slowly on • *white flesh*

white edge on gills •

• *free gills*

large, pendent double stem ring with scaly underside •

upper side of • ring stained by deposited spores

• *long, slender stem*

SECTION

• *crowded gills are pale pink then chocolate-brown*

• *basal swelling on stem, to 3cm wide*

FRUITING A few together or occasionally in rings.

Dimensions CAP ⊕ 6–12cm | STEM ↕ 8–12cm ↔ 1–2cm	Spores Chocolate-brown	Edibility

Family AGARICACEAE	Species *Agaricus arvensis*	Season Summer–autumn

HORSE MUSHROOM

This species has a rounded to convex cap with a smooth, yellow- to off-white surface that very slowly stains orange-yellow to ochre, particularly where bruised. The similarly coloured stem, which thickens towards the base, has a pendent ring with a wheel-like pattern on its underside. The thick, firm white flesh also stains very slowly. It smells similar to almonds and is edible but is high in cadmium.

• **OCCURRENCE** Often found in horse-grazed pasture and on lawns and in parkland. Widespread and common in northern temperate zones.

• **SIMILAR SPECIES** There are several similar species. *Agaricus augustus* (p.158). *A. macrosporus* is very fleshy, with scaly stem girdles. *A. sylvicola* (p.156) is a woodland form. *A. xanthoderma* (p.159).

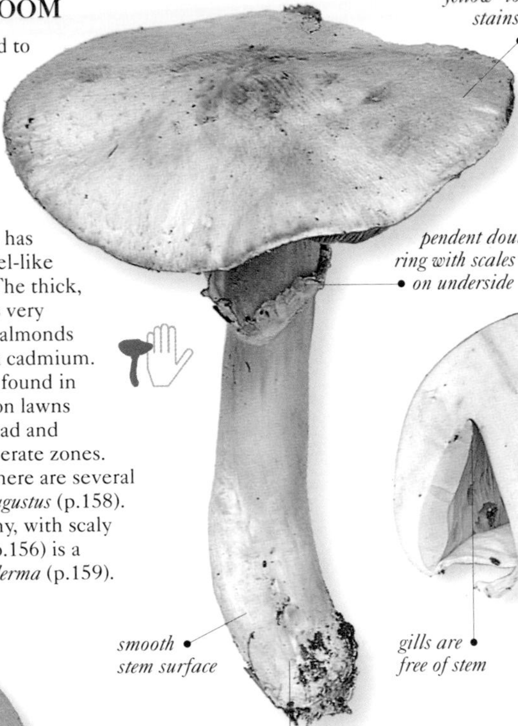

yellow- to off-white cap stains orange-yellow to ochre

pendent double ring with scales on underside

smooth stem surface

gills are free of stem

young cap is smooth with an inrolled margin

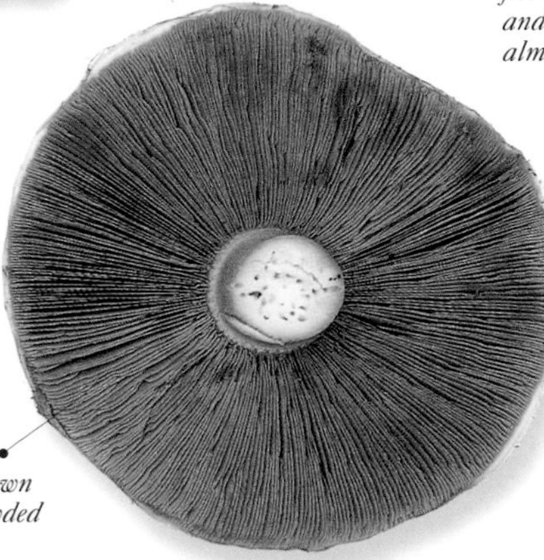

thick, but not bulbous, stem base

flesh is white and smells of almonds

SECTION

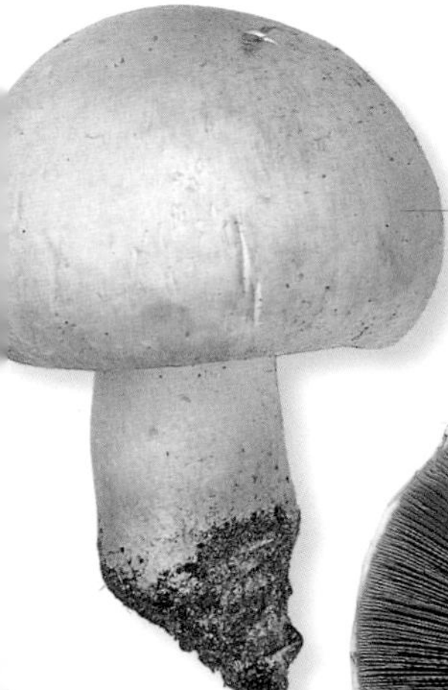

pale pink to chocolate-brown gills are crowded

FRUITING Mostly appears in fairy rings in grass.

Dimensions CAP ⊕ 7–15cm	STEM ↕ 7–15cm ↔ 1–3cm	Spores Chocolate-brown	Edibility

| Family AGARICACEAE | Species *Agaricus augustus* | Season Autumn |

THE PRINCE

Orange-brown scales on the
surface of both cap and stem,
together with yellow-staining
flesh that smells of almonds,
identify this species. The
scales are arranged in a
concentric pattern on the convex
to expanded cap, and the stem has
a large, pendent ring. With its firm,
abundant flesh, it makes a choice
edible, but should only be eaten
in small quantities as it contains a
large amount of cadmium.

• **OCCURRENCE** In all types of
woodland and parks, on rich soil,
and on garden compost. Widespread
in northern temperate zones.

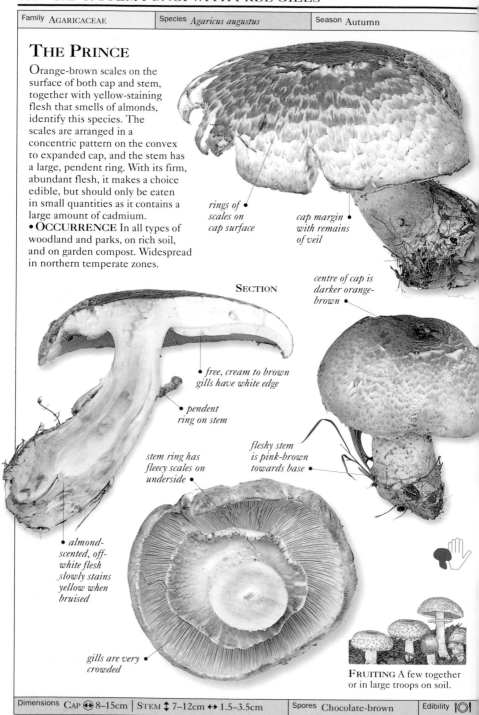

rings of •
scales on
cap surface

cap margin •
with remains
of veil

centre of cap is
darker orange-
brown •

SECTION

• free, cream to brown
gills have white edge

• pendent
ring on stem

fleshy stem
is pink-brown
towards base •

stem ring has
fleecy scales on
underside •

• almond-
scented, off-
white flesh
slowly stains
yellow when
bruised

gills are very •
crowded

FRUITING A few together
or in large troops on soil.

| Dimensions CAP ⊕ 8–15cm \| STEM ↕ 7–12cm ↔ 1.5–3.5cm | Spores Chocolate-brown | Edibility |

Family AGARICACEAE	Species *Agaricus xanthoderma*	Season Summer–autumn

YELLOW-STAINING MUSHROOM

Despite having a yellow-staining surface and flesh, this poisonous fungus appears whiter, almost chalk-white, in comparison with the other, slower-staining *Agaricus* species. Its most obvious characteristics are its stem base, which is very bright yellow at the tip when cut lengthwise, and its smell, which is very similar to that of ink.

• **OCCURRENCE** On bare soil or in grass in parkland, cemeteries, and similar places. Widespread throughout northern temperate zones and elsewhere.

• **SIMILAR SPECIES** *A. arvensis* (p.157) and *A. sylvicola* (p.156) have a distinctive smell of almonds. They are slower to stain yellow, and are edible. *A. moelleri* (p.160) is darker in colour and poisonous.

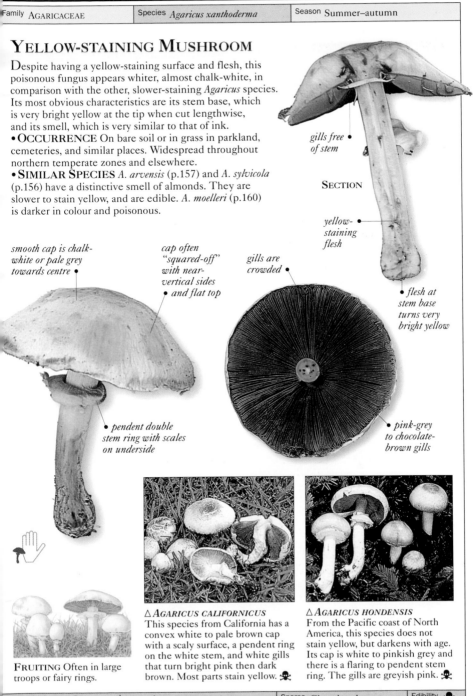

gills free of stem

SECTION

yellow-staining flesh

smooth cap is chalk-white or pale grey towards centre •

cap often "squared-off" with near-vertical sides and flat top

gills are crowded •

• flesh at stem base turns very bright yellow

• pendent double stem ring with scales on underside

• pink-grey to chocolate-brown gills

FRUITING Often in large troops or fairy rings.

△ *AGARICUS CALIFORNICUS*
This species from California has a convex white to pale brown cap with a scaly surface, a pendent ring on the white stem, and white gills that turn bright pink then dark brown. Most parts stain yellow. ☠

△ *AGARICUS HONDENSIS*
From the Pacific coast of North America, this species does not stain yellow, but darkens with age. Its cap is white to pinkish grey and there is a flaring to pendent stem ring. The gills are greyish pink. ☠

| Dimensions CAP ⊕ 5–13cm | STEM ↕ 5–10cm ↔ 1–2cm | Spores Chocolate-brown | Edibility ☠ |

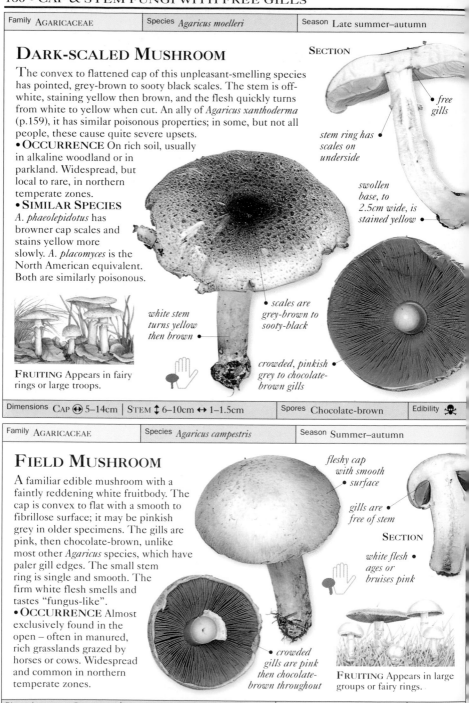

Family AGARICACEAE	Species *Agaricus moelleri*	Season Late summer–autumn

DARK-SCALED MUSHROOM

SECTION

The convex to flattened cap of this unpleasant-smelling species has pointed, grey-brown to sooty black scales. The stem is off-white, staining yellow then brown, and the flesh quickly turns from white to yellow when cut. An ally of *Agaricus xanthoderma* (p.159), it has similar poisonous properties; in some, but not all people, these cause quite severe upsets.

• **OCCURRENCE** On rich soil, usually in alkaline woodland or in parkland. Widespread, but local to rare, in northern temperate zones.

• **SIMILAR SPECIES** *A. phaeolepidotus* has browner cap scales and stains yellow more slowly. *A. placomyces* is the North American equivalent. Both are similarly poisonous.

• free gills

stem ring has • scales on underside

swollen base, to 2.5cm wide, is stained yellow •

FRUITING Appears in fairy rings or large troops.

white stem turns yellow then brown •

• scales are grey-brown to sooty-black

crowded, pinkish • grey to chocolate-brown gills

Dimensions CAP ⊕ 5–14cm | STEM ↕ 6–10cm ↔ 1–1.5cm	Spores Chocolate-brown	Edibility ☠

Family AGARICACEAE	Species *Agaricus campestris*	Season Summer–autumn

FIELD MUSHROOM

A familiar edible mushroom with a faintly reddening white fruitbody. The cap is convex to flat with a smooth to fibrillose surface; it may be pinkish grey in older specimens. The gills are pink, then chocolate-brown, unlike most other *Agaricus* species, which have paler gill edges. The small stem ring is single and smooth. The firm white flesh smells and tastes "fungus-like".

• **OCCURRENCE** Almost exclusively found in the open – often in manured, rich grasslands grazed by horses or cows. Widespread and common in northern temperate zones.

fleshy cap with smooth • surface

gills are • free of stem

SECTION

white flesh • ages or bruises pink

• crowded gills are pink then chocolate-brown throughout

FRUITING Appears in large groups or fairy rings.

Dimensions CAP ⊕ 4–10cm | STEM ↕ 3–7cm ↔ 0.8–1.5cm	Spores Chocolate-brown	Edibility ⦿

Family AGARICACEAE	Species *Agaricus bitorquis*	Season Summer–autumn

PAVEMENT MUSHROOM

This species has several distinguishing features: it has a prominent double stem ring, which is sheathed and upturned; its acid-smelling, firm flesh slowly turns pink; and it has a "squared" cap with an inrolled margin. Although it is edible, its roadside habitat makes eating it undesirable.

• OCCURRENCE Mostly found in urban areas, in soil or between paving stones. Widespread and common in Europe and North America.

• SIMILAR SPECIES *Agaricus bernardii* (p.162), which is foul smelling and has a cracked cap surface, is found in similar sites.

cap has distinct shoulders

smooth cap is white to off-white

stem ring is double and upturned

cap surface is often soiled

free gills are pink then chocolate-brown

FRUITING A few together. They can be found emerging from hard soil or even tarmac.

Dimensions CAP ⊕ 5–12cm	STEM ↕ 4–8cm ↔ 1–3.5cm	Spores Chocolate-brown	Edibility 🍽

Family AGARICACEAE	Species *Agaricus bisporus*	Season Late summer–autumn

CULTIVATED MUSHROOM

SECTION

This species is perhaps the best known of all edible fungi. It is cultivated on a huge scale; only species like *Volvariella volvacea* (Padistraw Mushroom), *Pleurotus ostreatus* (Common Oyster Mushroom, p.178), and *Lentinula edodes* (Shii-take) compete in commercial importance. Its convex cap varies from white to dark brown, and its stem has an upturned ring. Its flesh stains very slightly red.

• OCCURRENCE By roadsides, in cemeteries, and other sites with rich, disturbed soil. Widespread throughout northern temperate zones.

crowded gills are free

stem ring turns upward when young

convex to flat cap with smooth, dry surface

veil remains at margin

white to dark brown cap

faint carrot-red stain on stem from handling or bruising

gills are chocolate-brown when mature

FRUITING Appears in troops and fairy rings.

Dimensions CAP ⊕ 5–10cm	STEM ↕ 3–6cm ↔ 1–2cm	Spores Chocolate-brown	Edibility 🍽

| Family AGARICACEAE | Species *Agaricus bernardii* | Season Summer–autumn |

SALT-LOVING MUSHROOM

This very fleshy mushroom tolerates soil that is rich in salt. It has a flattened or convex, white to grey-white cap, the surface of which often cracks into a scaly pattern. The thickset stem has a sheathing ring with a narrow, upturned rim. Foul smelling, the Salt-loving Mushroom has firm white flesh that slowly turns pink with age. Although it is edible, it has a poor flavour and is not worth eating.

• **OCCURRENCE** In the salt-spray zones of coastal areas or along roads that are salted during the winter. Widespread in Europe.

• **SIMILAR SPECIES** *Agaricus bitorquis* (p.161) is found in similar sites.

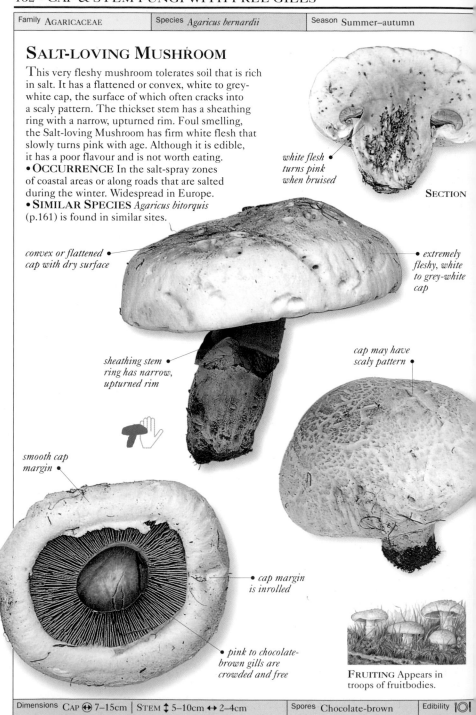

white flesh turns pink when bruised

SECTION

convex or flattened cap with dry surface

extremely fleshy, white to grey-white cap

sheathing stem ring has narrow, upturned rim

cap may have scaly pattern

smooth cap margin

cap margin is inrolled

pink to chocolate-brown gills are crowded and free

FRUITING Appears in troops of fruitbodies.

| Dimensions CAP ⊕ 7–15cm | STEM ↕ 5–10cm ↔ 2–4cm | Spores Chocolate-brown | Edibility 🔘 |

Family AGARICACEAE	Species *Agaricus sylvaticus*	Season Summer–autumn

RED-STAINING MUSHROOM

The convex to umbonate cap of this species is covered with fine brown fibres. The stem, with its pendent ring, may have a fibrous-scaly surface. Also known as the Pinewood Mushroom, Wood Mushroom, and Scaly Wood Mushroom, this choice edible has pleasant-smelling, off-white flesh that stains deep red, mostly after bruising, although the colour reaction is less marked than in some of its relatives.
• **OCCURRENCE** On softwood debris in woodland, plantations, and parks. Widespread in northern temperate zones.
• **SIMILAR SPECIES** *Agaricus langei*, also a good edible, is more fleshy and stains a deeper red. *A. phaeolepidotus* stains yellow and is poisonous.

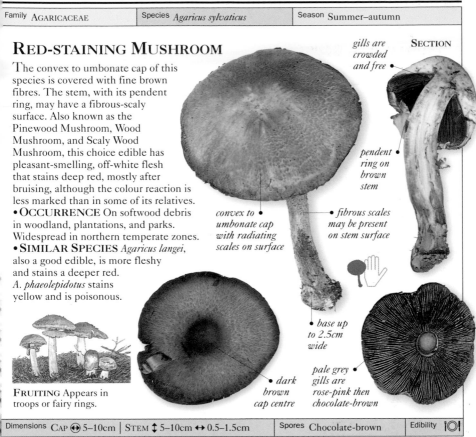

gills are crowded and free

SECTION

pendent ring on brown stem

convex to umbonate cap with radiating scales on surface

fibrous scales may be present on stem surface

base up to 2.5cm wide

dark brown cap centre

pale grey gills are rose-pink then chocolate-brown

FRUITING Appears in troops or fairy rings.

Dimensions CAP ⊕ 5–10cm | STEM ↕ 5–10cm ↔ 0.5–1.5cm	Spores Chocolate-brown	Edibility

Family AGARICACEAE	Species *Agaricus porphyrizon*	Season Throughout autumn

PORPHYRY MUSHROOM

This species is an unusually sturdy, fleshy member of a group of mostly small *Agaricus* species, called section *Minores*, that all have an almondy smell, yellow-staining flesh, and often purple cap colours. The cap of the Porphyry Mushroom is convex with a covering of fine, purple-lilac fibres on a paler background, and the stem is white with a bulbous, yellow to orange base and a fragile, narrow stem ring. The gills are grey-pink to purple-black. It has edible white flesh that slowly stains yellow.
• **OCCURRENCE** On soil and leaf litter in hardwood woodland, but also on softwood debris and in gardens. Widespread but local in Europe; world distribution not fully known.

fine, lilac-purple fibres

cap is convex and pale

grey-pink, free gills

FRUITING Appears singly or a few fruitbodies together on rich soil among leaf litter.

Dimensions CAP ⊕ 5–8cm | STEM ↕ 4–6cm ↔ 0.7–1cm	Spores Chocolate-brown	Edibility

| Family AGARICACEAE | Species *Leucoagaricus leucothites* | Season Late summer–autumn |

SMOOTH PARASOL

The convex cap of this white species has a smooth, dry surface. The stem has a thin ring, which may be loose, and a club-shaped base. The white flesh smells pleasant with a "fungus-like" taste, but is poisonous. Subtle colour differences have led some experts to divide *Leucoagaricus leucothites* into a small group of separate species; none are edible.
• **OCCURRENCE** In grass along road verges and in parks, gardens, and sand dunes. Widespread in Europe and North America.
• **SIMILAR SPECIES** Several *Agaricus* species are similar but their spore deposits and mature gills are chocolate-brown.

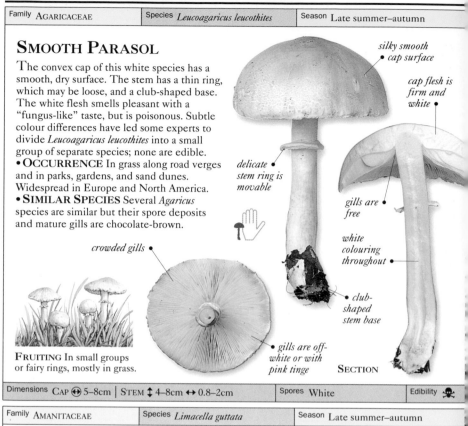

silky smooth cap surface

cap flesh is firm and white

delicate stem ring is movable

gills are free

white colouring throughout

club-shaped stem base

crowded gills

gills are off-white or with pink tinge

SECTION

FRUITING In small groups or fairy rings, mostly in grass.

| Dimensions CAP ⊕ 5–8cm | STEM ↕ 4–8cm ↔ 0.8–2cm | Spores White | Edibility ☠ |

| Family AMANITACEAE | Species *Limacella guttata* | Season Late summer–autumn |

WEEPING SLIME-VEIL

The slightly greasy, convex cap of this species is creamy ochre to very pale red-brown. Its dry stem has a bulbous base and a prominent, pendent ring that exudes drops of clear liquid, which dry as olive-brown spots. The white gills are free and crowded. Although this white-fleshed, mealy-smelling fungus is recorded as edible, it is not recommended.
• **OCCURRENCE** In hard- or softwood woodland, on rich soil among thick leaf litter. Widespread but local in Europe and North America.
• **SIMILAR SPECIES** *Limacella glioderma* is very slimy with an orange-brown cap. Some *Amanita* species are similar in appearance but have a dry cap surface, with veil remnants, and a volva at the base of the stem.

cap is creamy ochre, darker with age

pale red-brown centre of convex, greasy cap

crowded gills are white and free

pendent stem ring is very prominent

FRUITING Appears in troops of fruitbodies or singly in rich soil and litter in woodland areas.

| Dimensions CAP ⊕ 7–15cm | STEM ↕ 8–14cm ↔ 1–2.5cm | Spores White | Edibility ⬤◖ |

Family AGARICACEAE	Species *Macrolepiota procera*	Season Summer–autumn

PARASOL MUSHROOM

This spectacular large mushroom is distinguished by a beautiful snakeskin pattern on its stem, which also has a large, movable ring. The cap is umbrella-shaped to flat with a raised, dark grey-brown centre, and with a concentric pattern of attached scales. The pale flesh does not stain when bruised. Some consider this to be one of the best edible mushrooms.

• **OCCURRENCE** In dunes, dry grassland, and small grassy areas in woods and parks. Widespread and fairly common in Europe and North America.

• **SIMILAR SPECIES** *Macrolepiota permixta* has red-staining flesh. *M. rhacodes* (p.166). *Chlorophyllum molybdites* (p.166) is poisonous.

concentric brown scales on cap surface

cap centre is dark grey-brown

very tall stem with delicate snakeskin pattern

stem ring is large and movable

cap emerges egg-shaped, becoming umbrella-shaped or flat with a raised centre

crowded, free, white to cream gills

slightly bulbous stem base

stem may be 4cm wide at base

FRUITING In scattered troops on sandy grass or soil.

Dimensions CAP ⊕ 10–30cm	STEM ↕ 15–30cm ↔ 0.8–2cm	Spores White or pale pink	Edibility 🍴

| Family AGARICACEAE | Species *Macrolepiota rhacodes* | Season Summer–autumn |

SHAGGY PARASOL

This shaggy species has concentric, pale brown scales covering the surface of the convex cap, which flattens with age; very young specimens resemble flower bulbs. The stem has a prominent double ring. Its white flesh turns bright carrot-red when bruised. Although edible, some varieties cause stomach upsets, so only small quantities should be eaten (see also Similar Species).

• **OCCURRENCE** Mostly grows on rich soil in hedgerows, parks, and gardens. Widespread and common throughout Europe and North America.

• **SIMILAR SPECIES** *Macrolepiota permixta* and *M. procera* (p.165) are larger, with snakeskin-patterned stems. *Chlorophyllum molybdites* (inset, below) has a green spore deposit and is poisonous.

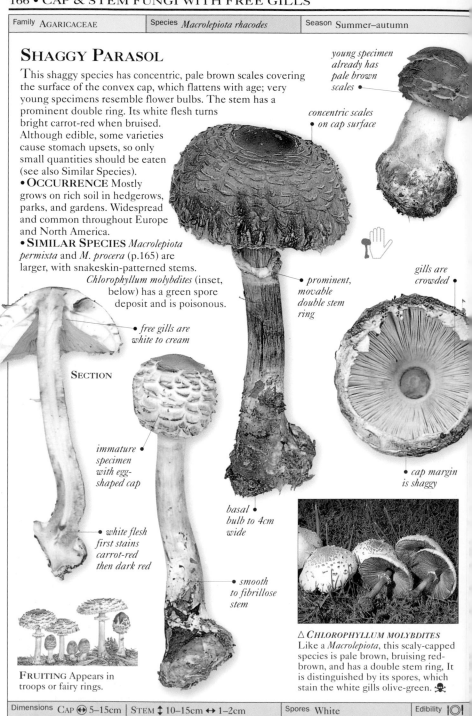

young specimen already has pale brown scales

concentric scales on cap surface

free gills are white to cream

SECTION

gills are crowded

prominent, movable double stem ring

immature specimen with egg-shaped cap

cap margin is shaggy

white flesh first stains carrot-red then dark red

basal bulb to 4cm wide

smooth to fibrillose stem

FRUITING Appears in troops or fairy rings.

△ ***CHLOROPHYLLUM MOLYBDITES***
Like a *Macrolepiota*, this scaly-capped species is pale brown, bruising red-brown, and has a double stem ring, It is distinguished by its spores, which stain the white gills olive-green. ☠

| Dimensions CAP ⊕ 5–15cm \| STEM ↕ 10–15cm ↔ 1–2cm | Spores White | Edibility ⲓⵔ |

Family AGARICACEAE	Species *Lepiota aspera*	Season Late summer–autumn

SHARP-SCALED PARASOL

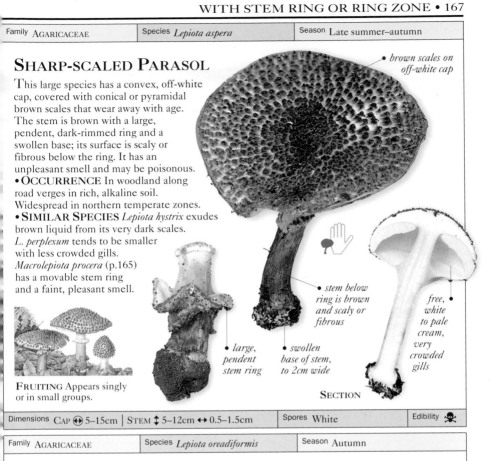

• *brown scales on off-white cap*

This large species has a convex, off-white cap, covered with conical or pyramidal brown scales that wear away with age. The stem is brown with a large, pendent, dark-rimmed ring and a swollen base; its surface is scaly or fibrous below the ring. It has an unpleasant smell and may be poisonous.

• **OCCURRENCE** In woodland along road verges in rich, alkaline soil. Widespread in northern temperate zones.

• **SIMILAR SPECIES** *Lepiota hystrix* exudes brown liquid from its very dark scales. *L. perplexum* tends to be smaller with less crowded gills. *Macrolepiota procera* (p.165) has a movable stem ring and a faint, pleasant smell.

stem below ring is brown and scaly or fibrous

free, white to pale cream, very crowded gills

FRUITING Appears singly or in small groups.

• *large, pendent stem ring*

• *swollen base of stem, to 2cm wide*

SECTION

Dimensions CAP ⊕ 5–15cm	STEM ↕ 5–12cm ↔ 0.5–1.5cm	Spores White	Edibility ☠

Family AGARICACEAE	Species *Lepiota oreadiformis*	Season Autumn

GRASSLAND PARASOL

A conical cap and crowded, thin, free white gills make this species typical of the genus; however, unlike most *Lepiota* species, the stem ring is hardly visible. The overall colouring of the fruitbody is off-white to cream, with the cap having a browner centre. The stem is girdled with the remains of the veil, and the cap margin also bears veil remnants. Some mycologists separate *L. oreadiformis* into three or more distinct species.

• **OCCURRENCE** In dry open grassland, often in coastal sites such as on sand dunes. Widespread in Europe; worldwide distribution is not fully understood.

• **SIMILAR SPECIES** *Marasmius oreades* (p.117) is superficially similar but has adnexed gills, tough flesh, and no sign of any veil remnants.

stem ring is hardly visible, if seen at all

free, crowded gills are pale cream

cap is off-white to cream with darker centre

FRUITING In troops of fruitbodies among lichens and short grass in open grassland and coastal sites.

Dimensions CAP ⊕ 2–6cm	STEM ↕ 3–5cm ↔ 0.8–1.2cm	Spores White	Edibility

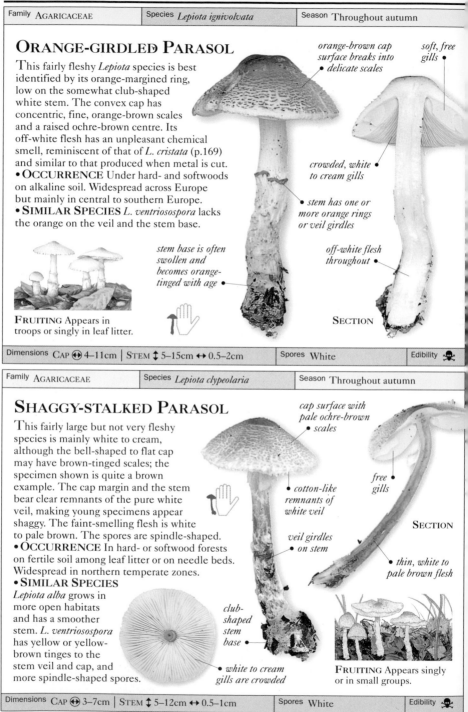

| Family AGARICACEAE | Species *Lepiota ignivolvata* | Season Throughout autumn |

ORANGE-GIRDLED PARASOL

This fairly fleshy *Lepiota* species is best identified by its orange-margined ring, low on the somewhat club-shaped white stem. The convex cap has concentric, fine, orange-brown scales and a raised ochre-brown centre. Its off-white flesh has an unpleasant chemical smell, reminiscent of that of *L. cristata* (p.169) and similar to that produced when metal is cut.
• **OCCURRENCE** Under hard- and softwoods on alkaline soil. Widespread across Europe but mainly in central to southern Europe.
• **SIMILAR SPECIES** *L. ventriosospora* lacks the orange on the veil and the stem base.

orange-brown cap surface breaks into delicate scales

soft, free gills

crowded, white to cream gills

stem has one or more orange rings or veil girdles

stem base is often swollen and becomes orange-tinged with age

off-white flesh throughout

FRUITING Appears in troops or singly in leaf litter.

SECTION

| Dimensions CAP ⊕ 4–11cm | STEM ↕ 5–15cm ↔ 0.5–2cm | Spores White | Edibility ☠ |

| Family AGARICACEAE | Species *Lepiota clypeolaria* | Season Throughout autumn |

SHAGGY-STALKED PARASOL

This fairly large but not very fleshy species is mainly white to cream, although the bell-shaped to flat cap may have brown-tinged scales; the specimen shown is quite a brown example. The cap margin and the stem bear clear remnants of the pure white veil, making young specimens appear shaggy. The faint-smelling flesh is white to pale brown. The spores are spindle-shaped.
• **OCCURRENCE** In hard- or softwood forests on fertile soil among leaf litter or on needle beds. Widespread in northern temperate zones.
• **SIMILAR SPECIES** *Lepiota alba* grows in more open habitats and has a smoother stem. *L. ventriosospora* has yellow or yellow-brown tinges to the stem veil and cap, and more spindle-shaped spores.

cap surface with pale ochre-brown scales

free gills

cotton-like remnants of white veil

SECTION

veil girdles on stem

thin, white to pale brown flesh

club-shaped stem base

white to cream gills are crowded

FRUITING Appears singly or in small groups.

| Dimensions CAP ⊕ 3–7cm | STEM ↕ 5–12cm ↔ 0.5–1cm | Spores White | Edibility ☠ |

Family AGARICACEAE	Species *Lepiota cristata*	Season Summer–autumn

STINKING PARASOL

This is the most common of the smaller *Lepiota* species. Its best identification characteristics are its pale colours, the concentric pattern of flat, orange-brown scales on the convex cap, and an unpleasant chemical smell. The stem ring is short lived but can be seen as an upturned cuff on younger specimens.
• **OCCURRENCE** In lawns, among mosses, or near nettles, at the edges of paths and roads, on fairly rich soil. Widespread and common in northern temperate zones.
• **SIMILAR SPECIES** The very poisonous *L. lilacea* is much rarer, with a similar shape but with purple to purple-brown colours.

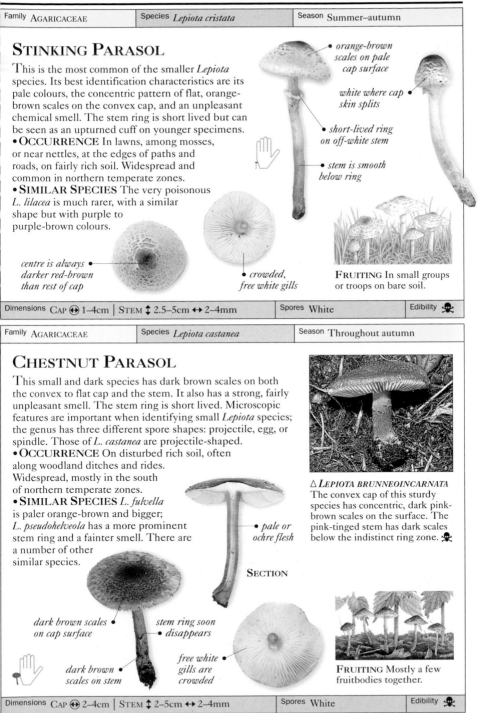

orange-brown scales on pale cap surface

white where cap skin splits

short-lived ring on off-white stem

stem is smooth below ring

centre is always darker red-brown than rest of cap

crowded, free white gills

FRUITING In small groups or troops on bare soil.

Dimensions CAP ⊕ 1–4cm	STEM ↕ 2.5–5cm ↔ 2–4mm	Spores White	Edibility 💀

Family AGARICACEAE	Species *Lepiota castanea*	Season Throughout autumn

CHESTNUT PARASOL

This small and dark species has dark brown scales on both the convex to flat cap and the stem. It also has a strong, fairly unpleasant smell. The stem ring is short lived. Microscopic features are important when identifying small *Lepiota* species; the genus has three different spore shapes: projectile, egg, or spindle. Those of *L. castanea* are projectile-shaped.
• **OCCURRENCE** On disturbed rich soil, often along woodland ditches and rides. Widespread, mostly in the south of northern temperate zones.
• **SIMILAR SPECIES** *L. fulvella* is paler orange-brown and bigger; *L. pseudohelveola* has a more prominent stem ring and a fainter smell. There are a number of other similar species.

△ *LEPIOTA BRUNNEOINCARNATA*
The convex cap of this sturdy species has concentric, dark pink-brown scales on the surface. The pink-tinged stem has dark scales below the indistinct ring zone. 💀

pale or ochre flesh

SECTION

dark brown scales on cap surface

stem ring soon disappears

dark brown scales on stem

free white gills are crowded

FRUITING Mostly a few fruitbodies together.

Dimensions CAP ⊕ 2–4cm	STEM ↕ 2–5cm ↔ 2–4mm	Spores White	Edibility 💀

Family AGARICACEAE	Species *Leucocoprinus badhamii*	Season Late summer–late autumn

RED-STAINING PARASOL

Initially almost white, with a pattern of delicate, pale brown scales on the flattened cap, any part of this agaric turns saffron-red or deep blood-red when handled, finally becoming nearly black. It belongs to a group of red-staining species that are rare and considered to be toxic. Prominent on the velvety stem, the ring is fragile and turns upwards. Some mycologists prefer to place this species in the genus *Leucocagaricus*.

• OCCURRENCE Found growing on alkaline or nutrient-rich soil, among leaf- and garden-litter, or on needle beds; particularly under yew trees but also under hardwoods. Widespread in the warmer parts of Europe; not known in North America.

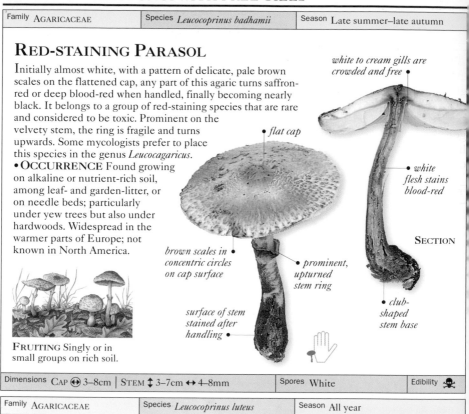

white to cream gills are crowded and free •

• *flat cap*

• *white flesh stains blood-red*

SECTION

brown scales in concentric circles on cap surface •

• *prominent, upturned stem ring*

• *club-shaped stem base*

surface of stem stained after handling •

FRUITING Singly or in small groups on rich soil.

Dimensions CAP ⊕ 3–8cm	STEM ↕ 3–7cm ↔ 4–8mm	Spores White	Edibility ☠

Family AGARICACEAE	Species *Leucocoprinus luteus*	Season All year

YELLOW PARASOL

This species has distinctive yellow colouring. The surface of the bell-shaped cap has fine, golden yellow to orange-yellow or yellow-brown scales on a sulphur-yellow ground. The stem is a similar colour with a short-lived ring, and becomes club-shaped towards the base, which is up to 6mm wide. The gills are also yellow, and are crowded and free. Inedible, possibly poisonous, it has thin yellow flesh. The fruitbodies are short lived, almost like those of the Ink-caps (*Coprinus*, pp.174–76); the genus name means White Ink-cap, a reference to the white spore deposit.

• OCCURRENCE In flowerpots and greenhouses in northern temperate zones, or in the wild in warm subtropical or tropical climates; widespread.

fine golden yellow scales on bell-shaped cap •

yellow stem ring is mostly short lived •

club-shaped stem base is yellow and powdery •

FRUITING Often found growing in tufts on soil that is rich in compost.

Dimensions CAP ⊕ 1–5cm	STEM ↕ 4–10cm ↔ 2–4mm	Spores White	Edibility ⵊ⊘

WITHOUT VEIL

THIS SUBSECTION FEATURES one genus, *Pluteus*. It is the only genus to combine gills that are free of the stem with a complete lack of a universal veil. All the species in the genus produce pink spore deposits and have very crowded gills. The majority of species grow on decayed wood, either in the form of fallen trunks or on beds of wood chippings or sawdust.

The genus *Volvariella* is a close relative of *Pluteus*, but *Volvariella* species, such as *V. bombycina* (p.154), have a universal veil that covers the immature fruitbody; the veil splits to leave a volva at the base.

Family PLUTEACEAE	Species *Pluteus cervinus*	Season Late spring–late autumn

FAWN SHIELD-CAP

Typically, this highly variable species has a dark brown cap and a white stem, with dark fibres that are particularly pronounced at the club-shaped base. The cap may be convex to umbonate or flat; its surface is felted at the centre and greasy when wet. It is edible but has an indistinct taste and smells rancid.
• **OCCURRENCE** On all kinds of decaying hardwood in woods, parks, and gardens; it reaches its most impressive dimensions when growing on sawdust or woodchips. Widespread in northern temperate zones and extending south.
• **SIMILAR SPECIES** *Pluteus pouzarianus*, found on softwoods, has no smell. It is distinguishable by the clamps on the hyphae (see p.11), visible under a microscope.

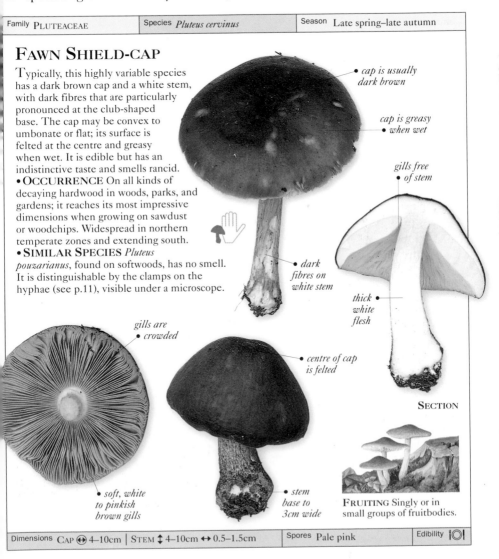

cap is usually dark brown

cap is greasy when wet

gills free of stem

dark fibres on white stem

thick white flesh

SECTION

gills are crowded

centre of cap is felted

soft, white to pinkish brown gills

stem base to 3cm wide

FRUITING Singly or in small groups of fruitbodies.

Dimensions CAP ⊕ 4–10cm	STEM ↕ 4–10cm ↔ 0.5–1.5cm	Spores Pale pink	Edibility

Family PLUTEACEAE	Species *Pluteus umbrosus*	Season Summer–autumn

VELVETY SHIELD-CAP

Velvety, dark brown cap and stem surfaces and dark gill edges make this *Pluteus* species easy to identify. Its cap is umbonate with a radiating vein pattern on the surface, while the pale stem is heavily dotted with brown scales. The flesh is white to pale brown and smells acidic. Its edibility is unknown.

• **OCCURRENCE** Often on naturally decaying hardwood trunks of large diameter; it frequently occurs alongside other *Pluteus* species. Widespread in northern temperate zones; mostly uncommon.

• **SIMILAR SPECIES** *P. cervinus* (p.171) is darker, with no vein patterning on the cap. *P. plautus* has white gill edges.

fringed cap
• margin

• umbo in cap centre

• radiating vein pattern on cap surface

• heavy brown dotting on pale stem

grows on decayed • hardwood

• paler cap flesh may be visible in places

gills are pale • pink-brown

gill edges are • downy and brown

SECTION

• cap surface is velvety dark brown

gills are free of stem •

• white to pale brown flesh in stem

gills are free of stem •

FRUITING Appears singly or in small groups.

• crowded, soft gills

Dimensions CAP ⊕ 4–11cm | STEM ↕ 5–8cm ↔ 0.4–2cm	Spores Pale pink	Edibility

| Family PLUTEACEAE | Species *Pluteus aurantiorugosus* | Season Summer–autumn |

FLAME SHIELD-CAP

This species has a vivid, flame-red cap that varies from convex to nearly flat; the colour makes it easy to distinguish it from its relatives. The cap surface consists of round cells, making it very delicate, in contrast to the fibre-covered *Pluteus cervinus* (p.171). The pale, more or less yellow stem curves, allowing the fruitbody to fit inside the cracks and hollows of decaying wood. It has no distinctive smell or taste.

• OCCURRENCE On fallen trunks or logs, or on pollarded trees such as poplar, ash, and elm. Widespread but uncommon in northern temperate zones.

• SIMILAR SPECIES *P. admirabilis*, a North American species, is more golden.

vivid, orange-red cap fades to yellow-orange

curved stem

convex to conical, umbonate, or almost flat cap

watery, off-white flesh

gills free of stem

SECTION

finely velvety cap surface is thin and very delicate

crowded, soft, pale pink gills

FRUITING Singly or in small groups on decaying wood.

| Dimensions CAP ⊕ 2–5cm | STEM ↕ 3–8cm ↔ 3–6mm | Spores Pale pink | Edibility |

| Family PLUTEACEAE | Species *Pluteus chrysophaeus* | Season Summer–autumn |

GOLDEN-GREEN SHIELD-CAP

There are many forms of this conspicuous species, thought by some experts to be separate species. Although all have yellow caps and pale yellow stems, the colour distribution and intensity varies. The cap is convex to umbonate with a smooth surface, the margins showing striations when wet. The stem is paler than the cap, and the off-white to yellow flesh is odourless and tasteless.

• OCCURRENCE On well-rotted hardwood stumps and moss-covered, fallen trunks. Widespread in Europe but world distribution not clear.

• SIMILAR SPECIES *Pluteus romellii* has a darker cap, and yellow colouring concentrated at the stem base. It mostly grows on wood mixed with soil.

free gills

SECTION

convex to umbonate cap

cap is mainly yellow

smooth cap has striations at margin

pale yellow stem has translucent quality

soft, crowded, pink-toned gills

FRUITING Singly or in small groups on rotten wood.

| Dimensions CAP ⊕ 1–6cm | STEM ↕ 3–8cm ↔ 3–8mm | Spores Pale pink | Edibility |

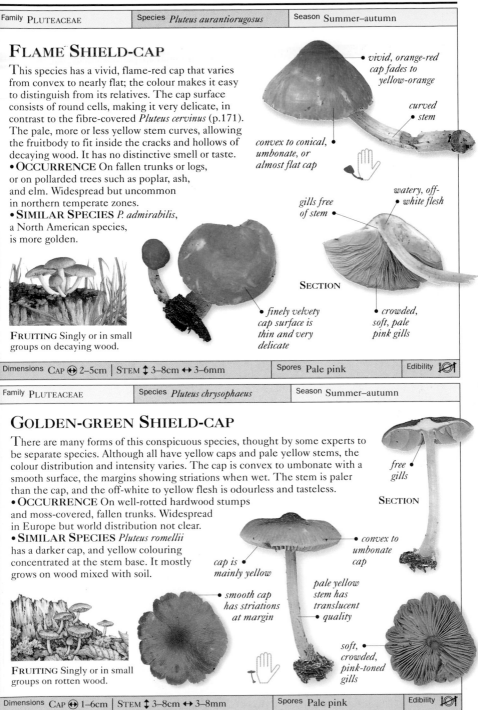

INKY WITH AGE

THIS SUBSECTION consists solely of a selection of members of the large genus *Coprinus*, the Ink-caps. Most species of *Coprinus* have gills that dissolve (deliquesce) from the margin inwards, into an ink-like liquid, coloured black by mature spores. Other spores are shot into the air, just before the dissolving process reaches the point on the gills where the spores are produced. The gills are usually much more crowded than in most agarics.

Coprinus species are often tiny with thin flesh, and many grow on the dung of herbivorous animals such as deer, cows, horses, and rabbits.

Family COPRINACEAE	Species *Coprinus comatus*	Season Autumn

LAWYER'S WIG

The cap of this species is either an elongated egg shape or broadly conical. It is 5–20cm high and has a shaggy or scaly surface that is off-white to pink tinged, soon becoming black from the margin. The stem has a distinctive ring that becomes black due to falling spores. This species deliquesces quickly and is more fleshy than most members of the genus. The very young fruitbodies are popular for eating due to their texture and mild, pleasant flavour. Specimens for eating should be collected early in the day and cooked soon after.

• **OCCURRENCE** In lawns and along roads and woodland paths, on disturbed soil. Widespread and common in northern temperate zones.

scaly cap surface becomes inky from margin

SECTION

extremely crowded, free gills become inky

mid-point stem ring, stained with spores

asparagus-like stem is tall and hollow

cap is elongated egg-shaped or broadly conical

stem base widens slightly

FRUITING Appears in large troops of fruitbodies.

Dimensions CAP ⊕ 2–6cm	STEM ↕ 10–35cm ↔ 1–2cm	Spores Black	Edibility 🍽

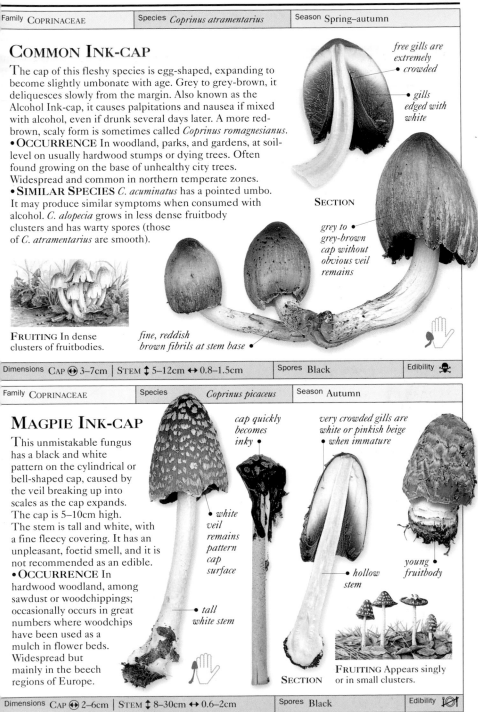

Family COPRINACEAE	Species *Coprinus atramentarius*	Season Spring–autumn

COMMON INK-CAP

The cap of this fleshy species is egg-shaped, expanding to become slightly umbonate with age. Grey to grey-brown, it deliquesces slowly from the margin. Also known as the Alcohol Ink-cap, it causes palpitations and nausea if mixed with alcohol, even if drunk several days later. A more red-brown, scaly form is sometimes called *Coprinus romagnesianus*.

• **OCCURRENCE** In woodland, parks, and gardens, at soil-level on usually hardwood stumps or dying trees. Often found growing on the base of unhealthy city trees. Widespread and common in northern temperate zones.

• **SIMILAR SPECIES** *C. acuminatus* has a pointed umbo. It may produce similar symptoms when consumed with alcohol. *C. alopecia* grows in less dense fruitbody clusters and has warty spores (those of *C. atramentarius* are smooth).

free gills are extremely crowded

gills edged with white

SECTION

grey to grey-brown cap without obvious veil remains

FRUITING In dense clusters of fruitbodies.

fine, reddish brown fibrils at stem base

Dimensions CAP ⊕ 3–7cm	STEM ↕ 5–12cm ↔ 0.8–1.5cm	Spores Black	Edibility ☠

Family COPRINACEAE	Species *Coprinus picaceus*	Season Autumn

MAGPIE INK-CAP

This unmistakable fungus has a black and white pattern on the cylindrical or bell-shaped cap, caused by the veil breaking up into scales as the cap expands. The cap is 5–10cm high. The stem is tall and white, with a fine fleecy covering. It has an unpleasant, foetid smell, and it is not recommended as an edible.

• **OCCURRENCE** In hardwood woodland, among sawdust or woodchippings; occasionally occurs in great numbers where woodchips have been used as a mulch in flower beds. Widespread but mainly in the beech regions of Europe.

cap quickly becomes inky

very crowded gills are white or pinkish beige when immature

white veil remains pattern cap surface

tall white stem

hollow stem

young fruitbody

SECTION

FRUITING Appears singly or in small clusters.

Dimensions CAP ⊕ 2–6cm	STEM ↕ 8–30cm ↔ 0.6–2cm	Spores Black	Edibility

| Family COPRINACEAE | Species *Coprinus micaceus* | Season Late spring–early winter |

GLISTENING INK-CAP

Grainy veil remnants create a sheen on the surface of the egg-shaped to slightly expanded, pleated, tawny brown cap of this species, which has a splitting or lobed margin. It has pale flesh. The mycelium can produce numerous fruitings in one season.

• **OCCURRENCE**
Abundant both in urban areas and in the heart of woodland, on and around old stumps and unhealthy trees. Widespread and common in northern temperate zones.

• **SIMILAR SPECIES** Some close relatives produce a thick, orange-yellow mat (ozonium) on the substrate. One of these, *Coprinus domesticus*, is often found in damp cellars. Along with others, it is also found behind loose bathroom tiles and in other damp sites. *C. truncorum* has a smoother stem and ellipsoid, non-flattened spores, each with a small pore; those of *C. micaceus* are flattened ellipsoid, each with a shortened germ pore.

pleated cap is shiny from grainy veil remains

cap is 1–3.5cm high

white to brown gills shrivel and become inky with age

SECTION

off-white stems are hollow and fragile

FRUITING In dense clusters of fruitbodies.

| Dimensions CAP ⊕ 2–4cm | STEM ↕ 4–10cm ↔ 2–5mm | Spores Black | Edibility 🚫🍴 |

| Family COPRINACEAE | Species *Coprinus niveus* | Season Summer–autumn |

SNOW-WHITE INK-CAP

Best identified by its snow-white colouring and the loose, mealy remnants of the veil over its cap surface, this species is quite small, although not the tiniest of the *Coprinus*. The conical to bell-shaped cap has an upturned margin, the crowded gills are grey when young, black when mature, and the stem has a slightly swollen base. The inedible flesh is very thin and pale.

• **OCCURRENCE** Nearly always found on fairly fresh horse manure in wet grass. Widespread and common in Europe; worldwide distribution is not known.

• **SIMILAR SPECIES** *C. cortinatus* grows on soil. *C. cothurnatus* often has brown scales at the cap centre. Tiny *C. friesii* is found growing on rotten grass. *C. stercoreus* has a slight, foetid smell.

fine mealy covering on cap may wash off in rain

rolled back cap margin

cap is egg-shaped when young

free gills are black and inky when mature

mealy white stem

FRUITING Appears in groups of a few fruitbodies.

| Dimensions CAP ⊕ 1–3cm | STEM ↕ 5–8cm ↔ 1–3mm | Spores Black | Edibility 🚫🍴 |

WITH GILLS JOINED TO A COLLAR

THIS SUBSECTION FEATURES species from a group of agarics that have gills attached to a "wheel" (collarium), rather than being free or joining the stem. The arrangement resembles the spokes of a bicycle wheel. Most species in the group are in the genus *Marasmius* and occur in the tropics.

Family TRICHOLOMATACEAE	Species *Marasmius rotula*	Season Midsummer–autumn

COMMON WHEEL MUMMY-CAP

The gills of this species are attached to a little "wheel", or collar, rather than the stem top. The convex ivory cap has a darker, navel-like centre with deep, radial grooves and thin, tough, off-white flesh. This fungus can revive after total desiccation.

• **OCCURRENCE** In mixed woodland, on hardwood twigs and branches. Widespread and common in northern temperate zones.

• **SIMILAR SPECIES** Many other *Marasmius* species also have a "wheel"; most occur in tropical rainforests, but a few tiny species can also be found in temperate zones: brick-red *M. curreyi* grows in grass; pale brown *M. bulliardii* occurs in swarms on leaf litter in damp woods; pale *M. limosus* grows on reeds. *Marasmiellus ramealis* (p.139), found in similar sites, lacks the gill "wheel" and the cap grooves.

radial grooves on cap surface

ivory gills attached to "wheel"

distinct dark navel in cap centre

upper stem is off-white

very tough black stem

FRUITING Appears in troops of fruitbodies.

Dimensions CAP ⊕ 0.5–2cm	STEM ↕ 2–4cm ↔ 1mm	Spores Off-white	Edibility

Family COPRINACEAE	Species *Coprinus plicatilis*	Season Early summer–autumn

LITTLE JAPANESE UMBRELLA

When fully expanded, the cap of this small *Coprinus* species has a pleated surface, resembling a Japanese umbrella. The cap is smooth, without hairs or veil remnants. The gills are joined to a "wheel", or collar, and are more distant, and become less inky than in most Ink-caps (pp.174–76).

• **OCCURRENCE** In lawns, appearing after rain has fallen. Widespread and common in northern temperate zones.

• **SIMILAR SPECIES** *C. auricomus* tends to be a bit bigger and has a browner cap. A microscope reveals thick-walled brown hairs, confirming its identity. Other similar species include *C. kuehneri*, *C. leiocephalus*, and *C. nudiceps*. They can only be distinguished by carefully measuring the spores.

very thin stem is delicate and smooth

conical to flat cap is smooth and pleated

rather distant gills are joined to a collar

FRUITING Singly or in small groups. Appears overnight and withers by noon.

Dimensions CAP ⊕ 0.8–2cm	STEM ↕ 4–8cm ↔ 1–2mm	Spores Black	Edibility

CAP FUNGI WITH STEM OFF-CENTRE OR ABSENT

Among the gilled fungi are some species with a stem that is not centrally placed under the cap. It may be attached to the side of the cap and, in some species, can be very small. Other gilled species lack a stem altogether. Most of these fungi are known as oyster mushrooms, but not all are related to each other.

stem off-centre

stem absent

Family POLYPORACEAE	Species *Pleurotus ostreatus*	Season Autumn–winter

COMMON OYSTER MUSHROOM

smooth cap surface •

The cap of this species is more or less oyster-shaped with a blue-grey colouring when young, becoming dark grey-blue to brown. The white stem is positioned at the cap margin or may be absent. The white flesh has a pleasant taste, but it is its firm texture that makes it popular for eating; it, and some close relatives, are commercially cultivated. This species prefers cold weather and appears later in the season than some similar species (see below).

• **OCCURRENCE** On a wide range of dead or dying hardwood trees; more rarely on softwoods. Widespread in northern temperate zones.

• **SIMILAR SPECIES** *Pleurotus dryinus* has a veil on the stem when young. *P. pulmonarius* is cream to pale brown; it appears earlier in the season.

• *dark grey-blue to brown cap*

• *more or less oyster-shaped cap*

stem at cap margin or • absent

crowded, decurrent, soft, • cream gills

FRUITING In tiers and rows on hardwood trees.

△ *LENTINELLUS URSINUS*
Although edible, this species has a bitter taste. The cap is densely hairy and pale brown, and the gills have toothed edges. |◉|

Dimensions CAP ⊕ 6–20cm | STEM ↕ 0–5cm ↔ 1–2cm	Spores Pale grey-lilac	Edibility |◉|

| Family POLYPORACEAE | Species *Pleurotus cornucopiae* | Season Spring–autumn |

TRUMPET OYSTER MUSHROOM

This species has a distinctive trumpet-shaped, pale leather-brown cap and a fairly central stem with decurrent gills that join together to form a net. The white flesh has a pleasant taste and smells floury.

• **OCCURRENCE** On hardwood trees, forming a white rot; often preferring elm, it has increased where Dutch elm disease has left abundant substrate. Widespread but mainly in southern Europe; world distribution unclear.

• **SIMILAR SPECIES** *Pleurotus citrinopileatus* occurs in east Asia and is yellow. *P. pulmonarius* has simple gills and less of a stem.

smooth cap surface

trumpet-shaped cap

off-white stem is tinged with cap colour

clustered fruitbodies are typical

△ *PLEUROTUS ERYNGII*
Found on umbellifer plants such as sea holly, this species has a pale cap with a suede-like surface and an inrolled margin. The stem is off-centre or may be absent. !◎!

• network of decurrent gills

FRUITING Appears in clustered groups or singly.

| Dimensions CAP ⊕ 4–12cm | STEM ↕ 1–5cm ↔ 0.5–2.5cm | Spores Pale lilac | Edibility !◎! |

| Family AURISCALPIACEAE | Species *Lentinellus cochleatus* | Season Late summer–autumn |

COCKLESHELL FUNGUS

This species has a more or less cockleshell-shaped, smooth, red-brown cap with an inrolled margin. The stem is attached to one side. The pale white-brown gills are decurrent and, like all *Lentinellus* species, have toothed edges. Some specimens have a pleasant, aniseed smell; others are odourless. The flesh tastes bitter.

• **OCCURRENCE** Rotting hardwood stumps. Widespread in northern temperate zones; locally common.

• **SIMILAR SPECIES** *L. castoreus* and *L. vulpinus* are more fleshy with felty caps. *L. micheneri* grows singly.

inrolled cap margin

smooth, red-brown cap surface

FRUITING Appears in layered clusters on rotting stumps of hardwood trees.

| Dimensions CAP ⊕ 2–6cm | STEM ↕ 2–5cm ↔ 0.8–1.5cm | Spores White | Edibility !◎! |

| Family TRICHOLOMATACEAE | Species *Pleurocybella porrigens* | Season Autumn |

ANGEL'S WINGS

This edible species is easily noticed from a distance as its light colouring contrasts strongly with the dark wood substrate. It has a clean, fan-shaped, stemless fruitbody with a distinct incurved margin and crowded gills. It is white, becoming tinted with yellow as it ages. The thin white flesh smells and tastes pleasant.

fruitbody is like an oyster mushroom

• **OCCURRENCE** On the decaying trunks and stumps of softwood trees such as spruce and fir. Widespread and locally common in northern temperate zones.

colour of fruitbody is overall white

• **SIMILAR SPECIES** *Panellus mitis* is similar but much smaller and grows on the twigs and branches of softwood trees.

fan-shaped cap has a smooth, dry surface

cap margin is distinctly incurved

gills are white and crowded

FRUITING Appears in large clusters on decaying softwood trees in open or dense woodland.

| Dimensions FRUITBODY ↕ 2–10cm ↔ 2–7cm | Spores White | Edibility ¶◎¶ |

| Family TRICHOLOMATACEAE | Species *Panellus serotinus* | Season Late autumn |

OLIVE OYSTER

Shaped like an oyster mushroom (*Pleurotus*, pp.178–79), the Olive Oyster has olive and yellow colouring, a velvety cap surface, and a short, indistinct stem, and is easy to identify. Not worthwhile as an edible, it has more or less gelatinous white flesh, which tastes mild to slightly bitter, and smells faintly "mushroom-like". Some mycologists prefer to classify *Panellus serotinus* in the genus *Sarcomyxa*.

• **OCCURRENCE** Often found fruiting near water on dead or living hardwood tree trunks and fallen branches, rarely on softwoods. Widespread throughout northern temperate zones.

• **SIMILAR SPECIES** The stemless, ochre-gilled *Phyllotopsis nidulans* is similar to old or atypical specimens but has an ochre-pink spore deposit.

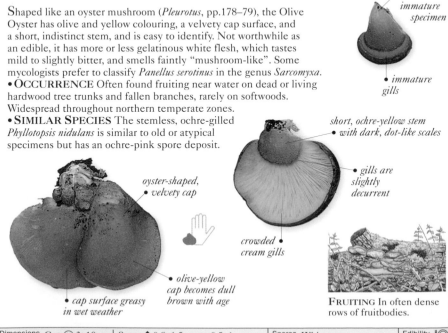

stem on immature specimen

immature gills

oyster-shaped, velvety cap

short, ochre-yellow stem with dark, dot-like scales

gills are slightly decurrent

crowded cream gills

olive-yellow cap becomes dull brown with age

cap surface greasy in wet weather

FRUITING In often dense rows of fruitbodies.

| Dimensions CAP ⊕ 3–10cm │ STEM ↕ 0.8–1.5cm ↔ 0.5–1cm | Spores White | Edibility ¶◎¶ |

Family TRICHOLOMATACEAE	Species *Panellus stypticus*	Season Autumn–winter

FALSE OYSTER

This small, oyster-shaped, pale leather-brown species has tough fruitbodies that usually survive until spring. It has a mealy cap surface and a very short stem. The off-white to pale yellow flesh has an aromatic, fruity smell but tastes bitter and astringent; it is inedible. American specimens have gills that glow in the dark, European ones do not.

• **OCCURRENCE** In woodland on stumps of hardwood trees such as beech and oak. Widespread in northern temperate zones.

• **SIMILAR SPECIES** *Panellus mitis* is whiter, smaller, and has a mild taste. It occurs, very late in the season, on softwood trees.

short stem at cap margin

brown gills with paler edges

well-spaced gills

pale leather-brown surface

FRUITING Appears in crowded tiers and rows.

oyster-shaped cap

cap surface cracks slightly with age

Dimensions CAP ⊕ 1–4cm │ STEM ↕ 0.1–1cm ↔ 2–7mm	Spores Off-white	Edibility

Family SCHIZOPHYLLACEAE	Species *Schizophyllum commune*	Season All year

SPLIT-GILL FUNGUS

This fan-shaped fungus belongs to a genus distinguished by gill-like structures that are split lengthways, the two parts curling inwards in dry conditions to protect the spore-bearing hymenium. Stemless, or with a short, stem-like base, it is covered with grey-white felt. The tough, pale flesh is reportedly eaten by certain tribal peoples and has been used like a chewing gum. Easily cultivated on artificial substrates, this species is popular for research in areas like genetics and anatomy.

• **OCCURRENCE** On a wide range of woody substrates, also on straw bales, mostly in exposed sites: it is able to grow on sun-baked or wind-dried wood, even driftwood. Locally, it can have substrate preferences – beech in northern Europe for example. Widespread and common in northern temperate zones; absent from northernmost areas.

pinkish beige "gills" radiate from attachment point

"gills" curl inwards when dry

felted, grey-white cap surface

split or lobed cap margin

green tinge from algae growing on cap

FRUITING Fans appear in often crowded tiers.

Dimensions FRUITBODY ⊕ 1–5cm	Spores White	Edibility

| Family PAXILLACEAE | Species *Tapinella atrotomentosus* | Season Summer–autumn |

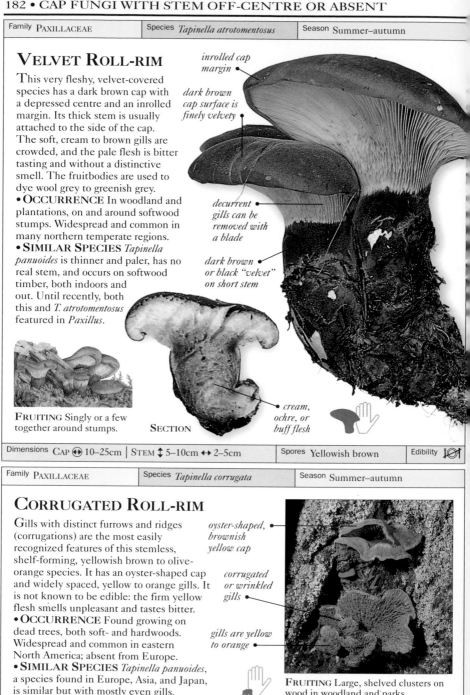

VELVET ROLL-RIM

This very fleshy, velvet-covered species has a dark brown cap with a depressed centre and an inrolled margin. Its thick stem is usually attached to the side of the cap. The soft, cream to brown gills are crowded, and the pale flesh is bitter tasting and without a distinctive smell. The fruitbodies are used to dye wool grey to greenish grey.
• **OCCURRENCE** In woodland and plantations, on and around softwood stumps. Widespread and common in many northern temperate regions.
• **SIMILAR SPECIES** *Tapinella panuoides* is thinner and paler, has no real stem, and occurs on softwood timber, both indoors and out. Until recently, both this and *T. atrotomentosus* featured in *Paxillus*.

inrolled cap margin

dark brown cap surface is finely velvety

decurrent gills can be removed with a blade

dark brown or black "velvet" on short stem

FRUITING Singly or a few together around stumps.

SECTION

cream, ochre, or buff flesh

| Dimensions CAP ⊕ 10–25cm \| STEM ↕ 5–10cm ↔ 2–5cm | Spores Yellowish brown | Edibility |

| Family PAXILLACEAE | Species *Tapinella corrugata* | Season Summer–autumn |

CORRUGATED ROLL-RIM

Gills with distinct furrows and ridges (corrugations) are the most easily recognized features of this stemless, shelf-forming, yellowish brown to olive-orange species. It has an oyster-shaped cap and widely spaced, yellow to orange gills. It is not known to be edible: the firm yellow flesh smells unpleasant and tastes bitter.
• **OCCURRENCE** Found growing on dead trees, both soft- and hardwoods. Widespread and common in eastern North America; absent from Europe.
• **SIMILAR SPECIES** *Tapinella panuoides*, a species found in Europe, Asia, and Japan, is similar but with mostly even gills.

oyster-shaped, brownish yellow cap

corrugated or wrinkled gills

gills are yellow to orange

FRUITING Large, shelved clusters on wood in woodland and parks.

| Dimensions FRUITBODY ⊕ 5–10cm | Spores Olive-buff | Edibility |

| Family CREPIDOTACEAE | Species *Crepidotus mollis* | Season Autumn |

SOFT SLIPPER

The gelatinous surface and flesh of this species distinguishes it from the many, mostly smaller, *Crepidotus* species. The smooth, oyster- to fan-shaped cap changes colour from grey-brown to off-white as it dries; when it is wet, radiating striations are clearly visible at the margin. The stem is very rudimentary or absent. The cap skin is easily peeled from the pale cap flesh, which may have a weak smell.

• **OCCURRENCE** On dead trunks of hardwood trees such as elm, ash, poplar, and beech. Widespread in northern temperate zones.

• **SIMILAR SPECIES** Closely related *C. calolepis* has pale brown scales towards the point where the cap is attached to its hardwood substrate.

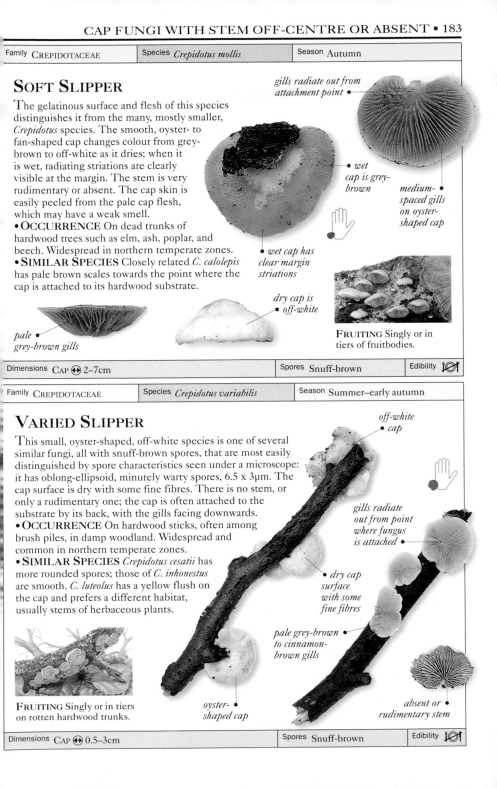

gills radiate out from attachment point

wet cap is grey-brown

medium-spaced gills on oyster-shaped cap

wet cap has clear margin striations

dry cap is off-white

FRUITING Singly or in tiers of fruitbodies.

pale grey-brown gills

| Dimensions CAP ⊕ 2–7cm | Spores Snuff-brown | Edibility |

| Family CREPIDOTACEAE | Species *Crepidotus variabilis* | Season Summer–early autumn |

VARIED SLIPPER

This small, oyster-shaped, off-white species is one of several similar fungi, all with snuff-brown spores, that are most easily distinguished by spore characteristics seen under a microscope: it has oblong-ellipsoid, minutely warty spores, 6.5 x 3µm. The cap surface is dry with some fine fibres. There is no stem, or only a rudimentary one; the cap is often attached to the substrate by its back, with the gills facing downwards.

• **OCCURRENCE** On hardwood sticks, often among brush piles, in damp woodland. Widespread and common in northern temperate zones.

• **SIMILAR SPECIES** *Crepidotus cesatii* has more rounded spores; those of *C. inhonestus* are smooth. *C. luteolus* has a yellow flush on the cap and prefers a different habitat, usually stems of herbaceous plants.

off-white cap

gills radiate out from point where fungus is attached

dry cap surface with some fine fibres

pale grey-brown to cinnamon-brown gills

FRUITING Singly or in tiers on rotten hardwood trunks.

oyster-shaped cap

absent or rudimentary stem

| Dimensions CAP ⊕ 0.5–3cm | Spores Snuff-brown | Edibility |

CAP & STEM FUNGI WITH PORES

This section consists of fungi that produce spores in crowded tubes. The spores are released through pores on the fruitbody underside. Some of these fungi look similar to agarics (see p.28). Boletes have soft flesh (see below). Polypores have tough flesh (see p.202). For bracket-like fungi with pores see p.211.

• *pores on underside*

WITH SOFT FLESH

THE FUNGI in this subsection are known as boletes. They all have fairly short-lived fruitbodies, which are characterized by their soft but firm flesh, combined with pores on the underside of the cap. The fruitbodies of many of the species that belong here are attractive as food to a wide range of animals, including human beings.

All of the boletes form mutually beneficial (mycorrhizal) associations with trees (see pp.18–19).

Family STROBILOMYCETACEAE	Species *Porphyrellus porphyrosporus*	Season Summer–autumn

PURPLE-BLACK BOLETE

This dark bolete is well camouflaged in its litter-rich habitat. Its convex cap is sepia coloured with a velvety-textured surface, which may crack into scales; the stem is the same colour with a velvety to smooth surface. The adnate or notched tubes, 1–2cm long, have wine-buff pores that become blue-green or black when they are bruised or otherwise damaged. The pale-coloured flesh smells and tastes unpleasant; on cutting, it turns blue, green, black, or sometimes red, and has been reported as poisonous.
• **OCCURRENCE** Mycorrhizal with both hardwood trees, such as beech, and softwoods. Widespread and common to locally absent in northern temperate zones.

pores are wine-buff, bruising blue-green or black •

cap surface may crack into scales •

velvety surface on convex cap •

pale flesh turns blue, green, or black •

stem is velvety to smooth, and sepia coloured

FRUITING Appears singly or in troops of fruitbodies, often in deep litter in woodland areas.

Dimensions CAP ⊕ 5–15cm	STEM ↕ 5–12cm ↔ 1–3cm	Spores Purple-brown	Edibility ☠

| Family STROBILOMYCETACEAE | Species *Strobilomyces strobilaceus* | Season Summer–autumn |

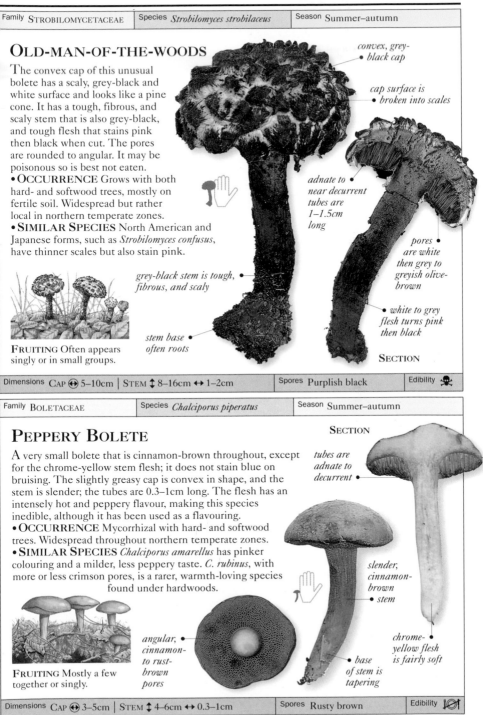

OLD-MAN-OF-THE-WOODS

The convex cap of this unusual bolete has a scaly, grey-black and white surface and looks like a pine cone. It has a tough, fibrous, and scaly stem that is also grey-black, and tough flesh that stains pink then black when cut. The pores are rounded to angular. It may be poisonous so is best not eaten.
• **OCCURRENCE** Grows with both hard- and softwood trees, mostly on fertile soil. Widespread but rather local in northern temperate zones.
• **SIMILAR SPECIES** North American and Japanese forms, such as *Strobilomyces confusus*, have thinner scales but also stain pink.

convex, grey-black cap

cap surface is broken into scales

adnate to near decurrent tubes are 1–1.5cm long

pores are white then grey to greyish olive-brown

grey-black stem is tough, fibrous, and scaly

white to grey flesh turns pink then black

FRUITING Often appears singly or in small groups.

stem base often roots

SECTION

| Dimensions CAP ⊕ 5–10cm | STEM ↕ 8–16cm ↔ 1–2cm | Spores Purplish black | Edibility ☠ |

| Family BOLETACEAE | Species *Chalciporus piperatus* | Season Summer–autumn |

PEPPERY BOLETE

A very small bolete that is cinnamon-brown throughout, except for the chrome-yellow stem flesh; it does not stain blue on bruising. The slightly greasy cap is convex in shape, and the stem is slender; the tubes are 0.3–1cm long. The flesh has an intensely hot and peppery flavour, making this species inedible, although it has been used as a flavouring.
• **OCCURRENCE** Mycorrhizal with hard- and softwood trees. Widespread throughout northern temperate zones.
• **SIMILAR SPECIES** *Chalciporus amarellus* has pinker colouring and a milder, less peppery taste. *C. rubinus*, with more or less crimson pores, is a rarer, warmth-loving species found under hardwoods.

SECTION

tubes are adnate to decurrent

slender, cinnamon-brown stem

chrome-yellow flesh is fairly soft

angular, cinnamon-to rust-brown pores

base of stem is tapering

FRUITING Mostly a few together or singly.

| Dimensions CAP ⊕ 3–5cm | STEM ↕ 4–6cm ↔ 0.3–1cm | Spores Rusty brown | Edibility |

Family STROBILOMYCETACEAE	Species *Tylopilus felleus*	Season Summer–autumn

BITTER BOLETE

Slightly to distinctly pink pores on the underside of the bun-shaped brown cap and a dark net on the thick stem are characteristic of this bolete. It has soft, white to cream flesh with an unpleasant smell and a taste that is too bitter to make it edible (see also Similar Species).

• **OCCURRENCE**
Mycorrhizal with soft- and hardwood trees on acid soil. Widespread and common in many areas of northern temperate zones.

• **SIMILAR SPECIES** The edible *Boletus edulis* (p.187) and *B. reticulatus* (p.189) are similar to young *Tylopilus felleus* specimens.

immature pores are off-white

brown cap feels like suede

notched tube layer, 1–2.5cm long, has fine pores

stem is thick with a prominent coarse, dark net

pores mature to deep pink

FRUITING Singly or in troops on well-drained, acid soil.

Dimensions CAP ⊕ 6–15cm	STEM ↕ 5–12cm ↔ 2.5–5cm	Spores Dingy pink	Edibility

Family BOLETACEAE	Species *Boletus barrowsii*	Season Summer

BARROW'S BOLETE

This species has a convex to flat, white to grey or tan cap with pores that are white when young, ageing to yellowish green. The tube layer, 2–3cm deep, is adnate to slightly depressed around the club-shaped stem, which is white with a distinctive off-white net pattern. The white flesh is thick and tastes sweet.

• **OCCURRENCE**
Mycorrhizal with both soft- and hardwoods. Widespread and common in North America; not found in Europe.

• **SIMILAR SPECIES** *Boletus edulis* (p.187) and closely related boletes have the white net patterning, but darker caps.

white pores age yellowish green

cap is dry and white to grey or tan

convex cap becomes flat with age

distinctive net pattern on upper stem

FRUITING Appears in large groups of fruitbodies, or scattered under soft- and hardwood trees.

Dimensions CAP ⊕ 7.5–25cm	STEM ↕ 10–25cm ↔ 2–4cm	Spores Olive-brown	Edibility

Family BOLETACEAE	Species *Boletus edulis*	Season Summer–autumn

PENNY BUN

Good markers for this species
include a white net pattern on
the upper stem and pale yellow
to olive-brown pores. It has a
bun-shaped, pale or dark
brown cap and a barrel- or
club-shaped stem. One of
the most sought-after of all
edible mushrooms, this
bolete has faint but pleasant-
smelling white flesh that tastes mild
and nutty and does not stain when cut.
• **OCCURRENCE** Mycorrhizal with
hard- and softwood trees in moss-rich
woodland. Widespread and common
in northern temperate zones.
• **SIMILAR SPECIES** Among several
similar boletes are *Boletus aereus* and
B. reticulatus (both p.189).

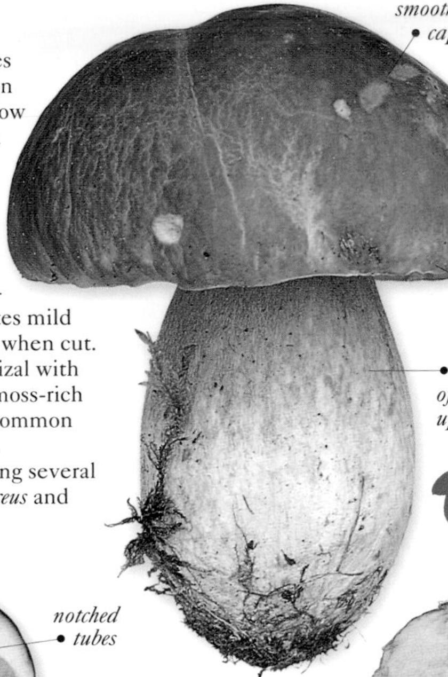

smooth, slightly greasy
• *cap surface*

• *bun-shaped
brown cap*

• *skin slightly over-
hanging cap margin*

• *white net
of veins on
upper stem*

*fine,
rounded,
white to
yellow
pores* •

notched
• *tubes*

• *tubes, 1–4cm long,
mature olive-brown and
are easily loosened*

• *white flesh may have maggot
holes or yellow staining from
the parasite* Sepedonium
chrysospermum *(inset, right)*

SECTION

FRUITING Singly or in
troops on well-drained soil.

△ *BOLETUS PINOPHILUS*
This rich brown species is found
under pine. It has a pale stem
net. The cap surface is slightly
sticky; it dries felty or granular,
often with distinct wrinkles. |◎|

△ *SEPEDONIUM
CHRYSOSPERMUM*
A parasite of boletes, this species
appears first as a white mould,
becoming powdery golden yellow
due to the asexual spores. |◎|

| Dimensions CAP ⊕ 10–25cm | STEM ↕ 10–20cm ↔ 3–10cm | Spores Olive-brown | Edibility |◎| |

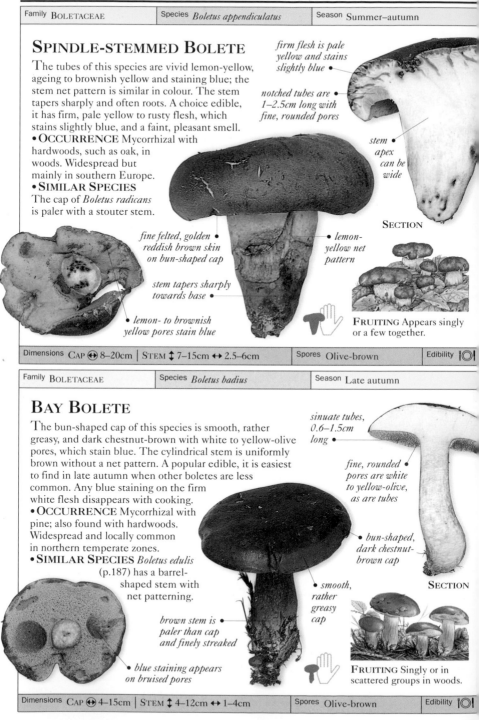

| Family BOLETACEAE | Species *Boletus appendiculatus* | Season Summer–autumn |

SPINDLE-STEMMED BOLETE

The tubes of this species are vivid lemon-yellow, ageing to brownish yellow and staining blue; the stem net pattern is similar in colour. The stem tapers sharply and often roots. A choice edible, it has firm, pale yellow to rusty flesh, which stains slightly blue, and a faint, pleasant smell.

• **OCCURRENCE** Mycorrhizal with hardwoods, such as oak, in woods. Widespread but mainly in southern Europe.

• **SIMILAR SPECIES**
The cap of *Boletus radicans* is paler with a stouter stem.

firm flesh is pale yellow and stains slightly blue •

notched tubes are 1–2.5cm long with fine, rounded pores

stem apex can be wide

SECTION

fine felted, golden • reddish brown skin on bun-shaped cap

• lemon-yellow net pattern

stem tapers sharply towards base •

• lemon- to brownish yellow pores stain blue

FRUITING Appears singly or a few together.

| Dimensions CAP ⊕ 8–20cm | STEM ↕ 7–15cm ↔ 2.5–6cm | Spores Olive-brown | Edibility |

| Family BOLETACEAE | Species *Boletus badius* | Season Late autumn |

BAY BOLETE

The bun-shaped cap of this species is smooth, rather greasy, and dark chestnut-brown with white to yellow-olive pores, which stain blue. The cylindrical stem is uniformly brown without a net pattern. A popular edible, it is easiest to find in late autumn when other boletes are less common. Any blue staining on the firm white flesh disappears with cooking.

• **OCCURRENCE** Mycorrhizal with pine; also found with hardwoods. Widespread and locally common in northern temperate zones.

• **SIMILAR SPECIES** *Boletus edulis* (p.187) has a barrel-shaped stem with net patterning.

sinuate tubes, 0.6–1.5cm long •

fine, rounded • pores are white to yellow-olive, as are tubes

• bun-shaped, dark chestnut-brown cap

• smooth, rather greasy cap

SECTION

brown stem is • paler than cap and finely streaked

• blue staining appears on bruised pores

FRUITING Singly or in scattered groups in woods.

| Dimensions CAP ⊕ 4–15cm | STEM ↕ 4–12cm ↔ 1–4cm | Spores Olive-brown | Edibility |

| Family BOLETACEAE | Species *Boletus reticulatus* | Season Summer–autumn |

SUMMER BOLETE

The bun-shaped cap of this species has a dry, matt skin that tends to crack; it is warm orange-brown. A white to brown net pattern covers the barrel-shaped, pale brown stem. An excellent edible, it has firm white flesh with a nutty flavour, which does not stain when cut.

• **OCCURRENCE** Mycorrhizal with hardwoods, such as beech and oak; with *Boletus luridiformis* (below) in some areas. Widespread in northern temperate zones; absent in North America.

• **SIMILAR SPECIES** *B. edulis* (p.187) has a darker cap and a less extensive, paler stem net.

sinuate, notched tubes, 1–1.5cm long

tubes are white then green-yellow to olive-brown

fine cracks may cover surface of dry, matt cap

white to brown net over surface of pale brown stem

cap skin tends to overhang at margin

SECTION

△ **BOLETUS AEREUS**
Fruiting late in the year, this chestnut-brown species has a velvety cap and pale stem net. The flesh stays white.

FRUITING In troops or a few together in woodland.

| Dimensions CAP ⊕ 7–15cm | STEM ↕ 6–15cm ↔ 2–5cm | Spores Olive-brown | Edibility |

| Family BOLETACEAE | Species *Boletus luridiformis* | Season Summer–autumn |

DOTTED-STEM BOLETE

Belonging to the group of boletes whose flesh turns blue when cut, this choice edible has a bun-shaped, dark brown cap with deep blood-red pores and yellow tubes. The yellow stem is densely covered with red dots and has no net pattern.

• **OCCURRENCE** Mycorrhizal with hard- and softwood trees, in well-drained, mostly acid and moss-rich, woodland soil. Widespread and common in Europe; world distribution not known.

• **SIMILAR SPECIES** *Boletus junquilleus* is a yellow form. *B. luridus* has a stem net. *B. queletii* has dots only at the stem base and orange pores.

notched yellow tubes, 1–3cm long, stain blue-black

SECTION

cap is velvety to smooth

dark rich brown cap

blood-red pores

yellow flesh stains blue-black

club-shaped stem

FRUITING Singly or a few fruitbodies together.

| Dimensions CAP ⊕ 5–20cm | STEM ↕ 5–15cm ↔ 2–6cm | Spores Brown to olive-brown | Edibility |

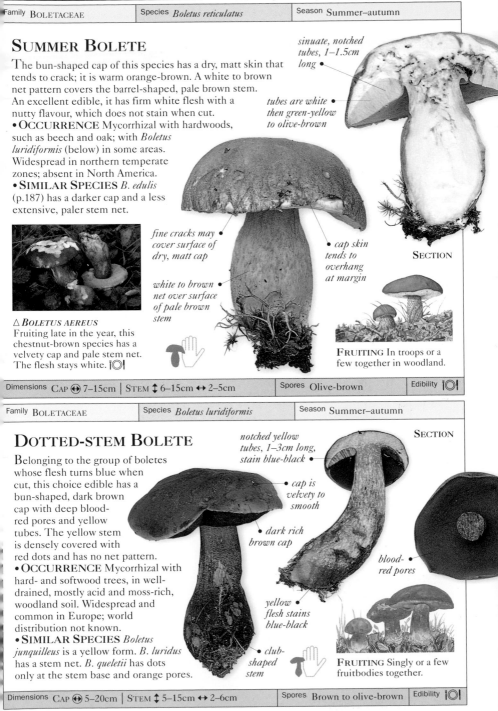

| Family BOLETACEAE | Species *Boletus calopus* | Season Summer–autumn |

SCARLET-STEMMED BOLETE

The skin on the bun-shaped cap of this bolete overhangs the margin and is felted, somewhat veined, and smoky grey or grey-brown. The cylindrical, barrel-shaped, or tapered stem is red at the base, yellow towards the top. It has a pale yellow net pattern, which is pale yellow above, darker and redder towards the base. The inedible, and possibly slightly poisonous flesh tastes bitter and is pale yellow, staining pale blue.

• **OCCURRENCE** Mycorrhizal with soft- and hardwood trees on acid, sandy soil. Widespread but mostly local in northern temperate zones.

• **SIMILAR SPECIES** Other pale-capped and red-stemmed boletes, such as *Boletus legaliae* (p.191), also tend to have red pores. *B. torosus*, with yellow pores, is an exception; it is distinguished by blue-black flesh staining, and a mild taste.

felted, • somewhat veined cap skin

• smoky grey or grey-brown cap sometimes olive flushed

• cylindrical, tapering, to barrel-shaped stem

cap skin overhangs at cap margin •

yellow and red • stem has striking pale yellow to red net pattern

• notched tubes, 0.5–1.5cm long, are lemon-yellow

• lemon-yellow pores stain pale blue

△ **BOLETUS LURIDUS**
This species has a prominent, orange-red stem net and lemon-yellow flesh that turns blue-black, as do the orange pores. There is a red line above the tube layer. |◎|

△ **BOLETUS BICOLOR**
A common summer species in eastern North America, this bolete has a bright rose-red cap and stem, and yellow pores. Its thick yellow flesh slowly bruises to blue. |◎|

FRUITING Appears singly or in troops under trees.

| Dimensions CAP ⊕ 6–14cm | STEM ↕ 6–10cm ↔ 3–5cm | Spores Olive-brown | Edibility |◎| |

| Family BOLETACEAE | Species *Boletus satanas* | Season Summer–early autumn |

SATAN'S BOLETE

A fleshy species with a bun-shaped, smooth, pale, almost white cap, Satan's Bolete is best identified by its orange to blood-red pores and the prominent yellow to blood-red net pattern on its fat, yellow to red stem. The yellow to white flesh stains slightly blue, as do the pores. The notched tubes, 1–3cm long, are yellowish green. Mild tasting, it is slightly poisonous, occasionally causing serious stomach problems. Mature fruitbodies smell unpleasant.
• **OCCURRENCE** Mycorrhizal with hardwood trees. Widespread, but mostly in southern Europe, and very local.

yellow to red stem with net pattern • • *smooth cap is pale, almost white*

FRUITING Singly, a few together, or in troops with trees such as beech and oak.

| Dimensions CAP ⊕ 10–25cm | STEM ↕ 5–15cm ↔ 4–12cm | Spores Olive-brown | Edibility ☠ |

| Family BOLETACEAE | Species *Boletus pulcherrimus* | Season Late summer–autumn |

PRETTY POISON BOLETE

This brightly coloured species is easily recognizable by its blood-red pores, bruising blue-black, its bun-shaped, felted, reddish to olive-brown cap, its firm yellow flesh, which turns blue on cutting, and its swollen reddish brown stem, which has a dark red net pattern covering the upper part. The notched tubes are 0.5–1.5cm long and yellow-green.
• **OCCURRENCE** Mycorrhizal with Tanbark Oak (*Lithocarpus*), Douglas Fir (*Pseudosuga menziesii*), and Giant Fir (*Abies grandis*) in mixed forests and woodland. Widespread on the west coast of North America and New Mexico. Not found in Europe.

stem is swollen and reddish brown • • *bun-shaped cap with felty covering*

FRUITING Appears singly or in troops in forests that consist of a mixture of trees.

| Dimensions CAP ⊕ 7.5–25cm | STEM ↕ 7.5–15cm ↔ to 10cm | Spores Brown | Edibility ☠ |

| Family BOLETACEAE | Species *Boletus legaliae* | Season Summer–early autumn |

LE GAL'S BOLETE

This spectacular species belongs to a group of red-coloured, net-stemmed boletes that are difficult to tell apart. It has a smooth, pink-orange cap and a similarly coloured stem with red netting at the top. The pores are red and the notched tubes are 1–2cm long. Smelling faintly pleasant, the off-white to pale yellow flesh bruises light blue; the stem base stains pale pink. It has a mild taste but is poisonous.
• **OCCURRENCE** Mycorrhizal with hardwoods, preferring alkaline soil. Widespread in Europe, but mostly local and in the south.
• **SIMILAR SPECIES** The cap of *Boletus rhodoxanthus* is purple-orange.

pink-orange stem is swollen, with a net • • *smooth, bun-shaped cap is pink-orange*

FRUITING Appears singly or a few fruit-bodies together; rarely occurs in troops.

| Dimensions CAP ⊕ 5–15cm | STEM ↕ 8–16cm ↔ 2.5–5cm | Spores Olive-brown | Edibility ☠ |

Family BOLETACEAE	Species *Boletus pulverulentus*	Season Summer–autumn

BLACKENING BOLETE

When bruised, all parts of this distinctive bolete almost immediately turn black. It has a convex, brown to red-brown cap with pointed, dull yellow pores on the underside. The red-dotted, yellow stem is comparatively thin. The slightly notched to slightly decurrent tubes are 0.5–1.5cm long and pale yellow to olive-yellow; the firm flesh is yellow. Although it has a mild taste, it does not rate as a choice edible.
• **OCCURRENCE** Mycorrhizal with hardwood trees, often oak, on fertile soil. Widespread in northern temperate zones, but rather local.
• **SIMILAR SPECIES** *Boletus luridiformis* (p.189) has a similar, but typically thicker, stem and has red pores. Its flesh turns blue when cut.

cap is brown to red-brown and convex •

pale yellow pores stain black •

yellow stem has red surface • dotting

FRUITING Appears singly or a few fruitbodies together; rarely, it may occur in troops.

Dimensions CAP ⊕ 4–10cm	STEM ↕ 4–10cm ↔ 1–3cm	Spores Olive-brown	Edibility |O|

Family BOLETACEAE	Species *Boletus pascuus*	Season Summer–autumn

RED-CRACKING BOLETE

One of the smaller, less fleshy boletes, this species has a convex, red-brown cap, with skin that tends to crack, revealing a red layer. The thin, cylindrical, yellow to red stem is streaked but lacks distinct patterning. The angular, yellow to olive pores bruise slightly blue; the white or pale yellow flesh hardly blues at all. It is edible, but tastes bland.
• **OCCURRENCE** Mycorrhizal with hardwood trees, often beech trees, on well-drained "mor" soil – humus-rich soil that is formed under acid conditions. Widespread and common in some parts of northern temperate zones.
• **SIMILAR SPECIES** The cap of *Boletus pruinatus* tends not to crack.

cap surface cracked, showing red • underlayer

△ *BOLETUS POROSPORUS*
This bolete has a white-cracked brown cap and lemon-yellow flesh, pores, and tubes that stain blue. It is best identified by its truncated, spindle-shaped spores, 13 x 5μm |O|

• convex cap is red-brown, often with red edge

• stem is streaked in yellow and red

slightly • notched to decurrent tubes, to 1cm long

FRUITING Often in large troops but also singly.

• yellow to olive pores stain slightly blue

• pale yellow young pores

SECTION

Dimensions CAP ⊕ 3–10cm	STEM ↕ 3–10cm ↔ 0.5–2cm	Spores Olive-brown	Edibility |O|

| Family BOLETACEAE | Species *Boletus rubellus* | Season Summer–autumn |

RED-CAPPED BOLETE

A small species with a deep red cap and stem. The cap is convex; the stem may have a thickened, pointed base. The yellow-olive pores stain blue when bruised; the yellow tubes are 0.5–1cm long. It has slowly blue-staining, pale yellow flesh. It is often placed in the genus *Xerocomus* with similarly coloured species such as *Boletus pascuus* (p.192).
• **OCCURRENCE** Mycorrhizal with hardwood trees, often in grassy areas, open woodland, and parks. Widespread but rather local in northern temperate zones.
• **SIMILAR SPECIES** *B. bicolor* (p.190). *B. sensibilis* has flesh that turns blue.

yellow tubes are notched to decurrent •

smooth, convex cap is dark red, becoming • browner with age

SECTION

pale • yellow flesh

• angular, yellow-olive pores stain blue

• stem is paler red than cap

stem base may be thickened and • pointed

FRUITING Mostly in troops of fruitbodies.

| Dimensions CAP ⊕ 3–6cm | STEM ↕ 3–8cm ↔ 0.5–1cm | Spores Olive-brown | Edibility |

| Family BOLETACEAE | Species *Boletus subtomentosus* | Season Summer–autumn |

YELLOW-CRACKING BOLETE

Despite its common name, the surface of the bun-shaped, golden brown cap of this species very rarely cracks. The stem is also golden brown, and the angular pores and the tubes, 0.5–1.5cm long, are yellow. The pores stain slightly blue when they are bruised. Although it is edible, the soft, pale yellow flesh has a bland flavour.
• **OCCURRENCE** Mycorrhizal with hard- and softwood trees. Widespread and fairly common in northern temperate zones, extending into sub-arctic and alpine regions.
• **SIMILAR SPECIES** *Boletus pruinatus* is smaller. *B. ferrugineus*, possibly just a form of *B. subtomentosus*, is darker and has a distinct raised net on the stem.

• felty surface of bun-shaped cap

golden brown to olive-brown • cap

yellow tube layer is notched •

faint streaks on pointed stem •

large, yellow to olive pores bruise slighlty blue •

pale • yellow flesh stains slightly blue

golden brown • or pale yellow stem

SECTION

FRUITING Singly or a few fruitbodies together.

| Dimensions CAP ⊕ 6–10cm | STEM ↕ 6–10cm ↔ 1–2.5cm | Spores Olive-brown | Edibility |

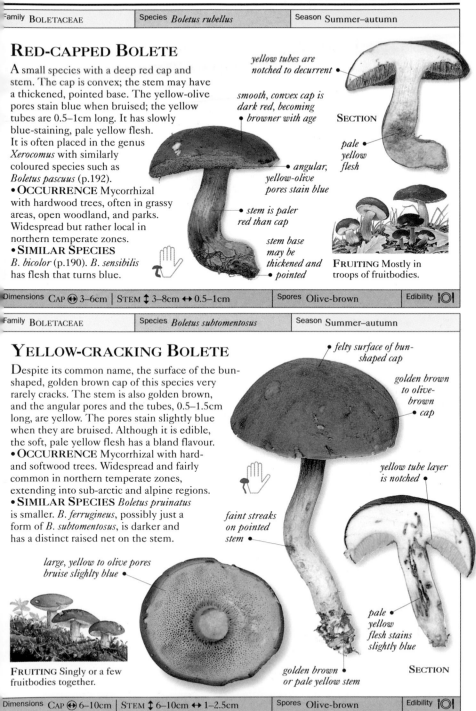

Family BOLETACEAE	Species *Boletus parasiticus*	Season Summer–autumn

PARASITIC BOLETE

An unusual habitat helps to distinguish this small bolete (see Occurrence). Fairly uniformly ochre-brown all over, with no blue staining reaction, it has a convex cap and quite a thin stem. The yellow to ochre tubes are 3–7mm long and decurrent. The flesh is pale yellow. Its rarity and inferior taste mean it is not recommended for eating.

• **OCCURRENCE** Mycorrhizal with hardwood trees in association with the fungus *Scleroderma citrinum* (p.256), to which it does little or no damage. Widespread in Europe and at least in eastern North America.

convex, ochre-brown cap •

surface of • cap is slightly velvety and a little greasy

• coarse pores are lemon-yellow to rust-brown

grows on the fruitbodies of Scleroderma citrinum

FRUITING In clusters on *Scleroderma citrinum*.

Dimensions CAP ⊕ 2–7cm	STEM ↕ 3–6cm ↔ 0.8–1.5cm	Spores Olive-brown	Edibility |O|

Family PAXILLACEAE	Species *Gyroporus castaneus*	Season Summer–autumn

CHESTNUT BOLETE

As with all *Gyroporus* species, the Chestnut Bolete has pale spores, a fragile, chambered stem, and off-white to pale brown tubes, 3–6mm long, which are almost free. The convex to flat cap and smooth stem are a distinctive rich orange-brown. Its flesh, which does not stain when cut, tastes pleasantly nutty.

• **OCCURRENCE** Mycorrhizal with hardwood trees, especially oak, and also with pine. Often found on sandy soil. Widespread and locally quite common in northern temperate zones.

• **SIMILAR SPECIES** There is an apparently poisonous species in coastal Portugal.

pores are • off-white to pale brown

• smooth, pale orange-brown stem

brittle, off-white • flesh does not stain

velvety cap surface •

rich orange-brown • cap is convex to flat

FRUITING Singly or a few together under hardwoods.

SECTION

Dimensions CAP ⊕ 3–8cm	STEM ↕ 4–7cm ↔ 1–3cm	Spores Pale yellow	Edibility |O|

| Family PAXILLACEAE | Species *Gyroporus cyanescens* | Season Summer–autumn |

CORNFLOWER BOLETE

SECTION

The most distinctive feature of this species is revealed when it is cut or its tube layer is scratched – the off-white flesh and tubes turn cornflower-blue; other blue-staining boletes (mainly *Boletus* species) typically turn darker blue or even blue-black. Otherwise, it has the characteristic fragile flesh, almost free tubes, 5–10mm long, and chambered stem of the genus. It has small, rounded pores and a bulbous stem base that tapers abruptly to a point. A choice edible, it has a pleasantly nutty flavour.

• **OCCURRENCE** Mycorrhizal with soft- and hardwood trees in woods. Widespread and locally common but rare in most northern temperate zones.

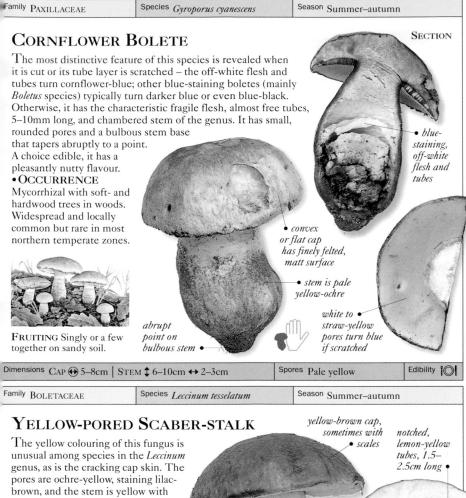

FRUITING Singly or a few together on sandy soil.

• blue-staining, off-white flesh and tubes

• convex or flat cap has finely felted, matt surface

• stem is pale yellow-ochre

abrupt point on bulbous stem •

white to • straw-yellow pores turn blue if scratched

| Dimensions CAP ⊕ 5–8cm │ STEM ↕ 6–10cm ↔ 2–3cm | Spores Pale yellow | Edibility |○| |

| Family BOLETACEAE | Species *Leccinum tesselatum* | Season Summer–autumn |

YELLOW-PORED SCABER-STALK

The yellow colouring of this fungus is unusual among species in the *Leccinum* genus, as is the cracking cap skin. The pores are ochre-yellow, staining lilac-brown, and the stem is yellow with ochre-yellow spotting, becoming net-like and brown towards the base; the bun-shaped cap is yellow-brown with a slightly velvety surface. The pale yellow flesh slowly stains wine-red to violet-black. It is edible but not distinctive in taste.

• **OCCURRENCE** Mycorrhizal with oak trees. Mostly in warmer parts of Europe; world distribution is unclear.

FRUITING Singly or a few together; prefers fertile soil.

yellow-brown cap, sometimes with • scales

notched, lemon-yellow tubes, 1.5–2.5cm long •

firm, pale • yellow flesh stains wine-red to violet-black

club-shaped • *stem*

SECTION

| Dimensions CAP ⊕ 4–10cm │ STEM ↕ 5–12cm ↔ 1–3cm | Spores Olive-ochre | Edibility |○| |

Family BOLETACEAE	Species *Leccinum scabrum*	Season Summer–autumn

BROWN BIRCH SCABER STALK

A brown cap with grey-white pores and a
white to grey stem covered with grey-
black scales are key identification
marks of this species, which is
treated in a broad sense here:
distinguishing between it and
its near relatives is difficult, and
Leccinum scabrum is often used as
a collective name for all brown-
capped *Leccinum* species (see also
L. variicolor, inset). The flesh is soft in the
bun-shaped cap, fibrous in the club-shaped
stem; unlike that of some relatives, it hardly
stains. Although edible, it is not choice and,
once gathered, does not keep well.
• **OCCURRENCE** Mycorrhizal with birch,
often on damp ground. Widespread in northern
temperate zones; precise distribution unclear.

*bun-shaped cap
• is brown*

*• slightly
overhanging
skin on cap*

*sturdy,
club-
shaped
stem •*

*• grey to
black scales
cover stem*

*• soft, grey-
white tubes,
1.5–2.5cm
long, are
notched*

*firm, fibrous
• flesh in stem*

SECTION

*• colour of flesh
hardly changes at
all when cut*

FRUITING Singly, a few
together, or in troops.

△ *LECCINUM VARIICOLOR*
This species has a mottled, sooty brown
cap with white or cream pores. The base
of the grey-scaled, white stem usually
has a pale blue stain. The white stem
flesh stains pink and turquoise; the cap
flesh is pink with grey-white tubes. 🍴

Dimensions CAP ⊕ 6–15cm	STEM ↕ 10–20cm ↔ 1–3cm	Spores Ochre-brown	Edibility 🍴

Family BOLETACEAE	Species *Leccinum versipelle*	Season Summer–autumn

ORANGE BIRCH BOLETE

A very handsome fungus, this species has a bun-shaped, orange cap contrasting with its tall, black-scaled, white stem; the cap skin overhangs the cap margin and has a finely felted surface. The pores vary from pale grey to ochre-grey, while the notched tubes, 1–3cm long, are dirty white. Staining grey-black, the firm, off-white flesh is reasonably tasty but lacks the quality of some of the *Boletus* species.

• **OCCURRENCE** Mycorrhizal with birch in damp woodland. Widespread and common in northern temperate zones.

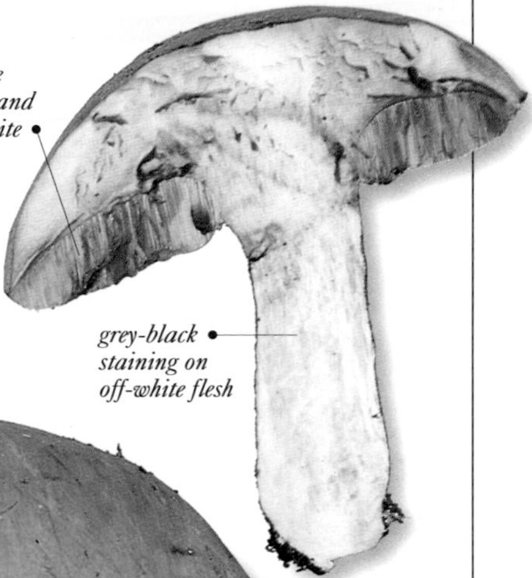

tubes are notched and dirty white

grey-black staining on off-white flesh

SECTION

bun-shaped mature cap

cap skin overhangs cap margin

pores may be pale grey to ochre-grey

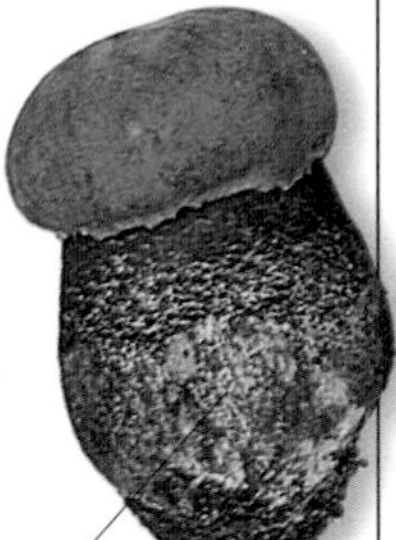

black scales cover tall stem

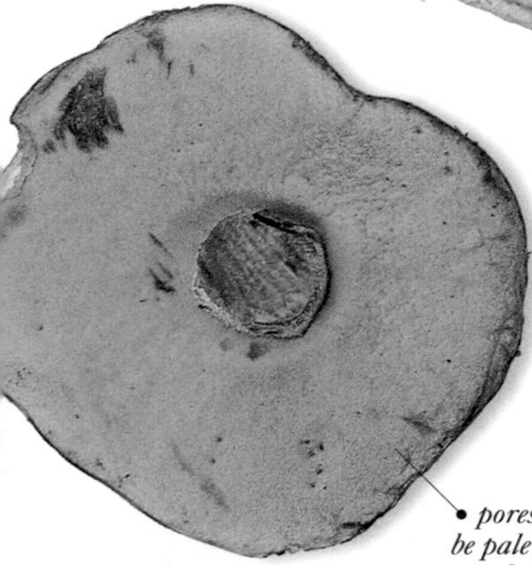

very dark stem of immature specimen

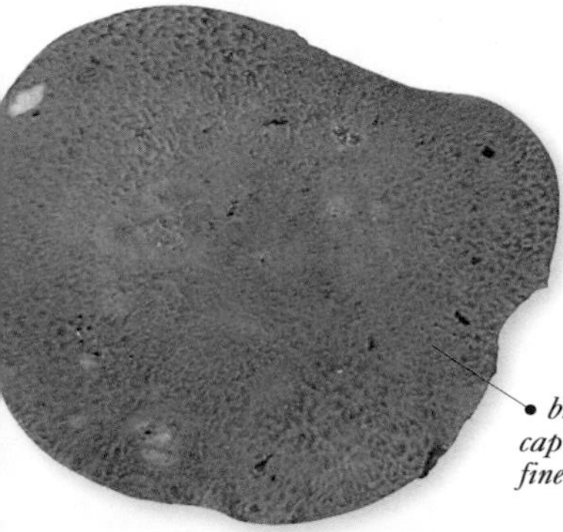

bright orange cap surface is finely felted

FRUITING Singly or a few fruitbodies together.

Dimensions CAP ⊕ 8–15cm	STEM ↕ 10–18cm ↔ 1.5–4cm	Spores Ochre-brown	Edibility

Family BOLETACEAE	Species *Leccinum quercinum*	Season Summer–autumn

RED OAK BOLETE

This bolete belongs to a group of red-capped *Leccinum* species and is distinguished in the group by its mycorrhizal partner (see Occurrence) and by the reddish brown scales on the stem. Its bun-shaped cap is orange-brown, the pores are off-white to grey or olive-yellow, and its firm white flesh stains almost black. It makes a good edible.

• **OCCURRENCE** Mycorrhizal with oak trees in woodland. Widespread and common in some regions of northern temperate zones.

• **SIMILAR SPECIES** *L. aurantiacum* has a more orange cap and is associated with aspen and poplar trees. *L. piccinum* and *L. vulpinum* grow with spruce and pine respectively.

cap is bun-shaped

pale grey tubes, 2–3cm long, are notched

SECTION

• *cap skin is dark chestnut-brown and overhangs margin*

almost black stains on firm white flesh

• *reddish brown scales cover stem surface*

• *almost cylindrical stem widens at base*

FRUITING Typically a few fruitbodies together.

Dimensions CAP ⊕ 8–15cm │ STEM ↕ 10–15cm ↔ 1.5–3cm	Spores Ochre-brown	Edibility

Family GOMPHIDIACEAE	Species *Suillus luteus*	Season Late summer–autumn

SLIPPERY JACK

Short-stemmed and slimy, this species has a convex, purple-brown cap, whose skin is easily peeled. It has adnate to slightly decurrent tubes, lemon-yellow pores. The stem ring has a dark purple underside. Below it, the stem is white, ageing purple; above, it is pale yellow with darker dots. Eat it with caution; some people experience allergic reactions.

• **OCCURRENCE** Mycorrhizal with pine trees. Widespread and common in northern temperate zones.

short tubes, 0.8–1.2cm long, are pale yellow

purple-brown cap

off-white or pale yellow flesh does not stain

SECTION

• *ring is off-white above, purple below*

fine, pale lemon-yellow pores

FRUITING Typically in troops under two-needled pine trees.

Dimensions CAP ⊕ 5–10cm │ STEM ↕ 5–10cm ↔ 1.5–3cm	Spores Ochre-brown	Edibility

| Family GOMPHIDIACEAE | Species *Suillus grevillei* | Season Autumn |

LARCH BOLETE

This vividly coloured bolete has a convex, bright yellow to yellowish orange cap, which is very slimy, and lemon-yellow pores that bruise cinnamon-brown. The white and yellow ring near the top of the yellow-brown stem is also slimy. It is edible, without a distinctive flavour, and, when young, has firm yellow flesh, which does not stain; the slimy cap skin is best peeled off when gathering for eating.

• **OCCURRENCE**
Mycorrhizal with larch trees in woodland, plantations, and gardens; may be found some distance from the host tree. Widespread and common in northern temperate zones.

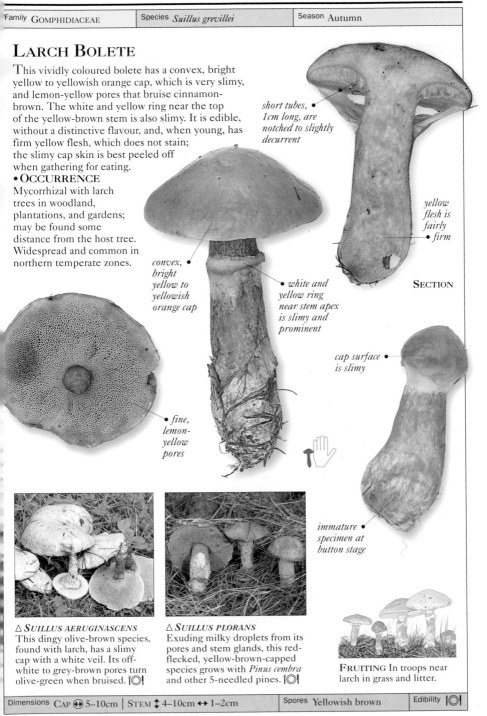

short tubes, 1cm long, are notched to slightly decurrent

yellow flesh is fairly firm

SECTION

convex, bright yellow to yellowish orange cap

white and yellow ring near stem apex is slimy and prominent

cap surface is slimy

fine, lemon-yellow pores

immature specimen at button stage

△ **SUILLUS AERUGINASCENS**
This dingy olive-brown species, found with larch, has a slimy cap with a white veil. Its off-white to grey-brown pores turn olive-green when bruised. |○|

△ **SUILLUS PLORANS**
Exuding milky droplets from its pores and stem glands, this red-flecked, yellow-brown-capped species grows with *Pinus cembra* and other 5-needled pines. |○|

FRUITING In troops near larch in grass and litter.

| Dimensions CAP ⊕ 5–10cm | STEM ↕ 4–10cm ↔ 1–2cm | Spores Yellowish brown | Edibility |○| |

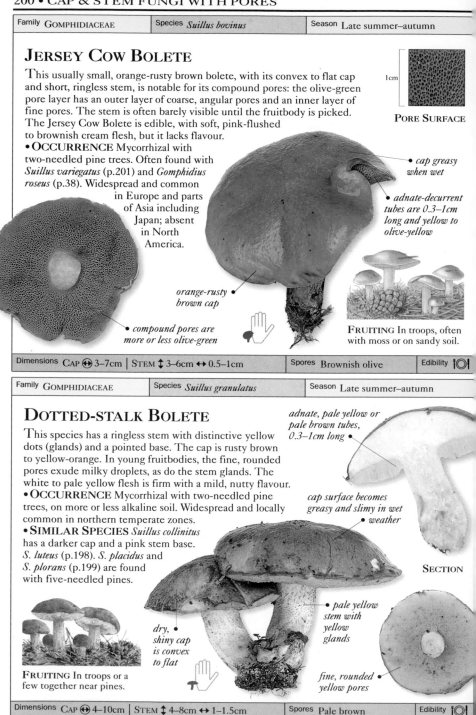

Family GOMPHIDIACEAE	Species *Suillus bovinus*	Season Late summer–autumn

JERSEY COW BOLETE

This usually small, orange-rusty brown bolete, with its convex to flat cap and short, ringless stem, is notable for its compound pores: the olive-green pore layer has an outer layer of coarse, angular pores and an inner layer of fine pores. The stem is often barely visible until the fruitbody is picked. The Jersey Cow Bolete is edible, with soft, pink-flushed to brownish cream flesh, but it lacks flavour.

• **OCCURRENCE** Mycorrhizal with two-needled pine trees. Often found with *Suillus variegatus* (p.201) and *Gomphidius roseus* (p.38). Widespread and common in Europe and parts of Asia including Japan; absent in North America.

1cm

PORE SURFACE

cap greasy when wet

adnate-decurrent tubes are 0.3–1cm long and yellow to olive-yellow

orange-rusty brown cap

compound pores are more or less olive-green

FRUITING In troops, often with moss or on sandy soil.

Dimensions CAP ⊕ 3–7cm | STEM ↕ 3–6cm ↔ 0.5–1cm	Spores Brownish olive	Edibility ⚭

Family GOMPHIDIACEAE	Species *Suillus granulatus*	Season Late summer–autumn

DOTTED-STALK BOLETE

This species has a ringless stem with distinctive yellow dots (glands) and a pointed base. The cap is rusty brown to yellow-orange. In young fruitbodies, the fine, rounded pores exude milky droplets, as do the stem glands. The white to pale yellow flesh is firm with a mild, nutty flavour.

• **OCCURRENCE** Mycorrhizal with two-needled pine trees, on more or less alkaline soil. Widespread and locally common in northern temperate zones.

• **SIMILAR SPECIES** *Suillus collinitus* has a darker cap and a pink stem base. *S. luteus* (p.198). *S. placidus* and *S. plorans* (p.199) are found with five-needled pines.

adnate, pale yellow or pale brown tubes, 0.3–1cm long

cap surface becomes greasy and slimy in wet weather

SECTION

dry, shiny cap is convex to flat

pale yellow stem with yellow glands

fine, rounded yellow pores

FRUITING In troops or a few together near pines.

Dimensions CAP ⊕ 4–10cm | STEM ↕ 4–8cm ↔ 1–1.5cm	Spores Pale brown	Edibility ⚭

| Family GOMPHIDIACEAE | Species *Suillus variegatus* | Season Summer–autumn |

VARIEGATED BOLETE

Rather tall-stemmed and fleshy, the Variegated Bolete rarely exhibits the sliminess that is characteristic of the genus *Suillus*. Its convex, orange-brown cap has a felty to finely scaly surface. The small pores are brown to olive-brown and, like the pale yellow flesh, stain blue when pressed. The stem is brown with olive-green or pale red tints. It is edible, but has a metallic smell and unpleasant taste.
• **OCCURRENCE** Mycorrhizal with two-needled pine trees, often found with heathers and other acid-loving plants, on sandy soil. Widespread and common in Europe and nearby parts of Asia.
• **SIMILAR SPECIES** *Scleroderma* species (pp.256, 263) smell like the Variegated Bolete, but are not similar in appearance.

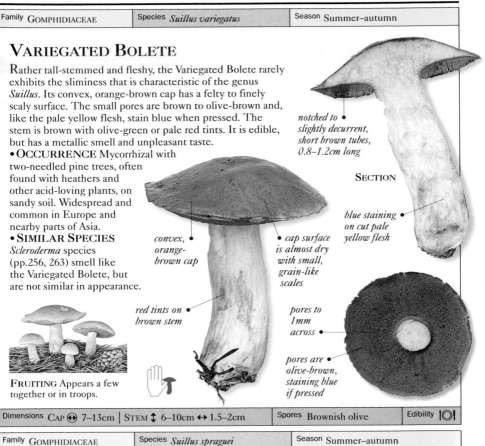

notched to • slightly decurrent, short brown tubes, 0.8–1.2cm long

SECTION

blue staining • on cut pale yellow flesh

convex, • orange-brown cap

cap surface • is almost dry with small, grain-like scales

red tints on • brown stem

pores to 1mm across •

pores are • olive-brown, staining blue if pressed

FRUITING Appears a few together or in troops.

| Dimensions CAP ⊕ 7–13cm | STEM ↕ 6–10cm ↔ 1.5–2cm | Spores Brownish olive | Edibility |⚬| |

| Family GOMPHIDIACEAE | Species *Suillus spraguei* | Season Summer–autumn |

PAINTED BOLETE

With its dry, scaly red cap, partial white veil, and large yellow pores, this species is very easily recognized. The cap is convex, and the red-flecked, yellow stem may be somewhat club-shaped. The partial veil, which covers the immature pores at first, leaves a cobweb-like ring on the upper part of the stem. The tubes are adnate to slightly decurrent. The yellow flesh, which becomes pink tinged on exposure to air, is firm in texture and has a mild taste.
• **OCCURRENCE** Mycorrhizal with Eastern White Pine (*Pinus strobus*) in woods and parks. Widespread and common in Eastern North America, wherever Eastern White Pine grows.

dry, convex cap is red with pale background •

scales cover surface of • cap

yellow stem is flecked with red •

FRUITING Appears in scattered fruitbodies or in large groups under Eastern White Pine trees.

| Dimensions CAP ⊕ 3–12cm | STEM ↕ 4–12cm ↔ 1–2.5cm | Spores Olive-brown | Edibility |⚬| |

WITH TOUGH FLESH

T HE FUNGI in this subsection are known as polypores, and have pores on the cap underside and tough flesh. The polypores described here also have a more or less distinct stem (for polypores with a bracket-like fruitbody and no stem see pp.211–233). Unlike the boletes (pp.184–201), the tube layer of polypores is not easy to separate from the flesh.

Family ALBATRELLACEAE	Species *Albatrellus ovinus*	Season Summer–autumn

SHEEP POLYPORE

From above, this creamy to pale grey-brown polypore looks like an agaric (see p.28) or a hedgehog fungus (p.238), but it has minute pores on the underside. It stains lemon or greenish yellow, particularly on the pores. The skin of the convex cap often cracks with age. It has a sturdy stem and very firm, mild to slightly bitter white flesh.
• OCCURRENCE Most probably mycorrhizal with spruce on moss-covered soil. Widespread throughout northern temperate zones; locally common.
• SIMILAR SPECIES *Albatrellus confluens* is more orange and does not stain yellow; it tastes bitter. *A. subrubescens* stains orange.

cap margin is often wavy

angular pores, 2–4 per mm on underside

short, sturdy, cream to grey stem

convex cap is creamy to pale grey brown

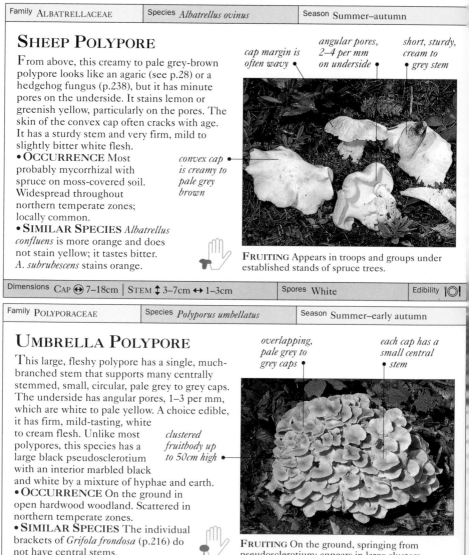

FRUITING Appears in troops and groups under established stands of spruce trees.

Dimensions CAP ⊕ 7–18cm	STEM ↕ 3–7cm ↔ 1–3cm	Spores White	Edibility

Family POLYPORACEAE	Species *Polyporus umbellatus*	Season Summer–early autumn

UMBRELLA POLYPORE

This large, fleshy polypore has a single, much-branched stem that supports many centrally stemmed, small, circular, pale grey to grey caps. The underside has angular pores, 1–3 per mm, which are white to pale yellow. A choice edible, it has firm, mild-tasting, white to cream flesh. Unlike most polypores, this species has a large black pseudosclerotium with an interior marbled black and white by a mixture of hyphae and earth.
• OCCURRENCE On the ground in open hardwood woodland. Scattered in northern temperate zones.
• SIMILAR SPECIES The individual brackets of *Grifola frondosa* (p.216) do not have central stems.

overlapping, pale grey to grey caps

each cap has a small central stem

clustered fruitbody up to 50cm high

FRUITING On the ground, springing from pseudosclerotium; appears in large clusters.

Dimensions CAP ⊕ 1–4cm	STEM ↕ 5–7.5cm ↔ 2–3cm	Spores White	Edibility

| Family POLYPORACEAE | Species *Polyporus squamosus* | Season Late spring–summer |

DRYAD'S SADDLE

A circular to fan-shaped bracket, covered with brown scales, a black stem positioned to one side, and a decurrent white tube layer, 0.5–1cm thick, make this fungus unmistakable. Early in the season, it seems to explode out of half-dead trees or stumps; it becomes very large, but is soon devoured by a multitude of insects, leaving only a dried-up carcass, which is broken down by other fungi. The white flesh is soft and smells strongly of meal. Dryad's Saddle can be eaten when very young.

• **OCCURRENCE** Parasitic or saprotrophic on hardwood trees in woods, on roadside trees, and in parks. Widespread and common in northern temperate zones.

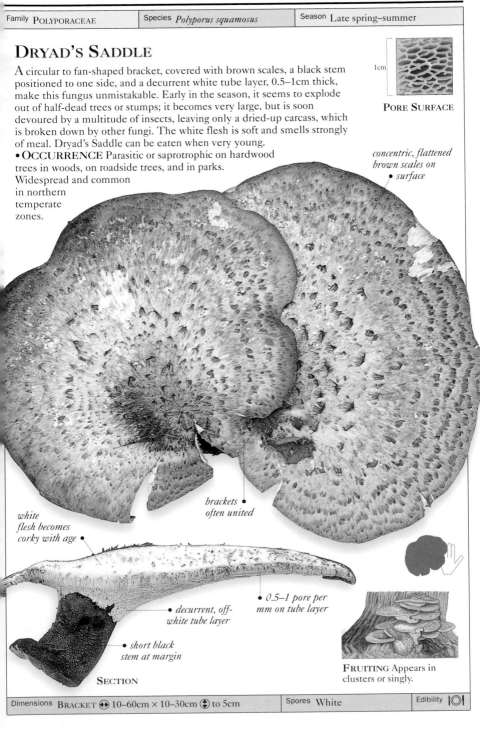

1cm

PORE SURFACE

concentric, flattened brown scales on • surface

white flesh becomes corky with age •

brackets • often united

• decurrent, off-white tube layer

• 0.5–1 pore per mm on tube layer

• short black stem at margin

SECTION

FRUITING Appears in clusters or singly.

| Dimensions BRACKET ⟷ 10–60cm × 10–30cm ⬍ to 5cm | Spores White | Edibility ⦿❙ |

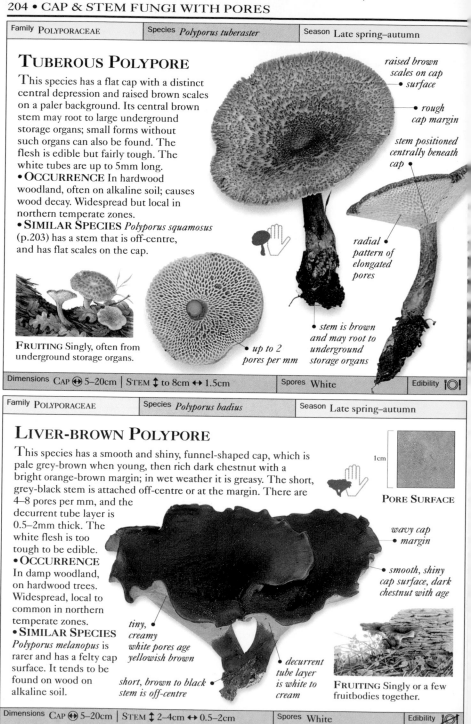

| Family POLYPORACEAE | Species *Polyporus tuberaster* | Season Late spring–autumn |

TUBEROUS POLYPORE

This species has a flat cap with a distinct central depression and raised brown scales on a paler background. Its central brown stem may root to large underground storage organs; small forms without such organs can also be found. The flesh is edible but fairly tough. The white tubes are up to 5mm long.
• OCCURRENCE In hardwood woodland, often on alkaline soil; causes wood decay. Widespread but local in northern temperate zones.
• SIMILAR SPECIES *Polyporus squamosus* (p.203) has a stem that is off-centre, and has flat scales on the cap.

raised brown scales on cap • surface

• rough cap margin

stem positioned centrally beneath cap •

radial • pattern of elongated pores

FRUITING Singly, often from underground storage organs.

• up to 2 pores per mm

• stem is brown and may root to underground storage organs

| Dimensions CAP ⊕ 5–20cm | STEM ↕ to 8cm ↔ 1.5cm | Spores White | Edibility |O| |

| Family POLYPORACEAE | Species *Polyporus badius* | Season Late spring–autumn |

LIVER-BROWN POLYPORE

This species has a smooth and shiny, funnel-shaped cap, which is pale grey-brown when young, then rich dark chestnut with a bright orange-brown margin; in wet weather it is greasy. The short, grey-black stem is attached off-centre or at the margin. There are 4–8 pores per mm, and the decurrent tube layer is 0.5–2mm thick. The white flesh is too tough to be edible.
• OCCURRENCE In damp woodland, on hardwood trees. Widespread, local to common in northern temperate zones.
• SIMILAR SPECIES *Polyporus melanopus* is rarer and has a felty cap surface. It tends to be found on wood on alkaline soil.

1cm

PORE SURFACE

wavy cap • margin

• smooth, shiny cap surface, dark chestnut with age

tiny, creamy white pores age yellowish brown

short, brown to black • stem is off-centre

• decurrent tube layer is white to cream

FRUITING Singly or a few fruitbodies together.

| Dimensions CAP ⊕ 5–20cm | STEM ↕ 2–4cm ↔ 0.5–2cm | Spores White | Edibility |O| |

Family POLYPORACEAE	Species *Polyporus varius*	Season Late spring–autumn

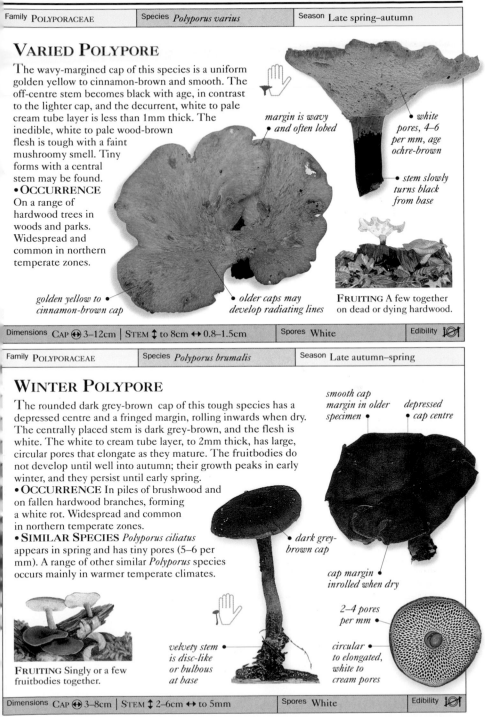

VARIED POLYPORE

The wavy-margined cap of this species is a uniform golden yellow to cinnamon-brown and smooth. The off-centre stem becomes black with age, in contrast to the lighter cap, and the decurrent, white to pale cream tube layer is less than 1mm thick. The inedible, white to pale wood-brown flesh is tough with a faint mushroomy smell. Tiny forms with a central stem may be found.

• OCCURRENCE
On a range of hardwood trees in woods and parks. Widespread and common in northern temperate zones.

margin is wavy and often lobed

white pores, 4–6 per mm, age ochre-brown

stem slowly turns black from base

golden yellow to cinnamon-brown cap

older caps may develop radiating lines

FRUITING A few together on dead or dying hardwood.

Dimensions CAP ⊕ 3–12cm │ STEM ↕ to 8cm ↔ 0.8–1.5cm	Spores White	Edibility

Family POLYPORACEAE	Species *Polyporus brumalis*	Season Late autumn–spring

WINTER POLYPORE

The rounded dark grey-brown cap of this tough species has a depressed centre and a fringed margin, rolling inwards when dry. The centrally placed stem is dark grey-brown, and the flesh is white. The white to cream tube layer, to 2mm thick, has large, circular pores that elongate as they mature. The fruitbodies do not develop until well into autumn; their growth peaks in early winter, and they persist until early spring.

• OCCURRENCE In piles of brushwood and on fallen hardwood branches, forming a white rot. Widespread and common in northern temperate zones.

• SIMILAR SPECIES *Polyporus ciliatus* appears in spring and has tiny pores (5–6 per mm). A range of other similar *Polyporus* species occurs mainly in warmer temperate climates.

smooth cap margin in older specimen

depressed cap centre

dark grey-brown cap

cap margin inrolled when dry

2–4 pores per mm

circular to elongated, white to cream pores

FRUITING Singly or a few fruitbodies together.

velvety stem is disc-like or bulbous at base

Dimensions CAP ⊕ 3–8cm │ STEM ↕ 2–6cm ↔ to 5mm	Spores White	Edibility

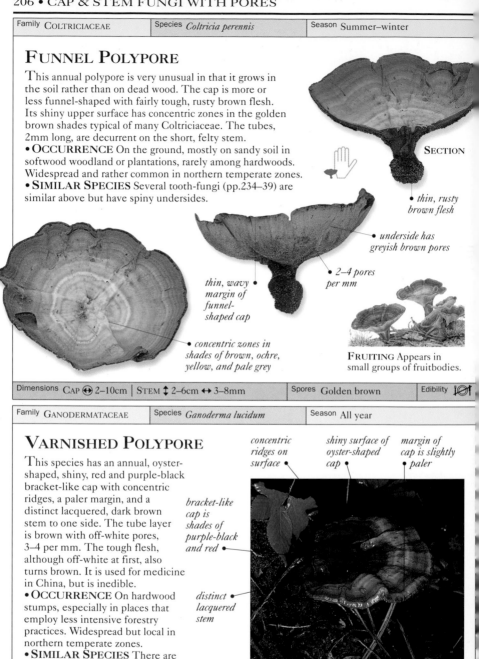

| Family COLTRICIACEAE | Species *Coltricia perennis* | Season Summer–winter |

FUNNEL POLYPORE

This annual polypore is very unusual in that it grows in the soil rather than on dead wood. The cap is more or less funnel-shaped with fairly tough, rusty brown flesh. Its shiny upper surface has concentric zones in the golden brown shades typical of many Coltriciaceae. The tubes, 2mm long, are decurrent on the short, felty stem.
• **OCCURRENCE** On the ground, mostly on sandy soil in softwood woodland or plantations, rarely among hardwoods. Widespread and rather common in northern temperate zones.
• **SIMILAR SPECIES** Several tooth-fungi (pp.234–39) are similar above but have spiny undersides.

SECTION

• *thin, rusty brown flesh*

• *underside has greyish brown pores*

• *2–4 pores per mm*

thin, wavy • margin of funnel- shaped cap

concentric zones in shades of brown, ochre, yellow, and pale grey

FRUITING Appears in small groups of fruitbodies.

| Dimensions CAP ⊕ 2–10cm | STEM ↕ 2–6cm ↔ 3–8mm | Spores Golden brown | Edibility |

| Family GANODERMATACEAE | Species *Ganoderma lucidum* | Season All year |

VARNISHED POLYPORE

This species has an annual, oyster-shaped, shiny, red and purple-black bracket-like cap with concentric ridges, a paler margin, and a distinct lacquered, dark brown stem to one side. The tube layer is brown with off-white pores, 3–4 per mm. The tough flesh, although off-white at first, also turns brown. It is used for medicine in China, but is inedible.
• **OCCURRENCE** On hardwood stumps, especially in places that employ less intensive forestry practices. Widespread but local in northern temperate zones.
• **SIMILAR SPECIES** There are several closely related species, including *Ganoderma carnosum*, some of which grow on softwood.

concentric ridges on surface •

shiny surface of oyster-shaped cap •

margin of cap is slightly • paler

bracket-like cap is shades of purple-black and red •

distinct • lacquered stem

FRUITING Singly or in groups of fruitbodies around the stumps of hardwood trees.

| Dimensions CAP ⊕ 10–30cm ⊕ to 3cm | STEM ↕ 5–20cm ↔ 1–3cm | Spores Brown | Edibility |

HONEYCOMB-, BRAIN-, OR SADDLE-LIKE CAP

Most of the species in this section are thought to have evolved from cup fungi (see p.264). Their "cup" is heavily folded and is raised on a stem. The spore-producing surface, or hymenium, is smooth and sited on the folds. The choice morels, with a honeycomb-like structure, are found here.

saddle-like cap

brain-like cap

Family HELVELLACEAE	Species *Helvella crispa*	Season Summer–autumn

COMMON WHITE SADDLE

This species is easily identified by its furrowed, hollow, and chambered stem, its saddle-shaped cap, and its pale creamy white colouring. It varies in size but is typically large. Edible, with rather thin flesh, it is not recommended and should only be eaten after being carefully dried until crisp or after a thorough boiling in water.

• **OCCURRENCE** In hard- or softwood woodland on alkaline soil, often along paths and roads. It, and several other *Helvella* species, is frequently found alongside species of *Peziza* (pp.266–67) and *Inocybe* (pp.98–102). Widespread and common in most northern temperate regions.

cap underside is tan or pale buff • SECTION

• convoluted, saddle-shaped cap is cream coloured

hollow • stem

chambers • in stem

smooth, spore-producing surface •

stem is white with longitudinal grooves

base is slightly rooting

△ *STEREOPSIS HUMPHREYI*
This North American species has a saddle-shaped, dull white cap and a white stem. It is thought to be related to coral fungi (pp.248–51) and appears in large troops. 🖐

FRUITING In troops of fruitbodies or singly.

Dimensions CAP ⊕ 2–6cm	STEM ↕ 3–12cm ↔ 0.5–2.5cm	Spores White	Edibility

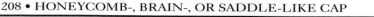

Family HELVELLACEAE	Species *Helvella lacunosa*	Season Summer–autumn

COMMON GREY SADDLE

Perhaps the most common *Helvella* species, this fungus is extremely variable in size, shape, and colour. It can be any shade of grey, and its cap is either saddle-shaped or convoluted and lobed. The stem has distinct grooves on the outside and is chambered within. The flesh is thin and grey to dirty white; like *Helvella crispa* (p.207), it is edible after thorough drying or boiling, but is not recommended.

• OCCURRENCE In woodland and more open areas on alkaline soil and gravel. Widespread in temperate and alpine zones of both the northern and southern hemispheres.

SECTION

• upper, spore-producing surface

grey to near black lobes are paler beneath •

• deep longitudinal grooves in stem

• chambers inside stem

• stem is any shade of grey

FRUITING In troops or singly on disturbed soil.

| Dimensions CAP ⊕ 1–5cm | STEM ↕ 2–8cm ↔ 0.5–1.5cm | Spores White | Edibility |

Family HELVELLACEAE	Species *Gyromitra esculenta*	Season Spring

FALSE MOREL

A brain-like, dark brown cap with a chambered interior characterizes this easily identified species. The short white stem is almost hollow, with white flesh. Despite being poisonous, in parts of Europe it is eaten after careful drying or repeated boiling in fresh water.

• OCCURRENCE Near softwoods on sandy soil or on wood chippings. Widespread in northern temperate zones; locally common.

• SIMILAR SPECIES *Gyromitra gigas*, *G. brunnea*, and *G. caroliniana* are often larger and more vivid orange-brown; they can be common in parts of North America.

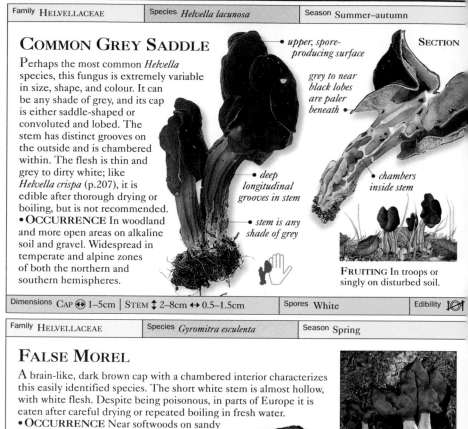

△ *GYROMITRA INFULA*
Appearing in autumn, this species has a lobed brown cap and a chambered, lavender to white stem. ☠

• brain-like cap surface

cap interior • is chambered

white flesh in hollow stem

SECTION

short white • stem with slightly grooved surface

FRUITING In troops, often on disturbed soil near pine.

| Dimensions CAP ⊕ 5–15cm | STEM ↕ 1–5cm ↔ 2–4cm | Spores White | Edibility ☠ |

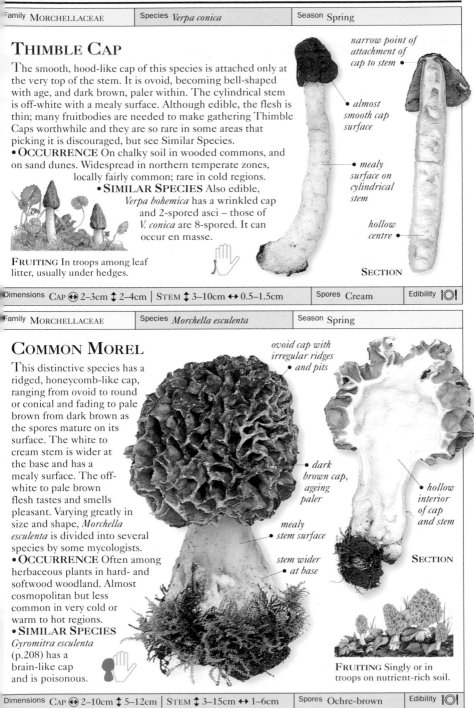

| Family MORCHELLACEAE | Species *Verpa conica* | Season Spring |

THIMBLE CAP

The smooth, hood-like cap of this species is attached only at the very top of the stem. It is ovoid, becoming bell-shaped with age, and dark brown, paler within. The cylindrical stem is off-white with a mealy surface. Although edible, the flesh is thin; many fruitbodies are needed to make gathering Thimble Caps worthwhile and they are so rare in some areas that picking it is discouraged, but see Similar Species.
• **OCCURRENCE** On chalky soil in wooded commons, and on sand dunes. Widespread in northern temperate zones, locally fairly common; rare in cold regions.
• **SIMILAR SPECIES** Also edible, *Verpa bohemica* has a wrinkled cap and 2-spored asci – those of *V. conica* are 8-spored. It can occur en masse.

FRUITING In troops among leaf litter, usually under hedges.

narrow point of attachment of cap to stem •

• *almost smooth cap surface*

• *mealy surface on cylindrical stem*

hollow centre •

SECTION

| Dimensions | CAP ⊕ 2–3cm ↕ 2–4cm | STEM ↕ 3–10cm ↔ 0.5–1.5cm | Spores Cream | Edibility |⊙| |

| Family MORCHELLACEAE | Species *Morchella esculenta* | Season Spring |

COMMON MOREL

This distinctive species has a ridged, honeycomb-like cap, ranging from ovoid to round or conical and fading to pale brown from dark brown as the spores mature on its surface. The white to cream stem is wider at the base and has a mealy surface. The off-white to pale brown flesh tastes and smells pleasant. Varying greatly in size and shape, *Morchella esculenta* is divided into several species by some mycologists.
• **OCCURRENCE** Often among herbaceous plants in hard- and softwood woodland. Almost cosmopolitan but less common in very cold or warm to hot regions.
• **SIMILAR SPECIES** *Gyromitra esculenta* (p.208) has a brain-like cap and is poisonous.

ovoid cap with irregular ridges • *and pits*

• *dark brown cap, ageing paler*

mealy • *stem surface*

stem wider • *at base*

• *hollow interior of cap and stem*

SECTION

FRUITING Singly or in troops on nutrient-rich soil.

| Dimensions | CAP ⊕ 2–10cm ↕ 5–12cm | STEM ↕ 3–15cm ↔ 1–6cm | Spores Ochre-brown | Edibility |⊙| |

Family MORCHELLACEAE	Species *Morchella elata*	Season Spring

BLACK MOREL

This morel has a conical cap with distinct black ridges and brown to smoky-grey pits. The stem is white with a rough, mealy or granular surface and a hollow centre. A popular edible with a crunchy texture and nutty flavour, the Black Morel can cause stomach upsets in some people.
• **OCCURRENCE** On the ground, in parks and open woods. Another form can appear in mountainous areas in summer. Widespread in northern temperate zones.
• **SIMILAR SPECIES** *Morchella esculenta* (p.209) is yellow and has pale ribs along the length of its cap. *Gyromitra* species (p.208), which are poisonous, lack the pitted cap and have chambered, rather than hollow, stems.

pits on cap are brown to smoky-grey •

cap is conical and tapers at top •

brown to black cap with longitudinal ridges •

white stem • with granular surface

FRUITING In large numbers under hard- and softwoods; especially in burnt areas.

Dimensions CAP ⊕ 5–10cm ↕ 2.5–5cm	STEM ↕ 5–10cm ↔ 2.5–5cm	Spores White to cream	Edibility |O|

Family MORCHELLACEAE	Species *Morchella semilibera*	Season Spring

HALF-FREE MOREL

The conical, dark grey-brown cap of this small morel is free at the rim, with honeycomb-like ridges and pits. It has a slender, hollow, white to cream stem with a mealy surface. It is edible but the cream flesh is too thin to make it choice.
• **OCCURRENCE** Dense woodland on rich soil, along paths in damp places. Widespread; more common in warmer regions of Europe.
• **SIMILAR SPECIES** *Verpa* species (p.209) have small hood-like caps that are attached only to the very top of the stem.

ridges and pits on cap surface

rim of cap is free of stem •

stem has • hollow centre

SECTION

cap is conical and taller than it is wide

stem is not • very fleshy

cap is dark grey-brown

stem is cylindrical • and white to cream

slender stem has mealy surface •

FRUITING Often in troops hidden in dense vegetation.

Dimensions CAP ⊕ 1–2.5cm ↕ 1–4cm	STEM ↕ 3–10cm ↔ 1–2cm	Spores Cream	Edibility |O|

BRACKET- OR SKIN-LIKE

This section features fungi that have shelf-like fruitbodies, which grow from trunks or branches, as well as species that grow flat (resupinate) against a woody substrate, forming a skin-like crust. The spore-producing surface (hymenium) may consist of tubes, with pores on the surface, or may be smooth to wrinkled.

• *bracket-like*

• *skin-like*

WITH PORES

THE SPECIES in this subsection are known as polypores. Their spores are produced in tubes sited on their undersides and are dispersed through pores that can be rounded to elongated or maze-like in shape. The fruitbodies can be produced annually or continue to grow as long as the substrate lasts.

Family PHAEOLACEAE	Species *Tyromyces stipticus*	Season Mainly autumn

BITTER BRACKET

A very bitter taste is one of the best indicators of this species, which produces semi-circular to kidney-shaped, off-white annual brackets. Distinctly triangular in cross-section, they have a rough, warty surface and soft white flesh. In humid weather the pores exude an off-white liquid that dries to cream-white. The tube layer is 0.5–1cm thick; there are 4–6 pores per mm.

• **OCCURRENCE** On stumps or trunks of softwood trees in woodland and plantations; sometimes on hardwood. Widespread and common in northern temperate zones, especially in the boreal regions.

• **SIMILAR SPECIES** Other white *Tyromyces* species are milder tasting; some bruise red, others grow on hardwood.

• *bracket has broad area of attachment*

• *white to grey or cream surface*

1cm

PORE SURFACE

• *soft flesh has cheese-like texture*

FRUITING Singly or a few together in woodland.

• *white to cream pores*

△ *POSTIA CAESIA*
The semi-circular annual brackets of this polypore are soft and spongy with a slightly felty white surface that ages blue-black.

Dimensions BRACKET ⊕ 5–12cm × 3–7cm ⊕ to 2.5cm	Spores White	Edibility

Family FOMITOPSIDACEAE	Species *Piptoporus betulinus*	Season All year

RAZOR-STROP FUNGUS

bracket often swollen near attachment point •

This semi-circular annual bracket fungus has a skin-like brown surface. It is stemless or has a rudimentary stem-like attachment. The soft but firm white flesh smells pleasant but is inedible. It was once used for sharpening razors and as a polishing agent in the watch-making industry. The brackets are often attacked by flask fungi: *Hypocrea pulvinata* when on the tree; the orange *Hypomyces aurantius* once the tree or polypore has fallen.

• **OCCURRENCE** In damp woodland, often alongside *Fomes fomentarius* (p.219). It is parasitic on birch trees, mostly older specimens, causing brown rot. The trees eventually die but the polypore can continue fruiting on them for some time. Widespread and common in northern temperate zones.

brown • surface may crack to reveal white flesh

SECTION

white tube layer is up to 1cm thick •

• white flesh is soft but tough

smooth, • rounded margin

• white pore surface with 3–4 pores per mm

FRUITING A few together on rotten birch trunks.

Dimensions BRACKET ⊕ 5–30cm × 5–20cm ⬧ 2–6cm	Spores White	Edibility

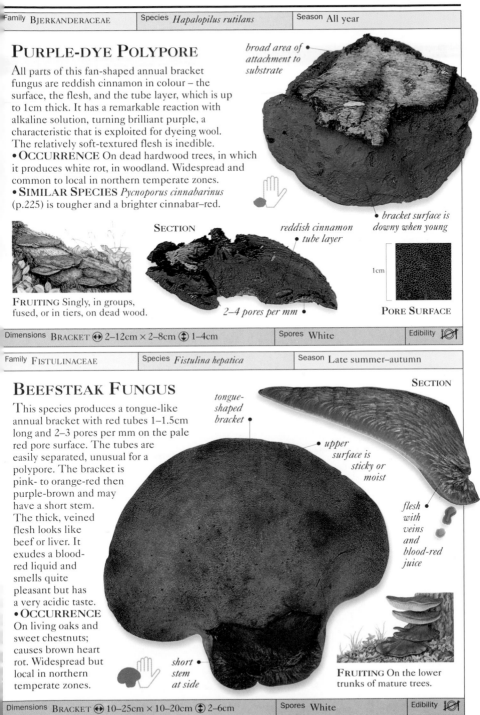

Family BJERKANDERACEAE	Species *Hapalopilus rutilans*	Season All year

PURPLE-DYE POLYPORE

All parts of this fan-shaped annual bracket fungus are reddish cinnamon in colour – the surface, the flesh, and the tube layer, which is up to 1cm thick. It has a remarkable reaction with alkaline solution, turning brilliant purple, a characteristic that is exploited for dyeing wool. The relatively soft-textured flesh is inedible.
• OCCURRENCE On dead hardwood trees, in which it produces white rot, in woodland. Widespread and common to local in northern temperate zones.
• SIMILAR SPECIES *Pycnoporus cinnabarinus* (p.225) is tougher and a brighter cinnabar-red.

broad area of attachment to substrate

bracket surface is downy when young

SECTION

reddish cinnamon tube layer

1cm

FRUITING Singly, in groups, fused, or in tiers, on dead wood.

2–4 pores per mm

PORE SURFACE

Dimensions BRACKET ⊕ 2–12cm × 2–8cm ⊕ 1–4cm	Spores White	Edibility

Family FISTULINACEAE	Species *Fistulina hepatica*	Season Late summer–autumn

BEEFSTEAK FUNGUS

SECTION

This species produces a tongue-like annual bracket with red tubes 1–1.5cm long and 2–3 pores per mm on the pale red pore surface. The tubes are easily separated, unusual for a polypore. The bracket is pink- to orange-red then purple-brown and may have a short stem. The thick, veined flesh looks like beef or liver. It exudes a blood-red liquid and smells quite pleasant but has a very acidic taste.
• OCCURRENCE On living oaks and sweet chestnuts; causes brown heart rot. Widespread but local in northern temperate zones.

tongue-shaped bracket

upper surface is sticky or moist

flesh with veins and blood-red juice

short stem at side

FRUITING On the lower trunks of mature trees.

Dimensions BRACKET ⊕ 10–25cm × 10–20cm ⊕ 2–6cm	Spores White	Edibility

| Family RIGIDOPORACEAE | Species *Meripilus giganteus* | Season Autumn |

BLACK-STAINING POLYPORE

This massive species produces several densely layered annual brackets from a single short stem; a composite fruitbody can be up to 1m across. Each fan-shaped bracket has a smooth surface with concentric, golden brown zones and a wavy margin. The pleasant smelling white flesh is soft and fibrous; it is edible when young – turning grey to black when cooked – but has a poor flavour. The off-white tube layer is up to 1cm thick.

• **OCCURRENCE** In woods and parks, around dead or dying hardwood trees, rarely on softwoods. Widespread and fairly common in northern temperate zones.

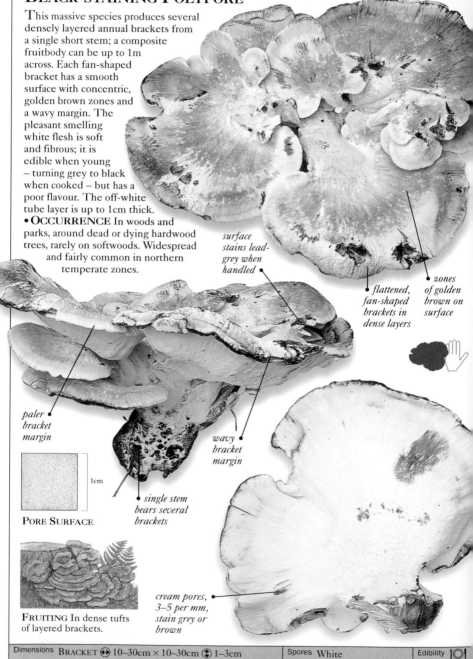

surface stains lead-grey when handled

zones of golden brown on surface

flattened, fan-shaped brackets in dense layers

paler bracket margin

wavy bracket margin

1cm

PORE SURFACE

single stem bears several brackets

FRUITING In dense tufts of layered brackets.

cream pores, 3–5 per mm, stain grey or brown

| Dimensions BRACKET ⊕ 10–30cm × 10–30cm ↕ 1–3cm | Spores White | Edibility ⏀ |

Family PHAEOLACEAE	Species *Laetiporus sulphureus*	Season Early summer–late autumn

CHICKEN-OF-THE-WOODS

This splendid, annual bracket fungus has an almost luminous quality with its large, quick-growing, yellow or yellow-orange fruitbodies. The thick, fleshy brackets are fan-shaped or irregularly semi-circular with an uneven, suede-like surface. The flesh is pale yellow with a crumbly texture, especially when old, and smells of lemon then mice. A choice edible, it requires thorough cooking; some people are allergic to it.

• **OCCURRENCE**
On hardwood in some regions, softwood in others; mostly attacks the heartwood. Widespread and common in northern temperate zones.

overlapping tiers of brackets

lustrous yellow to orange-yellow surface dulls with age

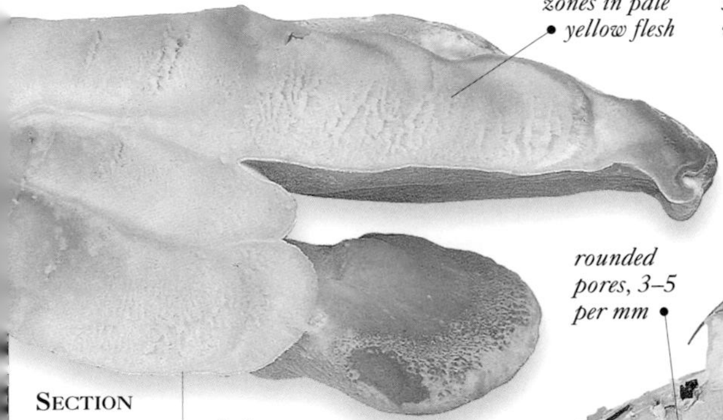

indistinct zones in pale yellow flesh

flesh becomes crumbly and cheese-like with age

rounded pores, 3–5 per mm

SECTION

• tube layer, to 5mm thick, is indistinct in young specimens

bracket • margin is fairly thick

striking yellow pores

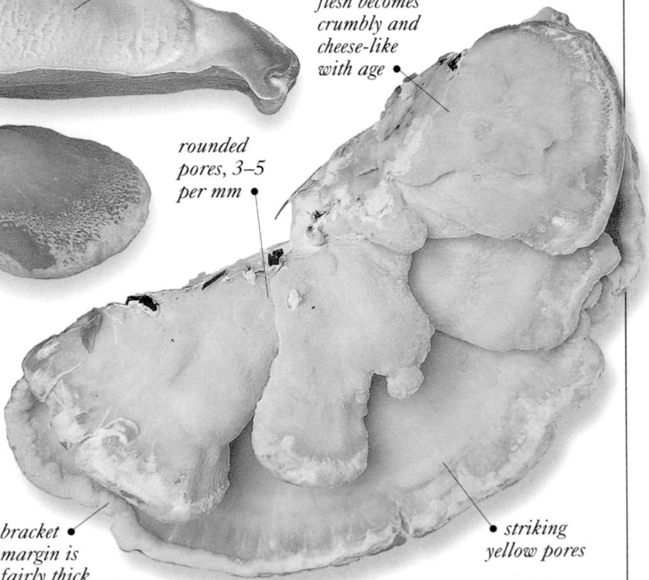

FRUITING Mostly in tiers, often high up in trees.

| Dimensions BRACKET ⊕ 10–50cm × 10–30cm ⊕ 1–5cm | Spores White | Edibility |O| |

| Family BJERKANDERACEAE | Species *Grifola frondosa* | Season Summer–autumn |

HEN-OF-THE-WOODS

This species has an annual fruitbody with tongue-shaped brackets branching off a central stem. Leathery with a wavy margin, the upper surface is grey, ageing to brown. The decurrent tube layer is up to 5mm thick and off-white. The white flesh smells of mice when it ages. It is edible when young but the species is rare, so eating it is not recommended.
• OCCURRENCE By oak and sweet chestnut, produces a white rot. Widespread but rather local in northern temperate zones.
• SIMILAR SPECIES *Meripilus giganteus* (p.214).

small, tongue-shaped bracket •

grey upper surface ages • to brown

wrinkled and streaky upper surface •

composite fruitbody, to 50cm wide •

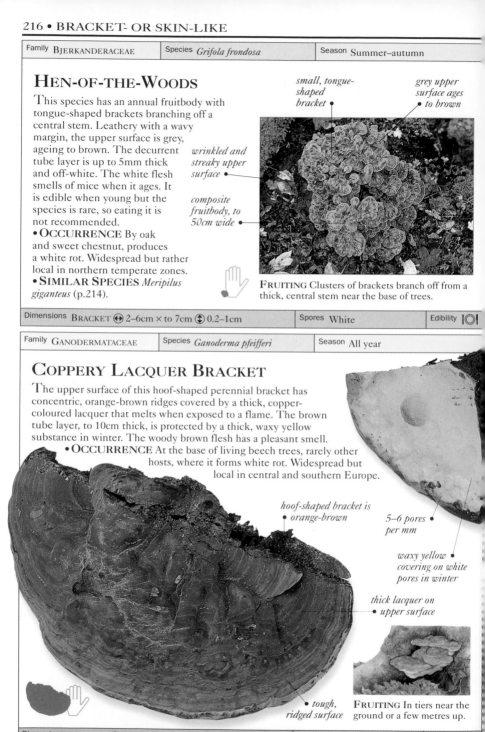

FRUITING Clusters of brackets branch off from a thick, central stem near the base of trees.

| Dimensions BRACKET ⊕ 2–6cm × to 7cm ⧀ 0.2–1cm | Spores White | Edibility |

| Family GANODERMATACEAE | Species *Ganoderma pfeifferi* | Season All year |

COPPERY LACQUER BRACKET

The upper surface of this hoof-shaped perennial bracket has concentric, orange-brown ridges covered by a thick, copper-coloured lacquer that melts when exposed to a flame. The brown tube layer, to 10cm thick, is protected by a thick, waxy yellow substance in winter. The woody brown flesh has a pleasant smell.
• OCCURRENCE At the base of living beech trees, rarely other hosts, where it forms white rot. Widespread but local in central and southern Europe.

hoof-shaped bracket is • orange-brown

5–6 pores • per mm

waxy yellow • covering on white pores in winter

thick lacquer on • upper surface

tough, ridged surface •

FRUITING In tiers near the ground or a few metres up.

| Dimensions BRACKET ⊕ 20–50cm × to 25cm ⧀ to 15cm | Spores Brown | Edibility |

Family GANODERMATACEAE	Species *Ganoderma applanatum*	Season All year

ARTIST'S FUNGUS

The upper surface of this semi-circular perennial bracket is uneven, with concentric ridges and a thin margin. Beginning off-white, it becomes pale ochre-brown and is often covered with a brown spore deposit. The lacquered upper surface is easily broken; the creamy white underside can be scratched with a sharp point to produce a brown "artwork", hence the common name. The tube layer is brown and 0.5–4cm deep. The thin, dark brown flesh, often with pockets of white tissue, has a bitter taste and a "mushroomy" smell.

• **OCCURRENCE** On stumps and trunks of trees in parks and woodland. Widespread and common in northern temperate zones.

• **SIMILAR SPECIES** *Ganoderma australe*, is slightly more southern in distribution, and has a more robust bracket with a thicker upper crust and darker flesh.

bracket
has grown around
• strand of ivy

• creamy
white pores,
4–6 per mm

uneven,
tough
bracket
• surface

thin layer of
lacquer just
visible •

SECTION

thick brown
spore deposit
partly covers
upper surface

FRUITING Singly or in groups, mostly on dead trees.

flesh is dark brown, typically •
with pockets of white tissue

• brown tubes

Dimensions BRACKET ⊕ 10–60cm × to 30cm ⬍ 2–8cm	Spores Brown	Edibility 🖐

Family HYMENOCHAETACEAE	Species *Phellinus igniarius*	Season All year

GREY FIRE BRACKET

Grey to almost black in colour, this perennial bracket is hoof-shaped and extremely woody, with thick margins. The bracket may remain on living host trees for many years. The hard flesh and tubes are rusty brown; new tubes, 1–5mm long, grow annually on the previous year's tubes. Tiny hairs, called setae, characteristic of the family, are concealed in the hymenium. Experts disagree on the exact identity of this species; a range of forms is covered here.

• **OCCURRENCE** Parasitic on a number of hardwood trees, commonly birch, willow, and apple, causing white rot. Widespread and fairly common in northern temperate zones.

moss and lichen grow on the upper surface of older specimens •

some cracking • often occurs on grey to almost black surface

• concentric ridges appear with age

broad area of • attachment

1cm

PORE SURFACE

• grey to grey-brown pores

5–6 pores • per mm

FRUITING Singly or a few together on living trees.

Dimensions BRACKET ⊕ 10–40cm × 10–20cm ✦ to 20cm	Spores White	Edibility

Family FOMITACEAE	Species *Fomes fomentarius*	Season All year

TINDER FUNGUS

This polypore has a hoof-shaped, woody perennial bracket with zones varying from dark brown in older areas to pale brown at the growing margin, which is downy or felty. A new brown tube layer grows annually. Each year's tube layer is 5mm thick. The pore surface is grey to grey-brown. Existing in several forms, depending on the host, this species has been used as tinder and to make hats and other clothing.
• **OCCURRENCE** Parasitic on hardwoods, especially beech and birch, and forms white rot. It will fruit on fallen wood. Widespread and often common in northern temperate zones.
• **SIMILAR SPECIES** *Fomitopsis pinicola* (inset, right).

△ *FOMITOPSIS PINICOLA*
This grey perennial species has bright yellow and red zones near its margin. The bracket surface feels lacquered and melts under a flame. The pores are pale yellow, and the hard flesh is white to yellow with a characteristic acidic smell. ⬤

this specimen has grown on beech

dark reddish brown zone behind pale margin •

more or less distinct zones on bracket surface •

hard, woody, smooth surface •

tough, fibrous, wood-brown flesh smells slightly fruity •

• *margin is downy or felty*

• *tube layer*

• *grey to greybrown pores, 2–3 per mm*

SECTION

FRUITING Appears singly or in rows of brackets.

Dimensions BRACKET ⊕ 5–30cm × to 25cm ⊕ 5–30cm	Spores White	Edibility ⬤

Family PHAEOLACEAE	Species *Phaeolus schweinitzii*	Season Summer–winter

PINE DYE POLYPORE

Impressive when actively growing, this annual
bracket fungus arises from a very short, more or less
central brown stalk, and has a brilliant sulphur-yellow
margin surrounding concentric zones of rusty brown.
As the bracket ages, it turns dirty brown then slowly
rots away. The sulphur-yellow tube layer is up to 1cm
thick with pores, 1–4mm in diameter, that are
greenish yellow when young, turning dark brown
when touched. The inedible, fibrous, yellow to
brown flesh contains a pigment that is used in dye.
• **OCCURRENCE** Around living or dead
softwood trees, especially pine, causing brown
rot. Widespread and common in northern
temperate zones; cosmopolitan.

*sulphur-
yellow
young
specimen*

*uneven surface
with colour
zones •*

*bracket •
surface is
very felty
or hairy*

1cm

PORE SURFACE

*• old specimen
is dark brown
all over*

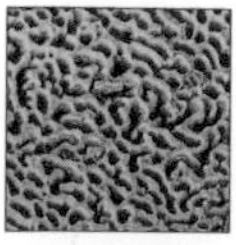

FRUITING Mostly solitary
from underground roots.

Dimensions BRACKET ⊕ 15–30cm × 10–25cm ⊛ 1–4cm	Spores White	Edibility

Family HYMENOCHAETACEAE	Species *Inonotus hispidus*	Season Summer–autumn

SHAGGY POLYPORE

The thick-fleshed, fan-shaped annual bracket of this species is distinguished by its shaggy surface. Flame-red when young, it gradually turns brown from the inner part of the fruitbody outwards; the pore surface is white to pale brown, becoming darker with age, and often appears shiny. There are 2–3 pores per mm. The pale brown tube layer is 1–3cm deep. Scattered, short, thick hairs (setae) are enclosed in the spore-bearing tissue (hymenium).
• **OCCURRENCE** Parasitic on hardwood trees such as ash, pear, apple, and walnut, causing white rot. Widespread and common to rare in northern temperate zones.
• **SIMILAR SPECIES** *Inonotus cuticularis* has smaller brackets and occurs on beech and oak. *I. rheades* is also smaller and occurs on aspen.

flame-red • bracket ages to brown

white to pale • brown pore surface becomes darker with age

bracket surface is very shaggy •

FRUITING Appears singly or in fused groups of brackets on living hardwood trees.

Dimensions BRACKET ⊕ 15–40cm × 10–20cm ⊕ to 10cm	Spores Yellow	Edibility 🖐

Family HYMENOCHAETACEAE	Species *Inonotus radiatus*	Season All year

ALDER BRACKET

SECTION

This polypore forms semi-circular, wavy-margined annual brackets. The upper surface is bright yellow to orange-red when young, becoming zoned in shades of rusty brown. When young and growing, the pore surface often has yellow drops on it; with age, it may appear "glancing" – shiny and silvery. The tubes are 1cm long, and the hymenium encloses tiny, short, curved hairs (setae).
• **OCCURRENCE** Parasitic, mostly on standing alder trunks or on birch trees. On fallen tree trunks it may develop just the tube layer over the bark (resupinate). Widespread and common in northern temperate zones.
• **SIMILAR SPECIES**
Inonotus nodulosus has less distinct brackets and occurs on beech.

• tough flesh is zoned with shades of rusty brown

• tube layer may be decurrent, running down the substrate

semi-circular brackets have • wavy margins

top surface is orange • when young

2–4 • pores per mm

• pore surface looks shiny silvery grey from some angles

FRUITING Tiers and rows on dead wood.

Dimensions BRACKET ⊕ 3–8cm × 1–3cm ⊕ to 3cm	Spores Pale yellow-brown	Edibility 🖐

Family PERENNIPORIACEAE	Species *Heterobasidion annosum*	Season All year

CONIFER-BASE POLYPORE

The perennial bracket of this species is irregular with a very uneven surface and a cork-like texture. Its light brown crust darkens with age; the margin is white, often with an orange band just behind it. The white to cream tube layer is up to 1cm thick, or more, and the inedible flesh is pale yellow. Occasionally this species grows against the substrate, without brackets (resupinate).
• **OCCURRENCE** On softwood stumps, rarely on hardwood trees. In densely planted softwood plantations, it can spread underground to infect healthy trees. Widespread and common in northern temperate zones.

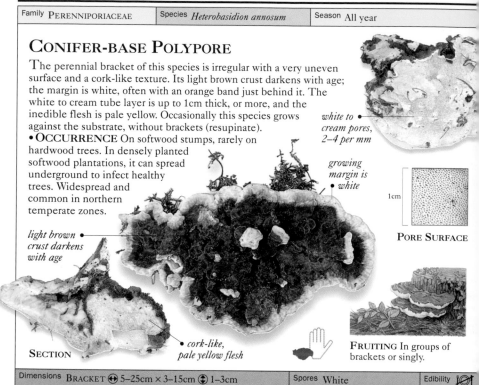

white to cream pores, 2–4 per mm

growing margin is white

1cm

PORE SURFACE

light brown crust darkens with age

cork-like, pale yellow flesh

SECTION

FRUITING In groups of brackets or singly.

Dimensions BRACKET ⊕ 5–25cm × 3–15cm ⊕ 1–3cm	Spores White	Edibility

Family FOMITOPSIDACEAE	Species *Gloeophyllum odoratum*	Season All year

SCENTED BRACKET

This species develops perennial brackets, which are cushion-shaped and slightly felted. The margin is golden yellow to orange; older parts are almost black. There are 1–2 golden yellow pores per mm and the tube layer is up to 1cm thick. The flesh is cork-like and rust-brown. This polypore has a pleasant smell of fennel and oranges.
• **OCCURRENCE** On softwoods, usually spruce; causes brown rot. Widespread in northern temperate zones.
• **SIMILAR SPECIES** Widespread and common, *Gloeophyllum abietinum* and *G. sepiarium* have gill-like pores and typically occur on sun-baked softwood.

dark brown to black inner area

golden yellow to orange margin

1cm

PORE SURFACE

golden yellow young specimen

FRUITING Mostly singly or in groups on tree stumps.

Dimensions BRACKET ⊕ 5–20cm × 5–20cm ⊕ 2–5cm	Spores White	Edibility

Family CORIOLACEAE	Species *Trametes gibbosa*	Season All year

BEECH BRACKET

Annual or perennial, the large brackets of this species are semi-circular with the inner part of the upper surface usually stained green by algae. Concentric colour zones occur near the smooth margin. Young specimens are chalk-white with a downy or minutely hairy surface, becoming smooth with age. The white flesh is tough and inedible; the tube layer, to 4mm thick, has elongated cream pores.

• **OCCURRENCE** In woodland, typically forms white rot on beech. Widespread and rather common in northern temperate zones.

• **SIMILAR SPECIES** *Trametes hirsuta* (p.224) is thinner and hairier with less elongated, greyer pores.

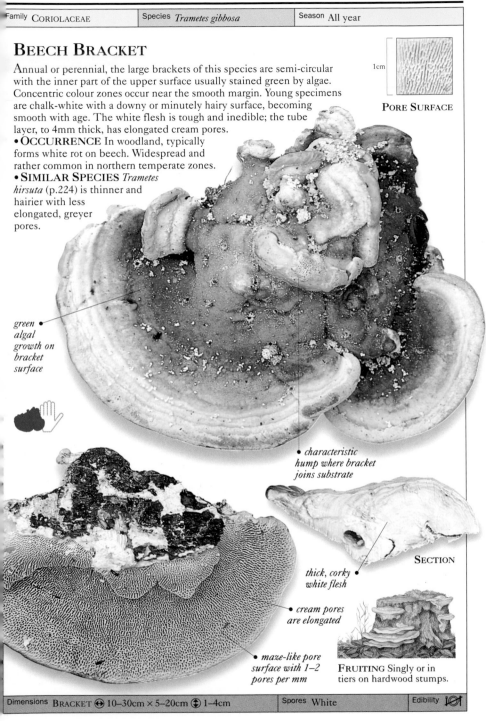

1cm

PORE SURFACE

green algal growth on bracket surface

• *characteristic hump where bracket joins substrate*

SECTION

thick, corky white flesh

• *cream pores are elongated*

• *maze-like pore surface with 1–2 pores per mm*

FRUITING Singly or in tiers on hardwood stumps.

Dimensions BRACKET ⊕ 10–30cm × 5–20cm ⊕ 1–4cm	Spores White	Edibility

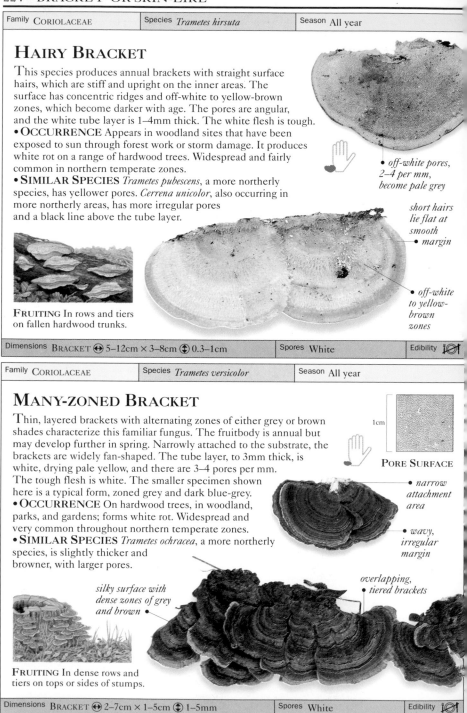

Family CORIOLACEAE	Species *Trametes hirsuta*	Season All year

HAIRY BRACKET

This species produces annual brackets with straight surface hairs, which are stiff and upright on the inner areas. The surface has concentric ridges and off-white to yellow-brown zones, which become darker with age. The pores are angular, and the white tube layer is 1–4mm thick. The white flesh is tough.
• **OCCURRENCE** Appears in woodland sites that have been exposed to sun through forest work or storm damage. It produces white rot on a range of hardwood trees. Widespread and fairly common in northern temperate zones.
• **SIMILAR SPECIES** *Trametes pubescens*, a more northerly species, has yellower pores. *Cerrena unicolor*, also occurring in more northerly areas, has more irregular pores and a black line above the tube layer.

• *off-white pores, 2–4 per mm, become pale grey*

short hairs lie flat at smooth • margin

• *off-white to yellow-brown zones*

FRUITING In rows and tiers on fallen hardwood trunks.

Dimensions BRACKET ⊕ 5–12cm × 3–8cm ⊕ 0.3–1cm	Spores White	Edibility

Family CORIOLACEAE	Species *Trametes versicolor*	Season All year

MANY-ZONED BRACKET

Thin, layered brackets with alternating zones of either grey or brown shades characterize this familiar fungus. The fruitbody is annual but may develop further in spring. Narrowly attached to the substrate, the brackets are widely fan-shaped. The tube layer, to 3mm thick, is white, drying pale yellow, and there are 3–4 pores per mm. The tough flesh is white. The smaller specimen shown here is a typical form, zoned grey and dark blue-grey.
• **OCCURRENCE** On hardwood trees, in woodland, parks, and gardens; forms white rot. Widespread and very common throughout northern temperate zones.
• **SIMILAR SPECIES** *Trametes ochracea*, a more northerly species, is slightly thicker and browner, with larger pores.

1cm

PORE SURFACE

• *narrow attachment area*

• *wavy, irregular margin*

overlapping, • tiered brackets

silky surface with dense zones of grey and brown •

FRUITING In dense rows and tiers on tops or sides of stumps.

Dimensions BRACKET ⊕ 2–7cm × 1–5cm ⊕ 1–5mm	Spores White	Edibility

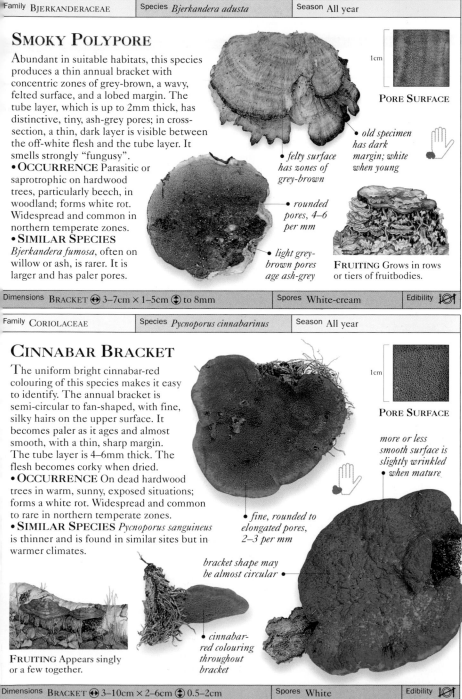

| Family BJERKANDERACEAE | Species *Bjerkandera adusta* | Season All year |

SMOKY POLYPORE

Abundant in suitable habitats, this species produces a thin annual bracket with concentric zones of grey-brown, a wavy, felted surface, and a lobed margin. The tube layer, which is up to 2mm thick, has distinctive, tiny, ash-grey pores; in cross-section, a thin, dark layer is visible between the off-white flesh and the tube layer. It smells strongly "fungusy".
• OCCURRENCE Parasitic or saprotrophic on hardwood trees, particularly beech, in woodland; forms white rot. Widespread and common in northern temperate zones.
• SIMILAR SPECIES *Bjerkandera fumosa*, often on willow or ash, is rarer. It is larger and has paler pores.

PORE SURFACE

• old specimen has dark margin; white when young

• felty surface has zones of grey-brown

• rounded pores, 4–6 per mm

• light grey-brown pores age ash-grey

FRUITING Grows in rows or tiers of fruitbodies.

| Dimensions BRACKET ⊕ 3–7cm × 1–5cm ⊕ to 8mm | Spores White-cream | Edibility 🚫 |

| Family CORIOLACEAE | Species *Pycnoporus cinnabarinus* | Season All year |

CINNABAR BRACKET

The uniform bright cinnabar-red colouring of this species makes it easy to identify. The annual bracket is semi-circular to fan-shaped, with fine, silky hairs on the upper surface. It becomes paler as it ages and almost smooth, with a thin, sharp margin. The tube layer is 4–6mm thick. The flesh becomes corky when dried.
• OCCURRENCE On dead hardwood trees in warm, sunny, exposed situations; forms a white rot. Widespread and common to rare in northern temperate zones.
• SIMILAR SPECIES *Pycnoporus sanguineus* is thinner and is found in similar sites but in warmer climates.

PORE SURFACE

more or less smooth surface is slightly wrinkled • when mature

• fine, rounded to elongated pores, 2–3 per mm

bracket shape may be almost circular •

• cinnabar-red colouring throughout bracket

FRUITING Appears singly or a few together.

| Dimensions BRACKET ⊕ 3–10cm × 2–6cm ⊕ 0.5–2cm | Spores White | Edibility 🚫 |

Family STECCHERINACEAE	Species *Trichaptum abietinum*	Season All year

CONIFER PURPLE-PORE

Tending to be abundant where it occurs, this widely fan-shaped annual bracket fungus has concentric grooves on the felty, pale grey surface, which is often tinged green by algae; the purple margin is typically wavy and lobed. When young, the tube layer, to 5mm thick, is purple, becoming reddish brown. The angular pores often split with age. It has tough, pale brown or purple flesh.
• **OCCURRENCE** On softwood trees, mostly spruce; it causes white rot. Widespread and common in northern temperate zones.
• **SIMILAR SPECIES** *Trichaptum biforme* has wider, less resupinate brackets, and grows on hardwood. Other *Trichaptum* species found on softwood trees, such as *T. fusco-violaceum* on pine, are distinguished by teeth or gills on the underside.

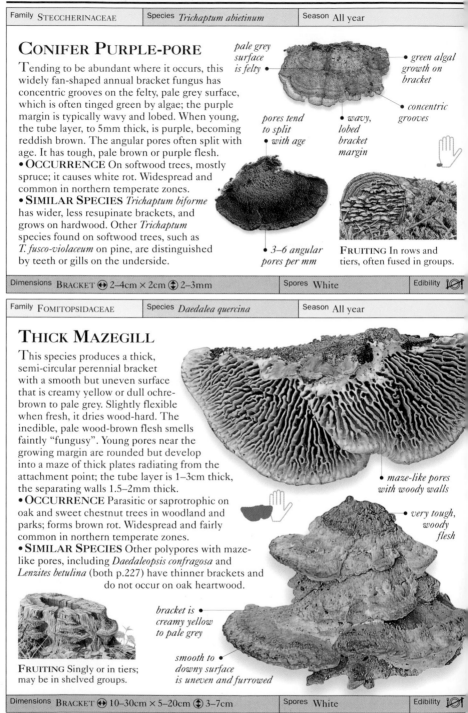

pale grey surface is felty •

• green algal growth on bracket

• concentric grooves

pores tend to split • with age

• wavy, lobed bracket margin

• 3–6 angular pores per mm

FRUITING In rows and tiers, often fused in groups.

Dimensions BRACKET ⊕ 2–4cm × 2cm ‡ 2–3mm	Spores White	Edibility

Family FOMITOPSIDACEAE	Species *Daedalea quercina*	Season All year

THICK MAZEGILL

This species produces a thick, semi-circular perennial bracket with a smooth but uneven surface that is creamy yellow or dull ochre-brown to pale grey. Slightly flexible when fresh, it dries wood-hard. The inedible, pale wood-brown flesh smells faintly "fungusy". Young pores near the growing margin are rounded but develop into a maze of thick plates radiating from the attachment point; the tube layer is 1–3cm thick, the separating walls 1.5–2mm thick.
• **OCCURRENCE** Parasitic or saprotrophic on oak and sweet chestnut trees in woodland and parks; forms brown rot. Widespread and fairly common in northern temperate zones.
• **SIMILAR SPECIES** Other polypores with maze-like pores, including *Daedaleopsis confragosa* and *Lenzites betulina* (both p.227) have thinner brackets and do not occur on oak heartwood.

• maze-like pores with woody walls

• very tough, woody flesh

bracket is • creamy yellow to pale grey

smooth to • downy surface is uneven and furrowed

FRUITING Singly or in tiers; may be in shelved groups.

Dimensions BRACKET ⊕ 10–30cm × 5–20cm ‡ 3–7cm	Spores White	Edibility

Family CORIOLACEAE	Species *Daedaleopsis confragosa*	Season All year

THIN MAZEGILL

Broadly fan-shaped with a smooth to warty surface, the annual brackets of this species are thin, only thickening towards the attachment area. The surface is smooth to warty and pale grey to yellow, ageing dingy red-brown – overall or in concentric zones. Cork-like in texture, the inedible flesh is pale wood-brown and the pores, which are pale grey when young, turn red when bruised. The tube layer, 0.5–1cm thick, is reddish brown.
• OCCURRENCE On a wide range of hardwoods in some areas, more restricted in others – willow is favoured; forms a white rot. Widespread and rather common in northern temperate zones.

lump at attachment area is typical

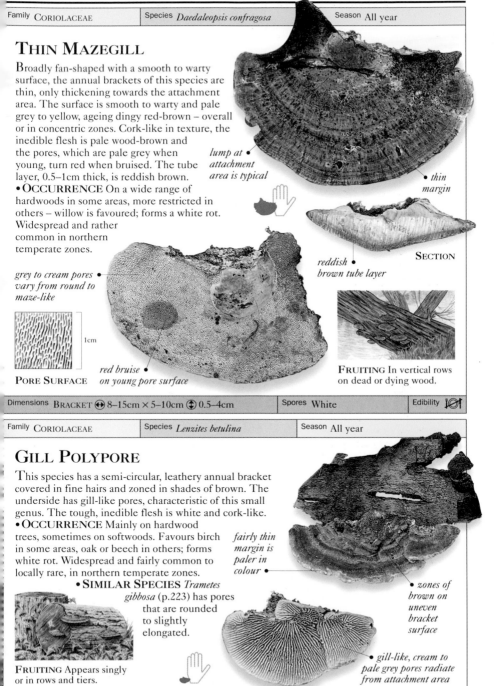

thin margin

reddish brown tube layer

SECTION

grey to cream pores vary from round to maze-like

red bruise on young pore surface

PORE SURFACE

1cm

FRUITING In vertical rows on dead or dying wood.

Dimensions BRACKET ⊕ 8–15cm × 5–10cm ⬍ 0.5–4cm	Spores White	Edibility

Family CORIOLACEAE	Species *Lenzites betulina*	Season All year

GILL POLYPORE

This species has a semi-circular, leathery annual bracket covered in fine hairs and zoned in shades of brown. The underside has gill-like pores, characteristic of this small genus. The tough, inedible flesh is white and cork-like.
• OCCURRENCE Mainly on hardwood trees, sometimes on softwoods. Favours birch in some areas, oak or beech in others; forms white rot. Widespread and fairly common to locally rare, in northern temperate zones.
• **SIMILAR SPECIES** *Trametes gibbosa* (p.223) has pores that are rounded to slightly elongated.

fairly thin margin is paler in colour

zones of brown on uneven bracket surface

gill-like, cream to pale grey pores radiate from attachment area

FRUITING Appears singly or in rows and tiers.

Dimensions BRACKET ⊕ 3–10cm × 1–5cm ⬍ 1–2cm	Spores White	Edibility

WRINKLED OR SMOOTH UNDERNEATH

NOT ALL BRACKET-LIKE fungi produce fruitbodies with a tube layer and pores on their underside (pp.211–27); some have the spore-producing cells (basidia) sited on a wrinkled, veined, warty, spiny, or completely smooth surface. This type of bracket is featured in this subsection. The other species featured here have tubes and pores but occasionally bear fruitbodies that grow flat against the substrate surface (resupinate). These species have a layer of flesh supporting the spore-producing tissue.

Family SCHIZOPHYLLACEAE	Species *Phlebia tremellosa*	Season Autumn–early winter

JELLY BRACKET

Exceptional among *Phlebia* species, which are usually resupinate, the Jelly Bracket has well-developed, protruding annual brackets, although part of the spore-producing layer runs down the bark. The upper side is velvety and almost white, while the underside is yellow to orange and covered with dense ridges and veins. The structure is soft and gelatinous.

• **OCCURRENCE** On the stumps of hardwood trees such as birch and beech; very rarely appears on softwoods. Widespread and common in northern temperate zones.

• **SIMILAR SPECIES** The closely related *P. radiata* is common on similar substrates, but is bright orange and thinner; it is fully resupinate, without brackets. The underside has radiating veins and wrinkles.

• velvety upper surface is almost white

• brackets have hairy margins and surfaces

• gelatinous, elastic, orange to pink flesh

veins and ridges cover spore-producing underside •

FRUITING In dense tiers of joined brackets.

• tiered brackets are semi-circular

Dimensions JOINED BRACKETS ⊕ 4–15cm × 2–4cm ‡ 1–3mm	Spores White	Edibility

Family THELEPHORACEAE	Species *Thelephora terrestris*	Season All year

COMMON EARTH-FAN

Similar in appearance to some lichens, the fringed, fan-shaped fruitbodies of this fungus are well camouflaged by their earth-like colours. The upper surface is uneven and fibrous; the spore-producing underside is warty and slightly paler in colour. The inedible flesh is thin and brown.

• OCCURRENCE Mycorrhizal with trees in woods and on heaths, on acid soil or decayed stumps; often found along rides and tracks. Also found in plant nurseries with conifer seedlings. Widespread and common in northern temperate zones.

• SIMILAR SPECIES *Thelephora caryophyllea* is deeply funnel-shaped and has a less felty surface. An uncommon resupinate form of *T. terrestris* is similar to species of *Tomentella*.

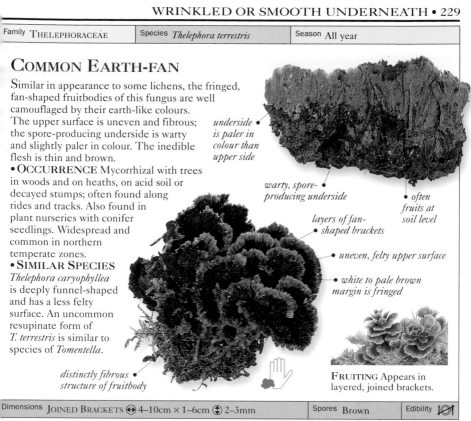

underside is paler in colour than upper side

warty, spore-producing underside

often fruits at soil level

layers of fan-shaped brackets

uneven, felty upper surface

white to pale brown margin is fringed

distinctly fibrous structure of fruitbody

FRUITING Appears in layered, joined brackets.

Dimensions JOINED BRACKETS ⊕ 4–10cm × 1–6cm ‡ 2–3mm	Spores Brown	Edibility 🚫

Family CONIOPHORACEAE	Species *Serpula lacrymans*	Season All year

DRY-ROT FUNGUS

This fungus is well known for the brown rot it causes, which severely weakens construction timber inside houses. The semi-circular, veined, resupinate or bracket-forming fruitbody is in shades of brown and exudes acidic white droplets from the growing margin. It stains red-brown when touched and is rubbery in texture. The fungus also produces a copious white weft of mycelium.

• OCCURRENCE Thrives inside poorly ventilated buildings where alkaline substances, such as mortar, neutralize its acidic droplets, which would otherwise make its growing environment too acid. Widespread and common in buildings; in the wild, known on the west coast of North America and in the Himalayan foothills of India.

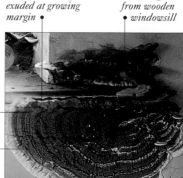

acidic white droplets exuded at growing margin

brackets growing from wooden windowsill

concentric zones in shades of brown

spreading fruitbody is mostly resupinate

FRUITING Fully resupinate or with brackets on timber, boards, and walls in houses.

Dimensions FRUITBODY ⊕ to 50cm × to 10cm ‡ 0.5–2cm	Spores Yellow to olive-brown	Edibility 🚫

Family AURICULARIACEAE	Species *Auricularia mesenterica*	Season All year

TRIPE FUNGUS

rubbery, jelly-like flesh

At first glance, this annual bracket could be mistaken for species of *Trametes* (p.223–24) or *Stereum* (p.232 and below) but it is distinguished by, among other features, its gelatinous flesh. The zonation on the top surface is due to fine velvety hairs. The spore-producing underside of the bracket is wrinkled and veined. Although edible, it is not worth eating.

• **OCCURRENCE** Almost confined to elm trees in parks and woods. Rarer than *A. auricula-judae* (p.281), but where there is dead elm, can be abundant alongside other elm-wood fungi. Widespread but fairly local in northern temperate zones; rare or absent to the north and in tropical areas.

velvety upper surface zoned in brown and grey-brown

wrinkled and veined spore-producing surface

green colouring due to algae

FRUITING In tiers on trunks and stumps.

Dimensions BRACKET ⊕ 4–15cm × 1–5cm ⬧ 2–5mm	Spores White	Edibility

Family PENIOPHORACEAE	Species *Stereum hirsutum*	Season All year

HAIRY LEATHER-BRACKET

This species produces a long-lived, fan-shaped, bright yellow to tan bracket with a smooth spore-bearing surface that often runs down the substrate. The upper surface is hairy, with indistinct concentric zones; it is paler at the margin. The similarly coloured flesh is thin but tough and does not stain. The spores are amyloid.

• **OCCURRENCE** On hardwoods, especially oak, birch, and beech; often on bark or on the cut surfaces of stored wood. Widespread in northern temperate zones; common.

• **SIMILAR SPECIES** *Stereum gausapatum* and *S. rugosum* (p.232) are more resupinate and stain red. *S. ochraceo-flavum* is smaller with duller undersides. *S. subtomentosum* (inset, right).

brackets can be densely layered

smooth, spore-producing underside

concentric zones in shades of yellow to tan

△ **STEREUM SUBTOMENTOSUM**
This species has wide, less resupinate brackets with more distinct zones. Its flesh stains yellow.

FRUITING Appears in abundant linked brackets.

wavy, lobed margin

hairy upper surface

Dimensions BRACKET ⊕ 2–6cm × to 3cm ⬧ 1–2mm	Spores White	Edibility

Family SCHIZOPHYLLACEAE	Species *Chondrostereum purpureum*	Season All year

PURPLE LEATHER-BRACKET

This fungus is easy to identify because of its habit of producing a multitude of wavy-margined brackets, which are purple when young. The upper surfaces are white-downy; the undersides are smooth and purple-brown. When dry, they tend to be horn-like in texture. The flesh is waxy and somewhat gelatinous. Unlike *Stereum* species, the spores do not develop a blue colouring with iodine reagents.

• **OCCURRENCE** Parasitic or saprotrophic on many hardwood trees; causes silver-leaf disease on cherry and plum trees, eventually producing white rot in the wood. Widespread in northern temperate zones; common in most regions.

fused and tiered brackets

tough, leathery flesh is somewhat gelatinous

smooth spore-producing surface is purple-brown

felty or downy upper surface often looks almost white

undulating bracket margin

FRUITING In tiers and rows of linked brackets.

Dimensions LINKED BRACKETS ⊕ 2–5cm × to 4cm ‡ 1–2.5mm	Spores White	Edibility

Family HYMENOCHAETACEAE	Species *Hymenochaete rubiginosa*	Season All year

RIGID LEATHER-BRACKET

This well-camouflaged, rigid, perennial bracket fungus with wavy margins occurs in abundant tiers. The top surface is marked with concentric brown zones, increasing in number and becoming very dark with age; the cocoa-brown underside seems smooth, but examination with a powerful hand-lens reveals a covering of tiny rigid hairs (setae). The flesh is very tough, thin, and cocoa-brown.

• **OCCURRENCE** Grows on the stumps or fallen branches of oak or sweet chestnut trees. Widespread in northern temperate zones.

zones increase with age

margins wavy and sometimes lobed

minute, stiff hairs cover underside

upper surface brown, becoming very dark with age

cocoa-brown underside

underside appears smooth

dark brown zones on upper surface

FRUITING In crowded tiers of brackets.

Dimensions BRACKET ⊕ 1–6cm × 1–4cm ‡ 1mm	Spores White-cream	Edibility

SKIN-LIKE, GROWING FLAT OR CRUST-LIKE

I N THIS SUBSECTION are some of the many fungi that produce fully resupinate, skin-like fruitbodies on the underside of fallen wood. They range from white to pink or deep blue. The spore-producing surface (hymenium) of these species can be smooth, warty spiny, or veined. (See also pp.228–31.)

Family PENIOPHORACEAE	Species *Stereum rugosum*	Season All year

COMMON LEATHER-BRACKET

This abundant woodland fungus, which may grow for several seasons, forms a thick, flat, rather featureless, pale grey skin on bark; brackets rarely occur. Scraping the surface of the fungus soon produces blood-red marks. The spores are amyloid.
• **OCCURRENCE** On hardwood trees, often standing dead trunks; frequently found on hazel, birch, and alder. Widespread and common in Europe; probably also in a wider area in northern temperate zones.
• **SIMILAR SPECIES** *Stereum sanguinolentum* also stains red when damaged, but it is found on bark of softwoods and has distinct brackets.

white growing margin

blood-red where surface is scratched

fungus is typically resupinate

smooth or warty spore-producing surface

fruitbody is smooth or warty

FRUITING Long, skin-like patches on dead wood.

Dimensions FRUITBODY ⊕ 10–50cm × 1–6cm ⧚ 2–5mm	Spores White	Edibility

Family CHAETOPORELLACEAE	Species *Hyphodontia paradoxa*	Season All year

DECEIVING POLYPORE

This fungus usually grows flat, but may produce tiny brackets when on vertical surfaces. It is fairly tough and white to creamy brown with cottony white margins and teeth up to 4mm long in the centre. The tube layer is 1–4mm thick and has 1–3 pores per mm; when examined under a hand lens, the pores often resemble flattened teeth.
• **OCCURRENCE** Grows mainly on hardwood trees, particularly beech, in woodland areas. Widespread and common in northern temperate zones; cosmopolitan.

white margins are cottony in texture

white to creamy brown centre with toothed surface

fruitbody usually resupinate

FRUITING Appears in skin-like, spreading patches on the underside of fallen branches.

Dimensions FRUITBODY ↕ 5–50cm × 2–10cm ⧚ 3–7mm	Spores White	Edibility

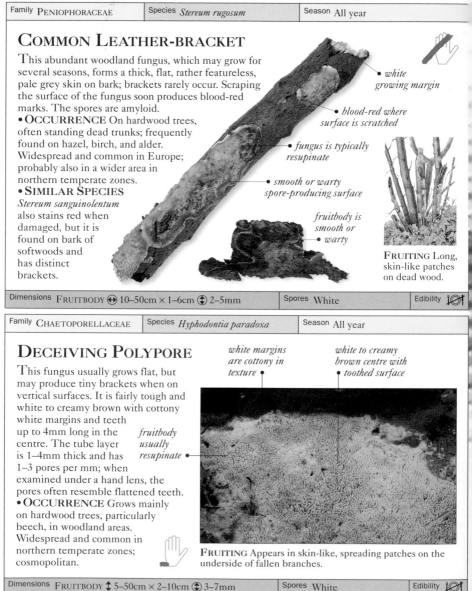

| Family CONIOPHORACEAE | Species *Coniophora puteana* | Season All year, mainly autumn |

CELLAR FUNGUS

The spreading fruitbodies of this wet-rot fungus are soft textured and grow flattened against the substrate, never forming brackets. Maturing spores make the centres yellow to olive-brown, whereas the margins are white and fringed. Typically, the fruitbody surface becomes wrinkly and warty with age. Unlike most resupinate species, which are firmly fixed to the substrate, Cellar Fungus fruitbodies can be prised gently off.

• **OCCURRENCE** On wet timber indoors, causing wet brown rot, and on all types of wood out of doors. Widespread in the wild and in buildings, in northern temperate zones.

• **SIMILAR SPECIES** *Serpula lacrymans* (p.229) exudes droplets and may form brackets.

creamy white new growth will turn pale yellow and then darken •

fringed • margin

centre stained brown by mature spores •

resupinate • fruitbody

fruitbody grows on woody substrate •

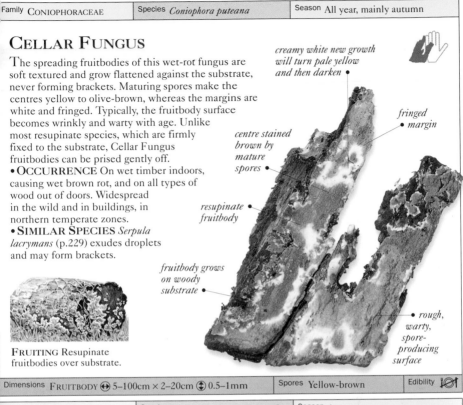

• rough, warty, spore-producing surface

FRUITING Resupinate fruitbodies over substrate.

| Dimensions FRUITBODY ⊕ 5–100cm × 2–20cm ⊕ 0.5–1mm | Spores Yellow-brown | Edibility |

| Family PHAEOLACEAE | Species *Oligoporus rennyi* | Season Autumn |

POWDER-PUFF POLYPORE

This spreading polypore is most easily recognized by its two growth stages, which occur almost simultaneously, next to each other. The resupinate, crust-like sexual stage is white at the edge, creamy white in the centre, with 2–3 pores per mm. The pores become torn with age and release white spores. The asexual stage is puffball-like at first, shredding open at maturity to expose a great mass of powdery, olive-brown spores.

• **OCCURRENCE** Small patches on stumps and fallen branches of softwood trees; produces a brown rot in the wood. Widespread and rare to common, but usually overlooked, in northern temperate zones.

puffball-like • asexual stage

crust-like • sexual stage

cream-white with pores in centre •

fuzzy white • periphery

FRUITING Grows in small patches, sometimes many together, along wood.

| Dimensions PATCHES ↔ to 7.5cm | "PUFFBALL" ↕ ↔ 2–4cm | Spores Olive-brown/white | Edibility |

FUNGI WITH SPINES

The fungi in this section are not closely related, but they all have their spore-producing cells (basidia) on a toothed or spiny surface. The spines are sited under the cap, on the underside of a bracket, or hanging from the branches of coral-like fruitbodies. Some resupinate species (not featured) have spines all over their surface.

• *spines on cap underside*

Family AURISCALPIACEAE	Species *Auriscalpium vulgare*	Season All year

EAR PICK-FUNGUS

Among the most distinctive of fungi, the Ear Pick-fungus has a characteristic kidney-shaped cap, which has a furry or hairy surface, with the stem attached to one side. The cap is brown with a paler margin, and its underside is hung with long, grey spines. The stem is a darker brown than the cap and has a felty covering. It is attached to the substrate by a felted pale brown mycelium. The brown colouring makes this species difficult to spot, despite the fact that it is common. It has tough, inedible flesh.
• **OCCURRENCE** On decaying pine and, to a lesser degree, spruce cones in needle litter, in mature softwood woods or plantations. Widespread in pine and spruce forests of northern temperate zones.

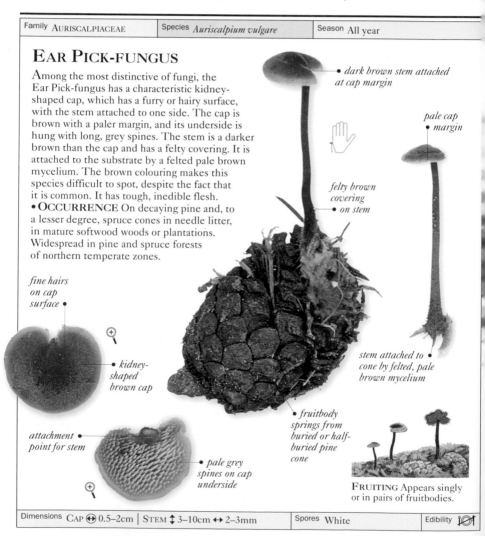

• *dark brown stem attached at cap margin*

pale cap • *margin*

felty brown covering • *on stem*

fine hairs on cap surface •

• *kidney-shaped brown cap*

attachment • *point for stem*

stem attached to • *cone by felted, pale brown mycelium*

• *fruitbody springs from buried or half-buried pine cone*

• *pale grey spines on cap underside*

FRUITING Appears singly or in pairs of fruitbodies.

Dimensions CAP ⊕ 0.5–2cm | STEM ↕ 3–10cm ↔ 2–3mm	Spores White	Edibility

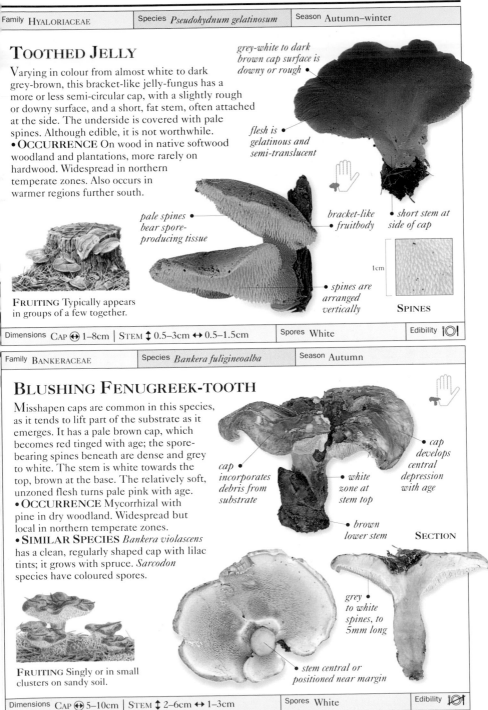

| Family HYALORIACEAE | Species *Pseudohydnum gelatinosum* | Season Autumn–winter |

TOOTHED JELLY

Varying in colour from almost white to dark grey-brown, this bracket-like jelly-fungus has a more or less semi-circular cap, with a slightly rough or downy surface, and a short, fat stem, often attached at the side. The underside is covered with pale spines. Although edible, it is not worthwhile.

• OCCURRENCE On wood in native softwood woodland and plantations, more rarely on hardwood. Widespread in northern temperate zones. Also occurs in warmer regions further south.

grey-white to dark brown cap surface is downy or rough •

flesh is gelatinous and semi-translucent

pale spines • bear spore-producing tissue

bracket-like • fruitbody

• short stem at side of cap

• spines are arranged vertically

1cm

SPINES

FRUITING Typically appears in groups of a few together.

| Dimensions CAP ⊕ 1–8cm | STEM ↕ 0.5–3cm ↔ 0.5–1.5cm | Spores White | Edibility |

| Family BANKERACEAE | Species *Bankera fuligineoalba* | Season Autumn |

BLUSHING FENUGREEK-TOOTH

Misshapen caps are common in this species, as it tends to lift part of the substrate as it emerges. It has a pale brown cap, which becomes red tinged with age; the spore-bearing spines beneath are dense and grey to white. The stem is white towards the top, brown at the base. The relatively soft, unzoned flesh turns pale pink with age.

• OCCURRENCE Mycorrhizal with pine in dry woodland. Widespread but local in northern temperate zones.

• SIMILAR SPECIES *Bankera violascens* has a clean, regularly shaped cap with lilac tints; it grows with spruce. *Sarcodon* species have coloured spores.

cap • incorporates debris from substrate

• white zone at stem top

• cap develops central depression with age

• brown lower stem

SECTION

grey to white spines, to 5mm long

• stem central or positioned near margin

FRUITING Singly or in small clusters on sandy soil.

| Dimensions CAP ⊕ 5–10cm | STEM ↕ 2–6cm ↔ 1–3cm | Spores White | Edibility |

| Family BANKERACEAE | Species *Phellodon niger* | Season Late summer–autumn |

BLACK TOOTH

Fruitbodies of this species are often fused together. The cap is flat or has a slightly depressed centre and is pale grey to purplish black; in young specimens the margin is a distinct pale blue. The spines are blue-grey at first, turning grey. The leathery black flesh smells of fenugreek, especially when it is dry.

• **OCCURRENCE** Mycorrhizal with softwood trees in woods or plantations, sometimes among hardwoods, on alkaline soil. Widespread but local in northern temperate zones.

• **SIMILAR SPECIES** *Phellodon melaleucus* smells similar but is thinner, paler, and less felty. It is found on poor, acid soil in woods. *Hydnellum* species have brown spores.

faint zones on cap surface, which is covered in dense felt

blue-grey spines, to 3mm long, darken with age

spines are decurrent

densely felty, dark brown stem

fused fruitbodies

FRUITING Singly or in dense clusters among moss.

| Dimensions CAP ⊕ 3–10cm | STEM ↕ 2–5cm ↔ 0.5–2cm | Spores White | Edibility |

| Family BANKERACEAE | Species *Phellodon tomentosus* | Season Late summer–autumn |

FUNNEL TOOTH

This tooth fungus has a centrally depressed cap with the surface marked in zones of shades of brown, vertical spines on the underside, and a fibrous dark brown stem. The growing margin on the cap is thin and white, and caps are often fused together. The inedible, tough flesh is thin and brown. Dried fruitbodies smell of curry or fenugreek.

• **OCCURRENCE** Mycorrhizal with soft- or, rarely, hardwood trees in woodland, on sandy soil. Widespread but local in northern temperate zones.

• **SIMILAR SPECIES** A range of tooth fungi look fairly similar, including some species of *Hydnellum* (see p.237), which have brown spores. *Phellodon confluens* has a more felty surface, fewer zones, and is paler in colour with more irregularly shaped caps.

spines, to 3mm long, are arranged vertically

fibrous, dark brown stem

stem slightly twisted and uneven

thin, sharp cap margin

cap flesh is thin but tough

cap has depressed centre and clear zones

FRUITING In groups among mosses and lichens.

| Dimensions CAP ⊕ 2–6cm | STEM ↕ 2–5cm ↔ 4–7mm | Spores White | Edibility |

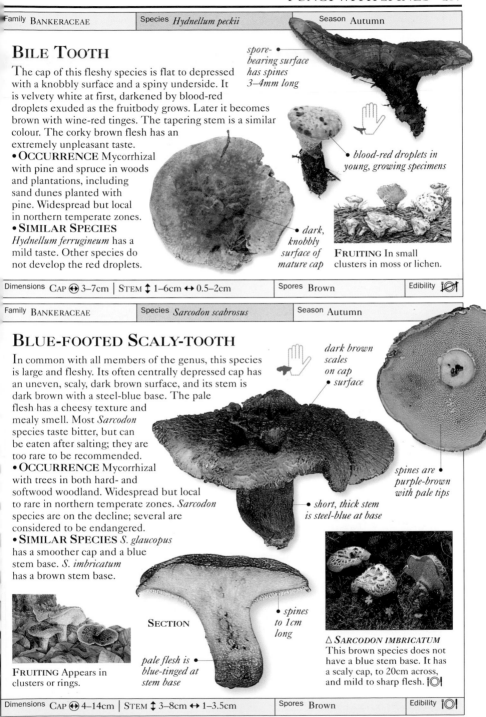

| Family BANKERACEAE | Species *Hydnellum peckii* | Season Autumn |

BILE TOOTH

The cap of this fleshy species is flat to depressed with a knobbly surface and a spiny underside. It is velvety white at first, darkened by blood-red droplets exuded as the fruitbody grows. Later it becomes brown with wine-red tinges. The tapering stem is a similar colour. The corky brown flesh has an extremely unpleasant taste.

• **OCCURRENCE** Mycorrhizal with pine and spruce in woods and plantations, including sand dunes planted with pine. Widespread but local in northern temperate zones.

• **SIMILAR SPECIES** *Hydnellum ferrugineum* has a mild taste. Other species do not develop the red droplets.

spore-bearing surface has spines 3–4mm long

blood-red droplets in young, growing specimens

dark, knobbly surface of mature cap

FRUITING In small clusters in moss or lichen.

| Dimensions CAP ⊕ 3–7cm | STEM ↕ 1–6cm ↔ 0.5–2cm | Spores Brown | Edibility |

| Family BANKERACEAE | Species *Sarcodon scabrosus* | Season Autumn |

BLUE-FOOTED SCALY-TOOTH

In common with all members of the genus, this species is large and fleshy. Its often centrally depressed cap has an uneven, scaly, dark brown surface, and its stem is dark brown with a steel-blue base. The pale flesh has a cheesy texture and mealy smell. Most *Sarcodon* species taste bitter, but can be eaten after salting; they are too rare to be recommended.

• **OCCURRENCE** Mycorrhizal with trees in both hard- and softwood woodland. Widespread but local to rare in northern temperate zones. *Sarcodon* species are on the decline; several are considered to be endangered.

• **SIMILAR SPECIES** *S. glaucopus* has a smoother cap and a blue stem base. *S. imbricatum* has a brown stem base.

dark brown scales on cap surface

spines are purple-brown with pale tips

short, thick stem is steel-blue at base

SECTION

spines to 1cm long

pale flesh is blue-tinged at stem base

FRUITING Appears in clusters or rings.

△ **SARCODON IMBRICATUM** This brown species does not have a blue stem base. It has a scaly cap, to 20cm across, and mild to sharp flesh.

| Dimensions CAP ⊕ 4–14cm | STEM ↕ 3–8cm ↔ 1–3.5cm | Spores Brown | Edibility |

Family HYDNACEAE-	Species *Hydnum repandum*	Season Autumn

COMMON HEDGEHOG FUNGUS

This very fleshy fungus has a massive, slightly off-centre stem and a large, convex or centrally depressed cap, which is often irregular in shape. It has a smooth or slightly felty upper surface and fragile spines on the underside. Pale cream to ochre in colour, the whole fruitbody stains orange with age and when bruised. This is a choice edible; older specimens should be cooked thoroughly, as the flesh can become bitter with age.

• **OCCURRENCE** Mycorrhizal with both hard- and softwood trees in woodland. Widespread in northern temperate zones, including cold regions.

• **SIMILAR SPECIES** *Hydnum albidum* has a white cap, smaller spores, and occurs on alkaline soil. Closely related *H. rufescens* is smaller and orange.

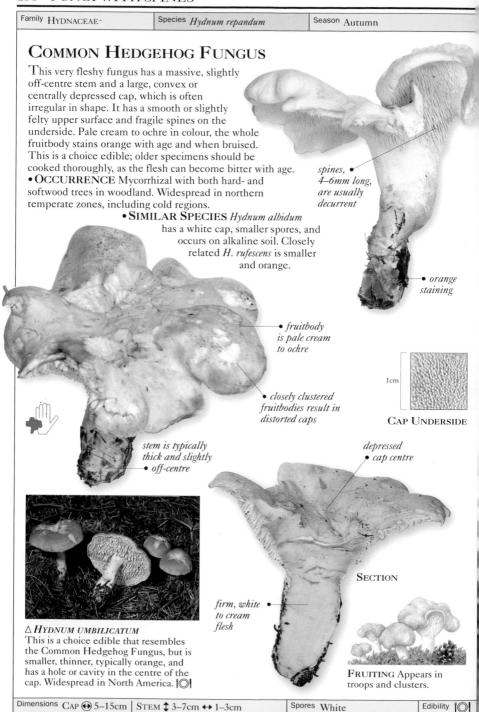

spines, 4–6mm long, are usually decurrent

orange staining

fruitbody is pale cream to ochre

closely clustered fruitbodies result in distorted caps

1cm

CAP UNDERSIDE

stem is typically thick and slightly off-centre

depressed cap centre

firm, white to cream flesh

SECTION

△ *HYDNUM UMBILICATUM*
This is a choice edible that resembles the Common Hedgehog Fungus, but is smaller, thinner, typically orange, and has a hole or cavity in the centre of the cap. Widespread in North America. |○|

FRUITING Appears in troops and clusters.

| Dimensions CAP ⊕ 5–15cm | STEM ↕ 3–7cm ↔ 1–3cm | Spores White | Edibility |○| |

Family HERICIACEAE	Species *Hericium coralloides*	Season Late summer–late autumn

CORAL TOOTH-FUNGUS

When it is spotted growing along a fallen trunk or similar substrate, this fungus is a breathtaking sight, with its off-white to dirty yellow fruitbody consisting of numerous brittle, coral-like branches, the lower surfaces of which are densely covered with long, pendent spines. The off-white to cream flesh tastes of radishes. Although this species is edible, it is scarce, so eating it is not recommended.

• OCCURRENCE
Found growing on fallen or standing, dead hardwood trees, such as beech and birch. Widespread in northern temperate zones; locally fairly common.

multi-branched, coral-like fruitbody

fruitbody becomes dirty yellow with age

off-white to cream flesh

pendent, off-white to dirty yellow spines

FRUITING Singly or in groups along dead trunks.

Dimensions FRUITBODY ⊕ 10–40cm × 5–20cm ⨪ 10–30cm	Spores White	Edibility

Family HERICIACEAE	Species *Creolophus cirrhatus*	Season Autumn

LAYERED TOOTH-FUNGUS

This species has a layered, fleshy, semi-circular fruitbody, which is creamy white and develops in tiers. The underside has long, pendent spines; the upper surface is felty. Although the thick, soft flesh is edible and smells and tastes pleasant, the species is rare so should not be gathered. It belongs to a very small genus, related and similar to *Hericium* (above).

• OCCURRENCE Mainly on hardwood trees, in woods. Widespread, in northern temperate zones.

• SIMILAR SPECIES The huge *Climacodon septentrionalis* has more regular and larger brackets and finer spines underneath. It is found in northeastern Europe, Japan, Siberia and northeastern North America to Tennessee.

spines on underside of fruitbody

felty upper surface

creamy white throughout

irregular layers of bracket-like fruitbodies

FRUITING Appears in tiers on stumps or, rarely, trunks.

Dimensions FRUITBODY ⊕ 10–20cm ⨪ to 10cm thick	Spores White	Edibility

CLUB-SHAPED FUNGI

The species in this section have more or less club-shaped fruitbodies. In most of those featured, the fruitbody is fertile over its entire surface, or the base may be sterile. In the flask-fungi (see p.244), the spore-producing surface (hymenium) is in tiny, flask-shaped fruitbodies embedded in a fleshy, club-shaped structure (stroma).

• *club-shaped fruitbody*

SMOOTH OR HAIRY

SPECIES FEATURED HERE have club-shaped fruitbodies with a smooth or hairy surface. (For species with a pimply or dusty surface see p.244.) They vary from the very slender *Typhula* species to the much thicker *Clavariadelphus pistillaris* (p.241). Some such as *Leotia lubrica* (p.243), have well-defined fertile heads, but in most the fertile part merges with the stem.

Family CLAVARIACEAE	Species *Clavulinopsis helvola*	Season Autumn

YELLOW SPINDLES

Just one of several unbranched, club-shaped yellow species in this genus, Yellow Spindles can only be correctly identified by examining the spores under a microscope: they have prominent warts on them, unlike the smooth spores of other members. The pale yellow flesh is rather brittle and odourless.
• **OCCURRENCE** In moss-rich meadows, mature lawns, and some wooded habitats. Widespread in temperate regions including southeast Asia; common in Europe.
• **SIMILAR SPECIES** *Clavulinopsis fusiformis* has large clubs and tends to grow in dense clusters. *C. laeticolor* is odourless and yellow to orange-yellow. *C. luteoalba* is apricot-orange and has an unpleasant smell. *Clavaria angillacea* is dull yellow-brown and grows on heathland.

tip may be darker in colour •

△ *CLAVARIA VERMICULARIS*
This species produces tufts of unbranched, club-shaped white fruitbodies. The tip of the club often dries yellow or tan. Fragile with brittle flesh, the fruitbody is hollow and may flatten as it ages.

more or less flattened fruitbody •

FRUITING Appears singly or a few together in small groups.

smooth, spore-producing surface •

• *club-shaped fruitbody with lengthwise groove*

Dimensions CLUB ↕ 3–7cm ↔ 2–4mm	Spores White	Edibility

Family CLAVARIADELPHACEAE	Species *Clavariadelphus pistillaris*	Season Autumn

GIANT CLUB

An impressive size for a club-fungus, this species is lemon flushed when young but becomes dull tan with age as the spores mature on the fruitbody surface. When bruised it stains reddish brown. Firm at first, becoming soft and spongy with age, the white flesh smells fairly pleasant but has a bitter taste.
• **OCCURRENCE** Found in woodland, often with beech. Widespread in northern temperate regions; local but can be common where habitats are suitable.
• **SIMILAR SPECIES** *Clavariadelphus ligula* and *C. sachalinensis* are smaller and less distinctly club-shaped; both occur with softwood trees. *C. truncatus* has a flat top and occurs in softwood woodland on rich soil.

large fruitbody is distinctly club-shaped

much of surface is covered with spore-bearing hymenium

fruitbody is lemon flushed when young, ageing dull tan

FRUITING Appears in troops on soil among leaf litter in alkaline woodland.

Dimensions CLUB ↕ 10–20cm ↔ 2–6cm	Spores White to pale yellow	Edibility

Family CLAVARIADELPHACEAE	Species *Macrotyphula fistulosa*	Season Late autumn

PIPE CLUB

Unmistakable when found, the Pipe Club has a slender, club-shaped, yellow to tawny-brown fruitbody; it looks similar to a leaf stalk so is easily overlooked. A fairly stunted and twisted form is less easy to identify and is sometimes considered an independent species, *Macrotyphula contorta*.
• **OCCURRENCE** On buried hardwood in damp leaf litter in woodland; especially among beech trees. Widespread in northern temperate regions and subarctic areas; common in Europe.
• **SIMILAR SPECIES** The closely related *M. juncea* has much thinner fruitbodies. It is common in damp woodland and grows on leaf litter.

spores produced all over surface except on stem

pointed tip of fruitbody

club varies considerably in thickness

club darkens from yellow to tawny brown with age

stem and spore-bearing area merge subtly

club looks like leaf stalk

club tapers towards base

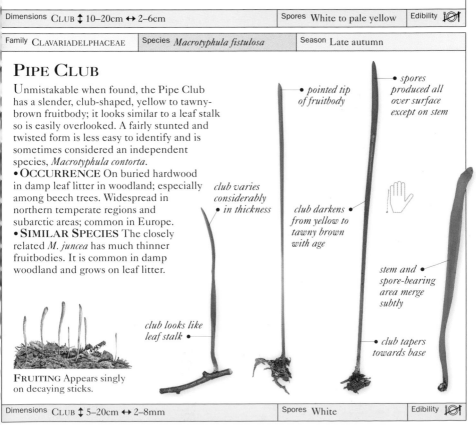

FRUITING Appears singly on decaying sticks.

Dimensions CLUB ↕ 5–20cm ↔ 2–8mm	Spores White	Edibility

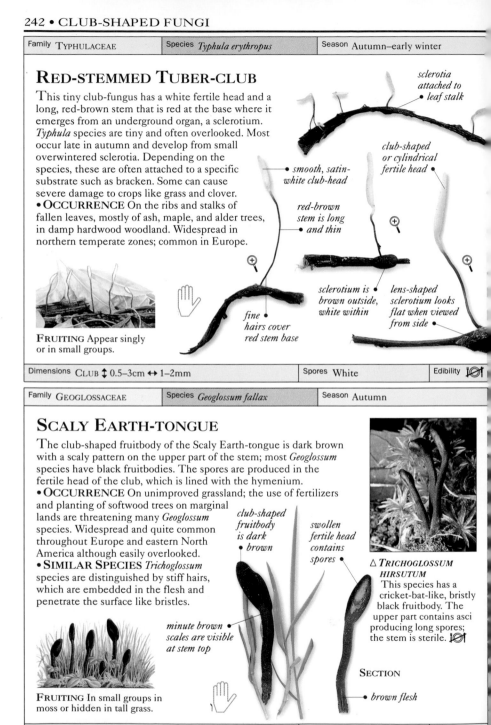

Family TYPHULACEAE	Species *Typhula erythropus*	Season Autumn–early winter

RED-STEMMED TUBER-CLUB

This tiny club-fungus has a white fertile head and a long, red-brown stem that is red at the base where it emerges from an underground organ, a sclerotium. *Typhula* species are tiny and often overlooked. Most occur late in autumn and develop from small overwintered sclerotia. Depending on the species, these are often attached to a specific substrate such as bracken. Some can cause severe damage to crops like grass and clover.
• OCCURRENCE On the ribs and stalks of fallen leaves, mostly of ash, maple, and alder trees, in damp hardwood woodland. Widespread in northern temperate zones; common in Europe.

sclerotia attached to leaf stalk

smooth, satin-white club-head

club-shaped or cylindrical fertile head

red-brown stem is long and thin

sclerotium is brown outside, white within

lens-shaped sclerotium looks flat when viewed from side

fine hairs cover red stem base

FRUITING Appear singly or in small groups.

Dimensions CLUB ↕ 0.5–3cm ↔ 1–2mm	Spores White	Edibility 🚫

Family GEOGLOSSACEAE	Species *Geoglossum fallax*	Season Autumn

SCALY EARTH-TONGUE

The club-shaped fruitbody of the Scaly Earth-tongue is dark brown with a scaly pattern on the upper part of the stem; most *Geoglossum* species have black fruitbodies. The spores are produced in the fertile head of the club, which is lined with the hymenium.
• OCCURRENCE On unimproved grassland; the use of fertilizers and planting of softwood trees on marginal lands are threatening many *Geoglossum* species. Widespread and quite common throughout Europe and eastern North America although easily overlooked.
• SIMILAR SPECIES *Trichoglossum* species are distinguished by stiff hairs, which are embedded in the flesh and penetrate the surface like bristles.

club-shaped fruitbody is dark brown

swollen fertile head contains spores

△ TRICHOGLOSSUM HIRSUTUM
This species has a cricket-bat-like, bristly black fruitbody. The upper part contains asci producing long spores; the stem is sterile. 🚫

minute brown scales are visible at stem top

SECTION

brown flesh

FRUITING In small groups in moss or hidden in tall grass.

Dimensions CLUB ↕ 3–7cm ↔ 3–7mm	Spores Dark brown	Edibility 🚫

Family LEOTIACEAE	Species *Leotia lubrica*	Season Autumn

JELLY BABIES

This distinctive species produces a small, pestle-shaped fruitbody with a rubbery texture and gelatinous flesh. The well-defined, convex, lobed head is greenish yellow with a clear, recurved margin, and contains the spore-producing tissue. The orange-yellow stem is covered with minute green scales or dots and is often hollow. Jelly Babies can develop a blackish green hue as a result of a fungal infection, but even healthy specimens often turn olive-green when they are fully mature.

• **OCCURRENCE** Found growing in damp woodland areas among leaf litter and moss. Widespread and common in most northern temperate zones; cosmopolitan.

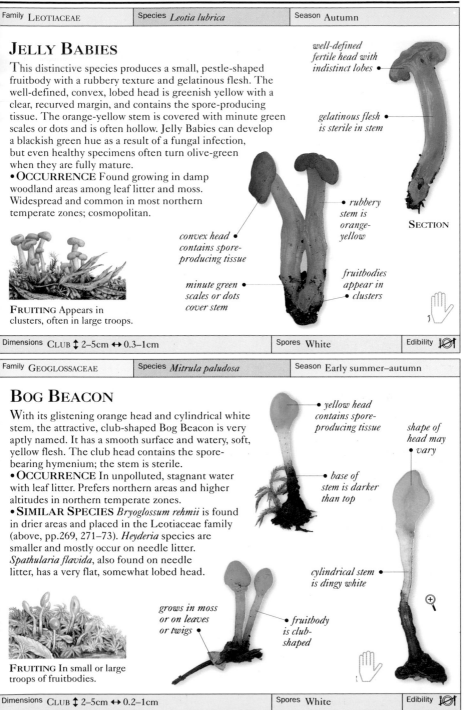

well-defined fertile head with indistinct lobes •

gelatinous flesh • is sterile in stem

SECTION

convex head • contains spore-producing tissue

• rubbery stem is orange-yellow

minute green scales or dots cover stem

fruitbodies appear in • clusters

FRUITING Appears in clusters, often in large troops.

Dimensions CLUB ‡ 2–5cm ↔ 0.3–1cm		Spores White	Edibility

Family GEOGLOSSACEAE	Species *Mitrula paludosa*	Season Early summer–autumn

BOG BEACON

With its glistening orange head and cylindrical white stem, the attractive, club-shaped Bog Beacon is very aptly named. It has a smooth surface and watery, soft, yellow flesh. The club head contains the spore-bearing hymenium; the stem is sterile.

• **OCCURRENCE** In unpolluted, stagnant water with leaf litter. Prefers northern areas and higher altitudes in northern temperate zones.

• **SIMILAR SPECIES** *Bryoglossum rehmii* is found in drier areas and placed in the Leotiaceae family (above, pp.269, 271–73). *Heyderia* species are smaller and mostly occur on needle litter. *Spathularia flavida*, also found on needle litter, has a very flat, somewhat lobed head.

• yellow head contains spore-producing tissue

shape of head may • vary

• base of stem is darker than top

cylindrical stem • is dingy white

grows in moss or on leaves or twigs •

• fruitbody is club-shaped

FRUITING In small or large troops of fruitbodies.

Dimensions CLUB ‡ 2–5cm ↔ 0.2–1cm		Spores White	Edibility

WITH PIMPLES OR A DUSTY SURFACE

T HE FUNGI in this subsection are mainly characterized by their pimply surface. The pimples are caused by flask-shaped fruitbodies embedded in the fleshy tissue (stroma). They are visible when the club is cut in half lengthways. One species featured here, *Paecilomyces farinosus* (below), produces masses of loose, asexual spores on its surface, making it look dusty.

Family CLAVICIPITACEAE	Species *Cordyceps militaris*	Season Summer–autumn

ORANGE CATERPILLAR-FUNGUS

This parasitic flask-fungus emerges from its host as a club-shaped, orange-red composite fruitbody, called a stroma. The spore-producing asci are contained in flasks seen as spikes breaking through the surface on the upper region of the club, which is slightly swollen. The spores themselves are long and cylindrical and break into segments. The stem is smooth and paler in colour.
• **OCCURRENCE** Mycelia invade and kill the larvae and pupae of moths, either in woodland or grassland. Widespread in northern temperate zones. Other *Cordyceps* species parasitize insects, spiders, or *Elaphomyces* truffles (p.259). The majority are tropical.
• **SIMILAR SPECIES** *C. bifusispora*, which is also parasitic on moths, is more yellow and has spores with club-shaped end cells.

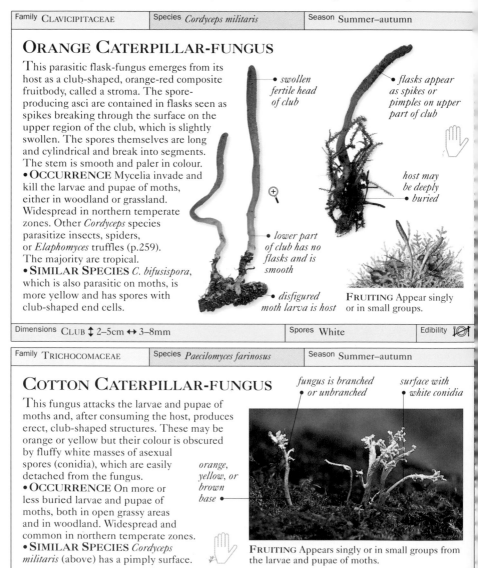

• *swollen fertile head of club*

• *flasks appear as spikes or pimples on upper part of club*

host may be deeply • *buried*

• *lower part of club has no flasks and is smooth*

• *disfigured moth larva is host*

FRUITING Appear singly or in small groups.

Dimensions CLUB ↕ 2–5cm ↔ 3–8mm	Spores White	Edibility 🚫

Family TRICHOCOMACEAE	Species *Paecilomyces farinosus*	Season Summer–autumn

COTTON CATERPILLAR-FUNGUS

This fungus attacks the larvae and pupae of moths and, after consuming the host, produces erect, club-shaped structures. These may be orange or yellow but their colour is obscured by fluffy white masses of asexual spores (conidia), which are easily detached from the fungus.
• **OCCURRENCE** On more or less buried larvae and pupae of moths, both in open grassy areas and in woodland. Widespread and common in northern temperate zones.
• **SIMILAR SPECIES** *Cordyceps militaris* (above) has a pimply surface.

fungus is branched • *or unbranched*

surface with • *white conidia*

orange, yellow, or brown base •

FRUITING Appears singly or in small groups from the larvae and pupae of moths.

Dimensions CLUB ↕ 2–5cm ↔ 2–5mm	Spores White	Edibility 🚫

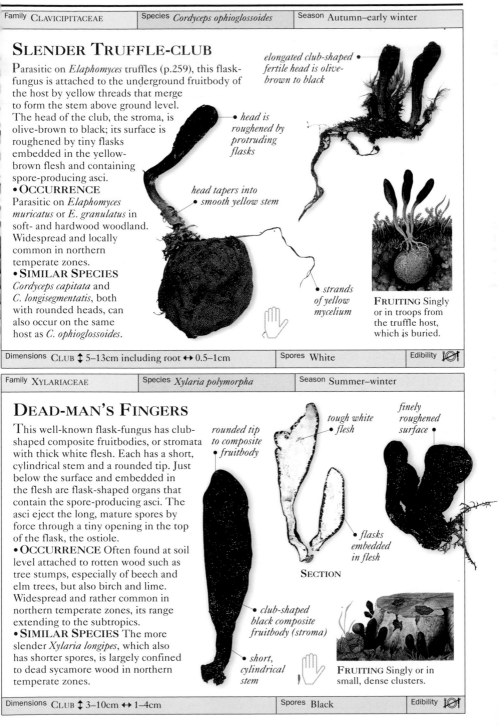

| Family CLAVICIPITACEAE | Species *Cordyceps ophioglossoides* | Season Autumn–early winter |

SLENDER TRUFFLE-CLUB

Parasitic on *Elaphomyces* truffles (p.259), this flask-fungus is attached to the underground fruitbody of the host by yellow threads that merge to form the stem above ground level. The head of the club, the stroma, is olive-brown to black; its surface is roughened by tiny flasks embedded in the yellow-brown flesh and containing spore-producing asci.

• **OCCURRENCE**
Parasitic on *Elaphomyces muricatus* or *E. granulatus* in soft- and hardwood woodland. Widespread and locally common in northern temperate zones.

• **SIMILAR SPECIES**
Cordyceps capitata and *C. longisegmentatis*, both with rounded heads, can also occur on the same host as *C. ophioglossoides*.

elongated club-shaped • fertile head is olive-brown to black

• head is roughened by protruding flasks

head tapers into • smooth yellow stem

• strands of yellow mycelium

FRUITING Singly or in troops from the truffle host, which is buried.

| Dimensions CLUB ↕ 5–13cm including root ↔ 0.5–1cm | Spores White | Edibility |

| Family XYLARIACEAE | Species *Xylaria polymorpha* | Season Summer–winter |

DEAD-MAN'S FINGERS

This well-known flask-fungus has club-shaped composite fruitbodies, or stromata with thick white flesh. Each has a short, cylindrical stem and a rounded tip. Just below the surface and embedded in the flesh are flask-shaped organs that contain the spore-producing asci. The asci eject the long, mature spores by force through a tiny opening in the top of the flask, the ostiole.

• **OCCURRENCE** Often found at soil level attached to rotten wood such as tree stumps, especially of beech and elm trees, but also birch and lime. Widespread and rather common in northern temperate zones, its range extending to the subtropics.

• **SIMILAR SPECIES** The more slender *Xylaria longipes*, which also has shorter spores, is largely confined to dead sycamore wood in northern temperate zones.

rounded tip to composite • fruitbody

tough white • flesh

finely roughened surface •

• flasks embedded in flesh

SECTION

• club-shaped black composite fruitbody (stroma)

• short, cylindrical stem

FRUITING Singly or in small, dense clusters.

| Dimensions CLUB ↕ 3–10cm ↔ 1–4cm | Spores Black | Edibility |

PHALLUS-LIKE

THIS SMALL SUBSECTION comprises fungi with phallic fruitbodies – the Stinkhorns – which belong to the genera *Phallus* and *Mutinus*. They bear spores in a sticky, slimy substance, known as the gleba. In *Phallus* the gleba sits on a cap-like structure; in *Mutinus* it is part of the top of the stem.

When young, the fruitbodies are egg-shaped and are surrounded by a skin-like structure called the peridium. It has a gelatinous, watery, inner layer that protects the maturing gleba.

All fungi in this group have a penetrating putrid smell when mature. This attracts flies to aid spore dispersal.

Family PHALLACEAE	Species *Mutinus caninus*	Season Summer–autumn

DOG STINKHORN

The long-stemmed, off-white to dirty orange fruitbody of this species emerges from an egg-shaped structure with a leathery, off-white skin. The orange stem tip merges with the stem. It is covered with a slimy, olive-green spore mass which is foul-smelling to attract insects for dispersal.
• **OCCURRENCE** On thick leaf litter or needle litter, often around rotten stumps, in hard- and softwood woodland. Fairly common in Europe; worldwide distribution unclear.
• **SIMILAR SPECIES** *Mutinus ravenelii*, from North America but also spreading in Europe, has red stem colouring. In Europe it prefers gardens and parks. *Phallus impudicus* (p.247) and its relatives have distinct caps at the stem tip.

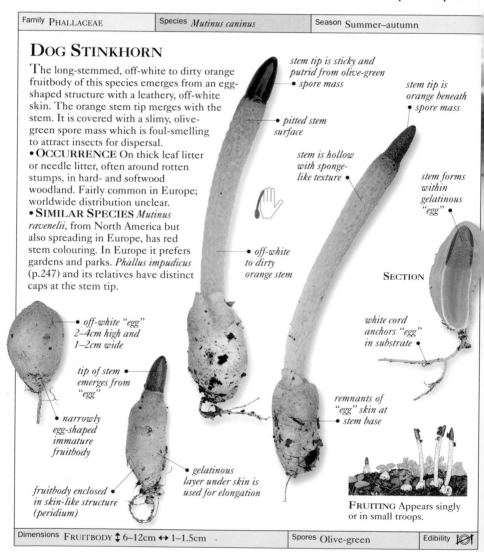

stem tip is sticky and putrid from olive-green • spore mass

stem tip is orange beneath • spore mass

• pitted stem surface

stem is hollow with sponge-like texture •

stem forms within gelatinous "egg"

SECTION

• off-white to dirty orange stem

white cord anchors "egg" in substrate •

• off-white "egg" 2–4cm high and 1–2cm wide

tip of stem • emerges from "egg"

• narrowly egg-shaped immature fruitbody

remnants of "egg" skin at • stem base

• gelatinous layer under skin is used for elongation

fruitbody enclosed • in skin-like structure (peridium)

FRUITING Appears singly or in small troops.

Dimensions FRUITBODY ↕ 6–12cm ↔ 1–1.5cm	Spores Olive-green	Edibility

Family PHALLACEAE	Species *Phallus impudicus*	Season Summer–autumn

COMMON STINKHORN

This species is often smelt before it is seen; members of the Phallaceae family are famous for their foul-smelling fruitbodies, which attract insects to disperse the spores. Mature specimens are easy to recognize by their phallic shape, formed by the white stem and the slimy, olive-green cap. Young fruitbodies are enclosed in an egg-like structure with a thin, leathery skin that breaks open as the stem emerges. The section that later becomes the stem is edible and can be extracted from the "egg".

• **OCCURRENCE** In soft- and hardwood woodland and in sand dunes. Widespread and common in areas of northern temperate zones.

• **SIMILAR SPECIES** *Phallus hadriani* has lilac egg skin and is mostly found in dunes. Other species, such as *P. duplicatus* (inset, below), have a skirt hanging from the cap.

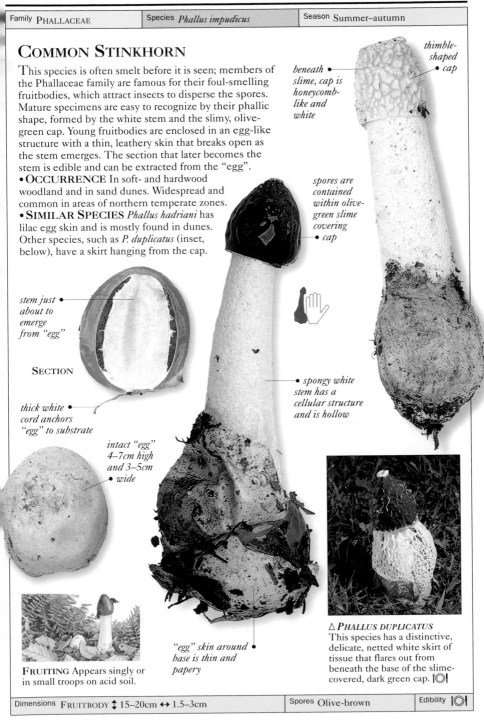

thimble-shaped cap

beneath slime, cap is honeycomb-like and white

spores are contained within olive-green slime covering cap

stem just about to emerge from "egg"

SECTION

thick white cord anchors "egg" to substrate

intact "egg" 4–7cm high and 3–5cm wide

spongy white stem has a cellular structure and is hollow

"egg" skin around base is thin and papery

FRUITING Appears singly or in small troops on acid soil.

△ *PHALLUS DUPLICATUS*
This species has a distinctive, delicate, netted white skirt of tissue that flares out from beneath the base of the slime-covered, dark green cap. |○|

Dimensions FRUITBODY ↕ 15–20cm ↔ 1.5–3cm	Spores Olive-brown	Edibility |○|

ANTLER- TO CORAL-LIKE FUNGI

These species are an elaboration of the club-shaped fungi on pp.240–45. Some have only a few branches, others are more complex. In most cases, the branches are entirely covered with spore-bearing tissue, however, those of Sparassis crispa *(p.252) are fertile on one side only and* Xylaria hypoxylon *is a flask-fungus (see p.244).*

coral-like fruit-body

Family XYLARIACEAE	Species *Xylaria hypoxylon*	Season All year

CANDLE-SNUFF FUNGUS

The young stromata, or composite fruitbodies, of this flask-fungus are very striking. Antler-shaped and white-powdered from asexual spores (conidia), they stand out strikingly on their hardwood stump substrate. The sexual spores develop within tiny, flask-shaped fruitbodies in the outer part of the stromata, and by late autumn they have turned the stromata coal-black and its tips have withered. The flesh is white, in common with most species of *Xylaria*.

• **OCCURRENCE** On hardwood, especially on stumps, in parks and woodland. Widespread and common throughout northern temperate zones.

• **SIMILAR SPECIES** *X. mellisii* is typically more branched when mature or has smoother stromata. It occurs in greenhouses and subtropical climates.

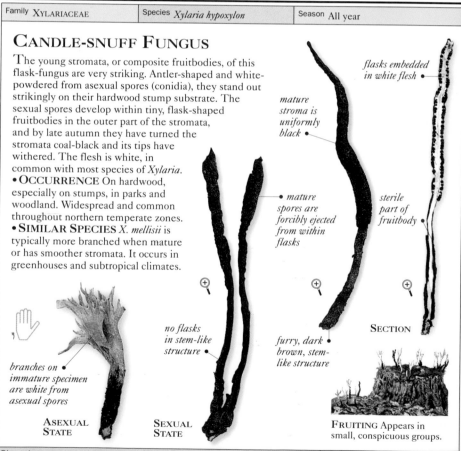

flasks embedded in white flesh

mature stroma is uniformly black

mature spores are forcibly ejected from within flasks

sterile part of fruitbody

no flasks in stem-like structure

furry, dark brown, stem-like structure

SECTION

branches on immature specimen are white from asexual spores

ASEXUAL STATE

SEXUAL STATE

FRUITING Appears in small, conspicuous groups.

Dimensions COMPOSITE FRUITBODY ↕ 1–6cm	BRANCH ↔ 1–4mm × 0.5mm	Spores Black	Edibility

Family CLAVARIACEAE	Species *Clavulinopsis corniculata*	Season Late autumn

MEADOW CORAL-FUNGUS

One of the more common *Clavulinopsis* species, the Meadow Coral-fungus typically has many antler-like branches, but the shape alters greatly with habitat. The fruitbody varies in colour from sulphur-yellow to orange or tan; the base is white and has a felt-like surface, which turns green in contact with either dissolved or solid iron sulphate ($FeSO_4$). The duller, thin, rather fragile flesh has a mealy smell.
• **OCCURRENCE** Mostly in unimproved, moss-rich grassland, but also in some coastal scrub with hawthorn, and in damp, ash-dominated woodland. Widespread in temperate regions.
• **SIMILAR SPECIES** *Ramariopsis crocea* has more pointed tips, is more golden, and does not react with $FeSO_4$; it typically occurs in woodland.

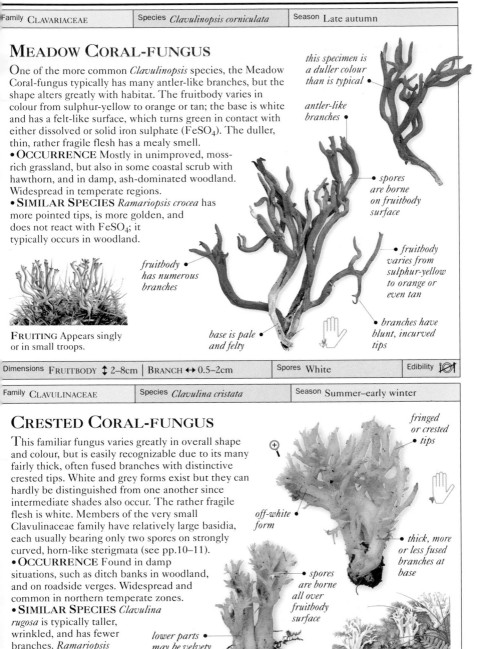

this specimen is a duller colour than is typical •

antler-like branches •

• spores are borne on fruitbody surface

• fruitbody varies from sulphur-yellow to orange or even tan

fruitbody has numerous branches

• branches have blunt, incurved tips

base is pale and felty •

FRUITING Appears singly or in small troops.

Dimensions FRUITBODY $\updownarrow$ 2–8cm | BRANCH $\leftrightarrow$ 0.5–2cm	Spores White	Edibility

Family CLAVULINACEAE	Species *Clavulina cristata*	Season Summer–early winter

CRESTED CORAL-FUNGUS

This familiar fungus varies greatly in overall shape and colour, but is easily recognizable due to its many fairly thick, often fused branches with distinctive crested tips. White and grey forms exist but they can hardly be distinguished from one another since intermediate shades also occur. The rather fragile flesh is white. Members of the very small Clavulinaceae family have relatively large basidia, each usually bearing only two spores on strongly curved, horn-like sterigmata (see pp.10–11).
• **OCCURRENCE** Found in damp situations, such as ditch banks in woodland, and on roadside verges. Widespread and common in northern temperate zones.
• **SIMILAR SPECIES** *Clavulina rugosa* is typically taller, wrinkled, and has fewer branches. *Ramariopsis kunzei* has branch tips that are not crested or fringed.

fringed or crested • tips

off-white • form

• thick, more or less fused branches at base

• spores are borne all over fruitbody surface

lower parts may be velvety and black due to fungal attack

FRUITING Appears singly or in small groups.

Dimensions FRUITBODY $\updownarrow$ 2–6cm $\leftrightarrow$ 0.5–3cm	Spores White	Edibility

Family DACRYOMYCETACEAE	Species *Calocera viscosa*	Season Autumn–winter

JELLY ANTLER

The many-branched fruitbody of this jelly-fungus is bright orange with tough, rubbery flesh. Members of the Dacryomycetaceae family are distinguished under a microscope by their "tuning-fork"-shaped basidia (see pp.10–11); spores are borne over most of the fruitbody.

• **OCCURRENCE** On decayed softwood in plantations and woodland. Widespread and common in northern temperate zones.

• **SIMILAR SPECIES** *Calocera cornea* has small, unbranched clubs and grows mainly on hardwood. *C. furcata* tends to be forked and grows on pine wood. Paler *C. pallido-spathulata* is flattened and irregular; it can be locally common. *Gymnosporangium clavariiforme*, found on juniper, is less erect and without branches at the tips. Club-fungi (pp.240–47) grow mainly on the ground and are more fragile.

flesh is rubbery and same colour as surface

branches are bright orange

forking branches of antler-like fruitbody

decayed softwood substrate

fruitbody is strongly attached to substrate

FRUITING Appears singly or in small, clustered groups.

Dimensions FRUITBODY ↕ 3–10cm ↔ 0.5–4cm	Spores White	Edibility

Family RAMARIACEAE	Species *Ramaria abietina*	Season Autumn

GREENING CORAL-FUNGUS

The verdigris colouring that stains the whole fruitbody of this fungus as it ages makes it easy to identify among the small, less fleshy *Ramaria* species. It is densely branched and dull brown to olive-brown when it first emerges, slowly turning green. The flesh is dull pale brown and fairly firm.

• **OCCURRENCE** On thick needle beds under softwood trees, especially spruce. Widespread in northern temperate zones; rather common.

• **SIMILAR SPECIES** Larger *R. apiculata* is green on the branch tips only. *R. eumorpha*, *R. flaccida*, and *R. myceliosa*, among others, are similar but do not stain green.

densely branched upper fruitbody

verdigris staining appears with age

detached spores collect in branch angles

short, felted, pale stem

FRUITING Almost always found in fairy rings.

Dimensions FRUITBODY ↕ 3–8cm ↔ 1.5–4cm	Spores Ochre	Edibility

Family RAMARIACEAE	Species *Ramaria botrytis*	Season Autumn

PINK-TIPPED CORAL-FUNGUS

Dense, white to pale brown branches with purple tips help to identify this fungus, which is typically very fleshy. The lower part of the stem is very thick and stubby. The white flesh is firm with a pleasant, fruity smell, but eating it cannot be recommended due to its rarity and identification problems (see Similar Species).
• **OCCURRENCE** In mature woodland, both soft- and hardwood. Widespread in northern temperate and warm-temperate zones; local to rather rare.
• **SIMILAR SPECIES** *Ramaria formosa* is a more colourful orange-pink without contrasting tips and is poisonous. There are over 20 other similar species.

distinct purple tips on dense • branches

△ *RAMARIA SANGUINEA* Rarer than *R. botrytis*, this species has thick yellow branches, the lower surfaces of which develop red spots with age or if bruised. |◎|

• numerous crowded branches with 5–7 forks

• white to pale brown fruitbody

• thick, stubby lower stem

FRUITING Appears singly or in fairy rings or lines.

Dimensions FRUITBODY ↕ ↔ 7–15cm	Spores Ochre	Edibility |◎|

Family RAMARIACEAE	Species *Ramaria stricta*	Season Later summer–winter

STRAIGHT CORAL-FUNGUS

This much-branched fungus is typically erect and taller than it is wide, but size and shape vary greatly. Its branches are pale orange-yellow, ageing to ochre-brown, and have pale yellow tips. The fairly firm, bitter-tasting flesh stains wine-red and has a spicy smell. Young fruitbodies can be citrus-yellow all over.
• **OCCURRENCE** Usually on half-buried hardwood, often beech, but also on sawdust. Widespread in northern temperate zones; mostly common.
• **SIMILAR SPECIES** *Ramaria gracilis* is paler with a distinct aniseed smell. It occurs mostly with softwood litter.

older specimens can be • fairly dark red-brown

branches have pale • yellow tips

detached spores collect in the • branch angles

• erect fruitbody

firm, comparatively thin base

white mycelial cords attach fruitbody to substrate •

FRUITING Singly or in lines on rotten branches.

Dimensions FRUITBODY ↕ 4–12cm ↔ 3–8cm	Spores Ochre	Edibility |◎|

Family SPARASSIDACEAE	Species *Sparassis crispa*	Season Late summer–autumn

CAULIFLOWER FUNGUS

A multitude of lobes forming an impressive fleshy, cream to pale yellow-brown fruitbody are characteristic of this species, which is borne on a short, thick, root-like stem. The lobes are branched, flattened or ribbon-like, and fairly firm; like all members of this small family, the spore-producing layer is on one side only. Although difficult to clean, its pleasant taste, along with its large size, makes the Cauliflower Fungus a very popular edible.

• **OCCURRENCE** Mostly on pine, in plantations and native woodland; causes brown rot. Widespread in northern temperate zones; locally quite common.

• **SIMILAR SPECIES** *Sparassis brevipes* is paler and tougher. It grows mostly on oak, beech, or fir. The North American *S. herbstii* is similar or the same species.

SECTION

• *densely packed, branched lobes*

strongly folded, cauliflower-like • fruitbody

spore-producing layer on one • side only

fruitbodies may • weigh up to 14kg; 1–9kg is typical

FRUITING Mostly singly on dead or dying softwoods.

Dimensions FRUITBODY ↕ ↔ 10–40cm	Spores White to pale yellow	Edibility

ROUNDED FUNGI

Many varieties of rounded fungi are shown in this section including puffballs and earthballs. The 'egg-stages' of stinkhorns can be found on pp.246–47, and species of Clathrus are featured on pp.277 and 280. Rounded fungi below ground include the truffles (pp.258–59), some of which are famous for their flavour.

rounded fruitbody

ABOVE GROUND

T HE FUNGI in this subsection are characterized by their stemless, rounded fruitbodies. (For rounded fruitbodies with stems see pp.260–63.) Some of the species are Basidiomycetes (see pp.10–11). They produce their spores within the fruitbody. The spores are released when its skin breaks down with age or when a pore develops on its top at maturity. Other species that are featured here are flask-fungi (see p.244). These have tiny, flask-shaped fruitbodies embedded in compound structures called stromata.

Family ENTOLOMATACEAE	Species *Entoloma abortivum*	Season Autumn

ABORTED PINK-GILL

A choice edible, the Aborted Pink-gill normally produces rounded, lumpy white fruitbodies. These are thought to be the result of the Aborted Pink-gill parasitizing the Honey Fungus, *Armillaria mellea* (p.80). Cap and stem fruitbodies are occasionally produced, with caps to 10cm across and stems to 10cm high and 1.5cm wide. They are grey with decurrent pink gills. The white flesh smells of cucumber or fresh meal; in aborted forms it is pink veined.
• **OCCURRENCE** On hardwood trees in open woodland. Widespread and common in eastern North America.
• **SIMILAR SPECIES** No other fungus produces aborted forms like this, but the cap and stem fruitbody is similar to other *Entoloma* species. However, they typically occur on the ground and lack decurrent gills. Many are poisonous, so it is unwise to eat isolated unaborted forms of *Entoloma abortivum*.

cap is convex and grey to grey-brown

decurrent, off-white gills age to greyish white or pink

stem is not always central under cap

firm white aborted form is irregularly rounded

pale yellow patches may be visible

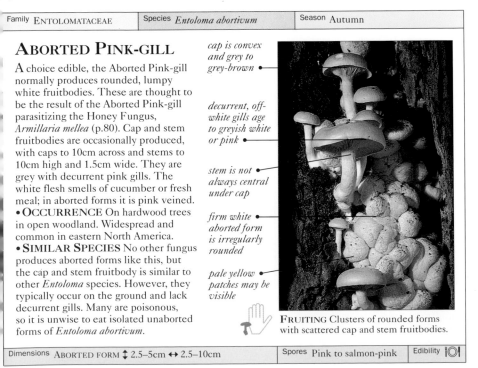

FRUITING Clusters of rounded forms with scattered cap and stem fruitbodies.

Dimensions ABORTED FORM ↕ 2.5–5cm ↔ 2.5–10cm	Spores Pink to salmon-pink	Edibility

Family LYCOPERDACEAE	Species *Calvatia gigantea*	Season Summer–autumn

GIANT PUFFBALL

This is one of the best known edible fungi. Its huge, football-shaped, white or cream fruitbodies regularly weigh above 4kg, and record finds are above 20kg. Most of the interior of the fruitbody consists of a vast number of spores; the lower, sterile part is much reduced. Its flesh is firm in texture and white when young.

• **OCCURRENCE** Saprotrophic; in disturbed sites with nutrient-rich soil, in fields, hedgerows, woodland edges, and parks. Widespread and locally common in northern temperate zones, except western North America.

SECTION

huge, ball-shaped, white or cream fruitbody

• flesh is edible when white and firm

leathery, smooth outer skin rots away to allow spores • to escape

spore-producing tissue becomes yellow then olive-brown with age

FRUITING Mostly appears in small fairy rings.

Dimensions FRUITBODY ↕ ↔ 20–50cm	Spores Olive-brown	Edibility

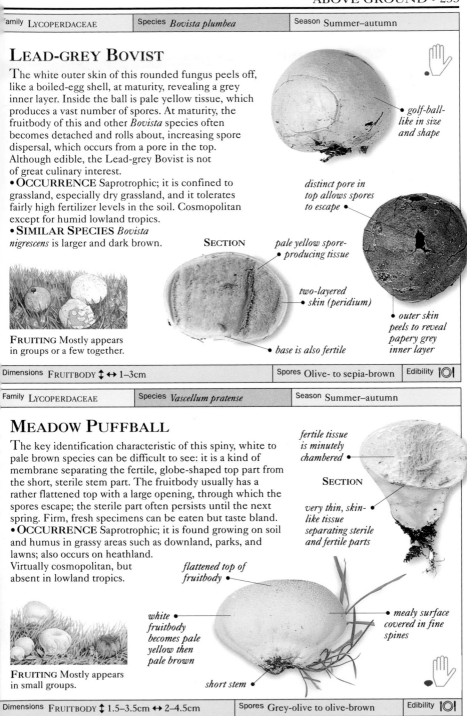

| Family LYCOPERDACEAE | Species *Bovista plumbea* | Season Summer–autumn |

LEAD-GREY BOVIST

The white outer skin of this rounded fungus peels off, like a boiled-egg shell, at maturity, revealing a grey inner layer. Inside the ball is pale yellow tissue, which produces a vast number of spores. At maturity, the fruitbody of this and other *Bovista* species often becomes detached and rolls about, increasing spore dispersal, which occurs from a pore in the top. Although edible, the Lead-grey Bovist is not of great culinary interest.

• **OCCURRENCE** Saprotrophic; it is confined to grassland, especially dry grassland, and it tolerates fairly high fertilizer levels in the soil. Cosmopolitan except for humid lowland tropics.

• **SIMILAR SPECIES** *Bovista nigrescens* is larger and dark brown.

golf-ball-like in size and shape

distinct pore in top allows spores to escape

SECTION

pale yellow spore-producing tissue

two-layered skin (peridium)

outer skin peels to reveal papery grey inner layer

base is also fertile

FRUITING Mostly appears in groups or a few together.

| Dimensions FRUITBODY ↕ ↔ 1–3cm | Spores Olive- to sepia-brown | Edibility |

| Family LYCOPERDACEAE | Species *Vascellum pratense* | Season Summer–autumn |

MEADOW PUFFBALL

The key identification characteristic of this spiny, white to pale brown species can be difficult to see: it is a kind of membrane separating the fertile, globe-shaped top part from the short, sterile stem part. The fruitbody usually has a rather flattened top with a large opening, through which the spores escape; the sterile part often persists until the next spring. Firm, fresh specimens can be eaten but taste bland.

• **OCCURRENCE** Saprotrophic; it is found growing on soil and humus in grassy areas such as downland, parks, and lawns; also occurs on heathland. Virtually cosmopolitan, but absent in lowland tropics.

fertile tissue is minutely chambered

SECTION

very thin, skin-like tissue separating sterile and fertile parts

flattened top of fruitbody

white fruitbody becomes pale yellow then pale brown

mealy surface covered in fine spines

FRUITING Mostly appears in small groups.

short stem

| Dimensions FRUITBODY ↕ 1.5–3.5cm ↔ 2–4.5cm | Spores Grey-olive to olive-brown | Edibility |

Family SCLERODERMATACEAE	Species *Scleroderma citrinum*	Season Summer–autumn

COMMON EARTHBALL

This hard, potato-like fungus, which is a familiar sight in damp woodland, has pale yellow skin covered with brown scales. It has a tough, pale yellow outer skin, which is 2–5mm thick, and its distinctive spore-filled, black interior is somewhat marbled. Inedible and poisonous, it has a strong metallic smell.
• OCCURRENCE Mycorrhizal with hardwood trees, mostly in damp woodland; it can be found with *Boletus parasiticus* (p.194). Widespread and common in areas of northern temperate zones.
• SIMILAR SPECIES Edible *Lycoperdon* species (pp.260–61) and *Tuber* species (pp.258–59) differ in overall shape, colour, smell, and spore shape.

firm black spore-bearing tissue is powdery when mature

SECTION

tough skin is 2–5mm thick

surface skin rots away, exposing spores for dispersal

fruitbody looks like a potato

brown scales on thick, pale yellow skin

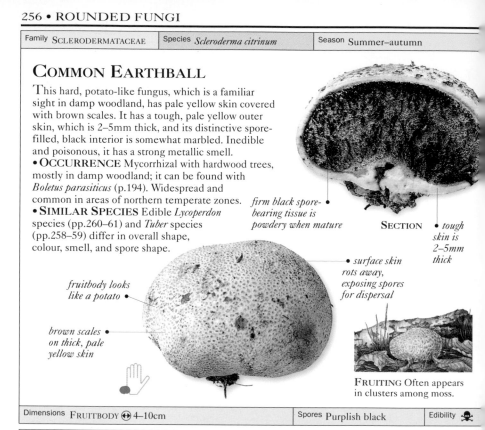

FRUITING Often appears in clusters among moss.

Dimensions FRUITBODY ⊕ 4–10cm	Spores Purplish black	Edibility 💀

Family RUSSULACEAE	Species *Zelleromyces cinnabarinus*	Season Summer–autumn

CINNABAR MILK-CAP TRUFFLE

Looking like a misshapen puffball, this species has the microscopic characteristics of a member of the *Lactarius* genus (pp.43–55) and, like *Lactarius* species, produces white "milk" when cut. The milk tastes mild and does not change colour as it dries. The spores are produced in chambers in the cinnamon-buff flesh. They are released as the fungus decays or are spread by animals, who eat the rounded fruitbodies.
• OCCURRENCE Mycorrhizal with pine trees in areas of open woodland. Widespread and common, but easily overlooked in its habitat, in eastern North America.

surface is smooth and dull

irregularly rounded to ovoid fruitbody

thin skin is cinnabar-red to cinnamon-brown

chambered, spore-bearing tissue is cinnamon-buff

FRUITING Scattered or several fruitbodies under pine, either on the soil surface or just beneath it.

Dimensions FRUITBODY ⊕ 3–5cm	Spores Pale cinnamon-buff	Edibility

| Family XYLARIACEAE | Species *Daldinia concentrica* | Season All year |

CRAMP BALLS

rounded, stemless composite fruitbody has rough surface •

surface is rusty brown when • young

The rounded, rusty brown composite fruitbodies, or stromata, of this flask-fungus are large, and have flesh that is zoned in dark and light bands. When the spores are mature, they are forcibly ejected from asci inside the spore-producing chambers, or flasks, just beneath the surface. The long-lasting stromata eventually turn black and become crumbly in texture.
• OCCURRENCE Mostly on still standing, dead or dying trunks, mainly of ash trees, but also birch and a range of other hardwoods in parks and woodland, especially following fire damage. Widespread in northern temperate zones; common in the British Isles, rarer in other parts of Europe.
• SIMILAR SPECIES *Hypoxylon* species (below) have unzoned flesh.

• minute, spore-producing flasks are found just beneath surface

flesh is silver-grey • and black in concentric zones

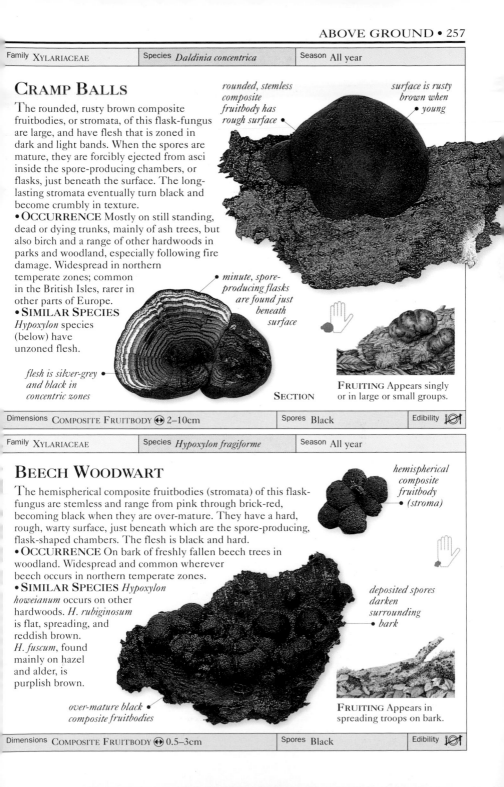

SECTION

FRUITING Appears singly or in large or small groups.

| Dimensions COMPOSITE FRUITBODY ⊕ 2–10cm | Spores Black | Edibility |

| Family XYLARIACEAE | Species *Hypoxylon fragiforme* | Season All year |

BEECH WOODWART

hemispherical composite fruitbody • (stroma)

The hemispherical composite fruitbodies (stromata) of this flask-fungus are stemless and range from pink through brick-red, becoming black when they are over-mature. They have a hard, rough, warty surface, just beneath which are the spore-producing, flask-shaped chambers. The flesh is black and hard.
• OCCURRENCE On bark of freshly fallen beech trees in woodland. Widespread and common wherever beech occurs in northern temperate zones.
• SIMILAR SPECIES *Hypoxylon howeianum* occurs on other hardwoods. *H. rubiginosum* is flat, spreading, and reddish brown. *H. fuscum*, found mainly on hazel and alder, is purplish brown.

deposited spores darken surrounding • bark

over-mature black • composite fruitbodies

FRUITING Appears in spreading troops on bark.

| Dimensions COMPOSITE FRUITBODY ⊕ 0.5–3cm | Spores Black | Edibility |

BELOW GROUND

T HE FUNGI featured here are among many that have tuber-like fruitbodies, produced below ground. The spore-bearing asci are enclosed in the fruitbodies. The *Tuber* species, "truffles", have fairly solid interiors and are related to *Peziza* (pp.266–67). Species of *Elaphomyces*, which have a powdery interior at maturity, have more obscure relationships with other genera.

Family TUBERACEAE	Species *Tuber aestivum*	Season Summer

SUMMER TRUFFLE

The least expensive of the true edible truffles, the Summer Truffle has a more or less round fruitbody with a rough surface covered in pyramidal black warts. Within the fungus, the solid flesh is grey-brown with white veins. It has a distinct aroma of rotten seaweed and a faint nutty taste.
Flies are attracted to *Tuber* fruitbodies, helping collectors to pinpoint truffle sites.
• OCCURRENCE Found growing among roots of beech, birch, and oak trees. Widespread in southern and central Europe and southern Scandinavia.

white veins run through solid, grey-brown flesh

SECTION

fruitbody surface is covered with pyramidal black warts

FRUITING Grows singly or in groups among tree roots.

Dimensions FRUITBODY ⊕ 2–5cm	Spores Yellow-brown	Edibility

Family TUBERACEAE	Species *Tuber melanosporum*	Season Late autumn–early spring

PERIGORD TRUFFLE

The rough, coal-black surface of the irregularly shaped Perigord Truffle consists of many tiny, polygonal warts. The solid flesh is made brown by the spores and turns black with age; it has white veins and a distinctive smell and taste. Perigord Truffles are collected from the wild by skilled pickers employing specially trained dogs or pigs, but inoculated seedlings of host trees are now commercially available.
• OCCURRENCE Under species of Mediterranean oaks and other host trees on alkaline, red Mediterranean soils. It is a warmth-loving species, confined to southern France, Italy, and Spain where the annual yield is about 300 metric tonnes.
• SIMILAR SPECIES
Tuber brumale is found further north, reaching the British Isles. *T. macrosporum* has an almost smooth surface. SECTION

rough rind is made up of hundreds of polygonal warts

coal-black surface on irregularly shaped fruitbody

solid brown flesh with white veins

FRUITING Grows singly, buried among tree roots.

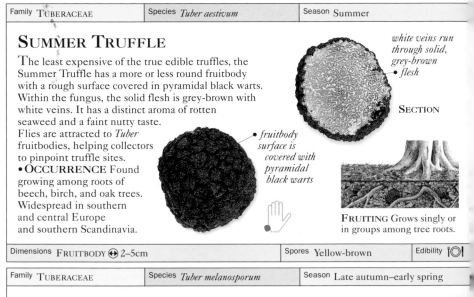

Dimensions FRUITBODY ⊕ 2–7cm	Spores Dark brown	Edibility

Family TUBERACEAE	Species *Tuber magnatum*	Season Autumn–winter

WHITE TRUFFLE

The fruitbody of this choice edible is irregularly round in shape, pale ochre to cream, and has a smooth surface. Its cream-coloured flesh has a spicy odour and flavour. The spores can be seen as darker cream-brown areas in the flesh. Attempts are being made to cultivate the species on a large scale by inoculating suitable host roots; if this is successful the prevalent high prices may drop.
• OCCURRENCE Buried in alkaline soil among the roots of oak, but also found among poplar and willow. Found in the Piemonte region of northwestern Italy and in France.
• SIMILAR SPECIES *Tuber gibbosum*, found in North America, also has pale flesh and is edible.

△ *TUBER CANALICULATUM*
This is a rounded to egg-shaped, warty, reddish brown truffle. Its flesh is tan with white streaks. At maturity, the fruitbodies push up above ground or are uprooted by animals. It is a choice edible of North America. |◯|

cream flesh is marbled with white veins •

• fruitbody looks somewhat like a potato

SECTION

FRUITING Grows singly, or in groups among tree roots.

Dimensions FRUITBODY ⊕ 2–8cm	Spores Brown	Edibility |◯|

Family ELAPHOMYCETACEAE	Species *Elaphomyces granulatus*	Season All year

GRANULATED HART'S TRUFFLE

powdery black interior at maturity •

This truffle has a thick-fleshed, scaly, warty, uniformly yellow-brown surface. Within the fruitbody, the spores are produced in a powdery mass that disperses when the skin breaks down at maturity.
• OCCURRENCE Mycorrhizal with a wide range of soft- and hardwood trees in woodland and parks. *Cordyceps ophioglossoides* (p.245) parasitizes it and can be used to locate it. Widespread and common in Europe; also found in North America and Japan.
• SIMILAR SPECIES
E. muricatus has a marbled outer layer, just beneath the warty, yellow-brown rind.

SECTION

SECTION

• fertile tissue is pale brown when immature

scaly, warty surface is golden brown •

FRUITING In large or small groups underground.

Dimensions FRUITBODY ⊕ 1.5–4.5cm	Spores Blackish brown	Edibility |◯|

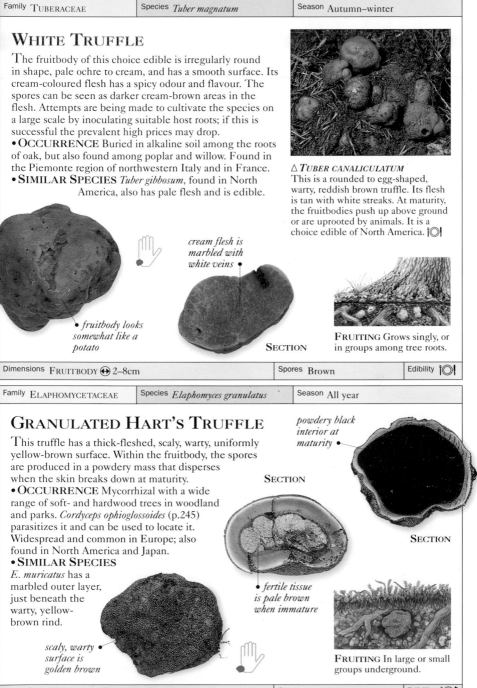

PEAR- TO PESTLE-SHAPED FUNGI

This section features puffballs and earthballs that typically have a short, stem-like base supporting the rounded, fertile top (see also pp.253–57). At maturity, the spores are released either through a pore in the top or as the outer skin breaks down. Drops of rain or other disturbance of the fruitbody helps to disperse the spores.

• *pestle-shaped fruitbody*

Family LYCOPERDACEAE	Species *Lycoperdon pyriforme*	Season Autumn–winter

STUMP PUFFBALL

This is one of the more easily identified *Lycoperdon* species: identification marks include its elongated pear shape, its smooth surface at maturity, white cords at the base, and its occurrence on woody substrates – others in the genus grow on the ground. Young fruitbodies have a warty to spiny skin. They can be eaten when their flesh is white and firm but are not choice.

• **OCCURRENCE** Saprotrophic; on rotten hardwood and, more rarely, softwood in woodland, parkland, and gardens. Almost cosmopolitan; absent in extreme climatic zones.

• **SIMILAR SPECIES** Found in open, sandy areas, *L. lividum* is also smooth, but is greyer and has warty spores (those of *L. pyriforme* are almost smooth).

young specimens have firm white flesh •

SECTION

• *skin soon becomes grainy to smooth*

• *pear-shaped fruitbodies*

• *dark spines on very young fruitbody*

• *spore-bearing tissue is olive-brown when mature*

skin becomes dark brown and papery • *when mature*

• *dense white sterile tissue in base*

SECTION

rounded pore in mature specimen through which spores escape •

FRUITING Typically in large, clustered groups.

Dimensions FRUITBODY ↕ 1.5–5cm ↔ 1–2.5cm	Spores Olive-brown	Edibility 🍴

| Family LYCOPERDACEAE | Species *Lycoperdon echinatum* | Season Autumn |

HEDGEHOG PUFFBALL

Long brown spines on the surface of the globe-shaped, tapering fruitbody give the Hedgehog Puffball its name. The spines fall off at maturity, leaving a distinctive net pattern on the dark brown surface. The spore-bearing tissue is white and firm when young, becoming brown at maturity when the lilac-tinted, chocolate-brown spores escape through a pore on the top; the sterile basal flesh also darkens with age.
• **OCCURRENCE** Saprotrophic; on alkaline soil, typically in beech woodland. Sometimes found beside the rarer, mealy, pink-tinted *Lycoperdon mammiforme*. In warmer parts of Europe and nearby parts of Asia.
• **SIMILAR SPECIES** *L. americanum* is very similar and occurs in North America.

groups of 3 or 4 long spines meet at tips •

pore in top of mature • fruitbody

• net pattern where spines have fallen off

• globe-shaped fruitbody tapers at base

white • mycelial cords attach fruitbody to litter

FRUITING A few together, often on ditch banks.

| Dimensions FRUITBODY ↕ 3–7cm ↔ 1–3cm | Spores Chocolate-brown | Edibility |

| Family LYCOPERDACEAE | Species *Lycoperdon perlatum* | Season Autumn |

COMMON PUFFBALL

Rounded, typically with a distinct stem, this white to yellowish brown species is covered with short spines, each surrounded by smaller, grain-like scales. A projection on the top marks where the pore, through which the spores escape, will form. At maturity, the spines fall off, leaving a regular pattern on the skin. The firm white flesh is edible when young, becoming darker and unpalatable with age.
• **OCCURRENCE** Saprotrophic; on soil, mainly in woods but also in grassland. Widespread; common in northern temperate zones.
• **SIMILAR SPECIES** *Lycoperdon nigrescens* has longer, darker spines in groups, like those of the much longer-spined *L. echinatum* (above). The surface of both has a similar pattern when the spines fall off.

pore •

spore mass brown and powdery when mature •

• cone-like spines are lost with age

SECTION

• projection where pore will form

spore-producing • tissue ages darker

SECTION

• grain-like spines around conical spines

sterile stem • tissue is spongy

FRUITING In dense groups or occasionally singly.

| Dimensions FRUITBODY ↕ 4–7cm ↔ 2–4cm | Spores Pale yellow to olive-brown | Edibility |

Family LYCOPERDACEAE	Species *Handkea excipuliformis*	Season Autumn

PESTLE-SHAPED PUFFBALL

This buff-brown fungus typically has a tall stem with a rounded upper fertile part; short-stemmed specimens also occur. When mature, the outer skin breaks open and the rich brown spores within are dispersed by wind and rain. When young and firm, the fruitbodies are edible, but fairly tasteless. The stem part becomes very tough as it matures and may persist into the following season.

• **OCCURRENCE** Saprotrophic; on soil or turf in woods or in the open. Widespread and common in most parts of northern temperate zones, extending to subarctic and subtropical zones.

• **SIMILAR SPECIES** *Lycoperdon molle* resembles a short-stemmed specimen. It is distinguished by microscopic examination.

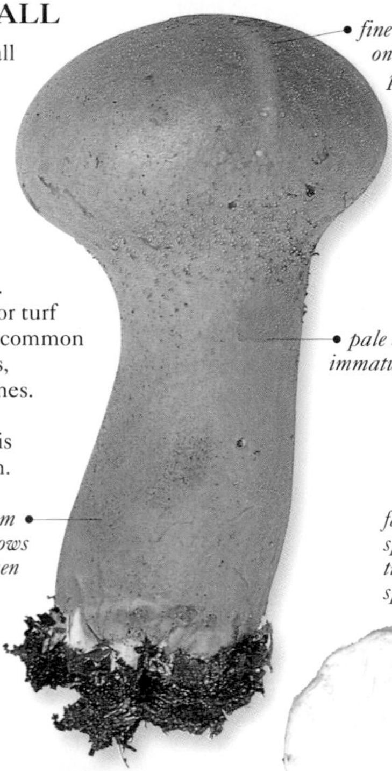

fine-pointed scales on surface of upper part when young

pale buff-brown immature fruitbody

outer skin breaks at maturity, revealing rich brown spore mass

fairly long stem develops furrows on surface when mature

fairly firm, white, spore-producing tissue in young specimen

SECTION

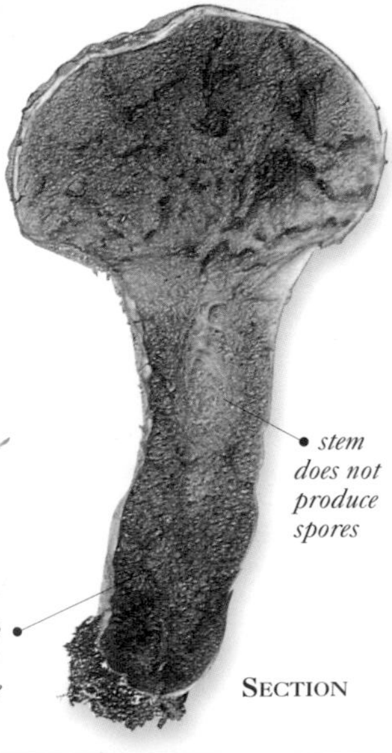

stem does not produce spores

appears among moss or leaf litter

stem flesh is spongy in texture

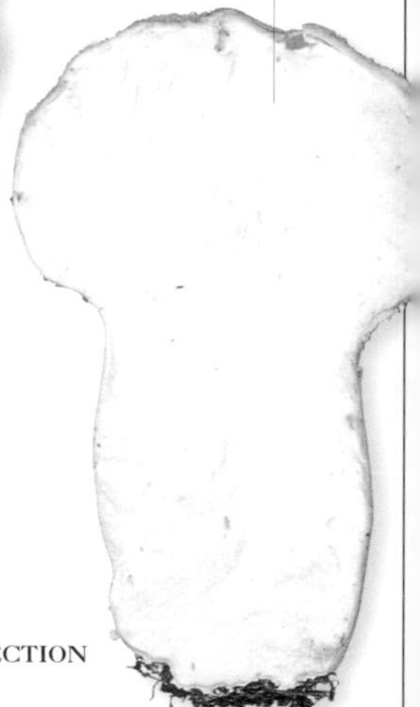

SECTION

FRUITING Mostly in small groups of fruitbodies.

Dimensions FRUITBODY ↕ 5–20cm ↔ 5–10cm	Spores Olive-brown to brown	Edibility

Family LYCOPERDACEAE	Species *Handkea utriformis*	Season Summer–autumn

MOSAIC PUFFBALL

Never taller than it is broad, this large *Handkea* species has pear-shaped fruitbodies with fairly coarse, mealy scales, which are more or less lost at maturity. The top skin rots away to reveal the powdery spore mass, which is brown, sometimes olive tinged. The lower, sterile part is white, ageing to brown. It is edible when very young, but not flavoursome.
• **OCCURRENCE** Saprotrophic; found growing in open, often coastal, areas. Widespread in northern temperate zones.

spore mass visible through hole in top •

coarse, mealy, white scales

pear-shaped • fruitbody with flat top

FRUITING Mostly in small groups among grasses, lichens, and low herbs.

Dimensions FRUITBODY ↕ 5–10cm ↔ 5–15cm	Spores Chocolate-brown	Edibility

Family SCLERODERMATACEAE	Species *Scleroderma verrucosum*	Season Autumn

SCALY EARTHBALL

This fairly large species is pale yellow to brown and covered with irregular brown scales. It has a stem-like projection and thin skin, to 1mm thick. The spore-bearing tissue smells metallic and is white, soon turning dark purple-brown as it matures. The spores are dispersed by wind as the outer skin of the fruitbody distintegrates.
• **OCCURRENCE** Mycorrhizal with hardwood trees such as oak and beech, growing in woodland areas and parks. Widespread and common in both northern and southern temperate zones.

brown scales on rounded fruitbody •

partly buried • "stem" under main fruitbody

white • mycelial cords

FRUITING Mostly a few together or singly, often on bare soil.

Dimensions FRUITBODY ↕ 5–10cm ↔ 2–5cm	Spores Purple-black	Edibility

Family CALOSTOMATACEAE	Species *Calostoma cinnabarina*	Season Late summer–autumn

PUFFBALL-IN-ASPIC

This species has a gelatinous outer layer and a red inner layer, breaking up to enclose the stem in a thick jelly, dotted with red pieces. The exposed, ovoid top is coated in a red powder that wears away to reveal a pale yellow ball with a cross-shaped opening for spore release.
• **OCCURRENCE** Found growing on the ground in open woods. Widespread and common in eastern North America.
• **SIMILAR SPECIES** *Calostoma lutescens* looks similar but is yellow. *C. ravenelii* is straw-yellow and not gelatinous.

red powder covers immature spore ball •

stem sheathed • in jelly filled with red pieces

red mouth for • spore release

FRUITING Appears in small groups on the ground in open woodland areas.

Dimensions FRUITBODY ↕ 2–5cm ↔ 1–2cm	Spores White to cream	Edibility

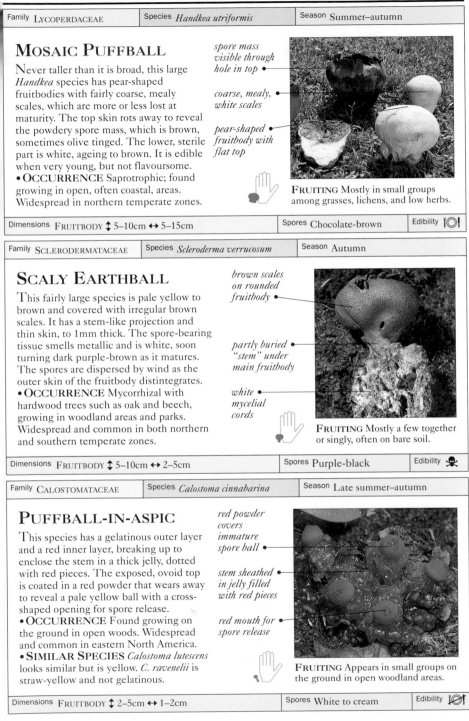

CUP- TO DISC-SHAPED

Although they all produce cup- or disc-shaped fruitbodies, the fungi in this section belong to two separate groups. The first group has more or less circular fruitbodies that are shallowly cupped or flat (pp.264–73); the second group has deeply cupped, bird's nest-like fruitbodies containing tiny, lentil-shaped structures (p.274).

• *cup-shaped fruitbody*

WITHOUT "EGGS"

THIS SUBSECTION features fungi that produce cup- or disc-shaped fruitbodies with a smooth, spore-bearing surface (hymenium) on the inner side of the cup or on the top of the disc. When mature, the spores are discharged violently (see p.16–17).

The morels (pp.209–10) evolved from simple cup-fungi, but have distinct stems and are more elaborate in shape.

Family SARCOSCYPHACEAE	Species *Sarcoscypha austriaca*	Season Late autumn–early summer

CURLY-HAIRED ELF-CUP

This fungus has tiny, corkscrew-like white hairs on the outside of the long-lasting, cup-shaped fruitbody, making it appear pale in contrast to the interior, which is bright scarlet. The cup margin is also fairly pale and may be finely toothed. The pale stem is often hidden in the substrate, and the pale red flesh is fairly firm but brittle. There is also a pure white form.
• **OCCURRENCE** Grows on wood substrates in hardwood areas. Widespread throughout Europe and probably in other parts of northern temperate zones.
• **SIMILAR SPECIES** *Sarcoscypha coccinea* has straight hairs on the outside of the cup. Other species of *Sarcoscypha* have more localized distributions and differ in spore characteristics and germination.

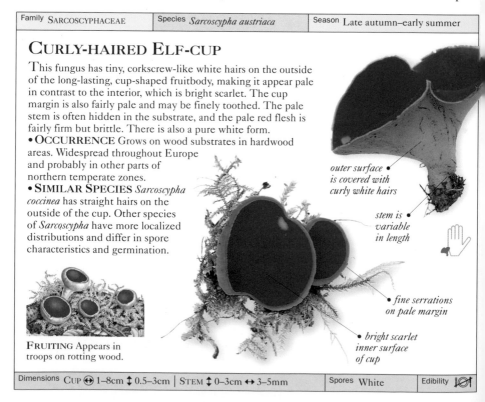

outer surface • is covered with curly white hairs

stem is • variable in length

• fine serrations on pale margin

• bright scarlet inner surface of cup

FRUITING Appears in troops on rotting wood.

Dimensions Cup ⊕ 1–8cm ↕ 0.5–3cm	Stem ↕ 0–3cm ↔ 3–5mm	Spores White	Edibility 🖐🍴

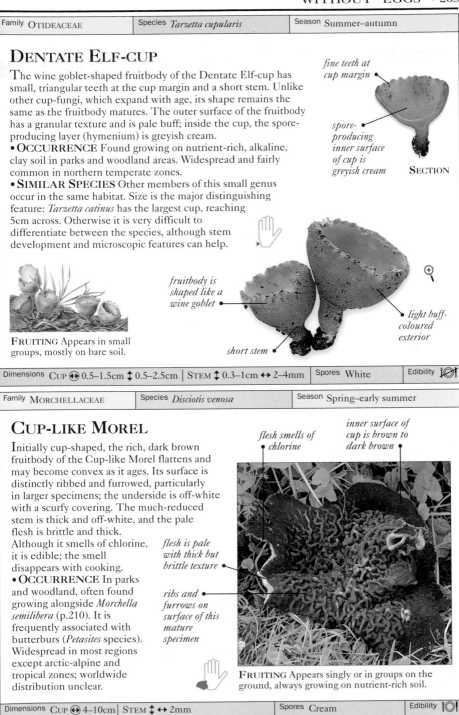

| Family OTIDEACEAE | Species *Tarzetta cupularis* | Season Summer–autumn |

DENTATE ELF-CUP

The wine goblet-shaped fruitbody of the Dentate Elf-cup has small, triangular teeth at the cup margin and a short stem. Unlike other cup-fungi, which expand with age, its shape remains the same as the fruitbody matures. The outer surface of the fruitbody has a granular texture and is pale buff; inside the cup, the spore-producing layer (hymenium) is greyish cream.
• OCCURRENCE Found growing on nutrient-rich, alkaline, clay soil in parks and woodland areas. Widespread and fairly common in northern temperate zones.
• SIMILAR SPECIES Other members of this small genus occur in the same habitat. Size is the major distinguishing feature: *Tarzetta catinus* has the largest cup, reaching 5cm across. Otherwise it is very difficult to differentiate between the species, although stem development and microscopic features can help.

fine teeth at cup margin

spore-producing inner surface of cup is greyish cream   SECTION

fruitbody is shaped like a wine goblet

light buff-coloured exterior

FRUITING Appears in small groups, mostly on bare soil.

short stem

| Dimensions CUP ⊕ 0.5–1.5cm ↕ 0.5–2.5cm | STEM ↕ 0.3–1cm ↔ 2–4mm | Spores White | Edibility |

| Family MORCHELLACEAE | Species *Disciotis venosa* | Season Spring–early summer |

CUP-LIKE MOREL

Initially cup-shaped, the rich, dark brown fruitbody of the Cup-like Morel flattens and may become convex as it ages. Its surface is distinctly ribbed and furrowed, particularly in larger specimens; the underside is off-white with a scurfy covering. The much-reduced stem is thick and off-white, and the pale flesh is brittle and thick. Although it smells of chlorine, it is edible; the smell disappears with cooking.
• OCCURRENCE In parks and woodland, often found growing alongside *Morchella semilibera* (p.210). It is frequently associated with butterburs (*Petasites* species). Widespread in most regions except arctic-alpine and tropical zones; worldwide distribution unclear.

flesh smells of chlorine

inner surface of cup is brown to dark brown

flesh is pale with thick but brittle texture

ribs and furrows on surface of this mature specimen

FRUITING Appears singly or in groups on the ground, always growing on nutrient-rich soil.

| Dimensions CUP ⊕ 4–10cm | STEM ↕ ↔ 2mm | Spores Cream | Edibility |

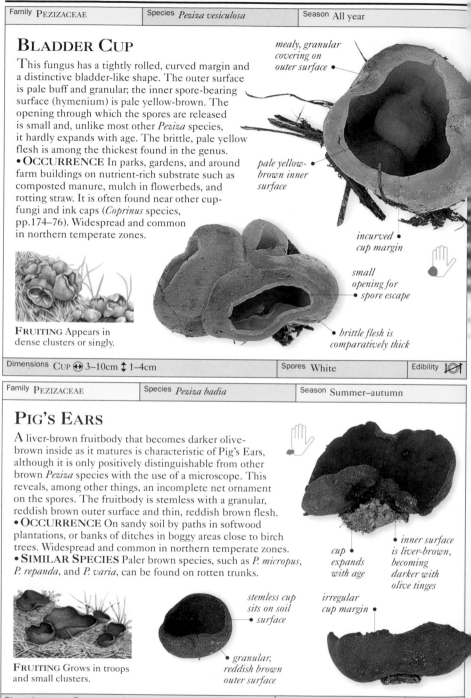

| Family PEZIZACEAE | Species *Peziza vesiculosa* | Season All year |

BLADDER CUP

This fungus has a tightly rolled, curved margin and a distinctive bladder-like shape. The outer surface is pale buff and granular; the inner spore-bearing surface (hymenium) is pale yellow-brown. The opening through which the spores are released is small and, unlike most other *Peziza* species, it hardly expands with age. The brittle, pale yellow flesh is among the thickest found in the genus.
• OCCURRENCE In parks, gardens, and around farm buildings on nutrient-rich substrate such as composted manure, mulch in flowerbeds, and rotting straw. It is often found near other cup-fungi and ink caps (*Coprinus* species, pp.174–76). Widespread and common in northern temperate zones.

mealy, granular covering on outer surface

pale yellow-brown inner surface

incurved cup margin

small opening for spore escape

brittle flesh is comparatively thick

FRUITING Appears in dense clusters or singly.

| Dimensions CUP ⊕ 3–10cm ↕ 1–4cm | Spores White | Edibility |

| Family PEZIZACEAE | Species *Peziza badia* | Season Summer–autumn |

PIG'S EARS

A liver-brown fruitbody that becomes darker olive-brown inside as it matures is characteristic of Pig's Ears, although it is only positively distinguishable from other brown *Peziza* species with the use of a microscope. This reveals, among other things, an incomplete net ornament on the spores. The fruitbody is stemless with a granular, reddish brown outer surface and thin, reddish brown flesh.
• OCCURRENCE On sandy soil by paths in softwood plantations, or banks of ditches in boggy areas close to birch trees. Widespread and common in northern temperate zones.
• SIMILAR SPECIES Paler brown species, such as *P. micropus*, *P. repanda*, and *P. varia*, can be found on rotten trunks.

inner surface is liver-brown, becoming darker with olive tinges

cup expands with age

irregular cup margin

stemless cup sits on soil surface

granular, reddish brown outer surface

FRUITING Grows in troops and small clusters.

| Dimensions CUP ⊕ 1.5–7cm ↕ 0.5–3cm | Spores White | Edibility |

| Family PEZIZACEAE | Species *Peziza succosa* | Season Summer–autumn |

YELLOW-MILK CUP

Cup-shaped and yellow- to grey-brown, the
Yellow-milk Cup is distinguished from most other
Peziza species by its reaction when cut open: the
thin, yellow-brown flesh exudes a milky yellow
juice and gradually turns bright yellow. With age,
the cup expands and becomes irregular in shape.
• OCCURRENCE Along road verges in hardwood
areas; often found growing alongside *Helvella* and
Inocybe species. Widespread and common in Europe;
also occurs in eastern and central North America.
• SIMILAR SPECIES Other *Peziza* species that have
yellow juice include *P. michelii*, which is smaller with lilac
tinges, and *P. succosella*, which is smaller, has a greenish
yellow flesh reaction, and has smaller spores.

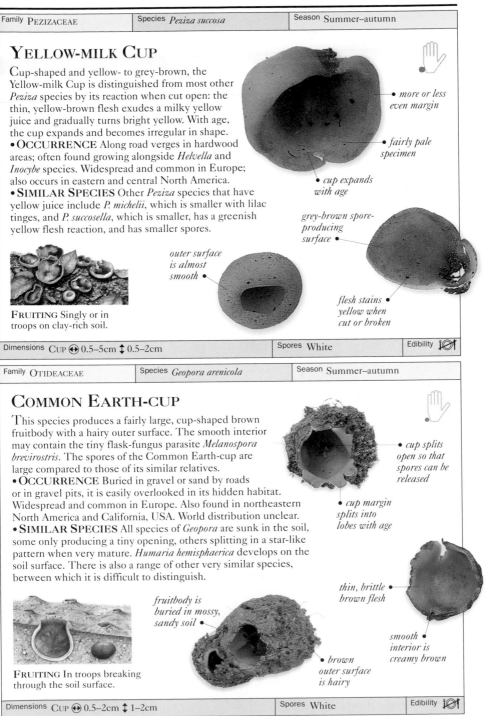

• *more or less
even margin*

• *fairly pale
specimen*

• *cup expands
with age*

*grey-brown spore-
producing
surface* •

*outer surface
is almost
smooth* •

*flesh stains
yellow when
cut or broken* •

FRUITING Singly or in
troops on clay-rich soil.

| Dimensions CUP ⊕ 0.5–5cm ↕ 0.5–2cm | Spores White | Edibility |

| Family OTIDEACEAE | Species *Geopora arenicola* | Season Summer–autumn |

COMMON EARTH-CUP

This species produces a fairly large, cup-shaped brown
fruitbody with a hairy outer surface. The smooth interior
may contain the tiny flask-fungus parasite *Melanospora
brevirostris*. The spores of the Common Earth-cup are
large compared to those of its similar relatives.
• OCCURRENCE Buried in gravel or sand by roads
or in gravel pits, it is easily overlooked in its hidden habitat.
Widespread and common in Europe. Also found in northeastern
North America and California, USA. World distribution unclear.
• SIMILAR SPECIES All species of *Geopora* are sunk in the soil,
some only producing a tiny opening, others splitting in a star-like
pattern when very mature. *Humaria hemisphaerica* develops on the
soil surface. There is also a range of other very similar species,
between which it is difficult to distinguish.

• *cup splits
open so that
spores can be
released*

• *cup margin
splits into
lobes with age*

• *thin, brittle
brown flesh*

*fruitbody is
buried in mossy,
sandy soil* •

• *smooth
interior is
creamy brown*

• *brown
outer surface
is hairy*

FRUITING In troops breaking
through the soil surface.

| Dimensions CUP ⊕ 0.5–2cm ↕ 1–2cm | Spores White | Edibility |

| Family OTIDEACEAE | Species *Aleuria aurantia* | Season Summer–autumn |

ORANGE-PEEL FUNGUS

With its vivid orange colouring, downy on the outside, the Orange-peel Fungus is one of the most attractive cup fungi. The cup margin is inrolled when young, becoming wavy. The cup flattens with age. It is occasionally eaten and has thin, brittle, white to very pale flesh.

• **OCCURRENCE** Found on gravelly soil in disturbed sites, such as between pavement stones or on dirt roads in wheel tracks, and on new lawns. Some *Scutellinia* species (see below) can also be found in similar sites. Widespread and common throughout northern temperate zones.

• **SIMILAR SPECIES** Found on similar sites, *Melastiza chateri* is smaller, reddish orange, and has very short, pale brown hairs at the cup margin. Other *Aleuria* species have smaller cups and are rarer; a microscope is required to identify them correctly.

cup becomes wavy and flattened • with age

outer surface covered with white down •

vivid orange inner surface

margin inrolled • when young

stem-like base is visible on • some specimens

FRUITING Appears in large groups and clusters.

| Dimensions CUP ⊕ 2–10cm ↕ 0.2–3cm | Spores White | Edibility |

| Family OTIDEACEAE | Species *Scutellinia scutellata* | Season Late spring–winter |

COMMON EYELASH-CUP

This highly distinctive cup-fungus has conspicuous long black "eye-lashes" at the margin of the disc-shaped, vivid orange-red cup; the outer surface is pale orange-brown. There are many similar species in this complex genus; under a microscope, spore shape and ornamentation offer the best clues for positive identification.

• **OCCURRENCE** On wet, mossy wood near pond edges and occasionally on humus-rich soil. Common among willow trees and in bogs and other marshy places. Other species in the genus favour damp, often alkaline soil. Widespread and common in northern temperate zones.

inner surface is bright orange-red, due to carotene pigment •

when fully mature, dark brown hairs point outwards

dark brown hairs project • inwards when young

grows on wet and rotten wood

FRUITING Typically appears in dense swarms on wood.

| Dimensions CUP ⊕ 0.5–1cm ↕ 2mm | Spores White | Edibility |

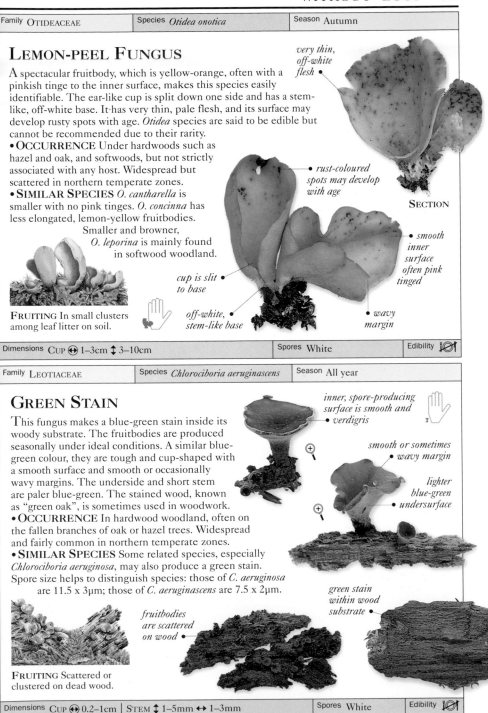

| Family OTIDEACEAE | Species *Otidea onotica* | Season Autumn |

LEMON-PEEL FUNGUS

A spectacular fruitbody, which is yellow-orange, often with a pinkish tinge to the inner surface, makes this species easily identifiable. The ear-like cup is split down one side and has a stem-like, off-white base. It-has very thin, pale flesh, and its surface may develop rusty spots with age. *Otidea* species are said to be edible but cannot be recommended due to their rarity.
• **OCCURRENCE** Under hardwoods such as hazel and oak, and softwoods, but not strictly associated with any host. Widespread but scattered in northern temperate zones.
• **SIMILAR SPECIES** *O. cantharella* is smaller with no pink tinges. *O. concinna* has less elongated, lemon-yellow fruitbodies. Smaller and browner, *O. leporina* is mainly found in softwood woodland.

very thin, off-white flesh

rust-coloured spots may develop with age

SECTION

smooth inner surface often pink tinged

cup is slit to base

FRUITING In small clusters among leaf litter on soil.

off-white, stem-like base

wavy margin

| Dimensions CUP ⊕ 1–3cm ↕ 3–10cm | Spores White | Edibility |

| Family LEOTIACEAE | Species *Chlorociboria aeruginascens* | Season All year |

GREEN STAIN

This fungus makes a blue-green stain inside its woody substrate. The fruitbodies are produced seasonally under ideal conditions. A similar blue-green colour, they are tough and cup-shaped with a smooth surface and smooth or occasionally wavy margins. The underside and short stem are paler blue-green. The stained wood, known as "green oak", is sometimes used in woodwork.
• **OCCURRENCE** In hardwood woodland, often on the fallen branches of oak or hazel trees. Widespread and fairly common in northern temperate zones.
• **SIMILAR SPECIES** Some related species, especially *Chlorociboria aeruginosa*, may also produce a green stain. Spore size helps to distinguish species: those of *C. aeruginosa* are 11.5 x 3µm; those of *C. aeruginascens* are 7.5 x 2µm.

inner, spore-producing surface is smooth and verdigris

smooth or sometimes wavy margin

lighter blue-green undersurface

green stain within wood substrate

fruitbodies are scattered on wood

FRUITING Scattered or clustered on dead wood.

| Dimensions CUP ⊕ 0.2–1cm | STEM ↕ 1–5mm ↔ 1–3mm | Spores White | Edibility |

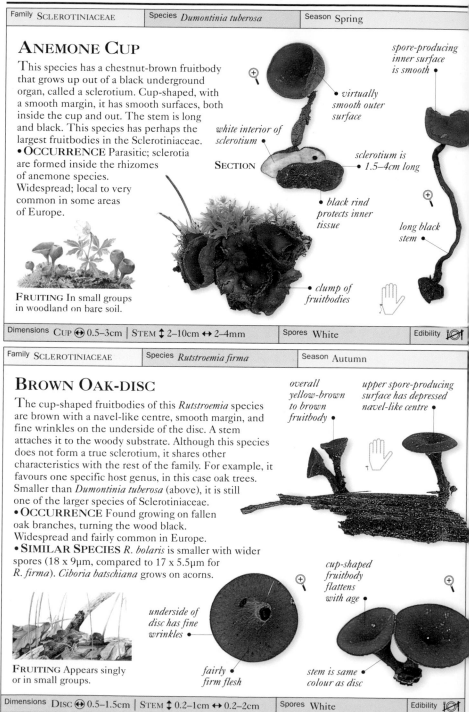

Family SCLEROTINIACEAE	Species *Dumontinia tuberosa*	Season Spring

ANEMONE CUP

This species has a chestnut-brown fruitbody that grows up out of a black underground organ, called a sclerotium. Cup-shaped, with a smooth margin, it has smooth surfaces, both inside the cup and out. The stem is long and black. This species has perhaps the largest fruitbodies in the Sclerotiniaceae.
• **OCCURRENCE** Parasitic; sclerotia are formed inside the rhizomes of anemone species. Widespread; local to very common in some areas of Europe.

spore-producing inner surface is smooth •

• virtually smooth outer surface

white interior of sclerotium •

SECTION

sclerotium is • 1.5–4cm long

black rind protects inner tissue

long black stem •

FRUITING In small groups in woodland on bare soil.

• clump of fruitbodies

Dimensions CUP ⊕ 0.5–3cm │ STEM ↕ 2–10cm ↔ 2–4mm	Spores White	Edibility

Family SCLEROTINIACEAE	Species *Rutstroemia firma*	Season Autumn

BROWN OAK-DISC

The cup-shaped fruitbodies of this *Rutstroemia* species are brown with a navel-like centre, smooth margin, and fine wrinkles on the underside of the disc. A stem attaches it to the woody substrate. Although this species does not form a true sclerotium, it shares other characteristics with the rest of the family. For example, it favours one specific host genus, in this case oak trees. Smaller than *Dumontinia tuberosa* (above), it is still one of the larger species of Sclerotiniaceae.
• **OCCURRENCE** Found growing on fallen oak branches, turning the wood black. Widespread and fairly common in Europe.
• **SIMILAR SPECIES** *R. bolaris* is smaller with wider spores (18 x 9µm, compared to 17 x 5.5µm for *R. firma*). *Ciboria batschiana* grows on acorns.

overall yellow-brown to brown fruitbody •

upper spore-producing surface has depressed navel-like centre •

cup-shaped fruitbody flattens with age •

underside of disc has fine wrinkles •

FRUITING Appears singly or in small groups.

fairly • firm flesh

stem is same • colour as disc

Dimensions DISC ⊕ 0.5–1.5cm │ STEM ↕ 0.2–1cm ↔ 0.2–2cm	Spores White	Edibility

Family LEOTIACEAE	Species *Neobulgaria pura*	Season Late autumn

BEECH JELLY-DISC

The fruitbodies of this fungus are pale pink, gelatinous, and translucent with a flat spore-producing surface and finely toothed margins. Tapering strongly to the base, they are cone-shaped in cross-section. Newly emerged specimens of Beech Jelly-disc are very firm and rubbery. Exposure to the weather eventually makes them collapse and become much thinner but they will persist into winter.
• OCCURRENCE On relatively fresh bark of fallen beech trunks and branches, often next to *Hypoxylon fragiforme* (p.257). Northern temperate zones; in most areas where beech occurs.
• SIMILAR SPECIES *Bulgaria inquinans* (below) is similar in habit and habitat but is harder and darker brown to black.

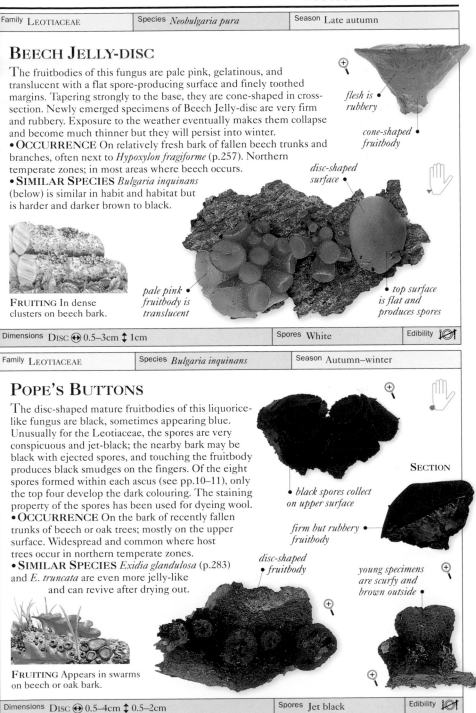

flesh is rubbery

cone-shaped fruitbody

disc-shaped surface

FRUITING In dense clusters on beech bark.

pale pink fruitbody is translucent

top surface is flat and produces spores

Dimensions DISC ⊕ 0.5–3cm ↕ 1cm	Spores White	Edibility 🚫

Family LEOTIACEAE	Species *Bulgaria inquinans*	Season Autumn–winter

POPE'S BUTTONS

The disc-shaped mature fruitbodies of this liquorice-like fungus are black, sometimes appearing blue. Unusually for the Leotiaceae, the spores are very conspicuous and jet-black; the nearby bark may be black with ejected spores, and touching the fruitbody produces black smudges on the fingers. Of the eight spores formed within each ascus (see pp.10–11), only the top four develop the dark colouring. The staining property of the spores has been used for dyeing wool.
• OCCURRENCE On the bark of recently fallen trunks of beech or oak trees; mostly on the upper surface. Widespread and common where host trees occur in northern temperate zones.
• SIMILAR SPECIES *Exidia glandulosa* (p.283) and *E. truncata* are even more jelly-like and can revive after drying out.

SECTION

black spores collect on upper surface

firm but rubbery fruitbody

disc-shaped fruitbody

young specimens are scurfy and brown outside

FRUITING Appears in swarms on beech or oak bark.

Dimensions DISC ⊕ 0.5–4cm ↕ 0.5–2cm	Spores Jet black	Edibility 🚫

Family LEOTIACEAE	Species *Ascocoryne cylichnium*	Season Autumn–winter

LARGE PURPLE-DROP

This species produces a disc-shaped, gelatinous, reddish purple fruitbody with a smooth, shiny, spore-producing surface and an often irregularly lobed margin. It has a short stem, which makes the fruitbody appear to be cone-shaped when viewed from the side.
• **OCCURRENCE** Found growing on the bark and exposed wood of hardwood trees. Widespread and fairly common in northern temperate zones.
• **SIMILAR SPECIES** *Ascocoryne sarcoides* (below) has narrower discs and shorter spores. Several other smaller species occur in the northern hemisphere. The best way to distinguish between them is by microscopic examination of features such as the spores.

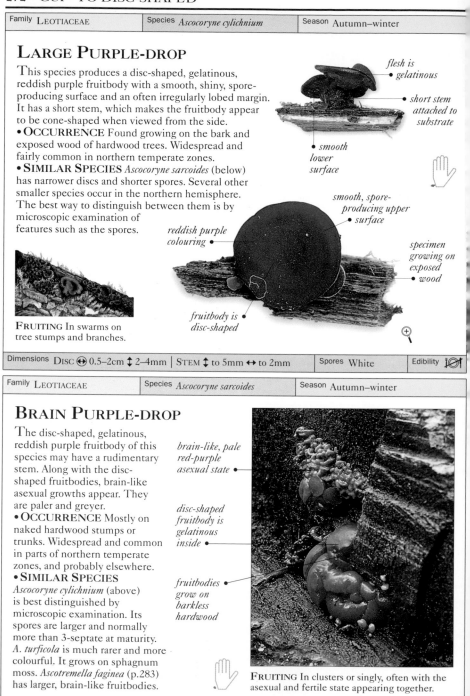

flesh is gelatinous

short stem attached to substrate

smooth lower surface

smooth, spore-producing upper surface

reddish purple colouring

specimen growing on exposed wood

FRUITING In swarms on tree stumps and branches.

fruitbody is disc-shaped

Dimensions DISC ⊕ 0.5–2cm ↕ 2–4mm	STEM ↕ to 5mm ↔ to 2mm	Spores White	Edibility

Family LEOTIACEAE	Species *Ascocoryne sarcoides*	Season Autumn–winter

BRAIN PURPLE-DROP

The disc-shaped, gelatinous, reddish purple fruitbody of this species may have a rudimentary stem. Along with the disc-shaped fruitbodies, brain-like asexual growths appear. They are paler and greyer.
• **OCCURRENCE** Mostly on naked hardwood stumps or trunks. Widespread and common in parts of northern temperate zones, and probably elsewhere.
• **SIMILAR SPECIES** *Ascocoryne cylichnium* (above) is best distinguished by microscopic examination. Its spores are larger and normally more than 3-septate at maturity. *A. turficola* is much rarer and more colourful. It grows on sphagnum moss. *Ascotremella faginea* (p.283) has larger, brain-like fruitbodies.

brain-like, pale red-purple asexual state

disc-shaped fruitbody is gelatinous inside

fruitbodies grow on barkless hardwood

FRUITING In clusters or singly, often with the asexual and fertile state appearing together.

Dimensions DISC ⊕ 0.2–1cm ↕ 1–4mm	Spores White	Edibility

Family LEOTIACEAE	Species *Bisporella citrina*	Season Autumn–early winter

LEMON DISC

The clustered habit and vivid yellow colour of this tiny species enable it to be seen from a distance. The discs have a smooth, flat or slightly concave upper surface and a paler lower surface. White discs may occur. There is no true stem.
• OCCURRENCE Found growing on fallen hardwood, often beech, oak, and hazel; mostly grows on wood that lacks its bark. Widespread and very common throughout northern temperate zones.
• SIMILAR SPECIES Some species of *Bisporella* are associalted with a blackish, powdery asexual form, called *Bispora antennata*. There are a number of other closely related yellow cup-fungi. Some may have a stem or may differ only in microscopic features.

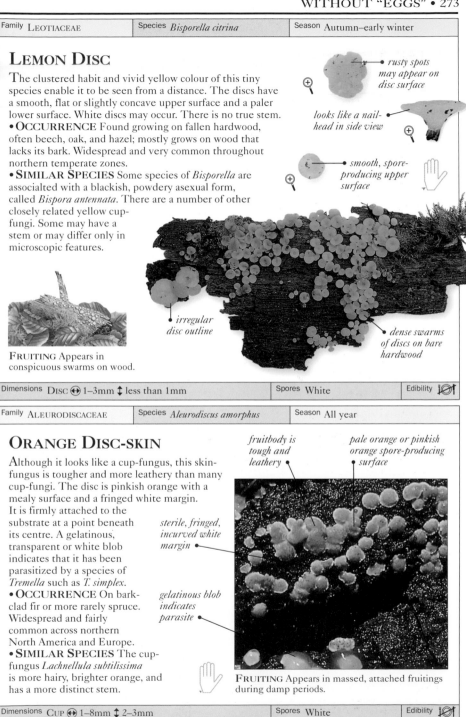

rusty spots may appear on disc surface

looks like a nail-head in side view

smooth, spore-producing upper surface

irregular disc outline

dense swarms of discs on bare hardwood

FRUITING Appears in conspicuous swarms on wood.

Dimensions DISC ⊕ 1–3mm ↕ less than 1mm	Spores White	Edibility 🚫

Family ALEURODISCACEAE	Species *Aleurodiscus amorphus*	Season All year

ORANGE DISC-SKIN

Although it looks like a cup-fungus, this skin-fungus is tougher and more leathery than many cup-fungi. The disc is pinkish orange with a mealy surface and a fringed white margin. It is firmly attached to the substrate at a point beneath its centre. A gelatinous, transparent or white blob indicates that it has been parasitized by a species of *Tremella* such as *T. simplex*.
• OCCURRENCE On bark-clad fir or more rarely spruce. Widespread and fairly common across northern North America and Europe.
• SIMILAR SPECIES The cup-fungus *Lachnellula subtilissima* is more hairy, brighter orange, and has a more distinct stem.

fruitbody is tough and leathery

pale orange or pinkish orange spore-producing surface

sterile, fringed, incurved white margin

gelatinous blob indicates parasite

FRUITING Appears in massed, attached fruitings during damp periods.

Dimensions CUP ⊕ 1–8mm ↕ 2–3mm	Spores White	Edibility 🚫

CUP-SHAPED CONTAINING "EGGS"

T HE FUNGI featured here have unique fruitbodies consisting of a "cup", inside which are tiny structures called peridioles. These contain the spore-producing hymenium. Initally, a protective skin covers the top of the "cup". It disappears at maturity and the peridioles are dispersed by raindrops.

Family NIDULARIACEAE	Species *Crucibulum crucibuliforme*	Season Autumn

WHITE EGG BIRD'S NEST

This species is the only member of the *Crucibulum* genus. It has cylindrical, nest-like, ochre-orange fruitbodies within which there are 10–15 (up to 20) lentil-shaped white "eggs" that contain the spores. Each "egg" is attached to the "nest" by a tiny cord. The outer surface of the "nest" is felty to smooth. Immature "nests" are covered with a protective ochre-orange skin; when this withers, the "eggs" are dispersed by raindrops.
• OCCURRENCE On litter, mulch, and sawdust, in woodland, parks, and gardens. Widespread and fairly common in northern temperate zones.
• SIMILAR SPECIES *Cyathus* species have cone-shaped fruitbodies and "eggs" that are darker in colour.

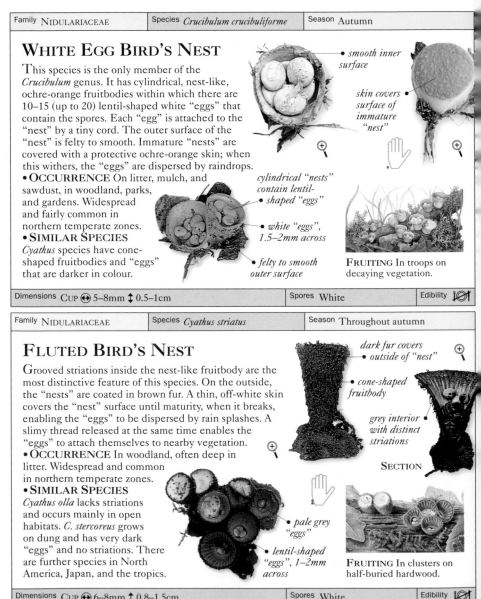

• smooth inner surface

skin covers • surface of immature "nest"

cylindrical "nests" contain lentil-• shaped "eggs"

• white "eggs", 1.5–2mm across

• felty to smooth outer surface

FRUITING In troops on decaying vegetation.

Dimensions CUP ⊕ 5–8mm ↕ 0.5–1cm		Spores White	Edibility 🚫🍴

Family NIDULARIACEAE	Species *Cyathus striatus*	Season Throughout autumn

FLUTED BIRD'S NEST

Grooved striations inside the nest-like fruitbody are the most distinctive feature of this species. On the outside, the "nests" are coated in brown fur. A thin, off-white skin covers the "nest" surface until maturity, when it breaks, enabling the "eggs" to be dispersed by rain splashes. A slimy thread released at the same time enables the "eggs" to attach themselves to nearby vegetation.
• OCCURRENCE In woodland, often deep in litter. Widespread and common in northern temperate zones.
• SIMILAR SPECIES *Cyathus olla* lacks striations and occurs mainly in open habitats. *C. stercoreus* grows on dung and has very dark "eggs" and no striations. There are further species in North America, Japan, and the tropics.

dark fur covers • outside of "nest"

• cone-shaped fruitbody

grey interior • with distinct striations

SECTION

• pale grey "eggs"

• lentil-shaped "eggs", 1–2mm across

FRUITING In clusters on half-buried hardwood.

Dimensions CUP ⊕ 6–8mm ↕ 0.8–1.5cm		Spores White	Edibility 🚫🍴

TRUMPET-SHAPED FUNGI

The fungi featured in this section have trumpet-shaped, hollow fruitbodies with the spore-producing hymenium lining the more or less smooth outer surface. Most of the species here belong to the Cantharellaceae family (see also pp.28 and 30). The fruitbodies have fairly tough flesh and may persist for several weeks.

• *trumpet-shaped fruitbody*

Family CANTHARELLACEAE	Species *Craterellus cornucopioides*	Season Summer–autumn

HORN OF PLENTY

The fruitbody of this dark brown species is hollow and trumpet-shaped, tapering towards the base. The outer side has a paler grey spore-bearing layer. The thin grey flesh is mild and pleasant tasting with an aromatic smell. Its dark colouring makes it difficult to spot at first, but where found it typically occurs *en masse*.
• **OCCURRENCE** Mycorrhizal with hardwood trees in woodland, on fairly rich, often alkaline soil; more rarely with softwoods. Widespread in northern temperate zones; abundant in some areas, but almost absent in others.
• **SIMILAR SPECIES** *Craterellus fallax*, a North American species, is more fragrant.

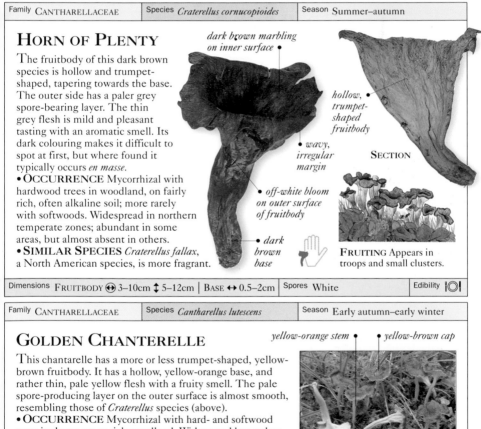

dark brown marbling on inner surface •

hollow, trumpet-shaped fruitbody

• *wavy, irregular margin*

SECTION

• *off-white bloom on outer surface of fruitbody*

• *dark brown base*

FRUITING Appears in troops and small clusters.

Dimensions FRUITBODY ⊕ 3–10cm ↕ 5–12cm	BASE ↔ 0.5–2cm	Spores White	Edibility

Family CANTHARELLACEAE	Species *Cantharellus lutescens*	Season Early autumn–early winter

GOLDEN CHANTERELLE

yellow-orange stem • • *yellow-brown cap*

This chantarelle has a more or less trumpet-shaped, yellow-brown fruitbody. It has a hollow, yellow-orange base, and rather thin, pale yellow flesh with a fruity smell. The pale spore-producing layer on the outer surface is almost smooth, resembling those of *Craterellus* species (above).
• **OCCURRENCE** Mycorrhizal with hard- and softwood trees in damp, moss-rich woodland. Widespread but rather local in temperate and warm-temperate regions, including North America, Europe, and Asia.
• **SIMILAR SPECIES** *C. tubaeformis* var. *lutescens* has distinct, vein-like gills on the outer surface.

FRUITING Appears in troops among mosses in alkaline woodland.

Dimensions FRUITBODY ⊕ 2–7cm ↕ 3–7cm	BASE ↔ 3–8mm	Spores Pale cream	Edibility

Family CANTHARELLACEAE	Species *Cantharellus lateritius*	Season Summer–autumn

SMOOTH CHANTERELLE

Trumpet-shaped with a pendent, wavy margin, this orange-yellow species is closely related to *Cantharellus cibarius* (p.28), and differs from it mainly in having a smooth to faintly or partly veined outer surface. It is generally denser, and stouter, but just as fragrant, with the same taste. It was formerly known as *Craterellus cantharellus*, because it looks like
C. cornucopioides (p.275) but with chanterelle colours.
• **OCCURRENCE**
Under oak. Widespread and very common in eastern North America.
• **SIMILAR SPECIES** *C. cibarius* (p.28), has well-formed, forked, gill-like folds on its outer surface. *C. odoratus* appears in dense, bouquet-like clusters.

poorly formed, gill-like folds sometimes occur •

cap margin is pendent and wavy •

trumpet-shaped, orange-yellow fruitbody •

smooth or nearly smooth undersurface •

FRUITING Appears singly or in large numbers on the ground under oak trees in open woodland and parks.

Dimensions FRUITBODY ⊕ ‡ 2.5–10cm	BASE ↔ 0.5–2.5cm	Spores Pale yellow-orange	Edibility

Family GOMPHACEAE	Species *Gomphus floccosus*	Season Summer–autumn

ORANGE PIG'S EAR

This large, trumpet- to vase-shaped species is brightly coloured, making it easy to spot where it occurs in open woods. It has a variably scaly, red-orange to orange-yellow cap. The flesh has the same strong colouring. The decurrent spore-producing surface is creamy white to ochre and veined. Eating it is not recommended because it may cause stomach upsets.
• **OCCURRENCE** On the ground under softwood trees and in mixed woodland areas. Widespread and common throughout North America.
• **SIMILAR SPECIES** *Gomphus bonarii* is bright red with a milk-white spore-producing surface. *G. kauffmanii* is larger, more coarsely scaly, and yellowish tan.

large, trumpet- to vase-shaped fruitbody •

cap surface is red-orange to orange-yellow •

scales on cap surface are red-orange •

creamy white to ochre spore-producing surface •

tapering, stem-like base is usually orange to yellow-orange

FRUITING Singly or in large groups of fruitbodies on the ground under softwoods and in mixed woods.

Dimensions FRUITBODY ⊕ 5–15cm ‡ 5–10cm	BASE ↔ 1.5cm	Spores Ochre-yellow	Edibility

STAR-SHAPED & CAGE-LIKE FUNGI

These fungi are called gasteroids because their spore-producing tissue (gleba) is enclosed in the fruitbody. The two Clathrus species (below and p.280) are related to stinkhorns (pp.246–47). The other species, the earthstars, have fruitbodies that split into a star with an inner spore-ball.

cage-like fruitbody •

• star-shaped fruitbody

Family CLATHRACEAE	Species *Clathrus archeri*	Season Summer–autumn

DEVIL'S FINGERS

This species produces spores in a foul-smelling slime to attract insects for dispersal. Its very characteristic fruitbody, with four to eight vivid red arms, emerges from a buff to pale pink "egg". The spore mass is on the inside of the arms. All Clathraceae have remarkable shapes; almost all are red tinged or white to off-white.

• OCCURRENCE Among woodland litter, or on sawdust or wood chippings; in woodland, parks, and flowerbeds. Inadvertently introduced from Australia or New Zealand and now well established in Europe.

• SIMILAR SPECIES *Pseudocolus fusiformis*, found in North America, has only three or four joined arms. *Aseroë* species, for example *A. coccinea* from Japan, have stem-like bases.

• joined at tips at first, arms soon separate

arms have honeycomb-like structure

• arms are vivid red

buff to pale pink "egg" is 3–6cm high •

• dark olive-brown spore mass on inside (upper surface) of arms

cords at • base of "egg"

• arms eventually spread out widely

• arms united at base

FRUITING In troops; may appear in mass fruitings.

EGG ⊕ 2.5–4cm	ARMS ↕ 5–10cm	Spores Olive-brown	Edibility 🍽

Family SCLERODERMATACEAE	Species *Astraeus hygrometricus*	Season All year

BAROMETER EARTHSTAR

The rounded, reddish brown immature fruitbody of this metallic-smelling species splits open into a star shape on maturity to reveal the skin-clad, grey-brown spore-ball within. It has amazing hygroscopic properties, even when detached from its mycelium: it curls back into a ball in dry weather and expands its rays in wet weather. Rain splashes are needed to release the spores through the central pore.

• **OCCURRENCE** Mycorrhizal; mostly found growing in dry, open woodland. Virtually cosmopolitan but absent in cold-temperate to arctic areas.

• **SIMILAR SPECIES** *Geastrum* species (below, pp.279–80) differ in microscopic details such as elastic threads in the spore-ball.

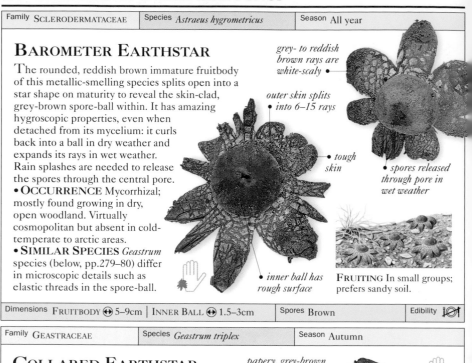

grey- to reddish brown rays are white-scaly •

outer skin splits • into 6–15 rays

• tough skin

• spores released through pore in wet weather

• inner ball has rough surface

FRUITING In small groups; prefers sandy soil.

Dimensions FRUITBODY ⊕ 5–9cm | INNER BALL ⊕ 1.5–3cm	Spores Brown	Edibility

Family GEASTRACEAE	Species *Geastrum triplex*	Season Autumn

COLLARED EARTHSTAR

One of the most widely distributed *Geastrum* species, the Collared Earthstar is comparatively large and fleshy. On maturity, the turnip- or onion-shaped fruitbody splits open, typically in two layers – an outer star shape and an inner collar – around a central ball. A pore on top of the ball allows the spores inside to be released by splashes of rainwater.

• **OCCURRENCE** In gardens, parks, and woodland. Widespread and fairly common in warmer regions in the northern temperate zones and almost cosmopolitan.

• **SIMILAR SPECIES** The inner ball of *Trichaster melanocephalus* has no skin or pore. The ball of *Myriostoma coliforme* has many holes through which the spores are released.

papery, grey-brown inner ball •

• brown to pink-brown collar, papery when dry

fleshy outer skin • arches back and splits into a star formation

• turnip- or onion-shaped when immature

finely fibrous hole in faint, • circular depression

smooth inner • surface of fruitbody

FRUITING In groups or fairy rings on rich soil.

Dimensions FRUITBODY ⊕ 4–12cm | INNER BALL ⊕ 2–4cm	Spores Chocolate-brown	Edibility

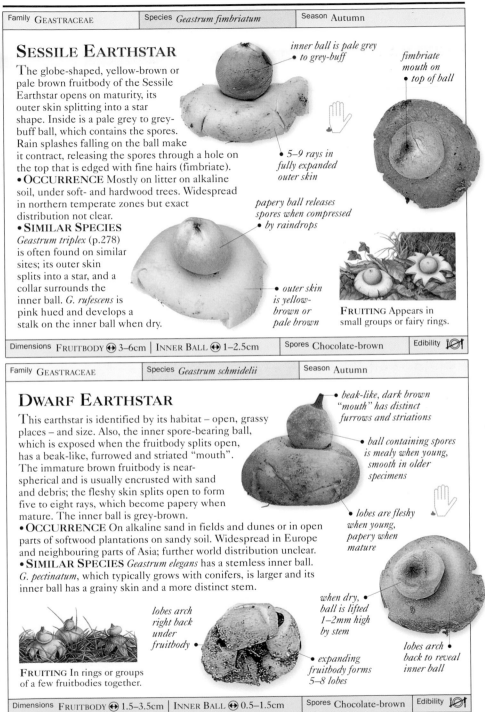

Family GEASTRACEAE	Species *Geastrum fimbriatum*	Season Autumn

SESSILE EARTHSTAR

The globe-shaped, yellow-brown or pale brown fruitbody of the Sessile Earthstar opens on maturity, its outer skin splitting into a star shape. Inside is a pale grey to grey-buff ball, which contains the spores. Rain splashes falling on the ball make it contract, releasing the spores through a hole on the top that is edged with fine hairs (fimbriate).
• OCCURRENCE Mostly on litter on alkaline soil, under soft- and hardwood trees. Widespread in northern temperate zones but exact distribution not clear.
• SIMILAR SPECIES *Geastrum triplex* (p.278) is often found on similar sites; its outer skin splits into a star, and a collar surrounds the inner ball. *G. rufescens* is pink hued and develops a stalk on the inner ball when dry.

inner ball is pale grey to grey-buff •

fimbriate mouth on top of ball •

• 5–9 rays in fully expanded outer skin

papery ball releases spores when compressed • by raindrops

• outer skin is yellow-brown or pale brown

FRUITING Appears in small groups or fairy rings.

Dimensions FRUITBODY ⊕ 3–6cm	INNER BALL ⊕ 1–2.5cm	Spores Chocolate-brown	Edibility

Family GEASTRACEAE	Species *Geastrum schmidelii*	Season Autumn

DWARF EARTHSTAR

This earthstar is identified by its habitat – open, grassy places – and size. Also, the inner spore-bearing ball, which is exposed when the fruitbody splits open, has a beak-like, furrowed and striated "mouth". The immature brown fruitbody is near-spherical and is usually encrusted with sand and debris; the fleshy skin splits open to form five to eight rays, which become papery when mature. The inner ball is grey-brown.
• OCCURRENCE On alkaline sand in fields and dunes or in open parts of softwood plantations on sandy soil. Widespread in Europe and neighbouring parts of Asia; further world distribution unclear.
• SIMILAR SPECIES *Geastrum elegans* has a stemless inner ball. *G. pectinatum*, which typically grows with conifers, is larger and its inner ball has a grainy skin and a more distinct stem.

• beak-like, dark brown "mouth" has distinct furrows and striations

• ball containing spores is mealy when young, smooth in older specimens

• lobes are fleshy when young, papery when mature

when dry, ball is lifted 1–2mm high by stem

• lobes arch back to reveal inner ball

lobes arch right back under fruitbody •

• expanding fruitbody forms 5–8 lobes

FRUITING In rings or groups of a few fruitbodies together.

Dimensions FRUITBODY ⊕ 1.5–3.5cm	INNER BALL ⊕ 0.5–1.5cm	Spores Chocolate-brown	Edibility

Family GEASTRACEAE	Species *Geastrum striatum*	Season Autumn

STRIATED EARTHSTAR

Like other earthstars, the outer skin of this species splits open to reveal a spore-ball. In the Striated Earthstar, the finely grainy, greyish white ball has a short stem, inserted into a collar-like rim. The immature fruitbody is near-spherical to onion-shaped and is strongly encrusted with soil and the debris of its habitat. After opening, the fleshy, grey-brown rays soon become papery in texture.
• **OCCURRENCE** On fertile soil, often under softwood trees in gardens and parks; also in mixed or softwood woodland. Widespread in Europe; world distribution unclear.

spore-ball is pale grey

the stem is most obvious in dry specimens

6–9 pointed rays

collar-like rim beneath spore-ball

furrowed and striated, beak-like, dark brown "mouth"

FRUITING In lines, rings, or a few together on mixed litter.

Dimensions FRUITBODY ⊕ 3–6.5cm	INNER BALL ⊕ 1–2.5cm	Spores Chocolate-brown	Edibility

Family CLATHRACEAE	Species *Clathrus ruber*	Season All year

RED CAGE FUNGUS

When mature, this fungus becomes striking red and develops a spherical, cage-like structure. It emerges from a white or buff "egg". Inside, the "cage bars" are smeared with an olive-brown spore mass, the foul smell of which attracts insects for spore dispersal.
• **OCCURRENCE** On leaf and wood litter, in parks and gardens; prefers warmth. Widespread but scattered; mostly in Mediterranean areas.
• **SIMILAR SPECIES** There are about 17 *Clathrus* species. They are mainly tropical. Some are bright red while others are white.

inner surface of "cage" is covered with slimy spore mass

"cage" is spongy in texture

bright red "cage"

buff or white "egg" is 3–6cm high

"egg" remains at base

FRUITING Appears in small groups or troops.

Dimensions FRUITBODY ⊕ to 9cm ↕ to 12cm	Spores Olive-brown	Edibility

EAR- OR BRAIN-LIKE, GELATINOUS FUNGI

Most of the fungi featured in this section have gelatinous flesh that desiccates in dry weather but rehydrates when wet and can then continue to shed spores. Their shape varies from brain-like, with the spore-bearing tissue (hymenium) all over, to pendent and ear-like, with the hymenium lining the inside and facing downwards.

brain-like
• *fruitbody*

ear-like •
fruitbody

Family AURICULARIACEAE	Species *Auricularia auricula-judae*	Season All year

JEW'S EAR

The fruitbody of this species is a distinctive ear-shape. It is gelatinous and smooth when fresh but becomes hard and folded as it matures and dries out. The outer surface is tan-brown and covered in downy hairs, while the inner, spore-producing surface is more grey in colour and veined and wrinkled. Considered a bland edible in the West, this fungus and related species are valued as both a food and a medicine in China.
• **OCCURRENCE** On hardwood trees, often elder, in damp woodland. Widespread in warmer parts of northern temperate zones.
• **SIMILAR SPECIES** *Auricularia polytricha* is the same colour or darker, and its upper surface is very velvety. It is found mainly in the tropics.

closely attached to
• *bark substrate*

downy hairs on
• *outer surface*

spore-producing •
surface is veined
and wrinkled and
faces downwards

tan-brown fruitbody •
is distinctly ear-shaped

• *folds develop*
as fruitbody ages
and dries out

• *flesh dries*
hard and horny

FRUITING Singly or in crowded tiers and rows.

Dimensions FRUITBODY ↔ 4–12cm ⊕ to 2mm	Spores White	Edibility

| Family | TREMELLACEAE | Species | *Tremella mesenterica* | Season | Mostly late autumn–winter |

YELLOW BRAIN-FUNGUS

fruitbody consists of soft, flabby lobes •

The striking, almost transparent, yellow colouring of the Yellow Brain-fungus makes it very easy to see. Prolonged rainfall can make it turn white, but occasionally it may also produce true albino forms. In dry weather the fruitbody shrivels up, but it will rehydrate when moist conditions return. Although its flavour is very bland, it can be eaten and used in soups.
• OCCURRENCE Parasitic on Corticiaceae species; growing on hardwood branches, often in piles of brushwood. Widespread and common in northern temperate zones.

• spores are produced all over surface

• prolonged wet weather causes colour loss

dried • flesh is brittle

• fruitbody dries to dark orange

FRUITING Mainly in small groups of lobed fruitbodies.

| Dimensions | JOINED FRUITBODIES ↔ 1–6cm ⊕ 0.5–4cm | Spores | White | Edibility |

| Family | TREMELLACEAE | Species | *Tremella foliacea* | Season | Autumn–winter |

LEAFY BRAIN-FUNGUS

flesh is brown and very gelatinous •

A strongly folded, highly gelatinous brown fruitbody, attached directly to bark with no stem, are features that make this species easy to identify. The spores are produced all over the surface of the fruitbody.
• OCCURRENCE Parasitic on species of *Stereum* and Corticiaceae growing on hardwoods, but also on pine, in parks and woods. Widespread in northern temperate zones.
• SIMILAR SPECIES *Ascotremella faginea* (p.283) and a folded form of *Neobulgaria pura* (p.271) may resemble this species; they are distinguished by purple tinges and more rounded, brain-like lobes.

fruitbody • is strongly folded

fresh specimens • are glossy brown

dried-up • fruitbody is shrunken and black

• water can reconstitute dried-up specimens

FRUITING Appears singly or a few together.

| Dimensions | FRUITBODY ↔ 4–12cm ↕ 3–7cm | Spores | White | Edibility |

| Family EXIDIACEAE | Species *Exidia glandulosa* | Season Late autumn–winter |

BLACK BRAIN-FUNGUS

Looking like blobs of tar, this jelly-fungus is comparatively firm and is less gelatinous to touch than *Tremella mesenterica* (p.282). The brain-like surface consists of numerous folds that become deeper and more wrinkled with age. As with most other jelly-fungi, wet weather causes shrivelled, dry specimens to rehydrate.
• OCCURRENCE On dead wood of hardwood trees in woodland. Widespread and common in northern temperate zones.
• SIMILAR SPECIES *Exidia truncata* is also common and is found mainly on hardwood trees such as oak. Its fruitbody is more button-shaped and has a fine velvety outer surface and a pimpled fertile surface.

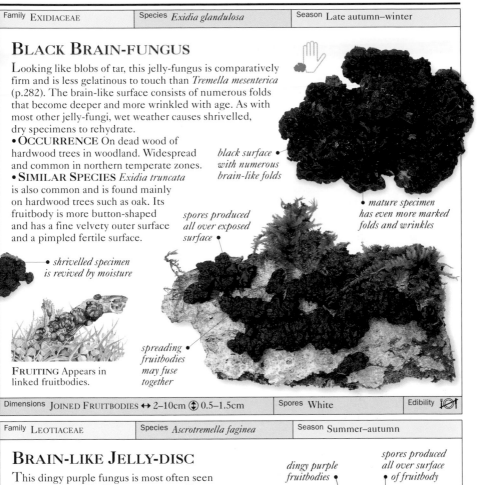

black surface with numerous brain-like folds

mature specimen has even more marked folds and wrinkles

spores produced all over exposed surface

shrivelled specimen is revived by moisture

spreading fruitbodies may fuse together

FRUITING Appears in linked fruitbodies.

| Dimensions JOINED FRUITBODIES ↔ 2–10cm ⊕ 0.5–1.5cm | Spores White | Edibility |

| Family LEOTIACEAE | Species *Ascotremella faginea* | Season Summer–autumn |

BRAIN-LIKE JELLY-DISC

This dingy purple fungus is most often seen in large, shiny, jelly-like groups, up to 10cm across. The fruitbody consists of a mass of gelatinous, irregularly shaped blobs, the whole effect being almost brain-like. It is attached to the substrate by a short, stem-like point. It looks like a jelly-fungus but microscopic characteristics, such as spores produced in cylindrical asci (pp.10–11), identify it as a cup-fungus.
• OCCURRENCE Typically on dead beech, but also on other hardwoods. Widespread and locally common in northeastern North America and most of Europe.

spores produced all over surface of fruitbody

dingy purple fruitbodies

fruitbody has jelly-like texture

brain-like, irregular fruitbody

FRUITING Mostly singly or a few together on branches and trunks of dead hardwood trees.

| Dimensions FRUITBODY ↕ 1–2cm ↔ 2–4cm | Spores White | Edibility |

SPORE CHART

SPORES occur in many colours, shapes, surface textures, and sizes, and offer important clues to precise identification of a species. Spore colour is included with each species main entry; size and shape are given in the table below. Spores vary from 2 to 500 microns (µm); average sizes are given here. A microscope is necessary to determine size and shape (see p.17). In the table below, ⊕ means diameter.

SPECIES	SIZE (µm)	SHAPE
Agaricus arvensis	7 × 5	broadly ellipsoid
Agaricus augustus	8.5 × 5	ellipsoid
Agaricus bernardii	6.5 × 5.5	broadly ellipsoid
Agaricus bisporus	6 × 5	broadly ellipsoid
Agaricus bitorquis	6 × 4.5	broadly ellipsoid
Agaricus californicus	5.5 × 4.5	ellipsoid
Agaricus campestris	8 × 4.5	ellipsoid
Agaricus hondensis	5 × 3.5	ellipsoid
Agaricus moelleri	5.5 × 3.5	broadly ellipsoid
Agaricus porphyrizon	5 × 3.5	ellipsoid
Agaricus sylvaticus	5.5 × 3.5	broadly ellipsoid
Agaricus sylvicola	7 × 4.5	ellipsoid
Agaricus xanthoderma	6 × 4	ellipsoid
Agrocybe cylindracea	10 × 5.5	ellipsoid with a pore
Agrocybe pediades	12 × 8	ellipsoid with a pore
Agrocybe praecox	9 × 5.5	ellipsoid with a pore
Albatrellus ovinus	4 × 3.5	near spherical, amyloid
Aleuria aurantia	17.5 × 9	ellipsoid, reticulate, 2 drops inside
Aleurodiscus amorphus	28 × 23	near spherical, spiny
Amanita caesarea	10 × 7	broadly ellipsoid
Amanita crocea	10 ⊕	near spherical
Amanita fulva	11 ⊕	near spherical
Amanita gemmata	10 × 7.5	broadly ellipsoid
Amanita mappa	9 × 8	near spherical, amyloid
Amanita muscaria and A. m. var. formosa	9 × 6.5	ellipsoid
Amanita pantherina	11 × 7.5	broadly ellipsoid
Amanita phalloides	8.5 × 7	near spherical to broadly ellipsoid, amyloid
Amanita porphyria	9 ⊕	near spherical, amyloid
Amanita rubescens	8.5 × 6.5	broadly ellipsoid, amyloid
Amanita smithiana	12 × 7.5	ellipsoid, amyloid
Amanita spissa	9.5 × 7.5	near spherical, amyloid
Amanita vaginata	11 ⊕	near spherical
Amanita virosa	7.5 ⊕	near spherical, amyloid
Armillaria cepistipes	8.5 × 5.5	broadly ellipsoid
Armillaria mellea	8.5 × 5.5	broadly ellipsoid
Armillaria tabescens	8 × 6	broadly ellipsoid
Ascocoryne cylichnium	24 × 5	narrow ellipsoid, 5–7 septate
Ascocoryne sarcoides	14 × 4	narrow ellipsoid
Ascotremella faginea	8 × 4	ellipsoide, faintly striate
Asterophora parasitica	5.5 × 3.5	broadly ellipsoid
Astraeus hygrometricus	9 ⊕	spherical, spiny
Auricularia auricula-judae	14 × 5.5	sausage-shaped
Auricularia mesenterica	16.5 × 6	broadly sausage-shaped
Auriscalpium vulgare	5 × 4	oval, minutely spiny
Baeospora myosura	3.5 × 1.5	ellipsoid
Bankera fuligineoalba	5 × 3	oval, spiny
Bispora citrina	12 × 4	ellipsoid, 0–1 septate

SPECIES	SIZE (µm)	SHAPE
Bjerkandera adusta	5 × 3	ellipsoid
Boletus aereus	15.5 × 5.5	spindle-shaped
Boletus appendiculatus	14.5 × 4.5	spindle-shaped
Boletus badius	14 × 5	spindle-shaped
Boletus barrowsii	14 × 4.5	spindle-shaped
Boletus bicolor	10 × 4.5	near spindle-shaped
Boletus calopus	14 × 5.5	spindle-shaped
Boletus edulis	15.5 × 5.5	spindle-shaped
Boletus legaliae	13 × 6	spindle-shaped
Boletus luridiformis	15 × 5	spindle-shaped
Boletus luridus	13 × 6	near spindle-shaped
Boletus pascuus	13 × 5	spindle-shaped
Boletus parasiticus	15 × 5	spindle-shaped
Boletus pinophilus	17 × 5	spindle-shaped
Boletus porosporus	13 × 5	spindle-shaped, some have a pore and appear truncate
Boletus pulcherrimus	14.5 × 6	spindle-shaped
Boletus pulverulentus	13 × 5	spindle-shaped
Boletus reticulatus	15 × 5	spindle-shaped
Boletus rubellus	12.5 × 5	spindle-shaped
Boletus satanas	13 × 6	near spindle-shaped
Boletus subtomentosus	12.5 × 5	spindle-shaped
Bovista plumbea	5.5 × 5	near spherical with a long pedicel, warty
Bulgaria inquinans	12.5 × 6.5	kidney-shaped; in asci top 4 spores are brown, lower 4 (slightly smaller) are hyaline
Calocera viscosa	11.5 × 4	curved with rounded ends
Calocybe carnea	5.5 × 3	egg-shaped
Calocybe gambosa	5.5 × 3.5	egg-shaped
Calocybe ionides	6 × 3	egg-shaped
Calostoma cinnabarina	17 × 8	ellipsoid, pitted
Calvatia gigantea	4.5 ⊕	spherical, warty
Cantharellus cibarius	8.5 × 5	ellipsoid
Cantharellus cinnabarinus	9 × 5	ellipsoid
Cantharellus lateritius	10 × 5.5	ellipsoid
Cantharellus lutescens	10.5 × 7	broadly ellipsoid
Cantharellus subalbidus	8 × 5	ellipsoid
Cantharellus tubaeformis	10 × 8	ellipsoid
Chalciporus piperatus	9.5 × 4.5	oblong
Chlorociboria aeruginascens	7.5 × 2	spindle-shaped
Chlorophyllum molybdites	11 × 7.5	egg-shaped to ellipsoid with a pore
Chondrostereum purpureum	7.5 × 3	ellipsoid
Chroogomphus rutilus	19 × 6.5	spindle-shaped
Clathrus archeri	6.5 × 3	narrowly cylindrical
Clathrus ruber	5 × 2.5	ellipsoid to cylindrical
Clavaria vermicularis	7 × 4.5	oval
Clavariadelphus pistillaris	13.5 × 8	broadly ellipsoid
Clavulina cristata	9 × 7.5	broadly ellipsoid
Clavulinopsis corniculata	6 ⊕	spherical

SPECIES	SIZE (μm)	SHAPE	SPECIES	SIZE (μm)	SHAPE
Clavulinopsis helvola	6.5 × 5	spherical to broadly ellipsoid, long warts, irregular outline	*Craterellus cornucopioides*	13 × 8	broadly ellipsoid
Clitocybe clavipes	8 × 4.5	ellipsoid	*Creolophus cirrhatus*	4 × 3	near spherical, amyloid, hyphae not amyloid
Clitocybe dealbata	5 × 3	tear-shaped	*Crepidotus mollis*	9 × 6	egg-shaped
Clitocybe geotropa	8 × 6	tear-shaped	*Crepidotus variabilis*	6.5 × 3	oblong-ellipsoid, warty
Clitocybe gibba	7 × 4.5	tear-shaped	*Crinipellus scabella*	7.5 × 5	broadly ellipsoid
Clitocybe metachroa	7 × 4.5	ellipsoid	*Crucibulum crucibuliforme*	8 × 4.5	oblong-ellipsoid
Clitocybe nebularis	7.5 × 4	ellipsoid	*Cyathus striatus*	17 × 10	oblong-ellipsoid
Clitocybe odora	7 × 4.5	ellipsoid	*Cystoderma amianthinum*	6 × 3	egg-shaped, amyloid
Clitopilus prunulus	10.5 × 5	egg-shaped to ellipsoid, ribbed lengthways	*Cystoderma carcharias*	5 × 4	near spherical, amyloid
			Cystoderma terrei	4.5 × 2.5	ellipsoid
Collybia butyracea	7 × 3.5	oblong-ellipsoid	*Daedalea quercina*	6.5 × 3	ellipsoid
Collybia confluens	8 × 3.5	egg-shaped	*Daedaleopsis confragosa*	7.5 × 2.5	cylindrical, curved
Collybia dryophila	5.5 × 2.5	egg-shaped to ellipsoid	*Daldinia concentrica*	14.5 × 7	ellipsoid to spindle-shaped, flattened on one side
Collybia erythropus	7 × 3.5	ellipsoid			
Collybia fusipes	5 × 3.5	broadly egg-shaped	*Disciotis venosa*	22 × 13.5	broadly ellipsoid
Collybia maculata	5 × 4.5	near spherical	*Dumontinia tuberosa*	15 × 7.5	ellipsoid
Collybia peronata	7.5 × 3.5	ellipsoid	*Elaphomyces granulatus*	30 ⊕	spherical, spiny
Coltricia perennis	7 × 4.5	ellipsoid	*Entoloma abortivum*	9 × 5	ellipsoid, angular
Coniophora puteana	13 × 7	ellipsoid	*Entoloma cetratum*	12 × 8	prism-shaped, nodular
Conocybe arrhenii	8 × 4.5	ellipsoid with a pore	*Entoloma clypeatum*	10 × 9.5	prism-shaped
Conocybe lactea	12.5 × 8	ellipsoid with a pore	*Entoloma conferendum*	10 × 9	cruciform, angular
Coprinus atramentarius	9 × 6	ellipsoid with a pore	*Entoloma incanum*	12.5 × 8.5	angular
Coprinus comatus	12 × 8	ellipsoid with a pore	*Entoloma nitidum*	8 × 7	angular
Coprinus disseminatus	8.5 × 4.5	ellipsoid with a pore	*Entoloma porphyrophaeum*	11 × 7.5	angular
Coprinus micaceus	8.5 × 6 × 4.5	flattened ellipsoid with a truncated pore	*Entoloma rhodopolium*	8.5 × 7.5	prism-shaped
			Entoloma sericeum	9 × 8	angular
Coprinus niveus	15 × 10.5 × 8	flattened ellipsoid, slightly hexagonal, with a pore	*Entoloma serrulatum*	10.5 × 7.5	angular
			Entoloma sinuatum	10 × 9	angular
Coprinus picaceus	16 × 11.5 × 9.5	flattened ellipsoid with a pore	*Exidia glandulosa*	13 × 4	sausage-shaped
			Fistulina hepatica	5.5 × 4	near spherical
Coprinus plicatilis	12 × 9 × 5	flat, heart-shaped with a pore	*Flammulina velutipes*	8.5 × 4	ellipsoid to cylindrical
Cordyceps militaris	4.5 × 1.5	very long, cylindrical, breaking into part spores	*Fomes fomentarius*	17 × 6	cylindrical
			Fomitopsis pinicola	7.5 × 4	slender ellipsoid
Cordyceps ophioglossoides	4 × 2	very long, cylindrical, breaking into part spores	*Galerina calyptrata*	11 × 6	broadly spindle-shaped, warty, loosening outer wall
Cortinarius alboviolaceus	8.5 × 5.5	ellipsoid, rugose	*Galerina unicolor*	12 × 6	almond-shaped, rugose, loosening outer wall
Cortinarius anserinus	10 × 6.5	lemon-shaped, rugose			
Cortinarius armillatus	10.5 × 6.5	almond-shaped, rugose	*Ganoderma applanatum*	7.5 × 5	ellipsoid, truncated, warty
Cortinarius bolaris	6.5 × 4	near spherical, rugose	*Ganoderma lucidum*	10 × 7	ellipsoid, truncated, warty
Cortinarius caerulescens	10 × 5.5	ellipsoid, rugose	*Ganoderma pfefferi*	10 × 7.5	ellipsoid, truncated, warty
Cortinarius calochrous	10 × 6	ellipsoid, rugose	*Geastrum fimbriatum*	3.5 ⊕	spherical, warty
Cortinarius cinnamomeus	7.5 × 4.5	almond-shaped, rugose	*Geastrum schmidelii*	5.2 ⊕	spherical, warty
Cortinarius elegantissimus	14 × 8.5	lemon-shaped, rugose	*Geastrum striatum*	4.5 ⊕	spherical, warty
Cortinarius mucosus	12.5 × 6.5	narrow lemon-shaped, rugose	*Geastrum triplex*	4 ⊕	spherical, blunt spiny
Cortinarius orellanus	10.5 × 6	ellipsoid, rugose	*Geoglossum fallax*	75 × 6	near cylindrical, 0–7 septate
Cortinarius paleaceus	8.5 × 5.5	ellipsoid, rugose	*Geopora arenicola*	25 × 15	ellipsoid, 1–2 drops inside
Cortinarius pholideus	7.5 × 5.5	near spherical, rugose	*Gloeophyllum odoratum*	8.5 × 4	cylindrical
Cortinarius rubellus	10 × 7.5	near spherical to broadly ellipsoid, rugose	*Gomphidius glutinosus*	19 × 5.5	near spindle-shaped
			Gomphidius roseus	19 × 5.5	near spindle-shaped
Cortinarius rufoolivaceus	13 × 7.5	almond- to lemon-shaped, rugose	*Gomphus floccosus*	13 × 7.5	ellipsoid, rugose
			Grifola frondosa	5.5 × 4	broadly ellipsoid to near spherical
Cortinarius semisanguineus	7 × 4.5	ellipsoid to lemon-shaped, rugose			
Cortinarius sodagnitus	11 × 6	ellipsoid to almond-shaped, rugose	*Gymnopilus junonius*	9 × 5.5	ellipsoid, rugose
			Gymnopilus penetrans	7.5 × 4.5	ellipsoid, rugose
Cortinarius splendens	9.5 × 5.5	almond-shaped, rugose	*Gyromitra esculenta*	20 × 10	ellipsoid
Cortinarius torvus	9.5 × 6	broadly ellipsoid to egg-shaped, rugose	*Gyromitra infula*	22 × 8.5	narrowly ellipsoid
			Gyroporus castaneus	9.5 × 5.5	ellipsoid
Cortinarius triumphans	12 × 6.5	almond-shaped, rugose	*Gyroporus cyanescens*	10 × 5	ellipsoid
Cortinarius violaceus	12.5 × 8	near spherical to almond-shaped, rugose	*Handkea excipuliformis*	5 ⊕	spherical, warty
			Handkea utriformis	4.5 ⊕	spherical, nearly smooth
			Hapalopilus rutilans	5 × 2.5	ellipsoid

Species	Size (μm)	Shape
Hebeloma crustuliniforme	11 × 6	almond-shaped, rugose
Hebeloma mesophaeum	9 × 5.5	ellipsoid, finely rugose
Hebeloma radicosum	9 × 5.5	almond-shaped, rugose
Helvella crispa	20 × 12	ellipsoid
Helvella lacunosa	19 × 12	ellipsoid
Hericium coralloides	4 × 3	oval, amyloid
Heterobasidion annosum	4.5 × 3.5	broadly ellipsoid to near spherical, warty
Hydnellum peckii	5.5 × 4	oval, warty
Hydnum repandum	7 × 6	oval
Hydnum umbilicatum	8.5 × 7	near spherical
Hygrocybe calyptraeformis	7.5 × 5	broadly ellipsoid
Hygrocybe chlorophana	8.5 × 5	ovoid to ellipsoid
Hygrocybe coccinea	9 × 5	ellipsoid to almond-shaped
Hygrocybe conica (4-spored)	9.5 × 6	ellipsoid or almond- to
(2-spored)	10.5 × 7	bean-shaped
Hygrocybe miniata	7.5 × 5.5	often pear-shaped
Hygrocybe pratensis	6 × 4.5	near spherical to ellipsoid or tear-shaped
Hygrocybe psittacina	8.5 × 5.5	oblong-ellipsoid
Hygrocybe punicea	9.5 × 5	oblong-ellipsoid
Hygrocybe virginea	8 × 5	narrowly ellipsoid
Hygrophoropsis aurantiaca	6.5 × 4	oblong-ellipsoid
Hygrophorus eburneus	8.5 × 4.5	ellipsoid
Hygrophorus hypothejus	8 × 4.5	ellipsoid
Hymenochaete rubiginosa	5.5 × 3	oblong-ellipsoid
Hyphodontia paradoxa	5.5 × 3.5	oval
Hypholoma capnoides	8 × 4.5	ellipsoid with a pore
Hypholoma fasciculare	7 × 4.5	ellipsoid with a pore
Hypholoma sublateritium	7 × 4	ellipsoid with a pore
Hypomyces hyalinus	19 × 5.5	spindle-shaped, 2-celled, warty
Hypomyces lactifluorum	40 × 4.5	spindle-shaped, 2-celled, warty
Hypoxylon fragiforme	13 × 6	ellipsoid to spindle-shaped, flattened
Inocybe asterospora	10.5 × 8.5	star-shaped, nodular
Inocybe erubescens	12 × 6	ellipsoid to bean-shaped
Inocybe geophylla	9.5 × 5.5	ellipsoid
Inocybe godeyi	10.5 × 6.5	almond-shaped
Inocybe griseolilacina	9 × 5.5	almond-shaped
Inocybe haemacta	9 × 5.5	ellipsoid to almond-shaped
Inocybe lacera	14 × 5.5	cylindrical
Inocybe rimosa	12 × 6	ellipsoid to bean-shaped
Inonotus hispidus	8.5 × 7	broadly ellipsoid
Inonotus radiatus	6 × 4.5	broadly ellipsoid
Kuehneromyces mutabilis	7.5 × 5	ellipsoid with a pore
Laccaria amethystina	9.5 ⊕	spherical or near spherical, spiny
Laccaria laccata	9 × 8	spherical or near spherical, spiny
Lacrymaria velutina	9.5 × 6	lemon-shaped with a big pore, warty
Lactarius blennius	7.5 × 6	near spherical, warty, veined, amyloid
Lactarius camphoratus	8 × 7	near spherical, spiny-rugose, veined, amyloid
Lactarius controversus	7 × 5	near spherical, rugose, veined, amyloid
Lactarius deliciosus	8.5 × 7	near spherical, warty, veined, amyloid

Species	Size (μm)	Shape
Lactarius deterrimus	9 × 7	near spherical, warty, veined, amyloid
Lactarius fuliginosus	9 ⊕	spherical, reticulate, crested, amyloid
Lactarius glyciosmus	8.5 × 7.5	near spherical, rugose, veined, amyloid
Lactarius helvus	8 × 6	near spherical, reticulate, veined, amyloid
Lactarius hepaticus	8 × 6.5	near spherical, reticulate, veined, amyloid
Lactarius hortensis	7 × 5.5	near spherical, reticulate, veined, amyloid
Lactarius hygrophoroides	8.5 × 7	near spherical, warty, veined, amyloid
Lactarius mitissimus	9 × 7	near spherical, rugose, amyloid
Lactarius necator	7 × 6	near spherical, veined, amyloid
Lactarius pallidus	8 × 6.5	near spherical, rugose, veined, amyloid
Lactarius piperatus	8.5 × 6.5	near spherical, warty, with connecting lines, amyloid
Lactarius quietus	8.5 × 7.5	near spherical, rugose, veined, amyloid
Lactarius rufus	9 × 6.5	broadly ellipsoid, reticulate, veined, amyloid
Lactarius sanguifluus	8.5 × 7	near spherical, warty, veined
Lactarius subdulcis	7.5 × 6	near spherical, reticulate, veined, amyloid
Lactarius theijogalus	8.5 × 6.5	near spherical, rugose, veined, amyloid
Lactarius torminosus	8.5 × 7	near spherical, rugose, veined, amyloid
Lactarius trivialis	9.5 × 8	near spherical, rugose, veined, amyloid
Lactarius vellereus	10.5 × 8.5	near spherical, warty, with connecting veins, amyloid
Lactarius volemus	8.5 ⊕	spherical, reticulate, veined, amyloid
Laetiporus sulphureus	6 × 4	broadly ellipsoid
Leccinum quercinum	13.5 × 4.5	near spindle-shaped
Leccinum scabrum	17 × 5.5	near spindle-shaped
Leccinum tesselatum	15 × 6	near spindle-shaped
Leccinum variicolor	14.5 × 5	near spindle-shaped
Leccinum versipelle	14.5 × 4.5	near spindle-shaped
Lentinellus cochleatus	4.5 × 4	near spherical, spiny
Lentinellus ursinus	4 × 2.5	egg-shaped, spiny, amyloid
Lentinus tigrinus	7.5 × 3.5	cylindrical
Lenzites betulina	5.5 × 2.5	more or less ellipsoid
Leotia lubrica	23 × 6	near cylindrical, somewhat curved, 4–5 septate
Lepiota aspera	8 × 3	ellipsoid
Lepiota brunneoincarnata	8 × 4.5	egg-shaped
Lepiota castanea	11 × 4	projectile-shaped
Lepiota clypeolaria	14 × 6	spindle-shaped
Lepiota cristata	7 × 3.5	projectile-shaped
Lepiota ignivolvata	12 × 6	broadly spindle-shaped
Lepiota oreadiformis	12.5 × 5	spindle-shaped
Lepista flaccida	3-4.5 ⊕	near spherical, fine spiny
Lepista irina	8 × 4.5	ellipsoid, rugose
Lepista nuda	7.5 × 4.5	ellipsoid, rugose
Lepista personata	7.5 × 5	ellipsoid, rugose

Species	Size (µm)	Shape	Species	Size (µm)	Shape
Leucoagaricus leucothites	8.5 × 5.5	broadly egg- to almond-shaped	Panellus serotinus	5 × 1.5	sausage-shaped
			Panellus stypticus	4.5 × 2	egg-shaped
Leucocoprinus badhamii	6.5 × 4.5	ellipsoid to spindle-shaped	Paxillus atrotomentosus	5 × 4	broadly ellipsoid
Leucocoprinus luteus	8.5 × 6	almond-shaped with a pore	Paxillus corrugatus	3 × 1.75	ellipsoid
Leucopaxillus giganteus	7 × 4	tear-shaped	Paxillus involutus	9 × 5.5	ellipsoid
Limacella guttata	5.5 × 4.5	near spherical	Peziza badia	18.5 × 8.5	ellipsoid, 2 drops inside
Lycoperdon echinatum	4.5 ⊕	spherical, warty	Peziza succosa	20.5 × 11	ellipsoid, 2 drops inside, warty
Lycoperdon perlatum	3.5 ⊕	spherical, warty			
Lycoperdon pyriforme	4 ⊕	spherical, nearly smooth	Peziza vesiculosa	22 × 12	ellipsoid without drops
Lyophyllum connatum	6 × 3.5	ellipsoid	Phaeolepiota aurea	12 × 5	narrowly ellipsoid
Lyophyllum decastes	5.5 ⊕	spherical	Phaeolus schweinitzii	7 × 4	ellipsoid
Lyophyllum palustre	7 × 4	ellipsoid	Phallus duplicatus	4 × 2	ellipsoid
Macrocystidia cucumis	9 × 4.5	ellipsoid	Phallus impudicus	5 × 2.5	ellipsoid
Macrolepiota procera	15 × 10	ellipsoid with a pore	Phellinus igniarius	6 × 5	near spherical
Macrolepiota rhacodes	10 × 6.5	ellipsoid with a pore	Phellodon niger	4 × 3	oval, spiny
Macrotyphula fistulosa	13 × 6.5	ellipsoid	Phellodon tomentosus	4 × 3	oval or spherical, spiny
Marasmiellus ramealis	9 × 3	spindle-shaped to ellipsoid	Phlebia tremellosa	4 × 1	sausage-shaped
Marasmius alliaceus	9.5 × 7	broadly ellipsoid	Pholiota alnicola	9.5 × 5	ellipsoid with a pore
Marasmius androsaceus	8 × 4.5	ellipsoid to tear-shaped	Pholiota aurivellus	9 × 5.5	ellipsoid with a pore
Marasmius oreades	9 × 5.5	broadly ellipsoid	Pholiota gummosa	7.5 × 4	ellipsoid with a pore
Marasmius rotula	8 × 4	ellipsoid or tear-shaped	Pholiota highlandensis	7 × 4.5	ellipsoid with a pore
Megacollybia platyphylla	7.5 × 6.5	near spherical	Pholiota lenta	6.5 × 3.5	ellipsoid with a pore
Melanoleuca cognata	9.5 × 6	ellipsoid, fine spiny, amyloid	Pholiota squarrosa	7 × 4	ellipsoid with a pore
Melanoleuca polioleuca	8 × 5.5	ellipsoid, fine spiny, amyloid	Phylloporus rhodoxanthus	12.5 × 4.5	ellipsoid to spindle-shaped
Meripilus giganteus	6 × 5	broadly ellipsoid to near spherical	Piptoporus betulinus	6 × 2	sausage-shaped
			Pleurocybella porrigens	7 × 5	near spherical to broadly ellipsoid
Micromphale foetidum	9 × 4	ellipsoid			
Mitrula paludosa	12.5 × 3	club-shaped to cylindrical	Pleurotus cornucopiae	10 × 4.5	elongated ellipsoid
Morchella elata	25 × 14	ellipsoid	Pleurotus eryngii	11 × 5	elongated ellipsoid
Morchella esculenta	20 × 12.5	ellipsoid	Pleurotus ostreatus	9.5 × 3.5	elongated ellipsoid
Morchella semilibera	26 × 16	ellipsoid	Pluteus aurantiorugosus	6 × 4	broadly ellipsoid
Mutinus caninus	5.5 × 2.5	ellipsoid	Pluteus cervinus	7.5 × 5.5	broadly ellipsoid
Mycena acicula	11 × 3.5	near spindle-shaped to near cylindrical	Pluteus chrysophaeus	7 × 6	near spherical
			Pluteus umbrosus	6.5 × 5	broadly ellipsoid
Mycena adonis	8.5 × 5	ellipsoid to oblong	Polyporus badius	7.5 × 3.5	cylindrical
Mycena arcangeliana	9 × 5.5	ellipsoid	Polyporus brumalis	5.5 × 2.5	cylindrical
Mycena crocata	8.5 × 5	broadly ellipsoid	Polyporus squamosus	13 × 5	cylindrical
Mycena epipterygia	10 × 5	ellispoid	Polyporus tuberaster	13 × 5	cylindrical
Mycena filopes	10 × 6	ellipsoid	Polyporus umbellatus	9 × 3	cylindrical
Mycena flavoalba	7.5 × 3.5	ellipsoid to near cylindrical	Polyporus varius	8.5 × 3	cylindrical
Mycena galericulata	10 × 7.5	egg-shaped to oblong	Porphyrellus porphyrosporus	14 × 6	near spindle-shaped
Mycena galopus	12 × 6	ellipsoid to near cylindrical	Postia caesia	5 × 1.5	sausage-shaped, amyloid
Mycena haematopus	8.5 × 6	ellipsoid	Postia stiptica	4.5 × 2	ellipsoid to cylindrical
Mycena inclinata	10 × 6.5	egg-shaped to ellipsoid	Psathyrella candolleana	8 × 4.5	ellipsoid with a pore
Mycena leptocephala	10 × 5	ellipsoid to near cylindrical	Psathyrella conopilus	15.5 × 7.5	ellipsoid with a pore
Mycena olivaceomarginata	10 × 5.5	ellipsoid	Psathyrella multipedata	7.5 × 4	ellipsoid with a pore
Mycena pelianthina	6.5 × 3.5	ellipsoid	Psathyrella piluliformis	6 × 3.5	ellipsoid with a pore
Mycena polygramma	9.5 × 6.5	ellipsoid	Pseudoclitocybe cyathiformis	9 × 5.5	ellipsoid, amyloid
Mycena pura	7 × 3.5	ellipsoid	Pseudohydnum gelatinosum	6.5 × 5.5	near spherical to broadly ellipsoid
Neobulgaria pura	9 × 4	ellipsoid, striped lengthways			
Oligoporus rennyi	4 × 2.5	oblong	Psilocybe cubensis	14 × 9	ellipsoid with a pore
Omphalina umbellifera	8.5 × 6	near spherical to egg-shaped	Psilocybe cyanescens	11.5 × 7 × 6	ellipsoid to almond-shaped with a pore
Omphalotus olearius	5.5 × 5	near spherical			
Otidea onotica	13 × 7	ellipsoid, 2 drops inside	Psilocybe semilanceata	13 × 8	ovoid to ellipsoid with a pore
Oudemansiella mucida	16 × 14	near spherical to spherical, thick-walled	Psilocybe squamosa	14 × 8	ellipsoid with a pore
			Pycnoporus cinnabarinus	5 × 2.5	ellipsoid
Oudemansiella radicata	13.5 × 10	broadly ellipsoid	Ramaria abietina	8 × 4	ellipsoid, short spiny
Paecilomyces farinosus	2.5 × 1.5	ellipsoid	Ramaria botrytis	15 × 5.5	narrowly ellipsoid, striped
Panaeolus foenisecii	13.5 × 8	lemon-shaped with a pore, warty	Ramaria sanguinea	10 × 4.5	narrowly ellipsoid, warty
			Ramaria stricta	9 × 4.5	ellipsoid, warty
Panaeolus papilionaceus	16 × 9	lemon-shaped with a pore	Rickenella fibula	4.5 × 2.5	narrowly ellipsoid
Panaeolus semiovatus	18 × 10	broadly ellipsoid with a pore	Rickenella setipes	5 × 3	ellipsoid

Species	Size (µm)	Shape
Rozites caperatus	12.5 × 8	almond-shaped, rugose
Russula aeruginea	8 × 6	near spherical, warty, veined, amyloid
Russula claroflava	8.5 × 7	near spherical, warty, veined, amyloid
Russula cyanoxantha	8.5 × 7	near spherical, warty, veined, amyloid
Russula delica	9.5 × 7.5	near spherical, rugose, amyloid
Russula emetica	9.5 × 8	near spherical, warty, veined, amyloid
Russula fellea	8.5 × 6.5	near spherical, veined, amyloid
Russula foetens	8.5 × 8	near spherical, warty, amyloid
Russula fragilis	8.5 × 7	near spherical, reticulate, warty, amyloid
Russula integra	10.5 × 8.5	near spherical, spiny, amyloid
Russula mairei	7.5 × 6	near spherical, reticulate, warty, amyloid
Russula nigricans	7 × 6.5	near spherical, reticulate, amyloid
Russula ochroleuca	9 × 7.5	near spherical, partly reticulate, warty, amyloid
Russula paludosa	9.5 × 8	near spherical, warty, some connecting veins, amyloid
Russula puellaris	8 × 6	near spherical, warty-spiny, amyloid
Russula rosea	8.5 × 7.5	near spherical, reticulate, warty, amyloid
Russula sanguinaria	8.5 × 7.5	near spherical, spiny, some connecting veins, amyloid
Russula sardonia	8 × 6.5	near spherical, warty-crested, veined, amyloid
Russula turci	8 × 7	near spherical, warty-crested, veined, amyloid
Russula undulata	8 × 6.5	near spherical, warty, partially reticulate, amyloid
Russula vesca	7 × 5.5	near spherical, warty, amyloid
Russula vinosa	10 × 8	near spherical, spiny, amyloid
Russula virescens	8 × 6.5	near spherical, reticulate, warty, amyloid
Russula xerampelina	9 × 8	near spherical, warty, amyloid
Rutstroemia firma	17 × 5.5	narrow ellipsoid, 3–5 septate
Sarcodon imbricatum	7.5 × 5	near spherical, warty
Sarcodon scabrosus	7.5 × 6	spherical with coarse warts
Sarcoscypha austriaca	28 × 13	narrowly ellipsoid
Schizophyllum commune	5 × 2	cylindrical or curved
Scleroderma citrinum	11.5 ⊕	spherical, spiny, partially reticulate
Scleroderma verrucosum	10 ⊕	spherical, spiny
Scutellinia scutellata	19 × 12	ellipsoid, warty
Sepedonium chrysospermum	20 ⊕	spherical, warty
Serpula lacrymans	12 × 7	ellipsoid
Sparassis crispa	7 × 4.5	ellipsoid
Spinellus fusiger	40 × 20	lemon-shaped, variable
Stereopsis humphreyi	7.5 × 4.5	ellipsoid to egg-shaped
Stereum hirsutum	6 × 2.5	ellipsoid to cylindrical, amyloid
Stereum rugosum	7.5 × 4	ellipsoid to cylindrical, amyloid
Stereum subtomentosum	6 × 2.5	ellipsoid to cylindrical, amyloid

Species	Size (µm)	Shape
Strobilomyces strobilaceus	11 × 10	near spherical, reticulate
Strobilurus esculentus	5 × 2	ellipsoid
Stropharia aurantiaca	14 × 7	ellipsoid with a pore
Stropharia coronilla	8.5 × 4.5	ellipsoid with a pore
Stropharia cyanea	8.5 × 4.5	ellipsoid with a pore
Stropharia rugoso-annulata	11.5 × 8	ellipsoid with a pore
Stropharia semiglobata	18 × 9	ellisoid with a pore
Suillus aeruginascens	11.5 × 5	near spindle-shaped
Suillus bovinus	9 × 3.5	near spindle-shaped
Suillus granulatus	9 × 3	near spindle-shaped
Suillus grevillei	9.5 × 3.5	near spindle-shaped
Suillus luteus	8.5 × 3.5	oblong to spindle-shaped
Suillus plorans	9 × 4.5	ellipsoid
Suillus spraguei	10 × 4	ellipsoid
Suillus variegatus	9 × 3.5	near spindle-shaped
Syzygites megalocarpus	25	globose
Tarzetta cupularis	20 × 13	narrowly ellipsoid, 2 drops inside
Thelephora terrestris	9 × 7	oval to ellipsoid, warty-spiny
Trametes gibbosa	5 × 2.5	cylindrical to curved
Trametes hirsuta	6 × 2	cylindrical
Trametes versicolor	6.5 × 2	cylindrical
Tremella foliacea	9.5 × 8	oval
Tremella mesenterica	12.5 × 8.5	oval
Trichaptum abietinum	7.5 × 2.5	cylindrical
Trichoglossum hirsutum	125 × 7	near cylindrical, pointed ends, 15 septate
Tricholoma atrosquamosum	6.5 × 4	ellipsoid
Tricholoma aurantium	5.5 × 3.5	ellipsoid
Tricholoma auratum	7 × 4.5	ellipsoid
Tricholoma caligatum	7 × 5	ellipsoid
Tricholoma fulvum	6.5 × 4.5	broadly ellipsoid
Tricholoma lascivum	7 × 4	ellipsoid to near spindle-shaped
Tricholoma magnivelare	6 × 5	ellipsoid to near spherical
Tricholoma pardinum	10 × 6.5	broadly ellipsoid
Tricholoma portentosum	6.5 × 4.5	ellipsoid
Tricholoma saponaceum	6 × 4	ellipsoid
Tricholoma scalpturatum	5 × 3	ellipsoid
Tricholoma sciodes	7 × 6	broadly ellipsoid
Tricholoma sejunctum	5.5 × 4	ellipsoid
Tricholoma sulphureum	10 × 6	ellipsoid to almond-shaped
Tricholoma terreum	6.5 × 4.5	ellipsoid
Tricholoma ustale	7 × 5	ellipsoid
Tricholomopsis rutilans	6.5 × 5	broadly ellipsoid to near spherical
Tuber aestivum	30 × 24	egg-shaped, reticulate, spiny
Tuber canaliculatum	60 × 50	ellipsoid to near spherical, reticulate
Tuber magnatum	40 × 35	egg-shaped, reticulate
Tuber melanosporum	35 × 25	ellipsoid, curved spiny
Tylopilus felleus	13 × 4.5	near spindle-shaped
Typhula erythropus	6 × 3	ellipsoid
Vascellum pratense	3.5 ⊕	spherical, warty
Verpa conica	22 × 13	ellipsoid
Volvariella bombycina	9 × 6	ellipsoid
Volvariella gloiocephala	15 × 9	egg-shaped to ellipsoid
Xylaria hypoxylon	12.5 × 5.5	spindle-shaped, flattened
Xylaria polymorpha	25 × 7	spindle-shaped, flattened
Zelleromyces cinnabarinus	15 × 12	ellipsoid, reticulate, amyloid

GLOSSARY

Many of the terms described here are illustrated in the introduction (pp.6–23). Words in **bold** type are defined elsewhere in the glossary.

• **ADNATE GILLS**
Gills that are broadly attached to the stem.

• **ADNEXED GILLS**
Gills with a narrow attachment to the stem.

• **AGARIC**
Fungus with a cap and stem **fruit-body** with **gills** under the cap.

• **AMYLOID**
Refers to a reaction with an iodine reagent resulting in a blue stain.

• **ASCUS (*pl.* ASCI)**
The sac-like organ in which ascomycetes (see p.11) produce sexual **spores**.

• **BASIDIUM (*pl.* BASIDIA)**
The club-shaped organ on which basidiomycetes (see p.11) form sexual **spores**.

• **BOLETE**
A bolete produces a fleshy cap and stem **fruitbody** with **pores** and soft **tubes** under the cap.

• **BOREAL**
Refers to northern conifer region.

• **CORTINA**
A web-like **veil**, found for example in the genus *Cortinarius*.

• **CYSTIDIUM (*pl.* CYSTIDIA)**
Special sterile cells that can be found in various places on **fruitbodies** of basidiomycetes (see p.8). Cystidia on the **gill** sides and the stem can be important in identifying species of *Conocybe* and *Inocybe*.

• **DECURRENT GILLS**
Gills that run down the stem.

• **DELIQUESCENT GILLS**
Gills that dissolve as they mature, releasing an inky liquid full of black **spores**. They are peculiar to the genus *Coprinus*.

• **FIBRILLOSE**
With thread-like fibres.

• **FIMBRIATE**
With prominent projecting hairs on the (cap) margin.

• **FLASK-FUNGUS**
Fungus with tiny, flask-shaped **fruitbodies**, sometimes enclosed within a protective **stroma**.

• **FREE GILLS**
Gills with no stem attachment.

• **FRUITBODY**
A structure that supports the cells required for sexual reproduction in fungi.

• **GILLS**
The blade-like, **spore**-bearing structures found under the caps of **agarics**.

• **GLEBA**
The fertile tissue occuring in the group of fungi that includes puffballs, stinkhorns, earthstars, earthballs, and bird's nest fungi.

• **HYALINE**
Colourless.

• **HYGROPHANOUS**
Usually refers to the caps of **agarics** drying from the centre and becoming paler in zones until they are completely dry. When damp, the dark colour reappears from the margin inwards. Such fungi are typically **striate** at the cap margin.

• **HYPHA (*pl.* HYPHAE)**
The thread-like structures that make up a fungus, including its **fruitbodies**.

• **KOH**
Potassium hydroxide. This aids identification by producing stains on the flesh of certain fungi.

• **MYCORRHIZAL**
A relationship between plants and fungi that benefits both partners.

• **NOTCHED GILLS**
Gills that are indented just before reaching the stem.

• **OSTIOLE**
The opening or neck of the **spore**-producing organ in **flask-fungi**.

• **PARTIAL VEIL**
Thin, skin- or thread-like tissue that protects the **gills** or **pores** of the immature **fruitbody**. It splits as the fruitbody matures, often leaving traces at the cap margin or as a ring around the stem.

• **PEDICEL**
A cylindrical or tapering appendage on the **spores** of some fungi, such as *Bovista plumbea*.

• **PORES**
The opening of the **tubes** through which the **spores** are released in fungi such as **boletes**.

• **RESUPINATE**
Refers to a **fruitbody** that grows completely flat against the **substrate** without producing a cap or free margin.

• **RETICULATE**
With a net pattern.

• **RHIZOIDS**
Tightly spun **hyphae**.

• **RUGOSE**
With a rough surface.

• **SCLEROTIUM (*pl.* SCLEROTIA)**
A storage organ with a dense pale interior and a black protective rind produced by some fungi. It contains nutrients that will enable the fungus to grow when conditions are favourable.

• **SEPTATE**
Refers to **hyphae** or **spores** with transverse partitions or walls.

• **SETA (*pl.* SETAE)**
Thick-walled hairs (on caps, **gills**, stems, or in the flesh).

• **SINUATE GILLS**
Curved **gills**.

• **SPORES**
Microscopic cells produced by fungi for reproduction.

• **STRIATE**
Refers to lines on the cap caused by underlying **gills**.

• **STROMA (*pl.* STROMATA)**
A protective tissue, formed by **flask-fungi** for example; it normally contains the tiny **fruitbodies**.

• **SUBSTRATE**
The medium, such as soil or bark, in which a fungus grows.

• **TUBES**
Tubular structures under the caps of fungi such as **boletes**, where the fertile, **spore**-producing tissue is found. Tubes are visible as **pores** on the undersurface.

• **UMBO**
A raised boss in the centre of a cap.

• **UNIVERSAL VEIL**
Thin, skin- or web-like tissue covering the whole of the immature **fruitbody**. It splits as the fruitbody grows, sometimes leaving a **volva** at the stem base or loose scales on the cap.

• **VEIL**
Thin, skin- or web-like tissue that may protect entire **fruitbodies** (universal veil) or just the **gills** or pores (partial veil).

• **VISCID**
Slimy-sticky.

• **VOLVA**
A sac-like remnant of the **universal veil** at a stem base.

INDEX

ACKNOWLEDGMENTS

THE AUTHOR would like to thank Colin Walton and Jo Weeks for their work on this book, as well as all those involved in *The Mushroom Book*, who did much of the groundwork for this project, including Paul Copsey, Neil Fletcher, Sharon Moore, Joyce Pitt, Bella Pringle, and Jo Weightman.

DORLING KINDERSLEY would like to thank: Margaret Cornell for the index, Peter Frances for additional editorial support, Chris Turner for proofreading, and Martin Lewy of Mycologue for supplying the equipment on p.22.

PICTURE CREDITS

All photographs are by Neil Fletcher with the exception of those listed below. Dorling Kindersley would like to thank the following illustrators and photographers for their kind permission to reproduce their artworks and photographs.

Illustrations by Pauline Bayne, Evelyn Binns, Caroline Church, Angela Hargreaves, Christine Hart-Davies, Sarah Kensington, Vanessa Luff, David More, Leighton Moses, Sue Oldfield, Liz Pepperell, Valerie Price, Sallie Reason, Elizabeth Rice, Michelle Ross, Helen Senior, Gill Tomblin, Barbara Walker, Debra Woodward.

Photographs by A-Z Botanical Collection Ltd 97tr (J M Staples), 20cl, 38tr, 187bc, 210tr, 219tr (Bjorn Svensson); Harley Barnhart 42cr, 81br, 84tr, 159crb, 237br; Kit Skates Barnhart 28crb, 35br, 43br, 81tr, 146br, 148br, 159bc, 170br, 186br, 191cr, 202cr, 207clb, 208cr; Biofotos 229br (Heather Angel), 32br, 110br, 138tr, 180tr, 272br (Gordon Dickson); Morten Christensen 187br, 275br; Bruce Coleman Collection 216tr (Adrian Davies); Dr Ewald Gerhardt 36crb, 97br, 192tr, 199bc; Jacob Heilmann-Clausen 163br; Emily Johnson 89tr, 147bl, 178br, 244br, 253br, 263br, 276tr; Peter Katsaros 114crb, 136crb; Thomas Læssøe 11br, 16c, 42tr, 60cra, 62cla, 63br, 72br, 96tr, 110tr, 110c, 128tr, 131br, 132cra, 141br, 150tr, 164br, 167br, 179br, 206br, 221tr, 232br, 242crb, 263tr, 265br, 283br; N W Legon 46bl, 230br; Natural History Photographic Agency 16cr (Stephen Dalton), 19c (Martin Garwood), 179cl, 184br (Yves Lanceau), 21tr (David Woodfall); Natural Image 68bl, 240crb, 263cr (John Roberts), 17c (courtesy of Olympus Microscopes), Alan R Outen 68tr; Jens H Petersen 11tr, 11cra, 11cr, 16cl, 17bl, 17bcl, 17bcr, 17br, 18br, 19bc, 124bc, 251tr; Planet Earth Pictures 18c (Wayne Harris); Erik Rald 169crb, 191br; Samuel Ristich 233br, 273br; William Roody 30tr, 42br, 52tr, 54br, 166br, 182br, 190bc, 202br, 238bl, 247br, 256br, 259tr, 276br; Royal Botanic Gardens Kew 8tc; A Sloth 11crb; Ulrik Søchting 6br, 20cra; Paul Stamets 84tr; Walter Sturgeon 201br; Jan Vesterholt 21cl, 46bc, 70br, 73tr, 74br, 76crb, 80tr, 102br, 116tr, 124crb, 130br, 143br, 153bl, 161tr, 177br, 189cla, 190bl, 191tr, 192cr, 196br, 199bl, 211br, 241tr.

(a=above; b=below; c=centre; l=left; r=right; t=top)

Mushroom silhouettes by Colin Walton

Jacket design by Nathalie Godwin